Fashion, Society, and the First World War

Fashion, Society, and the First World War

International Perspectives

*Edited by
Maude Bass-Krueger,
Hayley Edwards-Dujardin,
and Sophie Kurkdjian*

BLOOMSBURY VISUAL ARTS
LONDON • NEW YORK • OXFORD • NEW DELHI • SYDNEY

BLOOMSBURY VISUAL ARTS
Bloomsbury Publishing Plc
50 Bedford Square, London, WC1B 3DP, UK
1385 Broadway, New York, NY 10018, USA
29 Earlsfort Terrace, Dublin 2, Ireland

BLOOMSBURY, BLOOMSBURY VISUAL ARTS and the Diana logo are trademarks of Bloomsbury Publishing Plc

First published in Great Britain 2021
This edition published 2022

Selection, editorial matter, Introductions © Maude Bass-Krueger, Hayley Edwards-Dujardin and Sophie Kurkdjian, 2022
Individual chapters © Their Authors, 2022

Maude Bass-Krueger, Hayley Edwards-Dujardin and Sophie Kurkdjian have asserted their right under the Copyright, Designs and Patents Act, 1988, to be identified as Editors of this work.

For legal purposes the Acknowledgements on p. xiii constitute an extension of this copyright page.

Cover design by Adriana Brioso
Cover image: Two women wearing a Poiret military coat, c.1915. Postcard from authors' personal collection.

All rights reserved. No part of this publication may be reproduced or transmitted in any form or by any means, electronic or mechanical, including photocopying, recording, or any information storage or retrieval system, without prior permission in writing from the publishers.

Bloomsbury Publishing Plc does not have any control over, or responsibility for, any third-party websites referred to or in this book. All internet addresses given in this book were correct at the time of going to press. The author and publisher regret any inconvenience caused if addresses have changed or sites have ceased to exist, but can accept no responsibility for any such changes.

A catalogue record for this book is available from the British Library.

A catalog record for this book is available from the Library of Congress.

ISBN: HB: 978-1-3501-1986-4
PB: 978-1-3502-3117-7
ePDF: 978-1-3501-1987-1
eBook: 978-1-3501-1988-8

Typeset by RefineCatch Limited, Bungay, Suffolk
Printed and bound in Great Britain

To find out more about our authors and books visit www.bloomsbury.com and sign up for our newsletters.

To our colleagues, friends, families, and everyone in between.

Contents

List of illustrations x
Acknowledgments xiii
A note on translations xv
Timeline xvi

Introduction 1
Maude Bass-Krueger and Sophie Kurkdjian

Part One The reconfiguration of the international couture industry 15

1. Wartime marketing of Parisian haute couture in the United States, 1914–17 17
   Mary Lynn Stewart

2. Boué Sœurs: "Compelled by the War" 29
   Waleria Dorogova

3. "Gladdening the hearts of warriors": The relationship between Lucile's romantic fashions and morale in the First World War 46
   Georgina Ripley

4. *Die Kriegskrinoline*: A feminine fashion between past and future 59
   Birgit Haase

5. Fashion in Belgium during the First World War and the case of Norine Couture 72
   Nele Bernheim

Part Two The materiality of wartime fashion and textile industries 89

6   Dressed to quill: The origin and significance of the feathered showgirl in First World War Paris 91
    Emily Brayshaw

7   Between fashion and folk: Dress practices in Alsace during the First World War 108
    Sara Hume

8   The lace industry in France and Belgium during the First World War 122
    Marguerite Coppens

9   Industrial and homemade clothing production in the Netherlands: A neutral country during the First World War 134
    Marta Kargól

10 Wartime fabrics in the historical archives of Como weavers and in the collections of the Fondazione Antonio Ratti 151
    Margherita Rosina

Part Three Problematic uniforms: Male and female experiences and secondhand trade networks 163

11 "Breeched, booted, and cropped": A dress historical analysis of the uniform worn by members of Britain's Women's Land Army, 1917–19 165
    Amy de la Haye

12 The French home front in 1914–18: An investigation into female workwear 182
    Jérémie Brucker

13 Rushing to suit up: French aviation's adjustment to wartime uniforms, 1914–16 197
    Guillaume de Syon

14 The spoils of war: Use and transformations of secondhand uniforms during the First World War in France 208
    Manuel Charpy

Part Four Fashion in print: Questions of national fashion and gender 229

15 The gentleman turned "enemy": Men's fashion in the Hungarian press, 1914–18 231
Zsolt Mészáros

16 The politics of fashion: German fashion writings in times of war 246
Burcu Dogramaci

17 The Italian fashion magazine *Margherita*: The war, women, and the call for a "Moda Italiana," 1914–18 260
Enrica Morini

18 *Le Flambeau*'s fashion discourse during the First World War: Towards a retrograde femininity? 272
Nigel Lezama

19 Is beauty useless? Fashion, gender, and British wartime society in *Punch* Magazine, 1915 288
Andrea Kollnitz

Notes on contributors 309
Index 315

Illustrations

0.1	"Expansion of the War—Dates on which Declarations of War were made."	xxii
0.2	Two women and a French soldier wearing a Poiret military coat, *c.* 1915.	6
2.1	Baronne Jeanne d'Etreillis and Sylvie Montegut with their children Mounette and Philippe in the park of Château de Maison Rouge, Gagny, summer 1917. *c.* 1915.	30
2.2	"Robe Corbeau," taffeta and velvet dress with "new draped skirt and waistcoat effect."	33
2.3	"Ma Patrie," Summer Collection, 1916, pencil, ink, and watercolor sketch for presentation purposes, stamped "Boué Sœurs Ltd., 9, Rue de la Paix, Paris."	36
2.4	Mannequin wearing the "Manette" model, winter 1919.	38
2.5	Witold Gordon, Boué Sœurs advertisement, Newport Casino program, 1917.	39
3.1	"Carresaute," Lucile evening dress. Blue silk chiffon, lace, and metallic embroidery, London, 1905.	48
3.2	Woman's evening dress of shot silk, with gold embroidered net and passementerie, by Lucile Ltd, Paris, France, 1918	54
3.3	Page from Lucile sample album book of fashion designs of women's clothes, Great Britain, 1905.	54
4.1	Thomas Theodor Heine, caricature, "Die enttäuschte Pariserin" (The disappointed Parisian), *Simplicissimus*, 1916.	60
4.2	Annie Offterdinger, *Modebild II* (Two dancing women), 1916. Lithograph published in *Zeit-Echo: Kriegstagebuch der Künstler*, 1916.	63
5.1	Elvira De Baets sent photographs of herself in fashionable outfits to her fiancé, kept prisoner in Soltau, Germany, winter 1914.	75
5.2	Norine Deschryver and Paul-Gustave Van Hecke in their workshop, *c.* 1919.	76
5.3	The Belgian fashion magazine *Modes Élégantes*, October 1, 1915.	79
5.4	René Magritte, poster design for Norine, 1926.	81
6.1	*Quelques fantasies typiques de la mode d'hiver 1913* (Some trimmings typical of winter 1913 fashions), 1914.	98
6.2	Leonetto Cappiello, "Pupazzi var Cappiello," *Fantasio*, 1918.	101

7.1	Henri Bacher, *22 Novembre 1918: L'Entrée glorieuse des troupes Françaises à Strasbourg*, 1919.	109
7.2	Hansi, *Pages d'Album*, c. 1915.	114
7.3	Leven and Lemonier, *Alsace interprété par Mme Réjane*, 1916.	116
8.1	Propaganda photo for *Amies de la dentelle*, c. 1915. Postcard.	127
8.2	War Lace depicting the rooster, symbol of France. Volant in Malines lace.	128
8.3	War Lace depicting allies' banners. Needle-lace fan sheet. Dated and signed, 1915, Fernand Khnopff.	128
8.4	Paul Mussche, Comité de la dentelle, 1915, pl. 2. Catalogue of lace pieces offered for sale.	129
9.1	Fashion illustration. *Gracieuse*, no. 7: 16/5 (1916).	139
9.2	Fashion illustration. *Gracieuse*, no. 8: 16/3 (1915).	140
9.3	Knitting for soldiers. *Gracieuse*, no. 19: 13 (1914).	142
9.4	Knitting for soldiers. *Gracieuse*, no. 20: 9 (1917).	143
10.1	Lyon, Boisson & Fesquet, Sample of Taffetas rayé, 1915.	156
10.2	Lyon, Boisson & Fesquet, Sample of Poult de soie rayé, 1914.	157
10.3	Lyon (?), Fragment of ribbon, Gros de Tour broché, 1914.	159
11.1	Photographic portrait of member of Britain's Women's Land Army, postcard, 1917–19.	168
11.2	Satirical postcard, 1917–19.	171
11.3	Photographic postcard. A group of dairy workers (they wear white overalls).	176
11.4	Studio portrait of a uniformed member of Britain's Women's Land Army, 1917–19. Orphan photograph.	177
12.1	Women replacing male café waiters, 1914–18.	186
12.2	War-themed calendar, 1st year, August 1914–July 1915.	187
12.3	"La Françoise," trademark, May 16, 1916.	190
12.4	Drawing by Jean Villemot, "Les Usines de guerre."	192
13.1	The mix of uniforms of this military class at the Avord training airfield reflects the variety of arms that contributed flyers to the nascent French Air Force.	199
13.2	Pilot Adolphe Pégoud (1889–1915) sports a mix of clothing, combining leather pants with a leather coat over his military tunic in 1914, at the start of hostilities.	201
13.3	A postcard showing a typical reconnaissance crew wearing a combination of leather pants and fur coats or goat skins, c. 1915.	202
13.4	By the end of the war, two air force uniforms existed, one light blue, worn by French top ace René Fonck at the victory parade on July 14, 1919, and the other dark blue (almost black).	204
14.1	"Le Marchand d'habits militaires" (The military clothing merchant), 1914.	210
14.2	"Le tricot du combattant" (The soldier's knit), 1914.	214

14.3	Clothing distribution on the Front on the initiative of *La Revue hebdomadaire*.	215
14.4	The charity "Les Vêtements pour les combattants" (Clothing for soldiers).	216
14.5	Local leaders in European secondhand clothing. A common representation prewar, it disappeared with the involvement of Senegalese skirmishers.	221
15.1	Cover illustration, "A nők kedvence" (The ladies' sweetheart), artist: Dezső Bér.	233
15.2	Advertisement for Dr. Jutassy's cosmetic brand, *Színházi Élet*.	235
15.3	At the Budapest horse races, 1917.	240
16.1	Pamphlet cover, Hermann Muthesius, *Die Zukunft der deutschen Form* (The Future of German Form).	247
16.2	Book cover, Hermann Muthesius, *Der Deutsche nach dem Kriege* (The German after the War).	248
16.3	Book cover, Norbert Stern, *Die Weltpolitik der Weltmode* (Global Politics of Global Fashion).	249
18.1	Cover of *Le Flambeau*'s first issue, May 29, 1915.	273
18.2	Louise Faure-Favier's first fashion column, *Le Flambeau*, May 29, 1915.	274
18.3	Camille Duguet's fashion column, *Le Flambeau*, August 28, 1915.	278
18.4	Camille Duguet's fashion column, *Le Flambeau*, October 9, 1915.	279
18.5	Jeanne Tournier's first fashion column, *Le Flambeau*, November 13, 1915.	281
19.1	Arthur Wallis Mills, "More people we should like to see interned," *Punch*, March 24, 1915.	293
19.2	Lewis Baumer, "Well, Madam, we sell a good many of both …," *Punch*, August 18, 1915.	297
19.3	Lewis Baumer, "How Sir Benjamin Goldmore and his junior clerk …," *Punch*, April 28, 1915.	301

Acknowledgments

The process of gathering the papers and editing this volume has taken five years. We are immensely grateful to all those who supported us throughout this process, and particularly to our authors, whose patience with us has been tremendous. We received grants from the Mission du centenaire de la Première Guerre mondiale for the publication of this book. At the Mission du centenaire, we would like to thank Joseph Zimet, Quentin Tissot, and Richard Holding for their generosity and continued support of our work. Funds from Bijzonder Onderzoeksfonds (BOF) at Ghent University have also helped cover related publication costs.

Procuring the image rights has been a labor of love by our authors. We thank them, as well as Jack Glover Gun at the Victoria & Albert Museum (V&A) for assisting us with rights for the photos from that collection. The sharp eyes and precise corrections of Joannes van den Maagdenberg and Mathis Vanhee were of indispensable help in the formatting of all the notes and references. We are indebted to Frances Arnold, our editorial director, for providing unwavering support throughout this process. We would particularly like to thank her, as well as Yvonne Thouroude and Rebecca Hamilton, editorial assistants at Bloomsbury.

Amy de la Haye has provided unfailing support throughout this project. She very generously took the time to help us select, edit, and revise a first round of papers. In a gesture of professional graciousness, she bowed out from being named as co-editor in order to allow us, three young scholars, to come forward under our own names. She effectively sent the elevator back down, as the saying goes, and for this we are grateful.

These papers were originally presented at a conference organized by Maude Bass-Krueger and Sophie Kurkdjian as part of the seminar, "Histoire et Mode" at the Institut d'histoire du temps présent (IHTP-CNRS). At the time, the seminar was run by Sophie Kurkdjian and Thierry Maillet, who had taken over from its formidable founder, Dominique Veillon, assisted by Eléonore Testa. The IHTP has been a strong support for the seminar and its conferences since its foundation in 2001. We would like to thank Christian Delage, Christian Ingrao, and Henry Rousso at the IHTP.

The conference, "Fashion, Dress, and Society in Europe during World War I," was held in Paris on December 12–13, 2014. It was co-hosted by Dominique Veillon, Lou Taylor, and Adhelheid Rasche.

We would like to thank them for their mentorship and their encouragement. The careers of young fashion scholars stand on their shoulders. We are grateful for their friendship throughout the years. The conference received financial support from L'Oréal Recherche et Innovation, thanks to Isabelle Walter. We thank the Institut français de la mode, particularly Dominique Jacomet, David Zajtmann, and Lucas Delattre, for graciously lending us their space to organize our conference. Alexane Querrec was the graphic designer of the conference program.

Above all, we would like to thank everyone who spoke at the 2014 Paris conference. The two-day conference was enriching in more ways than one: not only did we hear about fascinating new research, but we also made friends and colleagues, whose continued presence in our lives has widened our networks and strengthened our own work. We would like to thank: Nuria Aragonès, Ana Balda, Beatrice Behlen, Ulrika Berglund, Nele Bernheim, Muriel Berthou Crestey, Cally Blackman, Emily Brayshaw, Maria Carlgren, Laura Casal-Valls, Manuel Charpy, Katy Conover, Marguerite Coppens, Ilaria Coser, Jennifer Daley, Gillian Davies, Burcu Dogramaci, Lourdes Font, Holly Grout, Didier Grumbach, Birgit Haase, Barton C. Hacker, Sara Hume, Stéphane Jacques-Addade, Catherine Join-Dieterle, Marta Kargól, Andrea Kollnitz, Regina Lee Blaszczyk, Nigel Lezama, Thierry Maillet, Chryssa Mantaka, Marie Mcloughlin, Zsolt Mészáros, Alisa Miller, Enrica Morini, Anna Novikov, Lewis Orchard, Alexandra Palmer, Victoria Pass, Emmanuelle Polle, Alan Price, Adelheid Rasche, Georgina Ripley, Jennifer Roberts, Margherita Rosina, Victoria Rovine, June Rowe, Suzanne Rowland, Änne Söll, Mary Lynn Stewart, Guillaume de Syon, Lou Taylor, Patricia Tilburg, Elena Trencheva, Dominique Veillon, Margaret Vining, Eva Maria Zangl, Johanna Zanon, and Steven Zdatny.

Maude Bass-Krueger, Hayley Edwards-Dujardin, and Sophie Kurkdjian

A Note on Translations

The texts of Jérémie Brucker, Manuel Charpy, Marguerite Coppens, Marta Kargól, Zsolt Mészáros, and Enrica Morini were translated from French by Tristan Bass-Krueger. Burcu Dogramaci's text was translated from German by Hayley B. Haupt. All citations and quotes within articles and footnotes are translated from their original language by the author, unless otherwise specified. The translation of names of associations, syndicates, unions, and magazines were done by the editors.

Timeline

Timeline of social and political history	Timeline of fashion and women's history
1914	

JUNE 28: Assassination of Archduke Franz Ferdinand of Austria. Austria suspects Serbia is responsible.

JULY 28: Austria-Hungary declares war on Serbia, beginning the First World War.

JULY 31: Full mobilization is announced in Austria-Hungary.

AUGUST 1: General mobilization order in France and Germany.

AUGUST 3: Germany declares war on France. Italy, part of the Triple Alliance with Germany and Austria-Hungary, remains neutral.

AUGUST 4: The German army Marches on neutral Belgium.

AUGUST 10: Austria-Hungary invades Russia.

END OF AUGUST: Beginning of the exodus of Belgians to France, England, and the Netherlands (which remains neutral during the war).

SEPTEMBER 2: The French government settles in Bordeaux.

SEPTEMBER 5–12: Beginning of the First Battle of the Marne. Allied forces halt German advance into France.

SEPTEMBER 20: German troops bombard Reims.

SEPTEMBER: Creation of the privately-run relief organization Comité national de secours et d'alimentation (National Committee for Food and Relief) in Brussels.

JULY: Suffragette demonstration in Paris, with 6,000 women led by Caroline Rémy de Guebhard, best known under the pen name Séverine.

AUGUST: Publication of the last issue of *La Gazette du Bon Ton*, edited by Lucien Vogel.

AUGUST: Decree closing entertainment establishments such as theaters and cinemas in Paris.

AUGUST 1–23: Presentation of new Parisian couture collections with the "crinoline" silhouette.

AUGUST 2: Mobilization of fashion designer Jean Patou to the rank of captain, on a temporary basis, of the 269th infantry regiment.

AUGUST 4: Mobilization of the couturier Paul Poiret, assigned to the 119th infantry regiment as a tailor.

AUGUST 7: René Viviani's "Call to Women," an appeal to peasant women to contribute to the war effort in France.

Timeline of social and political history	Timeline of fashion and women's history
OCTOBER 31: First Battle of Ypres. German and Allied troops are unable to win a decisive victory.	**OCTOBER 14:** Successful presentation of Boué Sœurs collections in New York.
NOVEMBER 5: Britain and France declare war on the Ottoman Empire.	
DECEMBER 2: End of maneuver warfare and beginning of trench warfare.	**DECEMBER 21:** The Chambre Syndicale de la Couture Parisienne is dissolved so as to expel foreign couture houses.
DECEMBER 8: French government returns to Paris.	**DECEMBER:** The Poiret greatcoat is issued to replace the 1877 coats worn by soldiers.
DECEMBER 15: Launch of the great Champagne offensive.	**DECEMBER:** Some theaters resume activity.

1915

JANUARY: German zeppelin raids on Great Britain begin, bringing the war home to British civilians.	**JANUARY:** French women begin to take up jobs previously reserved for men (public transportation, postal delivery, etc.).
FEBRUARY 16: Champagne offensive.	**FEBRUARY:** The Germans try to start their own fashion industry.
FEBRUARY 18: Germany begins naval blockade of Great Britain.	
	MARCH 7: Beginning of the controversy about the French fashion designer Christoph Drecoll's nationality.
APRIL 22: First successful use of toxic gas by the Germans. By the end of the war, both Allied and Central Powers will have used chemical weapons.	**APRIL 7:** The French couturiers Boué Sœurs open an American branch of their couture house in New York.
APRIL 24: Beginning of the Armenian genocide perpetrated by the Turks.	
APRIL 25: Allied forces land on the Gallipoli Peninsula in the Ottoman Empire.	
MAY 3: Italy withdraws from the Triple Alliance.	**MAY 5:** The Chambre syndicale de la Couture Parisienne is re-established without foreign couturiers or funding.
MAY 7: German submarine sinks the British passenger liner Lusitania during crossing from New York to Liverpool, England, killing 128 Americans.	**MAY:** Paul-Gustave Van Hecke and Honorine Deschryver open their couture house "Couture Norine" in Brussels, Belgium.
MAY 23: Italy declares war on Austria-Hungary, entering the First World War on the side of the Allies.	
	JUNE: Parisian fashion designers exhibit their models at the Panama Pacific International Exposition in San Francisco.

Timeline of social and political history	Timeline of fashion and women's history
JULY 1: Decision to grant leave of ten days to all French combatants.	**JULY:** Launch of *Le Style Parisien* by publisher Lucien Vogel.
	JULY 15: Gabrielle Chanel opens a couture boutique in Biarritz (after opening a hat shop in Paris in 1910 and another in Deauville in 1913).
	AUGUST: Double French-English issue of the *La Gazette du Bon Ton* published by Lucien Vogel and Condé Nast on the occasion of the Panama Pacific International Exposition in San Francisco.
OCTOBER 6: A combined force of Austro-Hungarians and Germans (and later Bulgarians) invade Serbia.	**OCTOBER:** The London couturière Lady Duff Gordon opens a branch of her couture house Lucile Ltd in Chicago.
DECEMBER 20: Beginning of the evacuation of Allied troops in the Dardanelles.	**NOVEMBER:** Organisation of the "Fête Parisienne" in New York, a charity event and play by Bernard Boutet de Monvel to support the French couture industry.
	NOVEMBER: The metallurgical industry begins to recruit women (*munitionnettes*) in France.

1916

FEBRUARY 21–DECEMBER 15: Germany begins the attack on Verdun, leading to the Battle of Verdun. The Battle ends with 550,000 French and 450,000 German casualties.	**FEBRUARY:** Foire de Lyon (Lyon Fair).
	APRIL: Launch of the newspaper *Les Élégances parisiennes* under the direction of Lucien Vogel at the Hachette Publishing House.
MAY 16: Sykes-Picot Agreement, a secret treaty between the UK and France to divide spheres of influence in the Ottoman Empire.	**MAY** and **JULY:** *Les Élégances parisiennes* presents the first jersey suits by "Gabrielle Channel" (*sic*).
MAY 31: Naval Battle of Jutland takes place between British and German fleets. Both sides declare victory over the largest naval battle of the war.	
JUNE 5: Arab nationalists revolt against Ottoman rule.	
JULY 1–NOVEMBER 18: Beginning of the Battle of the Somme, an Allied offensive.	**JULY 18:** In France, the Committee for Female Labor asks the Minister of Armaments to ensure that industries provide workers appropriate work wear.
	OCTOBER 1: English *Vogue* publishes "Channel" models (*sic*).
NOVEMBER 7: Woodrow Wilson is re-elected President of the United States.	
NOVEMBER: In Amsterdam, large demonstrations of women demand the right to vote.	

Timeline of social and political history	Timeline of fashion and women's history

1917

JANUARY: Intense cold and worsening food and coal shortages in France. In Great Britain, creation of the Women's Land Army (WLA) to support British farming and agriculture. Women, known as Land Girls, replace male farmers who had gone to war. **FEBRUARY:** Establishment of the Queen Mary's Army Auxiliary Corps (QMAAC) in Great Britain allowing British women to join the British Army. **FEBRUARY:** US severs diplomatic relations with Germany after Germany resumes its campaign of unrestricted submarine warfare. **MARCH 1:** British intelligence intercept the Zimmermann Telegram, a secret communication from Germany proposing an alliance with Mexico should the United States enter the First World War. **MARCH 5:** Creation of the Imperial War Museum in London. **MARCH 8:** Beginning of the February revolution in Russia. **MARCH 15:** Abdication of Nicolas II of Russia. **APRIL 6:** The United States declares war on Germany. **APRIL 16:** Offensive of the Chemin des Dames (The Second Battle of the Aisne). **MAY 4:** Mutinies begin in the French army. **JUNE:** American combat forces arrive in France.	**JANUARY:** Launch of the barrel silhouette in *Les Élégances parisiennes*. Ban on evening dresses with low-cut necklines at the Opera and in Parisian theaters. **FEBRUARY:** Paul Poiret opens a "Poiret Incorporated" branch in New York with the goal of selling ready-to-wear clothing. **FEBRUARY:** Callots Sœurs, Chéruit, Edouard, Lanvin, Paquin, Poiret, Rodier, and Worth register their models with the French Labour Court to counter eventual counterfeiting. **MAY:** French fashion exhibition organized in Madrid by the Syndicat de Défense de la Grande couture française (included Beer, Doeuillet, Jenny, Lanvin, Worth). **MAY 11:** Seamstress' strike in Paris initiated by the workers of the Jenny couture house. **JUNE 7:** Parisian seamstresses' demands are met and they receive the "English Week" and a cost-of-living allowance. **AUGUST:** US regulations impose textile length restrictions beyond 4.5 meters per dress. **AUGUST:** Jeanne Paquin is elected new director of the Chambre Syndicale, taking over the position of Jean Aine-Montaillé. She remains in the position for three years.

Timeline of social and political history	Timeline of fashion and women's history
	SEPTEMBER: Poiret appointed head of the Army's regimental tailors. The French Sewing Union assures the government that the length of the wool dresses will not exceed 4.3 meters.
OCTOBER 24: Chief General in charge of the French Armies Philippe Pétain's counteroffensive at Chemin des Dames.	**OCTOBER:** The US government bans the import of all wool dresses if the fabric blend is comprised of too much wool. American factories must reserve their raw materials for the army.
NOVEMBER 2: Balfour Declaration by the British government, announcing support for the establishment of a national home for the Jewish people in Palestine.	**NOVEMBER:** Implementation of a "national fashion" in France.
NOVEMBER 6: October Revolution in Russia. Vladimir Lenin and the Bolsheviks assume complete control over the new Soviet Russian state.	
NOVEMBER 16: Georges Clémenceau named Prime Minister of France.	
DECEMBER 9: The British capture Jerusalem from the Ottomans.	
DECEMBER 15: Armistice between Russian and Central Powers.	

1918

JANUARY 8: US President Woodrow Wilson delivers his Fourteen Points address, outlining his vision for a stable peace.	
FEBRUARY 23: Distribution of general food cards in France.	**FEBRUARY 6:** English women over the age of 30 obtain the right to vote.
MARCH 3: Treaty of Brest-Litovsk between the new Bolshevik government of Russia and the Central Powers (German Empire, Austria-Hungary, Bulgaria, and the Ottoman Empire), ends Russia's participation in the First World War.	
MARCH 8: Camp Funston at Fort Riley, Kansas first reports cases of influenza. The disease spreads overseas to the Western Front. Over the next year, this "Spanish flu" kills 20 million worldwide.	
JULY 15: Beginning of the Second Battle of the Marne.	
JULY 17: The Bolsheviks execute Nicolas II of Russia and his family.	
JULY 18–AUGUST 6: Aisne-Marne Offensive marks a major turning point in the fighting on the Western Front.	

Timeline of social and political history	Timeline of fashion and women's history
SEPTEMBER 26: Meuse-Argonne offensive, the largest offensive in US history, plays a major role in bringing about an end to the war.	
OCTOBER 23–NOVEMBER 3: Battle of Vittorio Venet. Austro-Hungarian forces are defeated by the Italian Army, ending the war on the Italian Front and ushering in the final dissolution of the Austro-Hungarian Empire.	
NOVEMBER 9: Abdication of William II, and the end of the German Empire. German Republic (later the Weimar Republic) proclaimed.	**NOVEMBER 1:** Austrian women obtain the right to vote.
NOVEMBER 11: Armistice between Germany and the Allies.	**NOVEMBER 30:** German women obtain the right to vote.
NOVEMBER 22: The French forces enter Alsace after the German defeat.	
DECEMBER: Allied troops move into Germany and begin Occupation.	**DECEMBER:** Chanel expands and opens a couture boutique at 31, rue Cambon, Paris.

1919

FEBRUARY 14: Allied nations at the Paris Peace Conference propose establishment of the League of Nations to promote international cooperation.	
JUNE 19: Germany is forced to sign the Treaty of Versailles. Germany cedes Alsace-Lorraine to France, recognizes Belgian sovereignty, disarms and agrees to pay war reparations. US Senate refuses to ratify the Treaty of Versailles, thus preventing the country from joining the League of Nations.	**MARCH 20:** Demobilized, Jean Patou presents his first postwar collection.
	MAY 20: Members of the European Parliament adopt female suffrage, but the French Senators reject it in November 1922.
AUGUST 10: Treaty of Sèvres imposed by the Allies on the Ottoman Empire. The treaty was designed to liquidate the Ottoman Empire and abolish Turkish sovereignty.	**SEPTEMBER 28:** Dutch women obtain the right to vote.

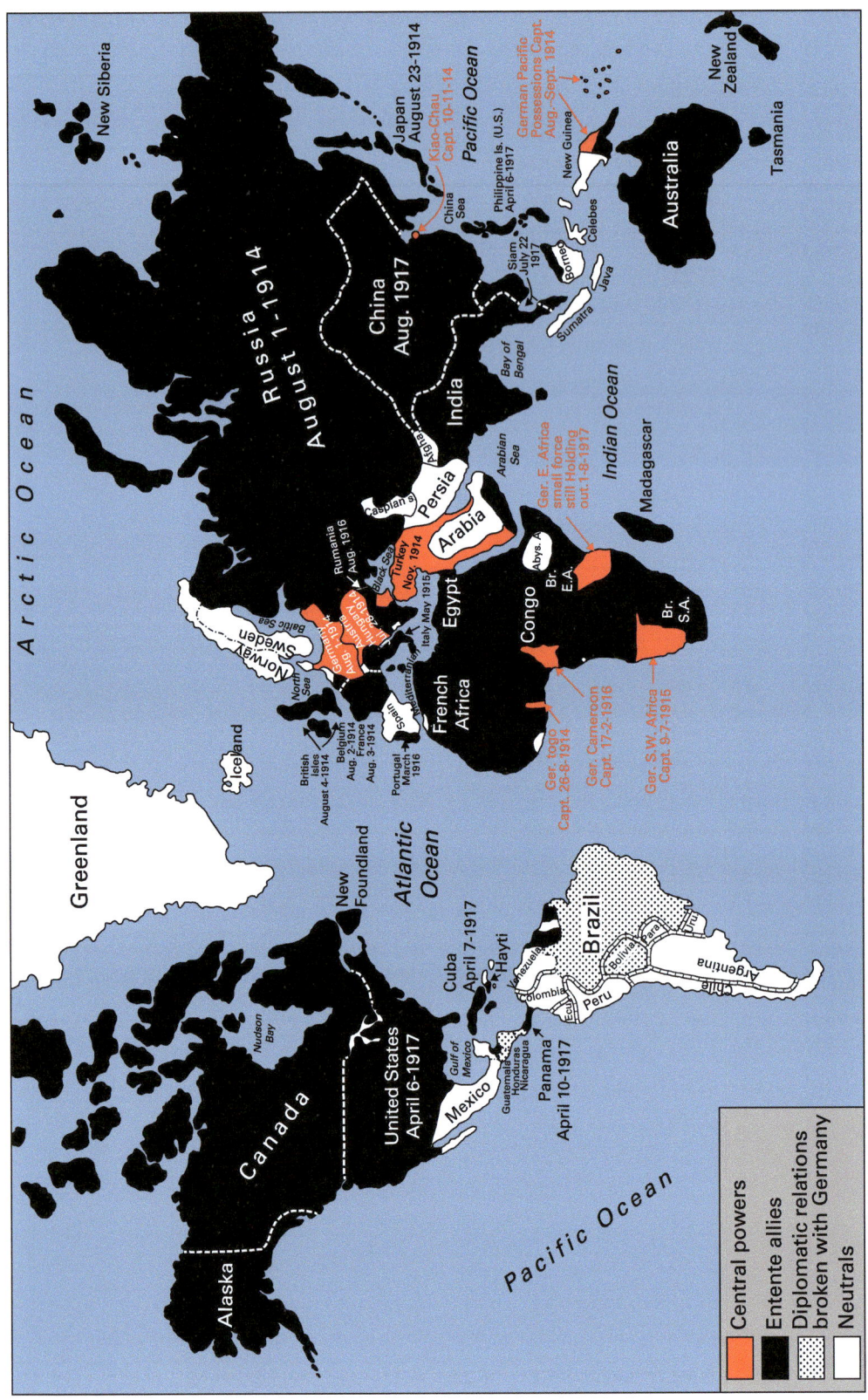

Figure 0.1 "Expansion of the War—Dates on which Declarations of War were made." Map from *The Story of the Great War*, vol. 5, Francis Joseph Reynolds, Allen Leon Churchill, and Francis Trevelyan Miller, eds. (New York: P.F. Collier & Sons, 1916), front insert.

Introduction

Maude Bass-Krueger and Sophie Kurkdjian

Inserting the international dimension into First World War fashion

This book examines fashion during the First World War from an international perspective. Fashion is addressed broadly: the essays in this book cover the garment, textile, and accessory trade—its objects, producers, consumers, and venues for dissemination—as well as fashion as an expression of personal identity. Earlier dress historians had written the First World War out of the history of fashion's evolution in the early twentieth century, while historians had written fashion out of sociocultural histories of the Great War. A few scholars have addressed this lacuna in the past few years, but primarily through a national perspective—recent monographs and exhibitions have addressed French, British, German, or American fashion during the First World War, for instance.[1] This book expands on their body of work, while challenging us to examine the international ties that bound together global fashion networks and fashion practices between 1914 and 1918.

The war altered the business of fashion on a national and international scale. The authors writing in this volume argue that the changes that occurred in the fashionable silhouette, while set in motion in the 1910s, were fixed into place during the war. Their essays highlight how the war restructured the international couture industry—not by decentering the axis away from Paris, but by finding a new economic balance with the US. "Problems" with the supposed reconfigurations of gender, which came to a fore in the interwar period, were rooted in new wartime fashion, workwear, and uniforms for men and for women. Fashion magazines, far from ceasing publication during the war, as some historians have suggested, honed their discourse during the war in order to guide consumers and address societal anxiety around new fashion practices. Read together, the essays in this volume broaden our understanding of the international networks of wartime fashion trade and dress practices, while also significantly adding to our knowledge of how fashion operated on national levels during a period of complex political alliances (Figure 0.1).

The papers weave fascinating connections between one another and the countries they address, which include France and its colonies, the US, Great Britain, Italy, Belgium, the Netherlands, Germany, and Hungary. Many of these countries opposed each other during the war, while others remained neutral. Some, like Belgium, were occupied, their economy at a standstill and their population reliant on foreign aid; others, like the US and the Netherlands, operated more or less "normally" throughout the war, whether as neutral parties or not. Although the essays in this volume all address how Western nations and their colonies responded to the war (France's colonies in Africa are included in Manuel Charpy's essay on secondhand clothing networks in Chapter 14), it should not be forgotten that the First World War was a total war, involving the Middle East and Japan. It would be fascinating to add to this first attempt to address Western fashion practices during the First World War with further discussions of fashion industries and practices in Asia, Africa, and the Middle East between 1914 and 1919.

While this book addresses fashion—an area seemingly far removed from the horrors of the war—the wounds of this massive conflict, which mobilized more than 65 million soldiers in more than thirty nations are an integral part of our authors' narratives (Figure 0.2). As Marie McLoughlin and Lou Taylor have written in the introduction to their recent edited volume on French fashion during the Second World War, "our commitment to examining fashion history in the midst of all [the slaughter and vast traumatic upheavals of this period] needs an explanation."[2] McLoughlin and Taylor quote Daniel Roche's use of clothing studies to "penetrate to the heart of social history" as justification.[3] Working on clothing, dress, textile, and fashion history does, indeed, allow us to have a better understanding of the lived experience of the past, and the social, economic, and cultural institutions of a nation. It also penetrates to the heart of cultural history, which includes the intellectual and artistic forces of a people and a nation. The essays in this volume look at fashion as an industry, as an artistic practice, and as a form of individual expression—all of which, we argue, are valid subjects to study in times of war as of peace.

While the topics of these essays and their disciplinary angle are broad in scope, each examines, in its own way, how fashion became a symbol and vehicle of nationalism during the war. For the French, maintaining the dominance and supremacy of Parisian haute couture throughout the war was an economic imperative; it was also a point of national pride. As we have written about in our own work on French fashion during the First World War, France relied heavily on revenue from their fashion and textile industry as well as the employment it generated.[4] French designers, supported by the government, fought hard to maintain their positions as the arbiters of fashionable taste from the very first days of the war (France's mobilization in early August coincided with scheduled couture showings, leading to several weeks of chaos for Parisian designers). The essays in this volume make clear that France's friends and foes alike tried to take advantage of the disorder of the first few months of the war to try and weaken Paris' influence: the US, Germany, and Italy each tried to create their own independent national fashion industries. Even countries with smaller fashion and textile industries, such as Belgian, Hungary, or the Netherlands, while they could not sustain an entire independent fashion industry, still strove to create "national fashions" as a point of national pride. Ultimately, the reader will learn, these attempts failed, and Paris triumphed. The reasons why are analyzed by our authors throughout the volume.

Many of these essays also speak to the relationship between fashion and gender. Examining discourses on fashion helps deepen our understanding of how gender is used as a referent to signal social "crises," as Mary Lou Roberts has eloquently written about in her exploration of the interwar *garçonne*.[5] On the eve of the war, women in the US and in most European nations appeared to be on the verge of obtaining female suffrage (some had already obtained voting rights for women, such as in Australia in 1902 or in Finland in 1907). During the war, feminists put their demands on hold and threw their support behind the war efforts of their home countries. The essays in this book evoke women who worked during the war in factories, as train conductors, as farmhands, as the head of couture houses, as seamstresses, as home-sewers of garments for soldiers, as organizers of war associations, as nurses, and in a whole range of other positions. In some countries, the women's contribution to the war effort helped society "see" women as "fit" to vote; female suffrage was passed in England, Germany, and Armenia in 1918, in Holland and Sweden in 1919, and in the United States in 1920. However, in France—a country which is the focus of several essays in this volume—women had to wait until the end of the Second World War to vote. The First World War was more of a hindrance to French women's suffrage than a facilitator.

Several of the essays in this volume address gender directly: fashion was a useful representational and rhetoric tool through which men and women could discuss the anxiety they felt about upheavals they perceived in society. Whether it was the "masculinization" of women who wore breaches, overalls, or uniforms, or the "feminization" of the non-combatant male, writing about or drawing cartoons about these subjects helped society externalize the range of emotions these changes evoked. Wartime throws much into crisis: political alliances, the economic balance, social networks, feelings of national pride, family dynamics, and gender norms. The essays in this volume study the rhetoric, representations, and objects of wartime fashion in order to shed light on how these alliances, dynamics, and networks were reinforced, reconfigured, or rebuked.

Recent research on fashion during the First World War

This volume has roots in a conference we organized in Paris on December 12–13, 2014, "Fashion, Dress, and Society in Europe during World War I." Co-hosted by Dominique Veillon, Lou Taylor, and Adhelheid Rasche, our conference was initiated within the framework of the monthly seminar on fashion history run by Sophie and Thierry Maillet at the Institut d'Histoire du Temps Présent (IHTP) in Paris. The conference was held at the Institut Français de la Mode.

At the time, governments across the globe were gearing up to celebrate the Centennial of the war with four years of events, conferences, exhibitions, and programs. We were aware of a few colleagues who had worked on women's uniforms, fashion seamstresses, and gender issues during the Great War, but we felt that the broader subject of wartime fashion was woefully understudied in 2014.[6] We sent out a call for papers, expecting perhaps a dozen or so responses. We were staggered when over 100 submissions came pouring in, from all points of the globe. In all, we convened 64 speakers that December in Paris.[7] Following the conference, we began the long process of inviting speakers to submit papers for publication, and then selecting and editing those contributions. Amy de la Haye helped us select and edit a first round of papers—her sharp eyes helped refine the focus of these essays in initial writing stages. Halfway through the project, we asked Hayley Edwards-Dujardin to reinforce our team. Hayley's painstaking editorial work has shepherded the essays into publication.

As stated above, at the time of our conference in 2014, there were only a few books and articles directly addressing the subject of female garments or fashion during the First World War, including Amy de la Haye's 2010 exhibition and catalogue on *Land Girls: Cinderellas of the Soil*.[8] Most historians either ignored the subject of wartime fashion or mentioned the era obliquely as a period when fashion came to a standstill.[9] With Centennial celebrations came renewed focus, and two more general interest books were published in 2014: Nina Edwards' *Dressed for War: Uniform, Civilian Clothing and Trappings, 1914 to 1918*, and Lucy Adlington's *Great War Fashion: Tales from the History Wardrobe*, which explores the lives and clothing of British women during the war.[10]

A great benefit of the Centennial programming was the funding of—and interest in—exhibitions on First World War fashion. In Germany, Adelheid Rasche organized the exhibition "Krieg und Kleider. Modegrafik zur Zeit des Ersten Weltkriegs" (Wardrobes in Wartime: Fashion Images during the First World War) at the Staatliche Museen in Berlin in 2014, which was accompanied by the edited volume, *Wardrobes in Wartime: Fashion, Art, Design during World War I*.[11] In England, an exhibition on "The Great War in Costume: Family and Fashion on the Home Front" was opened at the Fashion Museum in Bath in July 2014.[12] That same year in the US, Sara Hume, curator at Kent State University Museum, Ohio, and contributor to this volume, organized "The Great War: Women and Fashion in a World at War."[13] In 2016, the exhibition "Fashion & Freedom," organized in Manchester, displayed historic garments alongside contemporary fashions inspired by wartime fashion designs.[14] In France, we jointly curated "Mode & Femmes, 14/18," at the Bibliothèque Forney in Paris in 2017 and its subsequent American iteration, "French Fashion, Women, and the First World War," at the Bard Graduate Center in New York in 2019.[15]

Four years after our conference, in October 2018, British colleagues in the Association of Dress Historians organized a second conference, titled: "Dress and War: Clothing and Textiles at Home and

Abroad during the First World War Era, 1910–1920." Several of those proceedings were published in their online journal, *Journal of Dress History*, in the spring of 2019.[16] We are heartened to see so many new scholars working and writing on First World War fashion. Knowledge on the subject has expanded exponentially in the past five years. This volume gathers scholars with an aim to set on paper the current state of knowledge on fashion during the First World War from an international perspective; it is our hope that scholars will continue to build on this foundation.

Outline of the book

The nineteen essays in this book have been organized into four overarching parts. Part One, "The reconfiguration of the international couture industry," regroups the essays pertaining to the couture industry, its designers, and its designs. Part Two, "The materiality of wartime fashion and textile industries," takes the reader through other trades and dress practices within the fashion industry (feathers, folk dress, lace, handmade clothing, fabrics). Part Three, "Problematic uniforms: Male and female experiences and secondhand trade networks," includes four essays on women and men in uniform (or without it) and networks of sale for secondhand uniforms. Part Four, "Fashion in print: Questions of national fashion and gender," includes essays whose main focus is on the links between fashion discourse, nationalism, and gender within print culture. Although this organization breaks up a study of fashion as seen through the national lens (the two essays on Belgium are not in the same part, for instance), the hope is that the reader will be able to reconnect the dots if that viewpoint is desired.

Part One: The reconfiguration of the international couture industry

Although the couture industry was reconfigured during the war, the balance of power did not ultimately shift away from Paris. As the five essays in this chapter show, despite efforts made by the US, Germany, and Belgium to create national fashion industries, Paris managed to maintain the influence of its couture industry throughout the duration of the war. It did so by focusing on American clients, combatting copying and counterfeits, and launching new styles. But, while it survived the pressures of the war, the Parisian couture industry, reliant on foreign buyers and clients, was extremely hard hit when wartime alliances cut France off from many of its largest international markets. In their respective chapters, Mary Lynn Stewart, Waleria Dorogova, and Georgina Ripley look at how European designers turned to the US market in order to bolster sales.

Mary Lynn Stewart, in her article on the "Wartime marketing of Parisian haute couture in the United States, 1914–17" in Chapter 1, provides a general overview of how Parisian couturiers, working

Figure 0.2 *Two women and a French soldier wearing a Poiret military, c. 1915. Postcard from authors' personal collection.*

together in trade associations and syndicates—notably, the Syndicat de Défense de la Grande Couture, founded in 1914 by Paul Poiret and the Chambre Syndicale de la Couture Parisienne, founded in 1868 but reorganized in 1914 under the direction of Jean Aine-Montaillé—focused their attention on marketing to American buyers and clients. The couturiers sent new fashion designs to be shown in special fashion shows in New York; they also sent their best models to San Francisco and Saint Louis to be shown at the fairs and exhibitions held in those cities. Stewart examines the problem of illegal copying of models, which threatened to undercut much needed revenue, and reveals the ways in which the designers and trade associations attempted to combat this problem without angering important American partners.

Waleria Dorogova, in Chapter 2, "Boué Sœurs: 'Compelled by the war,'" focuses on one Paris-based couture house, Boué Sœurs, which, over the course of the war, began to shift the balance of their international business to the United States. Dorogova shows how the sisters captured the American market by opening a store in New York and forming partnerships with American department stores. The essay also addresses the problems and dangers associated with operating a transatlantic business, including high import taxes, dangerous boat crossings, and immigration laws.

Like the Boué Sœurs, the London-based designer Lucile, or Lady Duff Gordon, also marketed her romantic evening wear to an American clientele. In Chapter 3, "'Gladdening the hearts of warriors': The relationship between Lucile's romantic fashions and morale in the First World War," Georgina Ripley looks at extant garments Lucile designed during the war—mainly held in American collections—in order to see how the designer's dresses help promote an idealized image of womanhood while also responding to wartime morale.

In Chapter 4, "*Die Kriegskrinoline*: A feminine fashion between past and future," Birgit Haase argues that the war crinoline, which was the fashionable silhouette from September 1914 until early 1917 (when it was replaced by the barrel silhouette), expressed the ambivalent position of women during the First World War. Although the silhouette was historicizing—the flared skirts and defined waist harked back to eighteenth- and nineteenth-century crinolines—and helped reinforce gender norms, the new line was also conducive to the mobility and dynamism of modern life. Haase, like Burcu Dogramaci in Chapter 16, also investigates Germany's attempts to create a "national" style, free from Paris control. The Germans, like the Americans, hoped to use the chaos of the war to wrest control from Paris and impose their own style. Ultimately, Stewart, Dorogova, and Haase agree that these attempts fell flat and that Parisian fashion dictated international style throughout the war.

Nele Bernheim's essay, Chapter 5, "Fashion in Belgium during the First World War and the case of Norine Couture," is an apt conclusion to this section. The Belgian fashion industry was located at a crossroads between French, German, and Austrian influence. Belgium was almost fully occupied by the Germans during the war, who fought some of their bloodiest battles on Belgian soil. Hundreds of thousands of Belgians fled to the Netherlands, France, and England. Many of those who remained were largely dependent on foreign charity for food and clothing. Regardless, the Belgian elite still consumed fashion. Bernheim investigates the beginning of Norine Couture, a Belgian fashion house that was likely founded in 1915 by Paul-Gustave Van Hecke and his companion Honorine (Norine) Deschryver. Through a discussion of German and Austrian influences on Belgian fashion, Bernheim also addresses the issues of copying and counterfeits raised by Stewart. In her article, Bernheim traces the early history of Norine Couture, which can be considered the first genuine Belgian fashion house.

Part Two: The materiality of wartime fashion and textile industries

The second section of the book, "The materiality of wartime fashion and textile industries," deals with clothing industries and practices that lie outside of the couture industry but intersect with it in interesting ways. The section begins with Emily Brayshaw's cultural history of the feathered showgirl in Paris and ends with Margherita Rosina's close object analysis of the fabric and textile sample books held in the Fondazione Antonio Ratti. The arrangement of the chapters takes the reader from cultural history to material culture while moving eastward from Paris to Alsace, a region of heightened tension between France and Germany, through occupied Belgium, and to neutral Netherlands. The reader ends in Italy, which first joined the war as a neutral partner of the Triple Alliance, before negotiating a secret pact with Great Britain and France in April 1915.[17] By looking at specific products and practices—feathers, folk dress, lace, handmade clothing, silk textiles—these authors deepen our understanding of the wartime fashion and textile industries in Europe.

In Chapter 6, "Dressed to quill: The origin and significance of the feathered showgirl in First World War Paris," we learn of the opulent music-hall revue *Laisse les Tomber!*, which opened in 1917, in the midst of France's darkest year. It starred Gaby Desyls, a French music-hall star, wearing towering ostrich feather headdresses made by Maison Lewis. The decadent ostrich feathered fashions tapped into the audiences' nostalgia for Belle-Époque luxury and helped revive their use, despite a global crash of the raw plume market during the war. Designers consequently refashioned existing plumes, created cheaper pompons made from offcuts, and used precious stockpiles. Brayshaw's article also emphasizes how music-hall costumes influenced high fashion and department-store fashion in Paris, and as far abroad as Australia.

Sara Hume's essay on traditional Alsatian dress, Chapter 7, "Between fashion and folk: Dress practices in Alsace during the First World War," shows how the French and Germans placed their own meanings on the dress of this contested region during the war.[18] The French used heavily stylized imagery of the typical Alsatian dress and head bow to serve their own agenda. They created effective propaganda images that showed France fighting to free the costumed Alsacienne from her German captors and return her to the nation she loved. The Germans were less interested in the folk costume than they were in the logistics of governing the region and stamping out French influences on fashion.

In her essay in Chapter 8, "The lace industry in France and Belgium during the First World War," on the lace industry in Belgium and France, Marguerite Coppens explains that handmade lace production was promoted and financially subsidized in occupied Belgium during the war, despite the fact that machine-made lace had cornered most of the market. The plight of the Belgian lacemakers became a useful motif in propaganda campaigns aimed at supporting Belgian relief. Although lacemaking did not attract as much attention in France, the government did enforce a law to regulate salaries for work performed at home.

Although the Netherlands was neutral during the war, it also experienced fabric shortages, unemployment, and an economic crisis. Looking closely at Dutch women's magazines, Marta Kargól's essay, Chapter 9, "Industrial and homemade clothing production in the Netherlands: A neutral country during the First World War," examines how the Dutch responded to these problems by making their own clothing and hand-sewing garments and accessories for soldiers, Belgian refugees, and the poor. In the Netherlands, even more so than in France, Germany, or Belgium, handmade clothing became fashionable; it was even "recognized as typically Dutch." There was no Norine Couture equivalent in the Netherlands—no "Dutch" couture was created during the war—but the country did seek to emancipate itself from Parisian fashion, which was sometimes seen as too extravagant, by creating simple, practical, clothing embellished with needlework embroidery at home.

Margheria Rosina, in Chapter 10, "Wartime fabrics in the historical archives of Como weavers and in the collections of the Fondazione Antonio Ratti," looks closely at the sample books of textile manufacturers, dyers, and ribbon makers held in the archives of the Fondazione Antonio Ratti in Como in order to investigate the wartime production of French and Italian silk manufacturers. She finds that some manufacturers produced a few novelty "patriotic" pieces, but that for most manufacturers, production continued as normal during the war.

Part Three: Problematic uniforms: Male and female experiences and secondhand trade networks

"You are doing a man's work and so you are dressed rather like a man," read *The Women's Land Army L.A.A.S. Handbook*, quoted in Amy de la Haye's Chapter 11 essay on the reglementary uniforms worn by the women conscripted into the British Land Army between 1917 and 1919. De la Haye and Jérémie Brucker, the first authors in this part, tell two different stories about how the government on both sides of the Channel reacted to female workers during the First World War. Britain conscripted the Land Girls into a paid, uniformed Army. In France, the *remplaçantes*, or the women who replaced men in their jobs, were hired on a private or state level—they were not considered to be enlisted and were not provided with reglementary uniforms.

De la Haye, in Chapter 12, "'Breeched, booted, and cropped': A dress historical analysis of the uniform worn by members of Britain's Women's Land Army, 1917–19," investigates how the Land Girls reacted to their uniform: some were proud to wear it, while others disliked the performance of parading with it in public. She also looks at how some women personalized their uniform, turning it into a "non-uniform" uniform. In Chapter 12, "The French home front in 1914–18: An investigation into female workwear," Brucker's study of the situation in France shows that many women used their own clothes for workwear, signaling their status through armbands or items incorporated from the male uniform (waistcoats for female servers or hats with the company logo). Some French women wore men's overalls to work in factories. De la Haye and Brucker's essays both show that these "masculinized" female garments caused anxiety within civil society: these garments commanded respect, but also provoked ridicule and derision.

Guillaume de Syon and Manuel Charpy both look at male uniforms, but from very different angles. In Chapter 13, "Rushing to suit up: French aviation's adjustment to wartime uniforms, 1914–16," de Syon studies the challenges associated with the beginnings of French military aviation and charts the rise of the aviator's sartorial identity through the war. The adoption of a uniform fashion specific to aeronautics, de Syon argues, reflects a search for identity through style, ritual, and distinctiveness.

Manuel Charpy, Chapter 14, "The spoils of war: Use and transformations of secondhand uniforms during the First World War in France," is interested in what happens to the uniform once it is removed from the soldier's body and enters into civilian life, as it were. Although repurposed uniforms were a regular part of working-class dress in France in its overseas territories, Charpy's study shows that the war aggravated certain long-held fears about secondhand clothes as vectors of disease. There were also concerns about repurposed "civilian" uniforms posing a risk to army and police departments. Charpy concludes by looking at the ways in which secondhand uniforms in France and its colonies were subverted for patriotic, homoerotic, theatrical, or anti-colonial purposes. Like de Syon, Charpy sees the wearing of the uniform—for de Syon, on combattant aviators and in their civilian life, and for Charpy on non-combatant bodies—as a means of personal expression.

Part Four: Fashion in print: Questions of national fashion and gender

Print sources provide a rich venue for research on fashion during the Great War. Although some print publications ceased due to financial strain, most continued. New magazines were launched during the war as well: *Le Flambeau*, a luxury magazine studied by Nigel Lezama, was launched in May 1915 and ceased publication in January 1916.[19] Authors writing on France throughout this volume typically refer to articles and illustrations from *Le Style parisien*, the official magazine of the couture associations, which was published between July 1915 and April 1916; it was followed by *Les Élégances parisiennes*, published from April 1916 until September 1917.[20] All nineteen essays in this book make clear that information about fashion was printed outside of fashion journals as well: as sources, authors cite newspapers, satirical magazines, postcards, letters, diaries, and books.

However, the authors in Part Four look specifically at written texts from national perspectives. Three of the authors, Zsolt Mészáros, Burcu Dogramaci, and Enrica Morini analyze fashion writing in Hungary, Germany, and Italy, respectively, to see how each country tried to foster a national fashion industry. Mészáros, as well as Nigel Lezama and Andrea Kollnitz, trace shifting attitudes in print towards the recurring wartime tropes of "masculinized" women, "passive" female bodies, and "emasculated" men.

Zsolt Mészáros's essay, Chapter 15, "The gentleman turned 'enemy': Men's fashion in the Hungarian press, 1914–18," shows that in Hungary, men's fashion operated much like women's fashion in other European countries. There was a movement to bolster the national fashion industry which included abandoning French names for Hungarian ones, emphasizing local production, and positioning Hungarian men's fashion in opposition to English fashion, specifically as it was embodied by the figure of the "gentleman". However, Mészáros concludes, like other authors, that men's dress in Hungary during the war continued to follow the European standards. For womenswear, designers looked to Paris; for menswear, Mészáros shows that tailors looked to England.

The authors studied by Burcu Dogramaci in Chapter 16, "The politics of fashion: German fashion writings in times of war," wrote specifically about the need for German artists, designers, and manufacturers to free themselves from Paris and create an independent German fashion industry. Like Birgit Haase, Dogramaci looks at attempts to "Germanize" the war crinoline, or *Kriegscrinoline*, and to label it as a distinctly German design. However, Dogramaci concludes that these writers, who published their more salient fashion-related work in the year 1915, made no attempt to define a German style.

In Chapter 17, "The Italian fashion magazine *Margherita*: The war, women, and the call for a 'Moda Italiana,' 1914–18," Enrica Morini studies Italian attempts to create and define a "Moda Italiana" through the pages of the fashion magazine *Margherita*. Yet, like all the authors writing in this volume who touch on the attempted creation of national fashion industries—in the US, Germany, Belgium, and Netherlands—Italy failed as well. Morini also addresses questions of gender in the pages of *Margherita*. Her essay serves as a pivot to Nigel Lezama and Andrea Kollnitz's contributions. If *Le Flambeau*, studied by Lezama, promoted a retrograde femininity through its fashion pages, the Italian fashion *Margherita* did the opposite: it became even more politically and socially engaged during the war, and helped familiarize readers with the image of the new working woman.

Lezama's analysis of *Le Flambeau* in Chapter 18, "*Le Flambeau*'s fashion discourse during the First World War: Towards a retrograde femininity?," shows how the magazine's fashion column, which grew in size during the course of the war, promoted an ambivalent discourse on the relationship between fashion and femininity. Ultimately, it served to corral female behavior and limit the moral or social disorder that women were deemed capable of fostering.

In Chapter 19, "Is beauty useless? Fashion, gender, and British wartime society in *Punch* Magazine, 1915," Andrea Kollnitz analyzes the cartoons published in the British satirical magazine *Punch* in the year 1915. Looking closely at the illustrations that used fashion as signifier of social roles, gender norms, and class relationships, Kollnitz shows how the cartoons celebrated and ridiculed the creativity of fashionable women in war, mocked female vanity and fashionable ignorance, explored the trope of the uniform as a site of masculine vanity, and joked about the spectacularization of war. Kollnitz's conclusion to her essay is a fitting reminder for why studying fashion matters: "Buying into the largely pejorative tone on fashion and fashion practices that the jokes have communicated, historians may have unconsciously erased, hidden, or silenced other stories on fashion and fashionability as less politically correct in the (dress) history of the Great War in Britain." The same could be said for the histories of the other thirty nations engaged in the battles of the First World War.

Notes

1 A full overview of these works will be addressed further in this article.

2 Marie McLoughlin and Lou Taylor's complete sentence is as follows: "In the midst of the slaughter and the vast traumatic upheavals of this period, a text with its focus on couture clothes might seem positively shocking, even perverse, and our commitment to examining fashion history in the midst of all of this needs an explanation," in McLoughlin and Taylor, "Introduction," *Paris Fashion and World War Two: Global Diffusion and Nazi Control* (London: Bloomsbury, 2020), 13.

3 Daniel Roche, *The Culture of Clothing: Dress and Fashion in the Ancien Regime* (Cambridge: Cambridge University Press, 1994), 5, cited in McLoughlin and Taylor, "Introduction."

4 For a full overview of the economic, social, and political importance of French fashion during the war, see Maude Bass-Krueger and Sophie Kurkdjian, eds., *French Fashion, Women, and the First World War* (New Haven, CT: Yale University Press, 2019).

5 See Mary Louise Roberts, "'This civilization no longer has sexes': La Garçonne and cultural crisis in France after World War I," *Gender & History* 4, 1 (1992): 49–69, and ibid., *Civilization without Sexes: Reconstructing Gender in Postwar France, 1917–1927* (Chicago, IL: University of Chicago Press, 1994).

6 Amy de la Haye's exhibition on the "Land Girls" was held in 2010 (see n. 7). Other scholars who had published articles on First World War fashion include Cheryl Buckley, "'De-humanised females and Amazonians': British wartime fashion and its representation in *Home Chat*, 1914–1918," *Gender & History* 14, 3 (November 2002): 516–36; Patricia Tilburg, "Mimi Pinson goes to war: Taste, class and gender in France, 1900–18," *Gender & History* 23, 1 (April 2011): 92–110; Maude Bass-Krueger, "From the 'union parfaite' to the 'union brisée': The French couture industry and the midinettes during the Great War," *Costume* 47, 1 (2013): 28–44.

7 We thank all of those who spoke at the conference and attended as members of the audience. A full list of the speakers can be found in the Acknowledgments in this book. The conference program is available at: https://europeanfashionwwi.wordpress.com/ (accessed June 20, 2020); and "Fashion, dress, and society in Europe during WWI," Conference, Séminaire Histoire de la Mode, Paris, December 12–13, 2014. Available at: https://europeanfashionwwi.wordpress.com/ (accessed June 20, 2020).

8 Amy de la Haye, "Land Girls: Cinderellas of the soil," Exhibition, Brighton Museum & Art Gallery, October 2009–March 2010 (The Royal Pavilion & Museums, Brighton & Hove, 2019).

9 For the historiography within the French context, see Bass-Krueger and Kurkdjian, eds., *French Fashion*. Our "Introduction" in ibid., particularly pp. 43–51, refer specifically to the subject of wartime fashion within French Studies.

10 Lucy Adlington, *Great War Fashion: Tales from the History Wardrobe* (London: History Press, 2014) and Nina Edwards, *Dressed for War: Uniform, Civilian Clothing and Trappings, 1914 to 1918* (London: I.B. Tauris, 2014).

11 The exhibition, "Krieg und Kleider. Modegrafik zur Zeit des Ersten Weltkriegs," was held September 2014–January 2015, Kunstbibliothek, Staatlichen Museen, Berlin; see the exhibition catalogue, Adelheid Rasche, ed., *Wardrobes in Wartime: Fashion, Art, Design during World War I* (Leipzig: EA Seemann, 2014).

12 The exhibition, "The Great War in costume: Family and fashion on the home front," was held July 19–August 31, 2014, at the Fashion Museum in Bath.

13 "The Great War: Women and fashion in a world at war," Exhibition, Kent State University Museum, Ohio, July 24, 2014–June 7, 2015, available at: https://www.kent.edu/museum/event/great-war-women-and-fashion-world-war (accessed September 12, 2020).

14 "Fashion and freedom" was exhibited at the Manchester Art Gallery, May–November 2016, and a website was created to showcase the work, at: https://www.1418now.org.uk/fashion-freedom/?show_microsite_popup=3788 (accessed June 20, 2020).

15 "Mode & Femmes, 14/18" was open at the Bibliothèque Forney in Paris, February–June 2017. In 2019, the exhibition was augmented and modified for display at the Bard Graduate Center, New York. "French fashion, women, and the First World War" ran September 2019–January 2020.

16 See "Dress and war: Clothing and textiles at home and abroad during the First World War era, 1910–1920," *Journal of Dress History*, Special Issue, 3, 1 (Spring 2019), available at: https://dresshistorians.org/wp/wp-content/uploads/2019/05/The-Journal-of-Dress-History-Volume-3-Issue-1-Spring-2019.pdf. The conference, "Dress and war: Clothing and textiles at home and abroad during the First World War era, 1910–1920," organized by the Association of Dress Historians, was held in London on October 26, 2018.

17 Italy declared war on Austria-Hungary on May 23, 1915.

18 Located on the border between France and Germany, the region of Alsace had long been disputed by the two powers. From the seventeenth century until 1871, Alsace was part of France. Germany claimed Alsace as well as a portion of the neighboring Lorraine region, following France's defeat in the Franco-Prussian War (1870–1).

19 The magazine, whose full title was *Le Flambeau: Grand Magazine de Luxe Hebdomadaire* (The Torch: Weekly Luxury Magazine) was ultimately short-lived. Its first issue was dated May 1915 and its last, January 1916.

20 For more information on the French wartime fashion press, see Bass-Krueger and Kurkdjian, eds., *French Fashion*.

References

Adlington, Lucy. *Great War Fashion: Tales from the History Wardrobe*. London: History Press, 2014.
Bass-Krueger, Maude. "From the 'union parfaite' to the 'union brisée': The French couture industry and the midinettes during the Great War." *Costume* 47, 1 (2013): 28–44.

Bass-Krueger, Maude and Sophie Kurkdjian, eds. *French Fashion, Women, and the First World War*. New Haven, CT: Yale University Press, 2019.

Buckley, Cheryl. "'De-humanised females and Amazonians': British wartime fashion and its representation in *Home Chat*, 1914–1918." *Gender & History* 14, 3 (November 2002): 516–36.

"Dress and war: Clothing and textiles at home and abroad during the First World War era, 1910–1920," Conference, Association of Dress Historians, London, October 26, 2018.

"Dress and war: Clothing and textiles at home and abroad during the First World War era, 1910–1920." *Journal of Dress History*, Special Issue, 3, 1 (Spring 2019). Available at: https://dresshistorians.org/wp/wp-content/uploads/2019/05/The-Journal-of-Dress-History-Volume-3-Issue-1-Spring-2019.pdf (accessed June 20, 2020).

Edwards, Nina. *Dressed for War: Uniform, Civilian Clothing and Trappings, 1914 to 1918*. London: I.B. Tauris, 2014.

"Fashion and freedom," Exhibition, Manchester Art Gallery, May–November 2016. Available at: https://www.1418now.org.uk/fashion-freedom/?show_microsite_popup=3788 (accessed June 20, 2020).

"Fashion, dress, and society in Europe during WWI," Conference, Séminaire Histoire de la Mode, Paris, December 12–13, 2014. Available at: https://europeanfashionwwi.wordpress.com/ (accessed June 20, 2020).

"French fashion, women, and the First World War," Exhibition, Bard Graduate Center, New York, September 2019–January 2020.

la Haye, Amy de. "Land Girls: Cinderellas of the soil," Exhibition, Brighton Museum & Art Gallery, October 2009–March 2010. The Royal Pavilion & Museums, Brighton & Hove, 2019.

Le Flambeau: Grand Magazine de Luxe Hebdomadaire (The Torch: Weekly Luxury Magazine), May 1915–January 1916.

McLoughlin, Marie and Lou Taylor. "Introduction." *Paris Fashion and World War Two: Global Diffusion and Nazi Control*, 13–23. London: Bloomsbury, 2020.

"Mode & femmes, 14/18," Exhibition, Bibliothèque Forney, Paris, February–June 2017.

Rasche, Adelheid, ed. *Wardrobes in Wartime: Fashion, Art, Design during World War I*. Leipzig: EA Seemann, 2014. Exhibition catalogue of "Krieg und Kleider. Modegrafik zur Zeit des Ersten Weltkriegs," Kunstbibliothek, Staatlichen Museen, Berlin, September 2014–January 2015.

Roberts, Mary Louise. "'This civilization no longer has sexes': *La Garçonne* and cultural crisis in France after World War I." *Gender & History* 4, 1 (Spring 1992): 49–69.

Roberts, Mary Louise. *Civilization without Sexes: Reconstructing Gender in Postwar France, 1917–1927*. Chicago, IL: University of Chicago Press, 1994.

Roche, Daniel. *The Culture of Clothing: Dress and Fashion in the Ancien Regime*. Cambridge: Cambridge University Press, 1994.

"The Great War: Women and fashion in a world at war," Exhibition, Kent State University Museum, Ohio, July 24, 2014–June 7, 2015. Available at: https://www.kent.edu/museum/event/great-war-women-and-fashion-world-war (accessed September 1, 2020).

"The Great War in costume: Family and fashion on the home front," Exhibition, Fashion Museum, Bath, July 19–August 31, 2014.

Tilburg, Patricia. "Mimi Pinson goes to war: Taste, class and gender in France, 1900–18." *Gender & History* 23, 1 (April 2011): 92–110.

Part One

The reconfiguration of the international couture industry

1

Wartime marketing of Parisian haute couture in the United States, 1914–17

Mary Lynn Stewart

The First World War threatened Parisian haute couture's status as the center of international fashion. One of its largest and fastest growing markets, the United States, had its own expanding garment industry that might have challenged French domination of the luxury apparel business during a prolonged war. Because the United States did not enter the war for two years and because of its distance from the war front, Americans had more disposable income and fewer inhibitions about spending it on luxury goods than citizens of countries at war, making them an especially attractive wartime market. This essay assesses haute couture's marketing initiatives in the United States between August 1914 and April 1917, when America entered the war.

In America, the period between 1870 and 1914 is known as the Gilded Age, characterized by the emergence of corporate capitalism and a dramatic increase in the number of wealthy families with luxurious lifestyles. During this period, haute couture attracted many American ladies to Paris to acquire their wardrobes and about 500 American buyers—approximately one-third of them women—who regularly purchased between five and sixty models apiece. The buyers represented many dress shops and manufacturers.[1]

Before the war, haute couture was concerned about commercial copying of their models in the US. A provision of American copyright laws that required registration of a product before any promotion of that product was incompatible with the seasonal fashion shows in France, which identified the models worth importing and reproducing in America. Moreover, American officials often refused to register any item of practical utility, like clothing, under their design patent law.[2] Couturiers held early showings for foreign buyers, many of whom commissioned or bought sketches at the showings. Some cut swatches of material or tore trim off garments to have similar materials and notions for garments made by their clients in America.[3] For each model, a buyer received a certificate with information about the fabric and notions needed to produce the model and specified the number of reproductions allowed. Often American manufacturers made far more copies, or close copies, than the certificates specified.[4]

Couturiers also worried about losing control over the quality of their designs and models. They feared that Americans who altered designs before selling them as Parisian originals undermined the reputation and profits of haute couture. Their opinion was shared by the French government. According to the Minister of Commerce, American alterations lowered the "cachet of elegance and distinction" of the French originals—not to mention the revenue from exports to the US.[5]

In April 1913, *La Gazette du Bon Ton* (The Gazette of Good Taste), the society magazine sponsored by seven major Parisian couture houses (Cheruit, Doeuillet, Doucet, Paquin, Poiret, Redfern, and Worth) reported that fashion was the only French industry that was the major foreign competitor in a segment of the American market, yet their German competitors had far more business representatives in America. The magazine claimed that middle-class women were seduced by attractive fashion catalogs and magazines published by foreigners, mostly Germans, falsely advertising French styles. *La Gazette* urged couturiers to "redouble their efforts to uphold the prestige of our elegance."[6] When Paul Poiret visited the States later that year, he discovered knockoffs of his models selling for as little as $15 and duplicates of his dress labels being sold openly. On his return to France, he formed an association to protect couture's interests by ending "counterfeiting of labels and illicit use of their names." The initial members were Callot Sœurs, Cheruit, Doucet, Jeanne Lanvin, Jenny, Paquin, Poiret, Premet, and Worth, joined by textile manufacturers Bianchini-Férier and Rodier.[7] At the suggestion of Poiret's representative in the United States, they became the Syndicat de Défense de la Grande Couture Française (Syndicate for the Defense of French Haute Couture, hereafter the Syndicate) in June of 1914.[8]

On August 3, 1914, the day that Germany and France declared war, the Syndicate rallied to defend their domination of international fashion. They decided to hold the fall openings that month, even though four couturiers were mobilized and several others had closed shop or turned their workshops over to bandage making. Because buses, taxis, and trains were mobilized for the Battle of the Marne, the remaining designers found it difficult to get enough workers into the city and to procure adequate supplies of fabric and trim. Despite these obstacles, the Syndicate held openings in order to maintain the prestige of haute couture in the international market. They established a clearing house to ensure that there would be enough new models for the openings and required foreign buyers to pay in cash or certified checks when they placed their order, not when it was delivered. At least four major houses did not present collections; those who did have openings showed fewer models to fewer buyers than usual. All but one of the major houses followed the syndical line on payment at the time of purchase, which annoyed American buyers who found it difficult to acquire cash or certified checks in the "money panic" of the first few weeks of war. Some found ways to get their product to the market via ports in the south; others followed Worth to London, where American Express and other American businesses honored American cheques or offered credit.[9] The season was not profitable but made a statement about haute couture's continuing presence, if not its future domination, of the market.[10]

The situation was not promising. Even after German troops retreated, repeat customers avoided the capital. *La Gazette du bon ton* ceased publication.[11] *Le Style parisien* (Parisian Style), which replaced *La Gazette* a year later, informed American women accustomed to getting their wardrobes in Paris, what was being shown and worn in Paris.[12] Unfortunately, Parisian society was not lively because of early wartime closures of cafes, theatres, and other entertainment venues and because Parisiennes had adopted "sober" and practical clothing in deference to the war and their new occupations as nurses and drivers. American fashion columnists worried that American women might not find these sober styles attractive. Their concern proved to be exaggerated, but their attitude contributed to a depressed atmosphere.

Compounding haute couture's concerns, in September 1914, the Bureau of Foreign and Domestic Commerce in Washington urged American manufacturers to seize the opportunity to develop foreign trade.[13] The president of the American Ladies Tailoring Association argued that the situation "afforded an opportunity to demonstrate that American designers and dressmakers were the equal of any in Paris."[14] However, there were dissenting opinions. Chicago dressmakers pointed out that American designers could not quickly or economically replace established French designers, while *Women's Wear Daily*, the organ for the New York garment industry, praised the fall collections. The same daily newspaper recorded the resumption of weekly shipping from France to New York and the dates that imported models would arrive in New York.[15]

Vogue magazine, which had promoted Parisian fashion since 1892, had been trying to develop New York fashion since Condé Nast bought the magazine in 1909.[16] In the fall of 1914, the magazine organized a Fashion Fete showing American models, explaining that "there is a small prospect of new Paris styles for the midseason."[17] The Fete drew 700 people and raised money for an American charity for French women and children left destitute by the war. However, American fashion arbiters were quite critical because some contributors held back their best designs for their own openings later that month and some of the garments were not well designed. Influential fashion columnists found the gowns beautiful but not distinctively American. Several prominent society ladies publicly vowed that they would purchase their wardrobes in Paris. *Women's Wear Daily* admonished the "Made in America cabal" that what they really needed to do was improve the quality of American clothes.[18]

Despite a lukewarm reception in New York, the Fashion Fete galvanized couturiers in Paris.[19] As German troops pulled back in the fall of 1914, refugees from the capital straggled back to the city. But most American buyers had left, because there was little product to buy or transit to ship it. Many seats were empty at the fall 1914 openings. A *Vogue* article speculated that there would be no midwinter collections.[20] Although *Women's Wear Daily* correspondents liked the fall collections, one questioned whether the spring 1915 collections would be successful.[21] Much the same combination of positive coverage of the collections yet public doubt about the future occurred in the same newspaper in the spring of 1915.[22]

Haute couture had two major responses to the crisis. One was to participate in the Panama–Pacific International Exposition in San Francisco in the summer of 1915. Textile and clothing manufacturers associations had presented their creations at international trade fairs between 1900 and 1914. In 1904, several couturiers had taken part in the Louisiana Purchase Exposition (informally known as the Saint-Louis world fair). Despite regulations that prohibited copying goods on display "without the permission of the exhibitor," many French companies, including couture houses, complained about counterfeiting after the Saint-Louis fair.[23]

In May 1912, France had accepted an invitation to participate in an international exhibition in San Francisco to celebrate the completion of the Panama Canal. Although the war interrupted preparations, the government reaffirmed its commitment to the project late in 1914.[24] For two years, French ministers and officials lobbied the American government, legislators, and officials about tariffs and industrial property rights and recruited French companies to display their products. They encountered opposition in both endeavors. American manufacturers, patent agents, and senators tried to rescind or limit the protection offered foreign businesses willing to display products at the fair.[25] Many French exporters and associations like the Federation of the Fashion Industries (eleven syndicates including couture, confection and other branches of the garment industry) refused to take part on the grounds that their products and designs would not be protected from tariffs and copying. The Minister of Commerce reminded the Federation that French exports to the States had almost doubled between 1902 and 1912 and described how the French ambassador and other government agents had lobbied American legislators to vote for a September 1913 law conferring tariff immunity on all products destined for the fair and assuring exhibitors of their property in all goods sent to the fair for a term of three years.[26]

While these negotiations went on, the larger organization of French fashion designers, united under the Chambre Syndicale de la Couture Parisienne (Trade Association of Parisian Couture, henceforth Chambre Syndicale), reorganized itself after ousting twenty German- and Austrian-owned or -financed houses. A few of the ousted houses dissociated themselves from alleged German or Austrian ties, notably Drecoll and Redfern, and were readmitted. The newly reconstituted Chambre Syndicale unanimously agreed to contribute to the exhibition in San Francisco to counter the "campaign led against Parisian couture to the profit of American fashions."[27] The President of the Chambre Syndicale, Jean Aine-Montaillé, kept American buyers informed about these developments and portrayed German and Austrian houses as copyists who undersold Paris houses.[28]

The Syndicate, individual couturiers exhibiting at the fair, and *Women's Wear Daily* did advance publicity for the fashion exhibit at the fair.[29] Twelve prominent couturiers, including Beer, Callot Sisters, Cheruit, Doucet, Jenny, Paquin, Premet, and Worth, displayed as a collective.[30] Sixty outfits, ranging from evening gowns to children's clothing worth about $100,000, were shown on wax mannequins in three settings where French designs had been publicized before the war: Vichy, Longchamps, and the Côte d'Azur.[31] That publicity had included *Vogue*, *Women's Wear Daily*, and other American magazines and newspapers. As the three sites revived the following year, the same magazines and papers resumed reporting on them.[32] *La Gazette du bon ton* reappeared with a double issue on the San Francisco couture exhibit, one in English done in collaboration with *Vogue*. The English edition was a translation of the French original, minus one piece on financial exigencies in France.[33]

Both volumes claimed that the collection reflected "the elegance of war, a light and sporty elegance, loose, permitting easy gestures . . ." A long-time fashion columnist, Nada, specified that the skirts were gathered and the hemlines above the ankles, so women could run and move easily, while waistlines were relaxed "in order to lean over to console someone who suffers."[34] This kind of publicity reflected a trend toward practicality in wartime fashion.[35] Conversely, another article by an occasional reviewer added that women "must appear frivolous, even when we have never been less frivolous."[36] These commentators were expressing two French conceptions of American taste: one that American women wanted more practical clothing, the other that they desired spectacular outfits from Paris. Both types of publicity encouraged American consumption of haute couture.[37]

Couture's second response to the threat of American competition saw couturiers break with tradition by sending new models directly to New York before Parisians viewed them. Concerned that Americans might not buy subdued wartime styles, couturiers sent models that varied from the French versions.[38] This was precisely the kind of catering to American customers that worried pre-war couturiers. The nine houses and two textile manufacturers in the Syndicate sent 100 models and many new fabrics to New York. Poiret, who ran his company from the front, was permitted to return to the capital and advertised that he would make models for America alone.[39] He also persuaded *Le Style parisien* to set up a charity for war orphans to benefit from the New York event. The French Fashion Fete, held at the Ritz-Carlton Hotel in November 1915, was a success.[40] John Wanamaker bought all Poiret's models—the only Poiret models available that season—and many customers trusted other houses enough to pay in advance of delivery. *Vogue*, which co-sponsored the fete, devoted a special issue to it.[41]

In addition to these major initiatives, the Syndicate continued their campaign against copying. Some of this campaign was accomplished legally and amicably.[42] When the Women's Board of Trade in Massachusetts mobilized against foreign labels on American-made goods in early 1915, Aine-Montaillé expressed the full support of haute couture for the campaign.[43] The Chambre Syndicale also negotiated with American importers to impose certificates confirming that a design was a French original.[44] As President of the Chambre Syndicale until the spring of 1917, Aine-Montaillé wrote regularly to *Women's Wear Daily* to soothe recurring tensions about escalating anti-copying measures by the Syndicate. When the Chambre Syndicale ousted German and Austrian buyers and implicated German American buyers in early 1915, Aine-Montaillé wrote *Women's Wear Daily*, saying that German American buyers were only identified and shamed if they copied.[45]

In the winter of 1915–16, the Syndicate put out a stringent set of rules to protect their models from foreign buyers that, in their terms, "have perverted and vulgarized our designs." One of these rules designated the fashion magazines allowed to view the collections and one blacklisted any buyers who engaged in illegal copying. Although the principal targets were German and Austrian magazines and buyers, there was some spillover to German American houses and buyers. The spillover angered Americans. The *New York Times* suggested that importers ignore Poiret and deal with "others among the 402-odd French designers."[46]

When the Syndicate excluded a prominent New York buyer, Morris Weingarten of Weingarten and Pearl, he protested publicly until the Syndicate retreated from their position. Weingarten also criticized the Syndicate for their assumption that professional buyers, as opposed to manufacturers, were responsible for copying. The Syndicate also distributed entry cards for openings but refused to extend them to naturalized German Americans, who were labelled "Style Pirating Manufacturers."[47] In February 1916, many buyers announced that they would not apply for entry cards and some members of the Syndicate ignored the entry-card system.[48] Major American importers such as Bendel, Bergdorf-Goodman, and Bonwit Teller formed an Association that worked with the Chambre Syndicale and the Syndicate to set up a clearing house to handle shipping of models under a double seal.[49] But Callot Sœurs, Jenny, and Paquin soon withdrew and Worth's departure in the summer of 1916 signaled the dissolution of the Syndicate.[50] None of these efforts resolved the problem of illegal copying in the United States, and the couture syndicate repeatedly suggested solutions in the remaining years of the war and for decades thereafter.[51]

Throughout this turmoil, haute couture mounted seasonal collections and President Aine-Montaillé assured American buyers that the seasonal openings would be held on schedule.[52] In the spring of 1916, *Vogue* reported that "Bubbles of Fashion" were rising "to the Surface in Paris."[53] However, supply remained a problem. The German occupation of the northeastern departments amputated two-fifths of the textile industry's productive capacity.[54] To compensate for the dearth of wool and cotton, designers used more taffeta and serge. When serge became too scarce in 1916, couturiers introduced new, finer jerseys made by Rodier. To replace luxury fabrics, they used more decorative embroidery, ribbons, lace, tassels, or beads.[55] The number of workers employed in couture and confection ateliers nearly doubled from 48,880 in August 1914 to 85,077 in January 1917.[56]

In 1916 and 1917, the industry tried to attract American customers. The couture houses of Boué Sœurs and Marianne Buzenet acquired shops in New York in 1915 and 1916, respectively, and in 1917, Poiret opened a New York branch.[57] Over these two years, many other couturiers sent models to stores like J. M. Gidding and Co. of Fifth Avenue, which set up salons displaying Paris originals alongside salons with "modified" versions of these originals.[58] Individual couturiers combined openings in New York with support for charities or with exhibits of French paintings.[59] Couturiers also made designs more attractive for American buyers and improved deliveries.[60] Even before America entered the war in the spring of 1917 and imposed the famous restriction to four-and-a-half yards of wool for suits or dresses, couturiers had shifted from the barrel silhouette to a straighter line.[61] After the restrictions, they raised hems, slimmed skirts, shortened jackets, and eliminated "useless" pockets and flounces. Subsequent collections kept the silhouette but added draping and other details.[62]

Conclusion

When America entered the war, Paris and haute couture welcomed American intervention.[63] Some couturiers added items of clothing like tailored suits or shirtwaist dresses—outfits "beloved in America"—to their collections.[64] North and South American buyers—and even some British buyers, despite restrictions on luxury imports—made larger than usual purchases.[65] Over the next two years of war, couture continued to make and sell items of clothing like suits but also luxurious gowns, all of which attracted North and South American buyers. One consequence was steady sales of French designs in North and South American shops. After the war, Britain remained the largest foreign market for French clothing, but the United States took second place by the mid-1920s. Western European countries came third through seventh place in these years, but North and South American countries like Canada and Argentina moved up to eighth and ninth place among importers of French clothing.[66] Haute couture had held onto and expanded its American markets.

Notes

1 Allison Mathews David, "Vogue's New World: American fashionability and the politics of style," *Fashion Theory* 10, 1–2 (2006): 13–38. The figure for American buyers is from an advertisement for "Original Paris fashions," *Women's Wear Daily (WWD)*, September 18, 1914, 9.

2 Archives de la Chambre de Commerce de Paris, III 3.91 (18) Soleau Reports, 1905 and 1915, and Tailleur note.

3 "La Grande Couture française et quelques uns de ses clients," *Le Style parisien*, December 5, 1915.

4 Ibid. and Nancy Green, *Ready-to-Wear and Ready-to-Work:. A Century of Industry and Immigrants in Paris and New York* (Durham, NC: Duke University Press, 1997), 81.

5 Arsène Bonnaire, Director of Maison Laferriere, "American taste in dress," *New York Times*, May 24, 1912, 6; "American lifting Paris fashion yoke," ibid., July 14, 1912, 4; and "American women responsible for sensational French styles," ibid., July 5, 1914, 8.

6 André de Fouquières, "Du Prestige de la mode aux États-Unis," *La Gazette du bon ton*, April, 1913, 177–8.

7 Edna Woolman Chase and Ilka Chase, *Always in Vogue* (New York: Doubleday, 1954), 92–3. "Le Syndicat de Défense de la Grande Couture Française et des Industries s'y rattachant," *Le Style parisien*, November, 1915.

8 "Copyrighting clothes," *Vogue*, February 1, 1915, 17.

9 Anne Rittenhouse, "London honors American drafts," *WWD*, August 6, 1914; Anne Rittenhouse, "De Lange letters," ibid., August 28, 1914; Anne Rittenhouse, "Fashion under fire," *Vogue*, October 1, 1914, 11 and 40–1; Anne Rittenhouse, "Couturiers under arms," *Vogue*, October 15, 1921, 44; Lady Duff-Gordon, "Paris fashions that escaped the war zone," *The Washington Post*, October 22, 1914.

10 De Lange, "Couturiers will remain in Paris," *WWD*, November 30, 1914, 1. Reported no profit from the August showings. Paquin Ltd. had "a very heavy loss" of half a million pounds sterling in 1914 and offered no dividend that year, according to "Mme. Paquin has no idea of quitting Paquin Ltd.," ibid., May 7, 1915, 1, 7, and 11. No doubt, other houses suffered as well.

11 La Rédaction, "La Gazette du bon ton et la Guerre," *La Gazette du Bon Ton*, Summer 1914, 1.

12 La Rédaction, "Le Couturier," and Francine, "Lettre d'une Parisienne," *Le Style parisien*, September 2, 1915. Francine's "Letter from a Parisian" appeared monthly until the magazine folded in 1916.

13 "American trade activity. Bid for European markets," *London Times*, September 17, 1914.

14 "M. Greene, President of American Ladies Tailoring Association," *WWD (Fashion Illustrated Edition)*, September 3, 1914; "La Haute Couture," ibid., September 21, 1914, 1.

15 "Chicago dressmakers discuss fashion situation," ibid., September 8, 1914, 1; "Causerie de Paris," ibid., September 15, 1914; "Stern Brother's Opening," ibid., September 24, 1914.

16 David, "*Vogue*'s New World," 13–14.

17 "Editor's note," *Vogue*, September 15, 1914, 25; "Editorial," ibid., October 15, 1914, 29.

18 "The Ritz-Carlton Fashion Fête," *WWD*, November 6, 1914, 1, 5; "Costumes," ibid., November 13, 1914, 7; "A Reproach or A Recommendation," ibid., November 13, 1914.

19 "Fashion vs. The War Zone," *New York Times*, March 14, 1915, 1.

20 "The story of the Fashion Fête," "The latest, perhaps the last, Paris fashions," "Suggestions from Paris," *Vogue*, November 1, 1914, 51–61; "Designers who would rival Paris invited to society's Fashion Fête . . .," *The Washington Post*, October 1, 1914.

21 "Paris still live fashion center," *WWD*, November 10, 1914, 1; "Plenty of Paris models for early spring," ibid., November 14, 1914, 1; "Paris conditions better than expected," ibid., November 20, 1914, 1; "Doubt success of Paris Spring Openings," ibid., November 28, 1914, 1.

22 "Chez Doucet," ibid., March 11, 1915, 1; "Features of the Callot Collection," ibid., March 12, 1915, 1; "Belle Armstrong Whitney lauds Paris production," ibid., March 16, 1915, 1; "The Lanvin Collection," ibid., April 1, 1915, 1. See the lists of buyers in "Model buyers back from Paris," ibid., September 8, 1915, 14.

23 Archives Nationales (AN) AN/F/12/7431, Exposition de San Francisco, dossier Règlements, République Française, Ministère du Commerce, de l'Industrie, des Postes et des Télégraphes. *Exposition Universelle Internationale de Saint-Louis en 1904, Règlement général* (Paris: Imprimerie Nationale, Mars 1913).

24 AN/F/12/7431, Exposition, dossier "Débats parlementaires," *Journal Officiel*, 191 (July 15, 1914): 2744–65; dossier "Communiqués à la France": M. Gaston Thomson, Ministre du Commerce, de l'Industrie, etc., to the Conseil des

Ministres, undated but likely December 1914; and dossier "Crédits": Tirman, Commissaire général de l'Exposition, Rapport à M. le Ministre du Commerce, de l'Industrie etc., (December 2, 1914).

25 AN/F/12/7430 Exposition de San Francisco, dossier "Protection de la propriété industrielle et franchise douanière": Letters from Comité français des expositions à l'étranger to Minister of Commerce (February 18, 1913); from M. Jusserand, Ambassador to the United States, to Senator Dupon, President of the Comité des Expositions (June 20, 1913); from Jusserand to Minister of Foreign Affairs (November 14, 1913); copy of a confidential letter from President of the Commission française d'Étude de la Panama Pacific International Exposition to President Moore of Panama Pacific Exposition, undated; letter from Jusserand to M. Gaston Doumergue, Président du Conseil de Ministres, to Ministre des Affaires étrangères (December 18, 1913); telegrams to and from Charles C. Moore, President Panama Pacific International Exposition, sent on (December 15 and 17, 1913).

26 AN/F/12/7431, Exposition, dossiers "Objections du commerce française"; "Correspondance avec la Chambre de Commerce de Paris": Letters from the President of Chambre de Commerce de Paris, (March 7, 1914); from M. Danier, Président de la Fédération des Industries de la Mode, undated, except 1914, and from the Minister of Commerce, (March 18, 1914). See also Tirman Report subtitled "Historique de la participation française à l'Exposition de San Francisco" (December 2, 1914).

27 AN/F/12/7431, Exposition, dossier "Communiqués à la France": M. Gaston Thomson, Ministre du Commerce, to the Conseil des Ministres, undated but likely (December, 1914); Maude Bass-Krueger, "La mode en France durant la Première Guerre mondiale: Approches d'histoire culturelle," MA thesis, Bard Graduate Center, New York, 2009, 70–1 and 76.

28 "M. Aine thinks two fashion centers impossible," *WWD*, March 12, 1915, 1; "The German couturiers in Paris," ibid., March 17, 1915, 1; "Attitude today of French Syndicate," ibid., March 2, 1915, 1, 12.

29 "La Haute Couture," ibid., Feb. 10, 1915, 2; "The Paquin Models for San Francisco," ibid., March 16, 1915, 1; Edith L. Rosenbaum, "An exhibition worthy of France," ibid., April 20, 1915, 1.

30 *Exposition Universelle San Francisco, Panama Pacific International Exposition 1915, Section Française Catalogue Général* (1915), 441–4.

31 "Paris at the Panama Pacific Exhibition," *WWD*, June 15, 1915, 1.

32 E.g., "Deauville hotels gay with smart Parisians in holiday sports attire," ibid., July 17, 1916, 1; De Lange, "New models of Paris creations seen in Biarritz," ibid., September 26, 1916; "Biarritz styles forecast mode of the Season," ibid., October 29, 1916.

33 *La Gazette du Bon Ton* (Summer 1915).

34 Henri Adam, "La Coutume de Paris," *La Gazette du Bon Ton*, Summer 1915, 4–7 (quote 7); Nada, "A Tours simples," ibid., Summer 1915, 15–26 (quote 17); Jeanne Ramon Fernandez, "Grand-habits," ibid., Summer 1915, 51–61 (quote 91).

35 Florence Brachet Champsaur, "French fashion during the First World War," *Business and Economic History* 2 (2004): 1–4.

36 Princesse de Cleve, "Volants et Paniers," *La Gazette du Bon Ton*, Summer 1915, 33–45 (quote 33).

37 "War quiets fashions, makes them more sensible, say buyers arriving from France," *The Washington Post*, August 31, 1915; A. S., "Here comes the bride from Paris," *Vogue*, May 1, 1916.

38 E. G. (Elizabeth Gramont), "Paris by proxy," and G. H., "The city behind the Allies," *Vogue*, November 15, 1914, 42–6.

39 "France protects her industry," *WWD*, May 18, 1915, 1.

40 "Ritz-Carlton Fashion Show a success," ibid., November 23, 1915, 1; "What Edith thinks of the Fashion Fete," ibid., November 24, 1915, 1.

41 "Paris is Paris for a 'That,'" *Vogue*, December 1, 1915, 44; "The Paris Fashion Fete," ibid., December 15, 1915, 33ff.; Roger Boutet de Monvel, "Fashioning our first French Fashion Fete," ibid., 15 December, 1915, 34–5; Roger Boutet de Monvel, "The Blue Book of the Grands Maisons," ibid., December 15, 1915; "La Fête parisienne à New York," *Le Style parisien*; Francine, "Lettre d'une Parisienne," ibid., November 4, 1915, 22 ff.

42 "Campaign is successful against fake label makers and users," *WWD*, December 7, 1914, 1; "Another conviction in fake label campaign," ibid., December 19, 1914, 1; "Hickson denies charges in suit by Boué Sœurs," ibid., November 1, 1916, 1; "Copyright point made an issue in Hickson Defense," ibid., November 3, 1916, 1; "Hickson lost first point in Boué Sœur Suit," ibid., November 6, 1916, 1.

43 "Purchase only goods made in the U.S.A.," ibid., February 2, 1915, 1; "Paris welcomes 'Made in America' Movement," ibid., March 6, 1915, 1.

44 "Le Syndicat de Défense de la grande couture et des industries s'y rattachant fait la chasse aux contrefacteurs," *Les Élégances parisiennes*, June 1916; Bass-Krueger, "La mode en France," 47.

45 See "American citizens welcome to Paris," *WWD*, January 25, 1915; "The German couturiers in Paris," ibid., March 17, 1915, 1; "Attitude today of French Syndicate," ibid., March 24, 1915, 2; "M. Aine Tells of Paris Conditions," ibid., April 7, 1915, 1.

46 "Won't crown Poiret as Czar of Fashion," *New York Times*, December 20, 1915; "First news of French Syndicate's official plans," ibid., January 23, 1916, 2.

47 "Couturiers planning to eliminate certain buyers," *WWD*, June 1, 1915, 1; "France is firm against passports for buyers of German origin," ibid., July 7, 1915, 1; "La Haute Couture," ibid., October 39, 1915, 17; "Defense Syndicate of Paris breaks with exhibiting American importers," ibid., November 17, 1915, 1; "Plans for protection of American importers misunderstood, says Ortiz," "La Haute Couture," and "Ortiz discredits report of Defense Syndicate's impending dissolution," ibid., February 7, 1916.

48 "Most of Provisional Cards not renewed by Defense Syndicate," and "Supreme test of Defense Syndicate's strength made by Paris Spring Openings," ibid., 1, 10 and 13.

49 "Association of American Importers making good progress in organizing," ibid., January 9, 1916, 1; "New French–American Commission proposed to protect Paris Models," ibid., January 11, 1916, 1; "Peddling of Paris Models is abuse chiefly aimed at by Importers' Alliance," ibid., February 5, 1916, 1; "Importers," ibid., February 5, 1916, 13.

50 "La Haute Couture," ibid., December 3, 1915; "Further withdrawals," ibid., January 10, 1916, 1; "Withdrawals of Jenny,... confirmed," ibid., January 15, 1916, 1; "Defense Syndicate dissolution follows Worth resignation," ibid., August 9, 1916, 1.

51 "La Protection de la Propriété industrielle," *Les Élégances parisiennes* (Winter 1918–19); M. L. Stewart, "Copying and copyrighting haute couture," *French Historical Studies* 28, 1 (2005): 103–30.

52 "Views of M. E. Aine, President, Chambre Syndicale de la Couture," *WWD*, December 23, 1914, 1; "La Haute Couture," ibid., January 11, 1915, 1.

53 A. S., "Bubbles of fashion rise to the surface in Paris," *Vogue*, April 15, 1916, 35–40; "Paris rolls away the hoop," ibid., May 1, 1916, 46–8. Also see "Paris working hard to retain her prestige," *WWD*, February 24, 1916, 1.

54 Albert Aftalion, *L'Industrie textile en France pendant la guerre* (Paris: PUF, 1924), 41ff.

55 A. S., "The tale of the Paris Openings," *Vogue*, February 15, 1916, 3–6; "Paris passes judgment on the New Modes," *Vogue*, April 1, 1917, 45–6. See also "Paris revives Old Time ideas in embroidery," and De Lange, "Prints give way to embroideries in Paris," *WWD*, October 21, 1916, and December 1 and 18, 1916, 1.

56 "Les Industries de la mode et la reprise des affaires," *Les Élégances parisiennes*, January, 1917, 149.

57 "Boué Sœurs bring their Paris signature to New York," *Vogue*, June 1, 1916, 51; "Marianne Buzenet brings an atmosphere of Paris into her New York Salon," ibid., August 1, 1916, 52; Advertisement for Poiret Incorporated, 1239 Broadway, *WWD*, January 17, 1917, 26–7.

58 "The Paris shop of America: A bit of the Rue de la Paix transferred to Fifth Avenue," *Vogue*, October 1, 1916, 32; A. S., "The fashions of Paris lead the simple life," ibid., August 1, 1917; "The Paris shop of America," ibid., October 1, 1917. See also "Kurzman showing 350 models on mannequins in private fashion show," March 20, 1916; "Dresses," ibid., June 1 and 13, 1916, 1.

59 "New York clothes itself in dignity," ibid., December. 1, 1917, 161; "New York Interest . . .," ibid., May 1, 1918; "Fashion display at Palace," *New York Times*, December 4, 1917, 11.

60 "Offerings of Paris shops to tempt American buyers," *WWD*, July 1, 1916, 1; "Good deliveries please buyers," ibid., August 9, 1916, 1.

61 "Paris displays forecast New Season's modes," ibid., January 12, 1917, 1; "Paris views Jupe Tonneau, not a practical mode," ibid., January 22, 1917, 1; De Lange, "Revolution in fashion world," ibid., January 30, 1917, 1. See also "Forecast of the Spring Mode," *Vogue*, February 1, 1917.

62 "New York does its bit," *Vogue*, May 15, 1917, 35–6; "French designers, aided and abetted by American desires . . .," *New York Times*, August 5, 1917, 2.

63 "A star-spangled Paris," *Vogue*, 1 June 1917, 49–53; "Jenny makes coat gown—Lanvin calls her famous frock 'Pershing,'" *New York Times*, October 7, 1917, 38.

64 "Paris cuts its garments according to the times," *Vogue*, November 1, 1917, 54; "Paris suggests these new silhouettes," ibid., December 15, 1917, 41; "Uncensored news from the fashion front," ibid., December 15, 1917; J. R. F. (Jeanne Ramon Fernandez), "Paris sacrifices all things save elegance," ibid., April 15, 1918, 27 and 29.

65 "Bought more in Paris than ever—Henri Bendell," *WWD*, April 9, 1917; De Lange, "Business of Paris couture is improving," *WWD*, April 19, 1917, 1.

66 Didier Grumbach, *Histoire de la mode* (Paris: Seuil, 1993), 32–3, citing *Statistique Générale de France*.

References

Aftalion, Albert. *L'Industrie textile en France pendant la guerre*. Paris: PUF, 1924.
Archives de la Chambre de Commerce de Paris, III 3.9.
Archives Nationales (AN), F/12/7430 and 7431, Exposition de San Francisco.
Bass-Krueger, Maude. "La Mode en France durant la Première Guerre mondiale: Approches d'histoire culturelle," MA thesis, Bard Graduate Center, New York, 2009.
Champsaur, Florence Brachet. "French fashion during the First World War." *Business and Economic History* 2 (2004): 1–15.

Exposition Universelle Internationale de Saint-Louis en 1904, Règlement général. Paris: Imprimerie Nationale, Mars, 1913.

Exposition Universelle San Francisco, Panama Pacific International Exposition 1915, Section Française Catalogue Général. 1915.

Green, Nancy. *Ready-to-Wear and Ready-to-Work: A Century of Industry and Immigrants in Paris and New York.* Durham, NC: Duke University Press, 1997.

Grumbach, Didier. *Histoire de la mode.* Paris: Seuil, 1993.

La Gazette du bon ton, 1913–14 and 1915.

Le Style parisien, 1915–16.

Les Élégances parisiennes, 1916–19.

London Times, 1914–15.

Mathews David, Allison. "*Vogue*'s New World: American fashionability and the politics of style." *Fashion Theory* 10, 1–2 (2006): 13–38.

New York Times, 1912–17.

Stewart, Mary Lynn. "Copying and copyrighting haute couture." *French Historical Studies* 28, 1 (2005): 103–30.

The Washington Post, 1914–15.

Vogue, 1912–21.

Women's Wear Daily (WWD), 1914–18.

Woolman Chase, Edna and Ilka Chase. *Always in Vogue* (New York: Doubleday, 1954; and London: Victor Gollancz).

2

Boué Sœurs

"Compelled by the War"[1]
Waleria Dorogova

"Let's pretend there never was a war," said Boué Sœurs.[2]

The Great War must be emphasized as a principal force and an incomparable catalyst on the business development and the corporate identity of Boué Sœurs, a couture house that operated for sixty years from 1897 until 1957. Having become one of haute couture's successful pioneers of transatlantic expansion, an influential agent helping maintain Franco-American fashion trade, and a purveyor of a distinctly French stylistic narrative in support of national legitimation and the patriotic cause, the house of Boué Sœurs attests to the war's dual mechanics of cataclysm and progress, crisis and optimism.

In 1914, Sylvie Montegut née Boué (1872–1953) and Jeanne d'Etreillis née Boué (1876–1957) ran an internationally established couture house, whose principal premises was located at 9, rue de la Paix.[3] They also had branch stores in London at 39, Conduit Street (est. 1911), as well as in Cairo, Bucharest, and St. Petersburg.[4] The house catered to a high society clientele, who revolved in the Eastern court circles and grand centers of European elite tourism which were connected by luxury train lines such as the Orient Express.

Jeanne and her husband, Baron Achille d'Etreillis, had just returned from a business trip to St. Petersburg as the July crisis evolved, bringing growing international instability. When war broke out in August, business in the Orient and Eastern Europe was instantly terminated.[5] The Paris headquarters, along with the Conduit Street branch, were both maintained throughout the war. However, shipment of orders to Russia, Romania, and Egypt, all topographically placed on the opposite side of the Central Powers' territories, became entirely impossible.[6] So, too, did travel. Geographic constraint and the uncertainty of the conflict's outcome quickly disrupted the Boué Sœurs' trading network. Without a doubt, it was impossible for the house to survive solely under French, or even European, patronage.[7]

Figure 2.1 Left to right: *Baronne Jeanne d'Etreillis and Sylvie Montegut with their children Mounette and Philippe in the park of Château de Maison Rouge, Gagny, summer 1917. The C.M. Roussel Boué Sœurs Archive/Waleria Dorogova.*

When France found herself at war in early August of 1914, the collectivity of Paris couturiers, in the midst of their preparations for the autumn showings, was struck by the alarming unpredictability of the new season's outcome. Impending isolation from the immensely profitable US market and the gradually decreasing clientele, a consequence of Americans' cautiousness in travelling to Europe, threatened to become a financial threat to most high-profile dressmaking houses. Under severe pressure, Paris designers were forced to re-evaluate their strategies. Of utmost urgency was supplying American buyers with the current collections, and designers took advantage of the fact that American tourists were awaiting ships in England to be taken home. Fashion journalist Anne Rittenhouse reported that Boué Sœurs, who had "quite a reputation among American buyers," showed in London in October and had particular success with "American tourists who included at that time some of the richest women in the United States."[8] Meanwhile, in New York, it was hoped the European crisis would help a national American fashion force emerge that would "somewhat dim the prestige and luster" of

Paris imports.[9] In August of 1914, there could be no certainty about whether Parisian collections would even be presented or produced. However, trade professionals were doubtful about the prospects of America's sartorial independence from France, and dismissed the possibility of a downfall of Paris fashions: "They rest on too secure a foundation and the resourcefulness of the French is to be reckoned with," argued the *Brooklyn Daily Eagle*.[10]

Boué Sœurs' fall 1914 visit to America

Vastly experienced in international outreach, Boué Sœurs put together a delegation for a transatlantic expedition to America. They needed to sell the winter collection and it was also a good opportunity to evaluate future trade possibilities. US President Woodrow Wilson had no intention of entering the Great European War in 1914. This made investing in the ever-expanding metropolis of New York a promising prospect. The Tariff Act of 1913 had also considerably facilitated import regulations by lowering fees.[11]

Jeanne, who had been in charge of the international trade network since the inception of Boué Sœurs, set out for New York on the RMS *Lusitania* in late October of 1914 to present the winter collection in the luxurious Plaza and Biltmore hotels. The day before their American debut, Boué Sœurs placed advertisements in the daily papers, announcing that: "As New York Cannot Go to Paris During the War Paris Comes to New York."[12] The highly anticipated Plaza showing, beginning November 2, turned out to be a great success and was covered by all the major fashion columns. For two weeks, Boué Sœurs staged daily showings with live mannequins at the Plaza before moving the collection to be displayed at the Biltmore, where it received equally laudatory press reviews. Asserting that the war had not compromised or limited in any way the Boué Sœurs' access to fabric supply, Jeanne stated in an interview with *The New York Herald*: "we have certain materials that are especially reserved for us, like the veritable *chute d'eau*, a new wool velours, and a certain taffeta that is sold nowhere else and of which we will control the output for three years".[13] She added that the firm had ordered their fabrics earlier than usual, ensuring that Boué Sœurs would not be affected by the anticipated shortages. Only months after this statement was published, the German occupation of north-eastern France and its textile mills caused considerable loss for the couture industry. The invaded area included a cluster of "lingerie cities" between Lorraine and the Vosges, where Boué Sœurs' rural suppliers of fine cottons, whitework, and lace were located.[14]

The winter collection of 1914–15 consisted of the very first creations that were conceived before the rumblings of an impending war.[15] New York's newspapers were in agreement about the novel and unexpected features of the Boué collection. Coat-, dress-, and skirt-lengths as well as the waistline had noticeably risen; the hem was now up to 10 inches from the ground. Coats and dresses were characterized by a semi-fitted waistline that corresponded with new short, bolero-type jackets. Face-framing, high-standing lace collars were a picturesque detail of many designs, some reminiscent of sixteenth-century Medici collars. Equally delicate and historically inspired were the bell-shaped cuffs completing the long sleeves. Skirts, draped around the hips, were not only much shorter but also considerably more bouffant than in the designs for spring of 1914, when Boué Sœurs favored a lean and long silhouette, or what *Vanity Fair* believed to be a "possible forerunner of the fitted dress."[16]

Bright colors were entirely absent in the chromatic prism of the collection. Black, Russian green, navy blue, *corbeau* (raven) blue (launched by Boué), and peacock blue made up the dark color spectrum, while fawn and cream lightened the palette. The collection featured predominantly solid cloth; plush velvet and corduroy weaves were a novelty of the season. Wool velour, changeant taffeta, serge, and faille were softened with flounces of net, tulle, and chiffon. Tinsel brocade, characteristic of the evening wear designs, was overlaid with metallic net, gold, and silver lace, and bore rich adornments of jet and gold braid, some trimmed with monkey fur. The silk flower garlands, explicitly associated with Boué Sœurs in their 1920s *robes de style*, were already a recognizable trademark, as were distinct references to the Rococo aesthetics favored by the art-minded Boué sisters.

A second American visit in 1915 and the establishment of a New York branch

Despite hoping for the contrary, the winter months did not bring a resolution to the pan-European conflict. Given the satisfactory order outcome for the winter collection after the first Manhattan presentations, it was clear to the Boué Sœurs that they should conduct several showings of the spring collection for 1915 in the United States. In late February 1915, Jeanne brought an exhibition of gowns to the Ponce de Leon Hotel in St. Augustine, Florida, and in March to New York's Waldorf-Astoria on Fifth Avenue. The *Mercantile and Financial Times* pointed out the significance of this showing, appraising the presentation as: "A Fashion Exhibition of unusual Interest and Importance."[17] Visiting the daily showings required the holding of a special invitation or a card issued to members of the trade. Boué Sœurs succeeded in attracting New York's fashion professionals for a second time. The gossip sheet *Town Topics* reported that "the fashion-mongers of all the Peacock alleys in town" were to be found at the Waldorf, "feasting their eyes on the confections that, despite the vicissitudes of war, Mme. Boué has managed to bring over …" The sharp-tongued journalist added in regard to the unceasing appeal of fashion despite current geopolitical concerns: "I was convinced that, through thrones totter and crowns are humbled in the dust, the sway of fashion will hold forever."[18]

By the time of this second successful stay in New York, the Boué Sœurs had already made a decision to open a permanent American branch. The leasing of premises at 1 East 53rd Street was announced

Figure 2.2 *"Robe Corbeau," taffeta and velvet dress with "new draped skirt and waistcoat effect". Photograph by Joel Feder,* Town & Country, *September 1915, p. 35. The C.M. Roussel Boué Sœurs Archive/Waleria Dorogova.*

in early April of 1915.[19] For unknown reasons—perhaps the topographical or structural unsuitability of the 53rd Street store—a new lease was transacted in June of 1915 for a townhouse at 13 West 56th Street, a short walk from Fifth Avenue.[20] In accordance with the launch of the collection for winter of 1915–16, the new venue held a celebratory opening on September 1, 1915.[21] American *Vogue* portrayed the 56th Street venue in March 1916, observing that Boué Sœurs "have furthered [the] domestication of French shops in America by endeavoring to bring to New York the atmosphere of an historic French interior."[22] The feature highlighted the non-commercial ambiance of the reception area, which was found to be "without suggestion of 'shop'" with its Louis XIV armchairs, precious oriental carpets, enormous brocade floor cushions, and "window draperies … with garlands and roses, in a manner which suggests old French prints or the interiors painted by Nattier and Moreau." *Vogue* described the stage area as the "*petit théâtre des modes*," where "[t]he woman in search of a frock or a blouse may seat herself at ease in any one of a number of gilded, typically French chairs, and be as near to the stage as she desires."

In 1917, a visitor's account evoked the enticing atmosphere of the fanciful interior:

> I must admit that I felt very much as did Alice in Wonderland, when I stepped from the bright sunlight of Fifth avenue into the House of Boué Sœurs.... I must tell you about the beautiful Louis XIV setting, of gold and exquisite flowered tapestry, brought from the chateau of Baronne D. [sic] D'Etreillis, near Paris [Gagny, Château de Maison Rouge], which together with luxurious delicately shaded rugs gave the main salon more the appearance of a beautiful home than a place of business. Every detail has been thought out with infinite care, evidenced by the unique manner in which even the lace curtains were draped, and caught with bands of delicate blue silk and festoons of roses. Perfectly huge pillows made of gold brocade, gold filet lace and pompadour flowers studded with turquoise were thrown at the foot of a divan or near a table on the floor. As a proper setting... the Boué Sœurs have fitted up a stage with a background of blue grey and so lighted that each gown stands out like a cameo. In this room, as in the other, the touch of an artist appears. The windows are covered with delicate blue silk curtains gathered through the center with garlands of flowers. Little gold chairs are arranged in comfortable groups,....[23]

The trials of transatlantic business

American orders were not exclusively executed in Rue de la Paix. A secondary workshop was installed in 56th Street: "A gown can be ordered at the New York house and it will be made up in Paris or New York, just as the customer pleases. If the dress made in Paris requires any alteration, it will be made here."[24] From an economic perspective, the import of finished garments was disadvantageous, as opposed to the shipment of uncut embroideries, fragments and raw material on which tariffs were lower. The number of orders was so high in winter 1915, that the house deemed it necessary to interrupt order-taking for ten days "due to present overwhelming demands."[25]

Import taxes caused considerably high expenses and—purposely or not—the legal requirements for declaration of imported goods were neglected in at least one case in the winter of 1915. What the *New York Times* described as "an unusual kind of smuggling plot" was the violation of American customs law by undeclared import of garments for trade valued at $8,000.[26] These gowns were carried by Jeanne, Sylvie, and three of their employees as personal effects. In addition, a violation of labor law was detected when American employees of Boué Sœurs complained that they worked under different contracts than those workers who were employed at the Paris house and brought to New York. After an eight-day trial and pleading guilty on December 21, Sylvie and Jeanne were ultimately charged with a fine of $5,000 and sentenced to four hours in custody, spent in the police commissioner's room. The gowns were handed over to the customs inspectors to be processed as smuggled property. Both customs and labor law violations, imply the potential legal minefields that the transatlantic import of garments brought forth. The early period of business in the United States also confronted the sisters with the burning issue of design piracy and fraudulent practices of retailers copying Paris originals. In October 1916, an agent of the department store Hickson, misrepresenting herself as a private customer, had purchased gowns and a cape at Boué Sœurs. Shortly after, the garments—all labels removed—and counterfeits thereof were offered for sale at Hickson as their own models. In consequence, Boué Sœurs successfully sued Hickson, Inc. for $25,000 in damages.[27]

Apart from legal issues with import logistics and copyright protection, trading on both sides of the Atlantic grew to be a dangerous undertaking. The running of the Manhattan branch demanded regular travel by steamship, according to Sylvie six to eight trips annually.[28] When a German submarine sank the RMS *Lusitania* in May 1915, Jeanne and Sylvie continued traveling on the SS *Rochambeau*, where Sylvie organized a concert for the Secours de Guerre war relief in 1917.[29] The US declaring war on Germany on April 6, 1917 intensified the danger of transatlantic travel. Under the headline, "Parisian Dressmakers Risk Submarine Perils," a *New York Herald* report referred to the acute threat for dressmaking establishments, who seemed unreasonably "[u]ndismayed by German frightfulness."[30] Sylvie remembered that the ship captains marveled at her and Jeanne's seeming indifference to danger.[31] The sisters insisted on travelling together—Jeanne's granddaughter Christine Roussel remembers—for "as long as the war continued because if the ship was sunk, they wanted to die together. If one died, the other didn't want to have to go on without her sister."[32]

In wartime, the poetic idiom of the Boué sisters as "swallows in lace" was created. Sylvie credited this phrase to the soprano Emma Calvé, a close family friend and fellow traveler, while the writer Louis Roubaud wrote in 1928 that it originated because sailors dubbed the sisters the "les hirondelles en dentelles" (swallows in lace).[33] Calvé later wrote in her autobiography: "Two fairies of the couture parisienne, Mmes Boué, elegant, beautiful, wandered on deck, in light and floating costumes, two swallows in lace. Intrepid, they made the journey between New York and Paris all those years, with no worry of danger."[34]

Patriotic sentiments

Early in the war, the Paris atelier participated in the Œuvre de la Cocarde (Cocarde Charity Workshop) for the war effort, until human loss started to overshadow the cheerful testimony of patriotism that the cocarde symbolized. In a letter to Gustave Charpentier, founder of the Conservatoire Populaire de Mimi Pinson (Popular Conservatory of Mimi Pinson), dated October 21, 1915, an "unknown midinette" at Boué Sœurs regretfully expressed her feeling of moral ambiguity in the production of

Figure 2.3 *"Ma Patrie," Summer Collection, 1916, pencil, ink, and watercolor sketch for presentation purposes, stamped "Boué Sœurs Ltd., 9, Rue de la Paix, Paris," Musée de la Mode de la Ville de Paris, 1956.23.1.4.51. Photo: Waleria Dorogova.*

cockades.[35] The tokens of patriotism were put on display in Paris to be regarded by "indifferent people," while the men they were meant to be made for gave their lives in battle.

Discontented with the notion of competition between dressmakers that had started to dominate the cause, Boué Sœurs ended their charity work making cocardes. In November of 1915, when the Concours des Cocardes de Mimi Pinson (Contest of the Mimi Pinson Cocardes) was held in the Palais des Beaux-Arts (informally known as the Petit Palais), Boué Sœurs did not participate.[36] The creation of the design "Mimi Pinson" for the spring collection of 1916, a crinoline dress in lace with an eighteenth-century-style bodice, was a nod to the ongoing fascination with this patriotic heroine of the garment industries.[37]

By 1915, the collections had begun to show the impact of the omnipresent military conflict. This was a change from the collection of winter of 1914, which was mainly informed by a somewhat heterogeneous historicism and slight orientalist effects. Wartime designs began to display a striking duality between sumptuous romanticism in eveningwear and austere, military-inspired suits and coats. The effects of uniform appeared in the novel use of Hercules braid and metal embroidery. The so-called "Vivandière" apron, used to finish a dark blue taffeta afternoon gown baptized "Militaire" in the spring 1915 collection, was an echo to the eponymous female military canteen workers.[38] Other models designed between 1915 and 1917 were titled "Grenadier," "Mon Lieutenant," or "Mon Général." The winter collection of 1915–16 featured the "trouserette" suit with bloomers and a short flaring coat, adorned with metal braid that evoked the military.[39] Extant garments, notably a delicate embroidered blouse of white net in a private collection, exemplify the widespread vogue for sailor collars in wartime fashion.[40]

The design of the lingerie dress "Ma Patrie"—a historically inspired festive ensemble in the color scheme of the French flag—can be seen as a symbol of the pronounced patriotic sentiment characteristic of the war period, when the explicit demand for national dress design was regarded as being of strategic and psychological importance for the survival of the endangered fashion industry (Figure 2.3).[41] The rise of national self-consciousness could not but have been instrumentalized by the leading minds of haute couture, who were seen as forming a national art.

French art and Boué Sœurs' wartime marketing in America

Although the militaristic elements in the 1915 designs were a reflection and assimilation of social reality, and possibly even emblematic of solidarity, Boué Sœurs found their central wartime aesthetic in the artistic articulations of the eighteenth century. The seventeenth and eighteenth centuries, a golden age of French culture, were given particular importance in the wartime collections of many dressmaking establishments but Boué Sœurs began to build an all-encompassing corporate identity around the visual heritage of the Ancien Régime from 1916 on. The spring collection of 1916 formed a stylistic entity, serving as a sartorial manifestation of the strength of an entire nation as expressed by a national industry. These designs helped determine the very particular Boué Sœurs image, which persisted for several decades following the war.

The genre of the lingerie dress was first presented in spring 1916. Widely advertised as "The Boué Lingerie Dress," it combined delicately embroidered whitework, French lace, and strategically placed silk roses, as seen in the design "Ma Patrie." American *Vogue* proclaimed: "There are two kinds of lingerie frocks: just lingerie frocks and Boué lingerie frocks."[42] Those delicate full-skirted calf-length creations of whitework-embroidered batiste, organdy and tulle, baptized "Lutèce" (Lutecia, the Roman city that Paris was founded on) or "Versailles," complemented with buckled Louis XV shoes, picture hats and ruffled parasols were a suitable expression of a modern-day Rococo vogue and an unmistakable claim to French tradition. Among individual elements from eighteenth-century dress that were rendered to suit the current style was a fashion for aprons, which Boué Sœurs introduced during the war and revisited time and time again in subsequent seasons (Figure 2.4).

Elisabeth Vigée Le Brun's 1786 portrait of Madame Molé-Raymond became an integral element of Boué Sœurs' signature imagery and appeared in many advertisements. It helped support the nationalistic stylization that had been introduced in spring 1916. For a fashion house that was intrinsically tied to theatre, this dynamic portrait of a beautiful and stylish actress of the Comédie Française was in many respects a suitable emblem.[43] Other graphic advertising in the period after 1915 consisted of elaborate Louis XVI-style framework, ribbons, and rose festoons. Of particular artistry was an advertisement in the 1917 program of the Newport Casino club with an engraving by then young Witold Gordon (1885–1986), who was later to become well known for his cover designs

Figure 2.4 *Mannequin wearing the "Manette" model, winter 1919. Photograph by Ira L. Hill Studio. The C.M. Roussel Boué Sœurs Archive/Waleria Dorogova.*

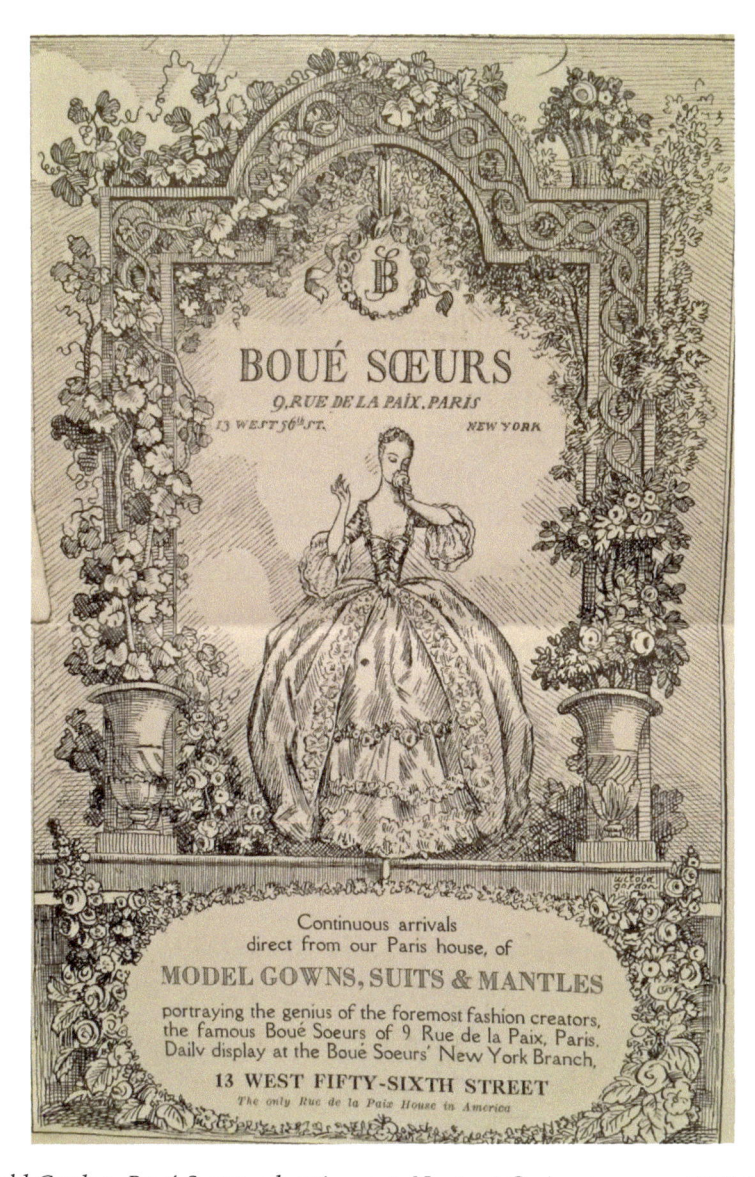

Figure 2.5 *Witold Gordon, Boué Sœurs advertisement, Newport Casino program, 1917. The C.M. Roussel Boué Sœurs Archive/Waleria Dorogova.*

for American *Vogue* and *The New Yorker* in the 1940s (Figure 2.5). The engraving showed a French beauty in 1750s court dress beneath a rose arbor, where she had plucked a rose to take delight in its perfume. She was a nod to François Boucher's 1759 painting of the Marquise de Pompadour in a garden.[44] This Rococo vision alluded to the crucial period of Louis XV's reign, when, for the first time in French history, "patriotic sentiment … infiltrated all aspects of French culture" leading to the emergence of a veritable "goût patriotique."[45] An updated French patriotic taste reemerged in Boué Sœurs' wartime collections and marketing.

This statement of historically legitimized national tradition, conceived to define the Boué Sœurs brand under the given political and social circumstances, was in part a well-strategized maneuver to gain recognition within New York's Francophile elite. The vivid enthusiasm towards French art in general that American patrons had initially expressed during New York's gilded age had a resurgence in wartime. The American upper class acted as a considerable financial support structure to help prevent the loss of French heritage; this played in haute couture's favor. The fascination with French court culture went so far as to cause a vogue for replicas of French interiors and even entire architectural structures in the United States.[46] The preservation of France's cultural heritage and the fashionable assimilation of a French style by America's financial elite were indicators of an unofficial cultural entente in wartime.

At the same time, collaborations between American department stores and Parisian couturiers became a mutual interest for commerce. At the opening of the spring season of 1916, the *Chambre Syndicale de la Couture Parisienne* (Trade Association of Parisian Couture) met with American buyers to forge an alliance between the fashion houses of New York and Paris and discuss strategies for economic growth in the transatlantic fashion trade.[48] At the house of Boué Sœurs, this alliance materialized in the spring season of 1918, when Boué Sœurs officially announced their first collaboration with the 5th Avenue department store Franklin Simon & Co, a regular importer of Paris models, in early May.[48]

The range of this diversified line of simplified models first comprised nightwear and undergarments (for the bridal trousseau) and was extended to gowns and blouses later in 1918. The line was permanently represented at the department store until well into the 1930s. All models were exclusively designed for Franklin Simon & Co and advertised as entirely handmade in the Paris atelier; they were priced lower than the Boué Sœurs lingerie offered in their branch shop. Aesthetically, there was little difference between the department store designs and the main line, except for a simplified execution in construction and decor of the collaboration pieces, which are distinguished by an addendum to the usual woven orange-on-white label "expressly for Franklin Simon & Co." In tune with the Franco-American trade alliance initiated by the *Chambre Syndicale* and the American Chamber of Commerce in 1916, this collaboration helped bolster the French fashion industry while strengthening the Boué Sœurs' presence and dissemination on the American market at a variety of price points.[49]

Conclusion: The Americanization of Boué Sœurs

In 1919, while the terms of peace were being set at Versailles, Boué Sœurs produced a collection inspired by the spirit of triumphant France. The "Trianon Collection" for spring 1920 was a nod to an ongoing conference at the Grand Trianon. The collection was meant to stand as a symbol for peace and showcase France's proud victory—which could transpire in something as seemingly trivial as the name of a couture collection. The designs were a testimony to French Rococo fashions and expressed the quintessential Boué Sœurs style as it had taken shape during wartime.

In retrospect, the First World War redefined the Boué Sœurs clientele: before 1914, the house dressed European aristocracy and the Parisian beau monde of the Belle Époque, but by the end of the war the house supplied an American bourgeoisie to a much greater extent. The multifold effect the war had on the development of Boué Sœurs was integral to the state of the fashion house from 1914 to 1957, the year it ceased to exist. Evolving from a branch store that was established to keep the Paris workshops afloat for the duration of the war, the Manhattan establishment soon became an equal counterpart of 9, rue de la Paix. Furthermore, the "trading links forged through the demands of wartime" proved to have a vital influence on the proceedings of the following decades.[50]

Only a few years after maison Boué set foot in the megapolis of New York in wartime, the house had become deeply rooted in New York's fashion landscape. Boué Sœurs gained a strong foothold on the American market by diversifying its range. After the success of simplified, yet elaborate lingerie at Franklin Simon & Co, Boué Sœurs opened an American wholesale division in 1921.[51] The house became one of the first Parisian couture businesses to venture into wholesale manufacturing for the American market. In the early 1920s, Boué Sœurs, Inc. was registered as an American corporation and in 1923 the firm Parfums Boué Sœurs was created at 565, 5th Avenue.[52] Later, Boué Sœurs opened branches in Palm Beach, Miami Beach and St. Francisco and enjoyed the patronage of illustrious clients in every corner of the United States. By 1936, the families of both Boué sisters had made New York their permanent residence. When in 1957, Boué Sœurs closed its doors at their last address at 16 West 58th Street, not very far from where their US expedition had begun in 1914 in the Plaza hotel, the house was legally and geographically an American fashion house.[53] As with many fashion houses, the Great War changed the history of the company Boué Sœurs and the life of its proprietors in a permanent way.

Notes

1 "Compelled by the war, Boué Sœurs show here. Remarkable Winter Models in Private View," cited in, "The Boué Collection," *Women's Wear Daily* (*WWD*), October 29, 1914, 1.

2 *Vogue*, July 15, 1918, 24.

3 In 1897, Sylvie and Jeanne Boué established their couture house at 13, Rue du Helder, and incorporated the Société Boué Sœurs in 1899 at 9, Rue de la Paix (Archives de Paris, D31U3 849). In 1906, Boué Sœurs became an English company limited by shares (The National Archives, Kew, BT 31/17764/88838). Technically, between 1906 and 1928, Boué Sœurs, Ltd. was a British business with a branch in Paris, but factually, the Rue de la Paix house remained the principal office and workshop of the firm.

4 The eastern subsidiaries of Boué Sœurs were established around 1908–13. The branch in Cairo was located at 36, Kasr El-Nil, a Europeanized boulevard, where French luxury trade flourished around 1900. The prewar address for the Bucharest branch remains unknown. There were plans for it to reopen in 1922 at 98, Calea Victoriei, under the patronage of longtime client Queen Marie of Romania. Boué Sœurs was one of numerous Parisian couture houses which acted as supplier to Russian nobility. Business in Russia was likely initiated with the aid of Jeanne's husband, Achille d'Etreillis, who ran a shipping insurance company in St. Petersburg since 1891 and created the *Revue Slave* in Russia, the first francolingual periodical dedicated to Eastern European literature. Achille-Clément Intering, Baron d'Etreillis (1854/55–1918), known under his *nom de plume* Servanine, married Jeanne Boué in 1904. He was a Dreyfusard and *homme de lettres*, owner and chief editor of the newspapers *La France* and *Paris*.

5 I am greatly indebted to Christine M. Roussel, granddaughter of the Baronne Jeanne D'Etreillis, whom she remembers very well, for sharing many fascinating stories of her family's history with me over the past years and providing tremendous help with my work on Boué Sœurs. Jeanne told Christine about this journey to Russia in the early summer of 1914. The closure of the Eastern branches is confirmed in: "Parisian gowns come to New York," *The New York Herald*, November 1, 1914.

6 In his article, Paul Kempf, then President of the Association des Tissus et Matières Textiles et de la Délégation des Industries Créatrices de la Mode, addresses the issue of transport in wartime. While inter alia shipments to Russia had been conducted by German companies before the war, this was now regarded as potential commercial espionage. Paul Kempf called for a reform of commercial transportation of goods, export tax, and international money transfer. Paul Kempf, "L'avenir de nos Industries de Luxe à l'Étranger," *Les Élégances parisiennes. Publication officielle des Industries Françaises de la Mode*, April, 1916, 50.

7 Jeanne addressed this issue in an interview: "We are a house that is patronized above all, by private customers abroad," *The New York Herald*, November 1, 1914.

8 Anne Rittenhouse, "Fashion world looks for invasion of America by Paris designers during European War," *The Sunday Star*, Washington DC, October 18, 1914, 6.

9 "Native fashions for Americans," *The Brooklyn Daily Eagle*, August 9, 1914, 11.

10 Ibid.

11 H. Parker Willis, "The Tariff of 1913 I–III," *Quarterly Journal of Economics*, January–March, 1914.

12 Advertisement in *The Evening Sun*, November 2, 1914.

13 "Parisian gowns come to New York," *The New York Herald*, November 1, 1914.

14 A report on the conditions in the textile and lace centers during the occupation: Blanche McManus, "Fashions affected by German hold on Northern France," *WWD*, September 3, 1915, 22–3.

15 Detailed descriptions of the collection can be found in the following articles: "Paris gowns come to New York," *The New York Herald*, November 1, 1914; "The Boué Collection," *WWD*, October 29, 1914, 1–2; "The new silhouette," *The New York Herald*, November 15, 1914.

16 "What they wear in *Vanity Fair*: The mode displays a dual personality," *Vanity Fair*, May 1914, 68.

17 "A fashion exhibition of unusual interest and importance," *The Mercantile and Financial Times*, March 25, 1915.

18 *Town Topics*, March 25, 1915.

19 "Paris dressmaker opens branch here: One of Boué Sisters will make permanent headquarters in New York," *The New York Herald*, April 7, 1915; 1 East 53rd Street is announced as the "Permanent American establishment" of Boué Sœurs in *Town Topics*, April 8, 1915.

20 "Boué Sœurs have taken a lease from Rosalie G. F. Barr, of the remodeled building at 13 West 56th st.....". In *New-York Tribune*, June 17, 1915, 13. In early August, they already occupied this new building. See *WWD*, August 10, 1915, 10.

21 Boué Sœurs was located at 13 West 56th Street until *c.* 1937.

22 "Shops which import the atmosphere of Paris," *Vogue*, March 15, 1916, 54–5.

23 Jean, "Bringing Rue de la Paix to America," *The American Jewish Chronicle*, 1917, 734.

24 "Paris dressmaker opens branch here: One of Boué Sisters will make permanent headquarters in New York," *The New York Herald*, April 7, 1915.

25 *WWD*, November 22, 1915, 16.

26 "Indict dressmakers in smuggling plot," *New York Times*, December 11, 1915, 13. The incident was widely covered in *WWD* between November 1915 and January 1916, and other American and French papers, for instance in, "Lenient with sisters who smuggled gowns," *The Evening World*, December 21, 1915, 7; "5,000 Dollair! Pouf! Reedicule!," *New-York Tribune*, December 21, 1915, 5; "Les Couturières parisiennes poursuivies à New-York," *Le Petit journal*, December 25, 1915, 2.

27 Case Montegut v. Hickson, Inc., Appellate Division of the Supreme Court of New York, 164 N.Y.S. 858. Covered by *WWD*, November 1916–October 1917.

28 Sylvie Montégut quoted in Jacques Makowsky, *Histoire de l'industrie et du commerce en France: L'Effort économique Français contemporain*, vol. 2 (Paris: Éditions d'Art et d'Histoire, 1926), 115.

29 "$600 is raised for Secours de Guerre. Mme Sylvie de Montagut and Mr. Jules Ratzkowski [Director of the Society of French Artists] organize concert on board ship," unattributed newspaper clipping, 1917, from a wartime press scrapbook in Christine Roussel's collection.

30 "Dressmakers risk submarine perils," *The New York Herald*, May 1, 1917.

31 Sylvie quoted by Makowsky, *Histoire de l'industrie et du commerce en France*, 115.

32 Christine Roussel, correspondence with the author.

33 "Une grande artiste française, Emma Calvé, connaissant le genre Boué et la fréquence de nos voyages, nous appela à bord 'les hirondelles en dentelles,'" Sylvie quoted in Makowsky, *Histoire de l'industrie et du commerce en France*, 115; "Mme Montegut et la baronne d'Etreillis (les sœurs Boué) ont bravé les torpillages pendant la guerre et se sont fait surnommer par les marins du bord 'les hirondelles en dentelles,'" Louis Roubaud, "Promenades dans le monde de la couture," *Le Petit parisien*, March 4, 1928, 1.

34 "Deux fées de la couture parisienne, Mmes Boué, élégantes, belles, se promènent sur le pont, en costumes légers et flottants, 'des hirondelles en dentelles.' Intrépides, elles font tous les ans le va-et-vient entre New-York et Paris, sans souci du danger," Emma Calvé, *Sous tous les ciels j'ai chanté: Souvenirs* (Paris: Librairie Plon, 1940), 264.

35 I am very grateful to Patricia Tilburg (Davidson College) for sharing this letter, that she has found and transcribed in the Fonds Gustave Charpentier/Bibliothèque Historique de la Ville de Paris [No. 471] and presented during the conference accompanied by this publication as part of an ongoing book project. In her article, Tilburg gives an excellent account of the midinette's social transformation, her symbolic role in the Cocarde campaign and her allegorical significance in wartime. Patricia Tilburg, "Mimi Pinson goes to war: Taste, class and gender in France, 1900–18," *Gender and History* 23, 1 (April 2011): 99f.

36 Palais des Beaux-Arts de la Ville de Paris, *Concours des Cocardes de Mimi Pinson: Catalogue* (Paris, 1915). Nearly 300 establishments and individuals of the Parisian luxury trade are listed as participants.

37 A gouache sketch of "Mimi Pinson" can be found at Musée de la Mode de la Ville de Paris, 1956.23.1.4.62.

38 "Militaire," and other military-inspired Boué Sœurs designs are illustrated in *The Washington Post*, May 2, 1915, 6.

39 Ibid., September 19, 1915, MS6.

40 This blouse is in the Joan Hart Collection and dates 1915–17. Another known example with a sailor collar from the period in question is a peacock blue velveteen dress with cut steel buttons in the Costume Collection of Mount Mary University, WI.

41 "Ma Patrie" is illustrated and described as "La Patrie" in *Vogue*, April 15, 1916, 43.

42 *Vogue*, April 15, 1916, 43.

43 Boué Sœurs dressed opera singers and theatre actresses in France from the onset and later in England and America. The firm was well connected to the stage with Philippe Montégut (1864–1933), Sylvie's husband since 1898, being a celebrated voice of the Opéra Comique, while Emma Calvé was a close family friend. Boué Sœurs was internationally promoted in theatre periodicals and, in 1919, they staged their own Broadway show, the *Parisian Fashion Frolic*.

44 François Boucher, *Madame de Pompadour*, 1759, oil on canvas, 91 x 68 cm. London, The Wallace Collection.

45 Colin Bailey, *Patriotic Taste: Collecting Modern Art in Pre-Revolutionary Paris* (New Haven, CT: Yale University Press, 2002), 16.

46 Pascale Richard, *Versailles: The American Story* (Paris: Alain de Gourcuff, 1999), 116ff. This publication offers an extensive account of the various contributions of wealthy American individuals in support of the French cultural heritage, for instance the restoration of Versailles and its neighboring buildings.

47 "À l'occasion de l'ouverture de la saison printanière de 1916, les membres du bureau de la Chambre Syndicale de la Couture Parisienne avaient décidé de se réunir aux principaux acheteurs américains, afin d'échanger leurs vues sur leurs intérêts réciproques. . . . en remerciant la nation américaine des marques de sympathie qu'elle n'a cessé de témoigner à notre population si éprouvée par la guerre. . . . En résumé, cette réunion est une première étape: elle laisse prévoir une entente, une alliance, entre les maisons de couture de New-York et de Paris, dans l'intérêt commun et pour le développement économique de nos relations avec les Etats-Unis," *Les Élégances parisiennes: Publication officielle des industries françaises de la mode*, April 1916, 54.

48 In addition to Boué Sœurs lingerie, Franklin Simon & Co also imported Premet, Agnès, Paquin, and Jeanne Lancret in 1919 (Advertisement in *The Brooklyn Daily Eagle*, September 21, 1919, 11). By 1924, the store claimed to be the "largest importers of Paris fashions in America," offering "Original Signed Models from every important member of the Haute Couture and Petite [sic!] Maisons, including the first and largest collection of original Vionnet models and the new Callot collection," ibid.; *WWD* pointed to the particular importance of lingerie in wartime: "experience in France and England has shown that, as the war burden increased, expensive outer clothes have been frowned upon as an extravagance and the expression of a lack of patriotism, but as the outer garments have lost in attractiveness there has been a greater demand for dainty things worn underneath or in the privacy of the boudoir," April 24, 1918, 27.

49 "Les Maisons de couture de Paris et les acheteurs de New-York," *Les Élégances parisiennes*, April 1916, 54. M. Flurshheim of Franklin Simon & Co attended a meeting of the trade alliance's supporters as one of many representatives for American department stores in early 1916.

50 Ross J. Wilson, *New York and the First World War: Shaping an American City* (Farnham: Ashgate, 2014), 2.

51 "Boué Sœurs to create simpler trade models," *WWD*, November 3, 1921, 1, 5.

52 The perfume company of Boué Sœurs was specifically established for the supply of the American market.

53 When Sylvie Montégut died in 1953, all business in Paris was liquidated.

References

Bailey, Colin. *Patriotic Taste: Collecting Modern Art in Pre-Revolutionary Paris*. New Haven, CT: Yale University Press, 2002.
Calvé, Emma. *Sous tous les ciels j'ai chanté: Souvenirs*. Paris: Librairie Plon, 1940.
Le Petit journal, 1915.
Le Petit parisien, 1928.
Les Élégances parisiennes, 1916.
Makowsky, Jacques. *Histoire de l'industrie et du commerce en France: L'Effort Économique Français contemporain*. Vol. 2, Paris: Éditions d'Art et d'Histoire, 1926.
New-York Tribune, 1915.
Parker Willis, H. "The Tariff of 1913 I–III," *Quarterly Journal of Economics*, January–March, 1914.
Richard, Pascale. *Versailles: The American Story*. Paris: Alain de Gourcuff, 1999.
The American Jewish Chronicle, 1917.
The Brooklyn Daily Eagle, 1914.
The Evening Sun, 1914.
The Evening World, 1915.
The Mercantile and Financial Times, 1915.
The New York Herald, 1914–17.
The Sunday Star, 1914.
The Washington Post, 1915.
Tilburg, Patricia. "Mimi Pinson goes to war: Taste, class and gender in France. 1900–18." *Gender and History* 23, 1 (April 2011): 92–110.
Town Topics, 1915.
Vanity Fair, 1914.
Vogue, 1916–18.
Wilson, Ross J. *New York and the First World War: Shaping an American City*. Farnham: Ashgate, 2014.
Women's Wear Daily (WWD), 1914–21.

3

"Gladdening the hearts of warriors"

The relationship between Lucile's romantic fashions and morale in the First World War

Georgina Ripley

The first London-based *couturière* to achieve international success, Lucile's pioneering spirit helped engineer designs that exemplified luxury and liberation for women at the turn of the twentieth century. In her own words, she "loosed upon a startled London, a London of flannel underclothes, woollen stockings and voluminous petticoats, a cascade of chiffons, of draperies as lovely as those of ancient Greece."[1] Hers was a romantic style, suited to the Edwardian age of opulence, but which successfully bridged the nineteenth and twentieth centuries. Lucile navigated between high society and the *demi-monde*, the artistry of the fashion designer and the personality of the client. Lucile, born Lucy Christiana (1863–1935), was among the first to develop the mannequin parade, the forerunner of the modern catwalk show, and to cultivate a social element to shopping; her contributions to haute couture, merchandising, and fashion-industry public relations helped to pave the way for the birth of modern fashion as we know it today.[2]

Such was her success that Lady Duff Gordon—as she became by marriage in 1900—went on to establish branches of Lucile Ltd in New York in 1910, Paris in 1911, and Chicago in 1915. Thus, just as war had descended on Europe and many male couturiers such as Paul Poiret and Jean Patou were called to the war effort, Lucile's star continued to rise and she gathered a prestigious clientele. Among them were royalty, high society ladies, Ziegfeld showgirls, the reigning stars of Hollywood's flourishing silent cinema, and three of the most beguiling fashion icons of the day—Mary Pickford, Lily Elsie, and Irene Castle.

The relationship between fashion and society is dependent upon a number of factors, which include the political and economic situation, cultural expectations, moral imperatives, class, and personal taste. Inevitably the impact of each of these on dress is heightened during wartime and as such, the fashion system arguably mirrors the greater political, economic, social and cultural impact of war on society as a whole. Prewar fashionable clothing was dictated by a strong sense of etiquette ensuring that women were *à la mode* for every occasion, but this set of rules did not allow for the incidence of war and the changing landscape in which dressing began to play less of a part in social life than it had before.[3] The fashion journals and consumers disagreed over whether economy in clothing was more, or less, patriotic. The fashion designer's response to this of course varied, but the complexity of the sartorial situation at this time can be considered in the context of Lucile's surviving body of work across fashion collections in Europe and America. Sensitive to the new demands on women's daytime clothing, she necessarily designed sensible suits in practical darker shades, but largely refused to compromise her eveningwear designs to suit the mood of war.

The "Lucile look"

Materialized in romantic and theatrically named creations such as "The Sighing Sound of Lips Unsatisfied" and "When Life's Young Pleasures Woo" the "Lucile look" was rendered in cascades of diaphanous chiffon, gossamer light wisps of lace, and shimmering silks in delicate color combinations. She believed that "dresses, if they are to give any pleasure to their wearer, must become a part of the personality" and called these ethereal evening dresses "gowns of emotion," honoring each one with a unique poetic name evocative of a mood, color, composition or her client's personality.[4] She also took inspiration from literature and popular culture. Often inspired by the prettiness and femininity of the late Rococo manner of Jean-Honoré Fragonard, and no doubt also by what Aileen Ribeiro refers to as the "eroticism and succulence which can best be seen in portraits by [François] Boucher in the 1740s," Lucile's handwriting was in the scalloped hemlines, obi-like sashes, *passementerie* comprised of the finest silk ribbon rosettes, and embroidery of almost incredible delicacy.[5]

A blue silk chiffon dress acquired by the Victoria & Albert Museum in 2007, dating from 1905 and corresponding to a fashion sketch also in their collection, encapsulates what came to be her signature look (Figure 3.1). Its subtly shifting color palette, complexity of design and decorative devices—metallic embroidery, lace trimming, silk ribbon flowers and self fabric ruffles—are all quintessentially Lucile, coming together to give an air of "indefinable shimmer."[6] Alongside its sketch, it is possible to

Figure 3.1 *"Carresaute," Lucile evening dress. Blue silk chiffon, lace, and metallic embroidery, London, 1905* © *Victoria and Albert Museum, London.*

tell that the garment is now missing its centre front corsage of silk flowers, as well as a trailing silver and white tissue sash with oval buckle and tasselled ends, but retains its feminine trimmings of ecru tape lace and pink silk ribbon rosebuds. The bodice is cut horizontally without the use of side seams, and is structured with nine internal bones; vertical shirred bands of silk chiffon and tiered flounces of shirred and accordion pleated silk on the sleeves create definition and texture, sculpting the female figure. The romance of the garment is also inherent to its structure, bearing as it does a rustle frill of pinked and scalloped taffeta at the hemline, which made an alluring rustling sound as the wearer walked and was thus an important seductive feature of dress of this era.[7]

These picture dresses, so called for their popularity with society ladies having their portraits painted, were Duff Gordon's favourites, and hence why she credited herself with being "the first dressmaker to bring joy and romance into clothes."[8] The mystique surrounding her designs was perpetuated by the calibre of the women who modeled them—handpicked for their combination of magnetism, charisma and compelling personal style, as their celebrity soared, so, too, did Lucile's reputation.

Lucile's romantic fashions and their American clientele

A Lucile gown promoted an idealized image of womanhood, and it is this which also appears to inform her outlook on wartime fashions. At a Pittsburgh press club anniversary dinner, Lady Duff Gordon was invited to follow a speech by Herbert Hoover on economy in food in wartime with one on dress, at which time she instead declared she did not believe in economy in dress at any time, least of all in wartime, suggesting it was the duty of every wife, sweetheart and mother to spend as much as they could possibly afford in order to make the best of themselves for the sake of the men in the trenches. Writing in her memoirs, she postured: "After all the men don't want to come back to frumps do they? And just think how fascinating the French women are. You simply can't afford to neglect your appearance."[9] As frivolous as this might be, her observations suggest Lucile saw clothes as a necessary weapon in social armoury and believed that women had a very personal relationship with their dress. Reflecting on the period 1914–18, she wrote:

> even the War could not make women forget the fashions, at least not altogether … Women, always personal in their outlook on everything, had translated the world's crisis in their own way. Their men were going to fight for them; they wanted themselves to represent everything feminine. So they put on frills and laces and big hats with ribbon bows to gladden the hearts of the returned warriors.[10]

However, when considering Lucile's design ethos during wartime, it is important to make the distinction of place, since fashion is an expression of the social and economic situation in which it flourishes.

Shortly after the outbreak of war, Duff Gordon closed her Paris branch and moved to New York, which had not been marked by war in the same way as Europe. Her former assistant designer in Chicago, Howard Greer, looked back on the period before America joined the war in 1917 in his memoirs: "The war, as I had brushed up against it in New York, was little more than a burst of wonton gaiety and spending. Everyone had money, and everyone was giving parties. Everyone who was anyone in my phony world rushed to Her Ladyship for a thousand dollar costume to wear to the latest charity ball."[11]

Even after America entered into conflict, there did not appear to be a wave of reduced spending as had been experienced in London and Paris. It is notable that the bulk of the romantic evening gowns that survive from the period between 1914 and 1918 tend to be the output of the Chicago or New York branches and thus remain today in American museums. It is not of course to say there are not good examples of her work in Europe; she is well represented in the collections of the Bowes Museum, the Museum of London, Brighton Museum and Art Gallery, the Fashion Museum, National Museums Scotland, and the Victoria & Albert Museum. However, many of these garments are daytime fashions dating from before or after the war period, and in the collection of the Musée des Arts Décoratifs in Paris there is only one garment, an evening coat currently dated to 1915–20.

The need for greater functionality in dress in Europe popularized simpler modes of fashion and the wearing, for the first time, of a sort of uniform for women. Influenced by men's tailoring, they tended to be costumes described as "wholly without sex appeal," based on real uniforms "worn indifferently by both sexes."[12] Lucile's designs, in contrast, were concerned wholeheartedly with retaining the gender distinction and clothed an intimated vulnerability; the historian Susan Glenn felt she, in fact, explored the relationship between "clothes as eroticized commodities and women as sexualized objects."[13]

Lucile gowns certainly emphasized the very feminine graces of their wearer and these styles fit what has been observed as "a natural heightening of sex appeal" as fashions became increasingly romantic at the beginning of war.[14] Thus, while tailor-mades in subdued tones and a looser cut and fit became the main order of the day in Paris and London—where it was said that even the most fashionable wore either black, or last season's purchases—there developed a marked contrast with the extravagant frills and laces of old.[15] We are therefore led to believe that the *décolletages*, transparencies, pastel shades and near-nudity of her evening dresses were reserved for the American market.

However, to reduce the global fashion system to this simple distinction would be naïve, and it is important to consider both the differences and similarities in the political and economic situation of an independent America, alongside that of a war-ravaged Europe. On the Continent there was never to be official rationing and utilitarian clothing of the kind that was to follow in 1941, but propaganda materials distributed by the National Organising Committee for War Savings promoted austerity measures, admonishing those who appeared to make little or no difference to their habits. A British propaganda poster from 1916 in the collection at the Imperial War Museum, simply states: "To dress extravagantly in war time is worse than bad form it is unpatriotic."[16] Mrs. Jack May of the British magazine *The Queen* wrote in 1915: "When the history of this wartime dress comes to be written, there will certainly be pointed out . . . that the dress designs emanating from Paris . . . are of the very simplest and most restrained order."[17]

Seemingly innocuous plain wool afternoon suits were produced by even the most exclusive Parisian couture houses and perfectly captured the patriotic mood: simple, functional, and practical for the new working woman. Subdued tones were also suggested to be patriotic, and certainly by 1916, "French grey," in reference to the blue-gray of the French military uniform, was a fashionable choice in London.[18] However, this was by no means a universal code of dress, as illustrated by an eye-catching purple silk satin and navy chiffon walking-suit with a day bodice in contrasting rich ochre chiffon and embroidered silk panels from *c.* 1916–19, in the National Museums Scotland's collection.[19]

Color choices more often than not owed much to practicality—as Mrs. Jack May again observed in June 1916, "the craze for delicate grey" was perhaps down to the "trying condition of the dye industry," as opposed to any concerted effort to align fashionable clothing with that of the Allied soldiers.[20] Certainly neutral shades were deemed practical, as suggested by *The Gentlewoman* in February of 1917 in an article entitled "Beige suits and black hats for spring," but the fashion journals also did not shy away from colorful reports where such garments were available.[21] An article in the same journal in May of that year describes a riot of color and richness in the new summer tea gowns, offered "in the choice of purple *crêpe de chine* overhung by purple, gold and silver woven brocade, pink and silver or mauve with orange lined with tinsel brocaded ninon, emerald with blue and white with silver."[22] The sources paint a more nuanced picture than an assumed blanket relinquishing of fashion and its superfluities.

For the most part, however, war had imprinted itself on fashion, be it superficially with ephemeral military-inspired trends, such as the decorative application of buttons or popularity of khaki, or through forced economic necessity. Even though women were encouraged to keep up their appearances by the fashion press, economy was still "the keynote of the moment."[23] Lucile herself subdued her designs for her European clients, and even in America introduced the "Ideal Office Gown" as advertised in *The New York Times* in 1916. She understood the fact that women attempted to present their new independence, patriotism and strength through tailored, military-influenced clothing and was clearly adept at adapting to consumer demand.

A wool gabardine tailor-made costume from *c.* 1915 in the Victoria & Albert Museum's collection is of course daywear, but it is more than that which puts it in stark contrast to the luxurious evening dresses clothing her American clients.[24] It clearly shows the influence of the First World War on fashion. The large pockets, belted waist and buttoned cuffs all nod to military style, while the straight cut, loose-fitting jacket and shorter, pleated skirt demonstrate the increasingly practical nature of women's clothing that allowed for greater freedom of movement. Change was not necessarily unwelcome either—fashion magazines of the time complimented the greater mobility and practicality in women's clothing: "what about the war-time pockets of our frocks and our coats; was ever fashion more glamorously amiable and helpful."[25]

The extant examples of fashionable wartime daywear suggest overall that there was little place for romance in the European landscape, but to assume Paris's importance as the centre of fashion production diminished would be misleading. After the outbreak of war, the Parisian fashion industry certainly faced a number of challenges: some textile mills had closed making it difficult to procure materials; with irregular shipping and prohibitively high insurance premiums transportation was brought to a standstill and there was a shortage of mannequins for the August openings as many of the women had signed up for war work. As the individual consumption of fashion was quickly considered unseemly, trade relations with America became even more important in the absence of a home market.

Thus, in October 1914, Callot Sœurs staged a fashion show with approximately 250 models "going about showing gowns in the same light-hearted way which marks their activities when there is no war."[26] Others did not initially fare so well—at Paquin, for example, there were only twenty-five models and no mannequins to show them on.[27] However, by the time of the spring openings of 1915, *Harper's Bazaar* was reporting to American readers that "Mannikins parade in the salons, always with a smile on their faces though their hearts may be breaking ... and all the signs of a busy session are in evidence."[27] This, coupled with the renewed romantic attitude of fashion encapsulated in the fuller, shorter silhouette known as the war crinoline, must surely have been a boost for morale.

To see new designs by some of the great couturiers circulating in the *Gazette du bon ton* in 1915 suggested a return to business as usual and an encouragement to the Parisian consumer to resume spending in the face of moral and economic restriction.[29] A more cynical view was expressed in the wartime diary of Helen Pearl Adam, who looked upon the new styles as an attempt to countermand the wave of economy—by decreeing "a change from narrow clothes to wide, [couturiers] knew they were making sure of their turnover for the Spring of 1915 ... we were new to war in those days and had no experience of profiteers."[30] Her observations, nonetheless, suggest that women were buying these fashions and certainly extant garments from the period show that luxurious fabrics and fanciful trimmings still found their way into the designs of the most exclusive Parisian houses such as Worth and Callot Sœurs.

Examples in the collection at The Metropolitan Museum of Art in neutral shades of oyster silk and sand-colored silk velvet, nonetheless exhibit metallic lace and seed pearl embroidery, floating tulle panels and luxurious fur trim.[31] Although they were probably made for the American market, they are interesting on two counts: first, they reiterate the significance of trade between Paris and America and, second, they evidence the fact that despite shortages, irregular shipping, and the struggling dye industry, Paris was still capable of producing romantic, extravagant fashions for the wealthy.

However, war brought about an inevitable change in lifestyle and the introduction of a new mood and modes which Lucile was less willing to countenance. A further distinction of class needs to be observed in relation to the Lucile client; she was designing for society's finest, described by her sister, the author Elinor Glynn, as "the fairy ring within which danced a circle of families entitled to enjoy its privileges on account of birth and tradition."[32] However, although this clientele was presumably less affected by wartime austerity and the society season did not altogether stop, American buyers in Paris reported a deserted city, devoid of the atmosphere of old. Lady Angela Forbes, a Lucile client, wrote in her memoirs that London was "overborne with a new sense of grave happenings, people ceased to concern themselves with changing their clothes. The hotel grill-rooms were crowded, but to dress for dinner became banal, almost an outrage."[33]

Fashion and morale

If Britain and France were out of sorts with the old theatre of dressing, then Lucile's picture dresses, which belonged to the grand ballrooms of the *Belle Époque*, were better suited to the wealthier American market. A pale blue silk chiffon dress in the collection of Philadelphia Museum is one of her wartime styles that most overtly hark back to the nostalgic romance of her Edwardian fashions, with the Rococo-inspired scalloped line of shirred silk taffeta around the midpoint of the skirt, and decorative silk rosebuds.[34] Named "Happiness," its color was no accident: Lucile imbued color with psychological importance and in her mind "blue stands for purity ... for homely love, and peaceful, happy things. It is a color all men love, and they will generally prefer a simple little homemade dress in blue to a model from one of the great houses in another color."[35] Far from a simple homemade dress, this evening gown was explicitly marketed to its American consumer; presumably the moniker of "Happiness" would not have sat well with a dispirited war-ravaged Europe and by this time Henri Bendel was reporting in *Harper's Bazaar* that evening gowns "were created solely for the American buyer—as French women wore only *tailleurs* (tailored suits)."[36]

Another garment that hints at a connection in Lucile's mind between fashion and morale in wartime is an evening dress of bright leaf green and red shot silk, trimmed with gold embroidered net, satin binding and silk flowers on display at the National Museum of Scotland (Figure 3.2). It bears the Paris label and is dated to around 1918, however as photocopies of Lucile designs and swatches were sent to Paris from America, we cannot be sure whether this is originally a Paris fashion, or a copy of an American design. Nevertheless, given that it was war's end that proved most disruptive to patterns of taste and consumption, as the general malaise prompted a definitive movement towards the discarding of old traditions and the shortages were felt most strongly, this dress is particularly interesting. It reflects the new, simpler silhouette and shorter skirt, the fewer layers and flounces, but it is nonetheless enriched with Lucile's handwriting, and is pertinent in comparison with a watercolor sketch in the Victoria & Albert Museum's collection dating from 1905 (Figure 3.3).

With a similar combination and choice of fabric colors and trimmings to create an overall emerald and gold effect, the later dress design bears the mark of a *couturière* lusting after the old standards of extravagant dressing in a rapidly modernising landscape and as such its color is most pertinent. Although often at the root of many a superstition for its unlucky connotations, for Lucile green signified hope and was "God's choice for a world that needed rest, it is the color of renewing, of re-birth"—a hint, perhaps, that her design ethos was intrinsically linked with both economic and social wartime morale.[37] Its Paris label is perhaps significant, for Duff Gordon's memoirs note that in France green has always been used as a symbol of hope, citing the example of the green caps of the unmarried Catherinettes on the Feast of Saint Catherine, where the color instead represents wisdom.[38] It is a color that she has revisited time and again but its romantic connotations are most

Figure 3.2 *Woman's evening dress of shot silk, with gold embroidered net and passementerie, by Lucile Ltd, Paris, France, 1918. © National Museums Scotland. A.1986.127.*

Figure 3.3 *Page from Lucile sample album book of fashion designs of women's clothes, Great Britain, 1905. © Victoria and Albert Museum, London. T.89A-1986.*

implicit in its use in wartime and immediately post-war garments. Surviving examples include an evening coat of taffeta and semi-transparent silk in the collection of National Museums Scotland,[39] made in Paris and dated 1914–19 and a silk and cotton evening dress trimmed with ecru lace and silk ribbon rosebuds from Chicago, now in The Metropolitan Museum of Art's collection,[40] dating from 1919.

Conclusion

Lucile was a shrewd businesswoman—she diversified her fashions, entered new markets, licensed her name, endorsed products and was one of the earliest of the *haute* couturiers to branch out into a ready-to-wear line through deals that she made with Sears in 1917. Her connection between fashion and morale could equally have been a judicious, profiteering move to encourage consumer demand for her romantic evening wear. Yet, it is important to reiterate that Lucile made her addresses dismissing economy in dress in America, where her "delicious blending of filmy fabrics" were still being praised with a hyperbole no longer suited to the malaise in Europe.[41] In March 1917, *Vogue* described a Lucile dress:

> [which] surely must be literally blown together or cunningly cajoled into having an appearance, as its little puffs seem full of air, and the silver flower flounces just float in space around its fortunate wearer. To think that this has been cut and stitched together is an anomaly which passes the imagination of the uninitiated."[42]

It is certainly true that fashion was capable of acting as a distraction and a means of lifting feminine spirits; Lucile herself staged two charity spectaculars in the vaudeville style in New York in 1916 and 1917 to raise money for war charities, turning to fashion as a means of uniting women in a common cause. In her memoirs, she placed a heavy importance on this aspect of the female personality:

> No man can possibly realise how women are influenced by the clothes they wear. Put even the plainest woman into a beautiful dress and unconsciously she will try to live up to it. It is as if for her the designer has created a new personality, her every movement reflects an increased self-confidence, a new joy of living.[43]

She was also not alone in harnessing fashion with the power "to gladden the hearts of the returned warriors."[44] In 1918, London magazine *The Queen* attacked the proposed National Standard Dress on grounds of individuality, patriotism and good taste, somewhat echoing Lucile's appraisal of the uniquely feminine charms of fashion, with the words "How [the men] would resent it if they found their women, whom they left clad in individuality and daintiness, all gowned in Government clothes like one huge orphan asylum!"⁴⁵ However, while in America, Lucile's evening dresses were flying out of the fitting rooms, in Europe there was perhaps little connection between her romantic fashions and morale, given that there was little market for romance—the very catalyst, perhaps, for the design of the hopeful green dress. In the end, it was, to quote Duff Gordon, "this passing of so much of the romance which made the world a very pleasant place" and the advent of what she rues as an era of "practical dressing" which diminished Lucile's place in the fashion market.⁴⁶

Notes

1 Lucile Duff Gordon, *A Woman of Temperament* (London: Attica Books, 2012 [1932]), 54–5.

2 Quote: "to her we owe the first conception of a dressmaker's shop as a *salon*, the social meeting place for a genuine aristocratic and artistic clientele. In many ways the advent of Lucile [*sic*] was a landmark in the history of modern beauty," Hon. Mrs C. W. Forester, *This Age of Beauty* (London: Methuen & Co., 1935) cited in Valerie D. Mendes and Amy de la Haye, *Lucile Ltd: London, Paris, New York and Chicago, 1890s–1930* (London: V&A Publishing, 2009).

3 Duff Gordon, *A Woman of Temperament*, 68.

4 Ibid., 54. In the *New York Examiner* in 1910, Lucile wrote: "there is only one real fashion, and that is different with every woman. It is the outward draping of the soul, her individuality, her physical ensemble; it's the thing that interprets and harmonises with her," Mendes and de la Haye, *Lucile Ltd.*; Duff Gordon, *A Woman of Temperament*, 68.

5 Aileen Ribeiro, *Dress in Eighteenth-Century Europe 1715–1789* (London: B. T. Batsford, 1984), 98.

6 Mendes and de la Haye, *Lucile Ltd.*; and Cecil Beaton wrote in *The Glass of Fashion* (London: Weidenfeld and Nicolson, 1954), 32:

> Lucile worked with soft materials, delicately sprinkling them with bead or sequin embroidery, with cobweb lace insertions, true lovers' knots, and garlands of minute roses. Her color sense was so subtle that the delicacy of detail could scarcely be seen at a distance, though the effect she created was of an indefinable shimmer. Sometimes, however, she introduced rainbow effects into a sash and would incorporate quite vivid mauves and greens, perhaps even a touch of shrimp-pink or orange.

7 Mendes and de la Haye, *Lucile Ltd.*

8 Duff Gordon, *A Woman of Temperament*, 54.

9 Ibid., 212.

10 Ibid., 250.

11 Howard Greer, *Designing Male* (London: Thomas Allen, 1952), 47.

12 Ibid.; and Cecil Willet Cunnington, *English Women's Clothing in the Present Century* (London: Faber and Faber, 1952), 127.

13 Susan Glenn, *Female Spectacle: The Theatrical Roots of Modern Feminism* (Cambridge, MA: Harvard University Press, 2000), 163.

14 Cunnington, *English Women's Clothing*, 126.

15 Caroline Evans, *The Mechanical Smile: Modernism and the First Fashion Shows in France and America, 1900–1929* (New Haven, CT: Yale University Press, 2013), 108.

16 Imperial War Museum (IWM), IWM ART.PST 10122.

17 May Jack, "Fashion's forecast," *The Queen*, July 24, 1915, 162.

18 Ibid., "Fashion's forecast," *The Queen*, May 20, 1916, 734.

19 National Museums Scotland, A.1922.227 A–C.

20 Jack, "Fashion's forecast," *The Queen*, June 10, 1916, 834.

21 Quote: "there isn't any doubt now about beige being the most insistent proposition for Spring. It is for rolls of beige gabardine the tailors are sharpening their shears just now and we are going to be shown practical darker shades of it as well," from Juno, "Beige suits and black hats for spring," *The Gentlewoman*, February 10, 1917.

22 "New summer gowns," *The Gentlewoman*, May 19, 1917.

23 "Dress and fashion," *The Queen*, August 28, 1915, 399.

24 Victoria and Albert Museum (V&A), T.27&A-1960.

25 "Fashion and the economic life of the nation," *The Gentlewoman*, February 17, 1917, 156.

26 Evans, *The Mechanical Smile*, 103.

27 Ibid.

28 Ibid.

29 National Museums Scotland, H.RHI 90.21.

30 Helen Pearl Adam, *Paris Sees it Through: A Diary, 1914–1919* (London: Hodder and Stoughton, 1919), 48.

31 Silk evening dress with metallic thread and glass embroidery, House of Worth, Paris, 1914–16, 1976.217.2; silk, tulle and lace evening dress, Callot Sœurs, Paris, Autumn/Winter 1915/16, 2009.300.3160; silk velvet evening coat, trimmed with fur, Callot Sœurs, Paris, 1916–17, C.I.51.97.6.

32 Mendes and de la Haye, *Lucile Ltd*.

33 Lady Angela Forbes, *Memories and Base Details,* 2nd edn (London, 1922), 151.

34 Philadelphia Museum of Art, 1962-190-1.

35 Duff Gordon, *A Woman of Temperament*, 215.

36 *Harper's Bazaar*, London, June 1916, 64–5.

37 Duff Gordon, *A Woman of Temperament*, 214.

38 Ibid.

39 National, Museums Scotland, A.1977.799.

40 The Metropolitan Museum of Art, 1979-569.4.

41 Mendes and de la Haye, *Lucile Ltd*.

42 *Vogue,* March 1917.

43 Duff Gordon, *A Woman of Temperament*, 58.

44 Ibid., 250.

45 Jack, "Fashion's forecast," *The Queen*, September 14, 1918, 224. Amidst the peak of shortages in 1918, the government attempted to introduce a "National Standard Dress," generally considered to have been the inspiration for the Utility Scheme of the Second World War. Its purpose was to introduce one garment that could be worn for a number of occasions, which would abolish the need for different changes of dress throughout the day.

46 Ibid., 68; Duff Gordon, *A Woman of Temperament*, 252.

References

Adam, Helen Pearl. *Paris Sees it Through: A Diary, 1914–1919*. London: Hodder and Stoughton, 1919.
Beaton, Cecil. *The Glass of Fashion*. London: Weidenfeld and Nicolson, 1954.
Cunnington, Cecil Willet. *English Women's Clothing in the Present Century*. London: Faber and Faber, 1952.
"Dress and Fashion." *The Queen*, August 28, 1915.
Duff Gordon, Lucile. *A Woman of Temperament*. 1932. Repr., London: Attica Books, 2012.
Evans, Caroline. *The Mechanical Smile: Modernism and the First Fashion Shows in France and America, 1900–1929*. New Haven, CT: Yale University Press, 2013.
"Fashion and the economic life of the nation." *The Gentlewoman*, February 17, 1917.
"Fashion's forecast." *The Queen*, September 14, 1918.
Forbes, Lady Angela. *Memories and Base Details*, 2nd edn. London, 1922.
Glenn, Susan. *Female Spectacle: The theatrical Roots of Modern Feminism*. Cambridge, MA: Harvard University Press, 2000.
Greer, Howard. *Designing Male*. London: Thomas Allen, 1952.
Harper's Bazaar, London, June 1916.
Jack, May. "Fashion's forecast." *The Queen*, July 24, 1915.
Jack, May. "Fashion's forecast." *The Queen*, May 20, 1916.
Jack, May. "Fashion's forecast." *The Queen*, June 10, 1916.
Juno. "Beige suits and black hats for spring." *The Gentlewoman*, February 10, 1917.
Mendes, Valerie D. and Amy De La Haye. *Lucile Ltd: London, Paris, New York and Chicago, 1890s–1930s*. London: V&A Publishing, 2009.
"New Summer Gowns." *The Gentlewoman*, May 19, 1917.
Ribeiro, Aileen. *Dress in Eighteenth-Century Europe 1715–1789*. London: B. T. Batsford, 1984.
Vogue, London, March 1917.

4

Die Kriegskrinoline

A feminine fashion between past and future

Birgit Haase

In January 1916, the satirical German weekly magazine *Simplicissimus* published a caricature by the German painter and illustrator Thomas Theodor Heine (1867–1948), which treated national fashion stereotypes in a kind of picture story.[1] Under the title "The disappointed Parisian," an elegantly dressed French woman speculates about the development of "German fashion" in wartime, making use of a number of common clichés in this context (Figure 4.1). The stereotypes quoted ironically by the satirist extend from dowdy and clumsy to "Teutonic" or "Prussian," and ultimately "Oriental" and "paradisaic." In the end, however, the Parisian discovers, much to her indignation, that women's fashion was identical on both sides of the border. The silhouette, with a tapered jacket and a mid-calf bell-shaped skirt, was in the internationally elegant style that came to be designated as the "war crinoline," or *Kriegskrinoline*.[2]

Seen in retrospect, this clothing style, which was widely disseminated and controversially debated, particularly around the midway point of war, can be seen as an indicator of contemporary ambivalences concerning modern aesthetics, gender, and economics.[3] With its flaring skirts and clearly defined waists, the style, which recalled fashionable silhouettes of the eighteenth and nineteenth centuries, appeared anachronistic in the midst of the war. A closer look, however, reveals a more differentiated picture. War crinolines, it can be argued, not only featured traits that were historicizing, but others that were up to date, and, in fact, decidedly modern. In the second decade of the twentieth century, the style simultaneously proved itself to be both backward-looking and farsighted, and it is precisely such ambiguity that, in recent years, has been characterized as a fundamental feature of modernism.[4]

Figure 4.1 *Thomas Theodor Heine, caricature, "Die enttäuschte Pariserin" (The disappointed Parisian), Simplicissimus, 40 (January 4, 1916): 472. Simplicissimus Online-Edition at: http://www.simplicissimus. info/uploads/tx_lombkswjournaldb/pdf/1/20/20_40.pdf (accessed July 7, 2019).*

The relatively short-lived war crinoline style, which hit its peak in 1915–16, revealed the break between the past and the future and was thus an adequate expression of the position of women during the First World War, who were, at the threshold, as it were, between yesterday and tomorrow. These connections will be discussed below, based on pictorial, textual, and material sources of mostly German provenance.[5]

The war crinoline's prewar genealogy

In terms of fashion history, the years prior to the outbreak of the First World War were designated as "l'époque Poiret," so named after the legendary French designer. Paul Poiret (1879–1944) left an indelible imprint on the look of women's fashion with his preference for clothing cut along straight lines and featuring a high waistline in the Empire style. Accordingly, prewar Western fashion showed a slender column-like silhouette varied by short overskirts, peplums and long jackets. Poiret also launched internationally trendsetting, highly extravagant creations, such as the "lampshade tunic."[6] This style was disseminated outside of Paris, as can be seen by a surviving garment from about 1914 with a probable Northern German provenance.[7] The evening dress of light-blue crêpe de Chine and decorations of artificial cherry blossoms has a narrow skirt overlaid with a mid-calf-length tunic of blue silk chiffon whose wire hem encircles the thighs, giving the tunic its characteristic "lampshade" effect.

Poiret's "lampshade tunic" might be identified as a kind of stylistic forerunner of the war crinoline, as indicated an article published in the Berlin-based journal *Elegante Welt*; it informed its readers in December 1913 that the "hoop skirt … can lay claim to being the most sensational innovation of this year's winter season."[8] The accompanying photographs show designs in an "Orientalizing style" with a variety of overskirts with inserted hoops from Paris and Berlin based tailors. The article was published under the headline: "Crinoline is back again!" A drawn vignette points to the historical prototype of the hoop skirt dating from the Second Empire while the text and pictures clearly indicate that the present style concerns "a coquette, delicate, and graceful great-granddaughter of that epoch's ostentatious clothing." "The hoop skirt sharply contradicts our hasty, fast-paced times," the journalist concluded.[9]

Ultimately, however, Poiret's "lampshade" style did not gain broad acceptance in German fashion magazines of the immediate prewar period. Yet, the crinoline, nevertheless, continued to be discussed in the fashion world. A richly illustrated special supplement published in the French fashion magazine *Fémina* in June 1914 featured a costume party given by the Duchess of Gramont. It was *the* event of Paris's social season; the theme of the party was *Le bal des crinolines*.[10] Germany's fashion-conscious public certainly would have followed such events in Paris with interest.

Die Kriegskrinoline: A fashionable style from the German perspective

Social life went on as before when Germany declared war on France several weeks after the Duchess' costume party. Despite predictions to the contrary, developments in the world of fashion did not come to a standstill. What did change on both sides of the Rhine, however, were the themes discussed in the fashion press and the tone of voice. German-language media called, once again, for the creation of a "German fashion," a concept that had been advocated repeatedly with nationalistic pathos since the Napoleonic Wars a century earlier.[11] Beginning in the fall of 1914, the slogan *Los von Paris!* (Freedom from Paris!) dominated the domestic fashion press. As imperialistic phrases of political propaganda aside, the discussion was in fact spurred by Germany's economic interests in developing Berlin as a strong fashion center in opposition to Paris and London.[12]

In search of stylistic examples that were *not* taken from French haute couture, German attention turned toward Vienna, whose status as fashion city of international significance had solidified since the late nineteenth century.[13] A decisive contribution to developing a characteristic Viennese style was made by the Wiener Werkstätte, founded in 1903, which had fostered a fashion department under the creative supervision of Eduard Wimmer-Wisgrill (1882–1961) since 1911. It organized regular fashion shows in Vienna and sometimes in Berlin as well, which received lively, although ambivalent, media attention, particularly after 1914.[14]

The distinct, experimental concept of design as well as the characteristic dress style of the Wiener Werkstätte is evident in a colored woodcut by the young Austrian visual artist Vally Wieselthier (1895–1945), from an album entitled *The Life of a Lady*, published in 1916.[15] It shows a group of visitors—a couple, a young girl, and two women—in front of a monkey-house at a zoological garden. The three women in the foreground wear variations of the tailored promenade suit with girded jackets and wide ankle-length skirts, combined with calf-high boots and hats pushed forward on top of pinned-up hair. There is no mistaking the historicizing references in the clothing depicted here: this silhouette, with its marked waist and bell-shaped skirt, was said to have taken its inspiration from the Biedermeier period (1815–48). Updated for the contemporary wearer, the suit was regarded as a typical example of Viennese fashion. In the fall of 1915, *Elegante Welt* wrote: "They [the Viennese designs] share by all means their short length with good German dresses. The little swinging skirt might be seen as the characteristic feature of this year's fashion."[16]

However, Viennese fashion of the time corresponded to an internationally applicable style, as it was introduced in Paris a year before: derived from various tunic shapes, a fundamental change in the female silhouette can already be observed by late summer of the first year of war with the widening of the dress skirts. A number of drawings of the French fashion illustrator Dartey (pseudonym of Anette Osterlind, 1882–1954) published from August 1915 to March 1916 by the short-lived Parisian fashion magazine *Le Style parisien* present the line perfectly.[17] Her illustrations show a variety of daytime ensembles, afternoon dresses and evening gowns from famous Parisian couture houses in mostly subdued colors with narrow-waist jackets and wide, mid-calf skirts that allowed the shoes and small boots to be seen. These elegant ensembles vary considerably from the columnar, ankle-length suits in fashion at the outbreak of the war. Ruffled taffeta petticoats recommended by fashionable magazines were required in order to attain the full-skirted silhouette, which was gathered at the waist and wide at the bottom.[18]

At first, there were some reservations in German fashion accounts about the "wide skirt" in terms of an all too sudden and revolutionary change in style. The additional material required to make these skirts was disapproved of, as were the historicizing echoes of former Rococo and Biedermeier styles. But approval for the fashionable style increased over the course of 1915 and a passionate plea in favor of the controversial garment was published in September by *Elegante Welt* in an article entitled, "The Battle of the Wide skirt," whose author called it a "true child of the time, a real war baby."[19]

In retrospect, this assessment has proven itself to be accurate. The line of the so-called war crinoline, whose name recalled historical models and whose full-skirted silhouette appeared backward-looking in terms of style, was interpreted on various occasions as a nostalgic reminiscence of the past, and, ostensibly, of better times. The Berlin fashion designer Otto Haas-Heye (1879–1959), known for the pronounced feminine style of his label "Moden Alfred-Marie," argued entirely in that vein when he stated in 1916: "I want precisely to create something that has nothing to do with this war, with the horrific events that have so terribly torn the harmony of our times and our lives asunder."[20]

Figure 4.2 *Annie Offterdinger,* Modebild II *(Two dancing women), 1916. Lithograph published in* Zeit-Echo: Kriegstagebuch der Künstler, *3 (1915–16), Otto Haas-Heye, ed., München. Berlin: Graphik-Verlag, 1916, 44.* © *Private collection.*

Two lithographs from the German illustrator Annie Offterdinger (1894–1987) created for Haas-Heye in 1916, one of an opening evening at the Berlin fashion house Alfred-Marie and the other showing two dancing women, illustrate his argument (Figure 4.2).[21] Haas-Heye's statement should also be seen in the context of the desire for a clearly recognizable differentiation between the sexes which, as the German artist Alice Trübner (1875–1916) discerned in 1916, arose from the charged wartime discourse on gender. She wrote: "The exclusively male trade of war emphasizes the contrasts between the sexes and women's clothing is logically seeking to borrow from the most feminine time of the whole Romantic period, namely from the fashion of the Biedermeier era."[22]

Other contemporary writers interpreted the decidedly feminine silhouette with marked waist and full, mid-calf skirts as a means of "cheering up" soldiers on furlough or as an erotic signal on the home front "lacking of men." The German physician and sexologist Magnus Hirschfeld (1868–1935) insinuated that "in the face of the reduced number of partners," the ankle-baring skirt "eased conquests with drastic means of attraction."[23]

The new line was, indeed, accompanied by an unprecedented shortening of the hemline. Although the development must have seemed almost revolutionary as compared with pre-war styles from the Belle Époque, it provoked, unlike comparable "revolutions" in previous decades, hardly any moral criticism. The more-or-less consistently positive echo was succinctly summed up by a French commentator in 1918: "and if the skirt is short, it's because one must be free to move."[24] With its wider and shorter skirts, the war crinoline style, which lasted until about 1917, permitted its wearers new freedom of movement, an advancement toward liberating the female body from the constraints of earlier fashion styles.[25]

The practical and elegant ankle boots that were often combined with the shorter skirts contributed to this impression, as did the only moderately marked waist, which made it possible, as Paul Poiret and other couturiers had already done before the war, to replace the constricting corset by softer versions of shaping garments.[26] Despite its historicizing elements, the new line appeared conducive to the mobility and dynamism of modern life. The ambivalence inherent here was already registered from a contemporary perspective: "We are experiencing the odd spectacle of seeing sedate great-grandmotherly attire translated into the era of exceedingly modern energy and mobility," a columnist wrote in *Elegante Welt* in February 1916.[27] At the same time, the writer clarified that the new skirts represented an interpretation and not an imitation of the historical prototypes.

A "modern fashion" in historicizing guise

The cultural historian Elizabeth Wilson has called the dichotomy between speed, variability, and innovation on the one hand, and reflexivity, tradition-consciousness, and nostalgia on the other a fundamental characteristic of modernism.[28] Wilson stated that this ambivalence found an adequate expression in (women's) fashion, declaring in this context, that: "Indeed, modernity repeatedly clothes itself in reconstructions of the past."[29] The prerequisite is that evocations of the past as expressed through clothing must comply with modern needs. This was also true for the war crinoline fashion, about which *Elegante Welt* wrote in September 1915:

> that is what is characteristic about the direction in taste, that it had been completely adapted to the altered demands made by life and makes no attempt whatsoever to defy life as it has now come to be lived. For the many women who are now doing social welfare work, the wide skirt is simply a necessity.[30]

Simplicity and functionality were the fashion watchwords of the day, not least in the face of the growing number of working women on the home front. In Germany as well in the other belligerent nations, this style was symbolized by the highly idealized nurse's uniform as well by the diverse female (work) uniforms that took a moderate course in following current fashion trends.[31]

Increasingly popular in civilian everyday life since the late nineteenth century, and often seen as an expression of female emancipation, the classic severe tailored ladies' suit—the so-called tailor-made that was judged to be the "ideal everyday dress"—was also seen in the silhouette of the war crinoline.[32] At the same time, patriotically connotated design elements were in fashion, particularly influences from military uniforms. These were often recommended in the media as appropriate means for women who wanted to express their love of fatherland.

Contemporary press accounts are dominated by a tone that oscillates between patriotism and fashion consciousness and which finds exemplary pictorial expression in a cover illustration for the November 1914 issue of *Elegante Welt*, drafted by Austrian illustrator and costume designer Ernst Deutsch (1887–1938).[33] Against the background of the colors of the German Empire—albeit in reversed order here, namely "red-white-black"—a striking young woman is captured in a three-quarter view. Her outfit, featuring an extravagant toque and braid trimmings *à la Brandebourg* on the gray suit jacket, resembles a free fashionable interpretation of the very topical uniform theme. In the same issue of *Elegante Welt*, journalist Ola Alsen (1880–1956) wrote: "The idea of tastefully modelling clothing after the uniform worn by our brave army equals a homage to the courageous warriors by German women."[34]

Inspired by military uniforms that were glorified by the official propaganda machinery, women's fashion featured patriotic design elements in cuts, trimmings, accessories, and dyes. "The colors of the day, dictated by time and mood, are reserved," wrote Alsen in September 1915.[35] Besides black, the shade *Feldgrau* (field gray) enjoyed enormous popularity in Germany, especially during the first year of the war. The gray-green protective and camouflage color introduced for functional reasons in 1907 advanced over the course of the war to the symbolic color of the front soldier.[36] As such, it acquired chauvinist connotations. In the winter of 1914–15, it was often recommended in the media as a very suitable hue for women who wanted to lend visual expression to their love of fatherland.

It can only be guessed at whether such motifs influenced the colors selected for an afternoon dress today in the Hamburg Arts and Crafts Museum.[37] It consists of a heavy silk twill featuring a stone-gray nuance, the top is overlaid with a shimmering green-gray silk chiffon and accentuated further with gray-blue silk embroideries in abstract patterns. The exquisite color and material schemes correspond to the good workmanship and meticulously conceived lines. The long-sleeved top, cut like a blouse, has a fashionable V-neck reminiscent of a sailor's collar. Embroideries accentuate the practical pocket mouths on both sides of the skirt, which is characterized especially by its considerable seam width measuring almost 4 meters. Making such a dress in the war-crinoline style required a considerable amount of material, and this fact triggered a controversial debate from the start. One repeated criticism was that it represented a "waste of fabric," while the style's supporters countered by stating the wide skirt style supported national textile manufacturers.[38] The discussion took a new turn by early 1916 at the latest with the increasing problem of shortages caused by the war.

In any case, the escalation of the war did nothing to change the parallel transborder developments in women's fashion styles. This insight became increasingly accepted in Germany as well, where the patriotic enthusiasm of the early war years gradually gave way to a more realistic view. *Elegante Welt* noted in September 1917:

> There are now absolutely no more attempts to impose 'German fashion' on the world. The fact that fashion is an international matter has been proven more convincingly over the course of the war. . . . Fashion today is still—with some very insignificant deviations—exactly the same here by us as it is in France, England or America.[39]

This statement was fully in tune with the caricature featured in the beginning of this article.

Conclusion

The war crinoline did not endure: in early 1917, the internationally effective imperative for the "strict restraint in the use of fabrics" promoted the development of a narrower silhouette.[40] The keywords of "simplification" and "shortening" characterized the basic tendencies that generally became noticeable in women's fashion at the end of the First World War. Preformed in the "modern" elements of the war crinoline style with its considerably shortened hemline, the borrowings from the design of military uniforms, as well as its predominantly subdued colors, these currents pointed the way to the future.

On the horizon was the "New Women," dressed in a short loose-fitting sack dress that would come to represent the epitome of modern life in the 1920s and whose genesis was closely linked to the flowering of Berlin's ready-made clothing industry.[41] "German fashion" once again overtly followed Paris's model, but the national clothing industry had by all means profited from the bundling of its forces made necessary by the war.

Seen in retrospect, the First World War seems to have had a catalytic impact on women's fashion in many regards. It demanded a "liberation of the woman" from traditional clothing constraints that had already been alluded to in prewar fashion but had not been completely realized. The turning point created by the outbreak of the war sharpened the awareness for one's own times through nostalgic touches in a way that is characteristic of modernism's ambivalence. This found its adequate expression in the temporarily fashionable war crinoline, which prepared the path for "modern fashion" in a historicizing guise.

Notes

1 This essay is an abridged and revised version of Birgit Haase, "Modern ambivalence: Women's fashions during the First World War from the German perspective," in *Wardrobes in Wartime: Fashion and Fashion Images During the First World War 1914–1918*, Adelheid Rasche, ed., catalogue of an exhibition at the Kunstbibliothek, Berlin (Berlin and Leipzig: E. A. Seemann, 2014), 18–29.

2 The term "war crinoline" is a translation of the term known in French and German fashion history as *crinoline de guerre* and *Kriegskrinoline*, respectively.

3 The debates focused particularly on the amount of fabric that was used to make the skirt and on the "romantic appeal" of the silhouette, with narrow waist and bell-shaped skirt, both of which seemed inappropriate in time of war, with its material as well as psychological challenges.

4 Regarding these thoughts, see further the seminal study by Elizabeth Wilson, "Fashion and modernity," in *Fashion and Modernity*, Christopher Breward and Caroline Evans, eds. (Oxford and New York: Berg, 2005), 9–14.

5 A focus on the German situation results from the sources used in the present case. The findings seem, however, to be applicable in other national contexts.

6 Paul Poiret, who headed an exclusive Parisian haute couture salon since 1903, worked in an imaginative, partly theatrical style that was inspired by avant-garde art. The idea for his orientalizing creations went back to the 1909 guest appearance of the Ballets Russes in Paris under the direction of Sergei Diaghilev and their sensational costumes designed by Léon Bakst, which caused a stir around the world. Poiret generated publicity for his designs by means of legendary celebrations, for example the costume ball he organized in 1911 under the motto *La 1002ème nuit* and costume designs for such successful theatre productions as *Le Minaret* in 1913. See Yvonne Deslandres, *Poiret—Paul Poiret, 1879–1944* (Paris: Éditions du Regard, 1986), 93–146; Nancy Troy, "Paul Poiret's minaret style: Originality, reproduction and art in fashion," *Fashion Theory: The Journal of Dress, Body and Culture* 6, 2 (2002): 117–144; Harold Koda and Andrew Bolton, *Poiret*, catalogue of an exhibition at the Metropolitan Museum of Art, New York, May 9–August 5, 2007 (New York, New Haven, CT, and London: Yale University Press, 2007), 17–23.

7 Museum für Hamburgische Geschichte, *Evening dress*, c. 1914, acc. no. 1914,212; see figure 15 in Rasche, ed., *Wardrobes in Wartime*. The dress has no label; its very contemporary lines, in combination with high-quality, if

not perfect, tailoring, allows us to assume that this model was made for a Hamburg customer by a good local dressmaker based on a French model.

8 Translated from Marion, "Die Krinoline ist wieder da!," *Elegante Welt*, 49, December 1913, 17.

9 Ibid.

10 E.g., "'Le bal des crinolines' chez Mme la duchesse de Gramont," *Fémina*, 322, June 15, 1914, supplement.

11 Starting from the call for "traditional German attire" propagated notably by Ernst Moritz Arndt around 1814–15, similar demands were made, for example, in conjunction with the Revolution of 1848–9 as well as with the unification of Germany in 1870–1. Siegfried Müller states that this was not a phenomenon unique to Germany: the topos of a national attire served throughout Europe as a nation-building element and the "politicization of fashion was ... part of a supranational discussion on nationalism or patriotism and national economics," translated from Siegfried Müller, "Einleitung," in *Kleider machen Politik. Zur Repräsentation von Nationalstaat und Politik durch Kleidung in Europa vom 18. bis 20. Jahrhundert*, catalogue for an exhibition at the Landesmuseum, Oldenburg (Oldenburg: Isensee Verlag, 2002), 8.

12 See Haase, "Modern ambivalence," 20.

13 See comprehensively Gerda Buxbaum, *Mode aus Wien 1815–1938* (Wien: Residenz Verlag, 1986), 94–101; Adelheid Rasche, "Wiener Mode in Berlin, 1907 bis 1932," in *Intermezzo Berlin. Wiener in Berlin 1890–1933*, catalogue for an exhibition at the Kunstbibliothek, Berlin, (Berlin: Kunstbibliothek, 1998), 29–36.

14 See Haase, "Modern ambivalence," 20–2.

15 Vally Wieselthier, *Im Tierpark* [At the Zoological Garden], 1916. Colored woodcut, 29.6 x 39.6 cm. From *Das Leben einer Dame*, Staatliche Museen zu Berlin, Kunstbibliothek, at: https://www.europeana.eu/de/item/2048202/europeana_fashion_DE_MUS_018313_1912048 (accessed June 19, 2020).

16 Translated from "Wiener Moden," *Elegante Welt*, 21, October 13, 1915, 21.

17 See Rasche, *Wardrobes in Wartime*, 154–9.

18 Ibid., 26, figure 10.

19 Translated from "Der Kampf um den weiten Rock," *Elegante Welt*, 19, September 15, 1915, 4–5.

20 Translated from Otto Haas-Heye, "Die Mode und diese Zeit. Bruchstücke aus einer Plauderei," in *Graphische Modeblätter* (Berlin: Graphik-Verl, 1916).

21 Annie Offterdinger: *Opening Evening at Berlin Based Couturier "Moden Alfred-Marie,"* 1916. Colored lithograph, 38.7 x 25.7 cm. Staatliche Museen zu Berlin, Kunstbibliothek, Lipperheidesche Kostümbibliothek—Sammlung Modebild, at: http://www.smb-digital.de/eMuseumPlus?service=ExternalInterface&module=collection&objectId=1888642 (accessed June 19, 2020).

22 Translated from Alice Trübner, "Arabeske," in *Graphische Modeblätter*, unpaginated. An analysis of the ideologically shaped dichotomy of the gender order in wartime is provided by Ute Daniel, "Frauen," in *Enzyklopädie Erster Weltkrieg*, 2nd edn, rev. Gerhard Hirschfeld, Gerd Krumreich, and Irina Renz, eds. (Paderborn: Schöningh, 2004), 116–17.

23 Translated from Magnus Hirschfeld and Andreas Gaspar, eds., *Sittengeschichte des Ersten Weltkrieges*, reprint of 2nd rev. edn (Frechen: Kiepenheuer, *c.* 1981), 84–6.

24 Translated from Maurice Guillemot, "L'esthétique de la mode," *Les Arts français*, 1916, 134. The German media had a similar judgment: "Short and wide is the motto of modern skirts and dresses. Very wide and very short. If they

are to be considerably shortened any further, then it is probably not due to coquetry but solely as a result of practical considerations." Translated from "Diskrete Indiskretionen," *Elegante Welt*, 10, May 12, 1915, 15.

25 See Florence Brachet-Champsaur, "De l'Odalisque de Poiret à la femme nouvelle de Chanel: Une victoire de la femme?," in Évelyne Morin-Rotureau, *Combats de femmes 1914–1918* (Paris: Autrement, 2004), 207.

26 See Patricia Cunningham, *Reforming Women's Fashion, 1850–1920: Politics, Health, and Art* (Kent, OH, and London: Kent State University Press, 2003), 219.

27 Translated from "Berlin als Modestadt," *Elegante Welt*, 3, February 2, 1916, 9.

28 See Wilson, "Fashion and modernity," 10–12.

29 Ibid., 10. Various scholars have arrived at similar conclusions in the age of postmodern historicism in fashion; see, for example, Richard Martin and Harold Koda, *The Historical Mode: Fashion and Art in the 1980s*, catalogue for an exhibition at the Fashion Institute of Technology (New York: Rizzoli, 1989), 89.

30 Translated from "Der Kampf um den weiten Rock," 5.

31 See "Unter dem Roten Kreuz," *Elegante Welt*, 32, August 3, 1914, 4–7; Klara Sander, *Die Mode im Spiegel des Krieges* (Essen: G. D. Baedeker, 1915), 18–19; "Special édition: Le Costume et la mode de 1914 à 1918," *Les Arts français*, 19, 1918, 133–4 and 144. See also comprehensively and with regards to women's emancipation aspirations: Brachet-Champsaur, "De l'Odalisque de Poiret," 205–6; Enrica Morini and Margherita Rosini, eds., *Le Donne, la moda, la guerra. Emancipazione femminile e moda durante la Prima guerra mondiale*, catalogue for an exhibition at the Museo Storico Italiano della Guerra, Rovereto, December 13, 2003–March 14, 2004 (Roverto: Museo Storico Italiano della Guerra, 2003), 31–9 and 61–2; Raffaella Sgubin, "Women and work during the First World War: Aspects of clothing," in Rasche, ed., *Wardrobes in Wartime*, 38–45.

32 Translated from "Tailor-made. Das ideale Gebrauchskleid," *Elegante Welt*, 2, January 22, 1914, 4. On the topicality of the tailor-made suit during the First World War, see further Xavier Chaumette, Emmanuelle Montet, and Claude Fauque, *Le Tailleur. Un vêtement-message* (Paris: Syros-Alternatives, 1992), 53–4; Brachet-Champsaur, "De l'Odalisque de Poiret," 208–11.

33 See figure 9 in Rasche, ed., *Wardrobes in Wartime* and in Rasche, "Krieg und Kleider: Modegrafik zur Zeit des Ersten Weltkriegs." *Museumsjournal* 4 (2014): 45, at: https://smart.smb.museum/export/downloadPM.php?id=3098 (accessed June 19, 2020).

34 Translated from Ola Alsen, "Die Dame in Feldgrau," *Elegante Welt*, 46, November 18, 1914, 6.

35 Translated from Ola Alsen, "Farben der Zeit," *Elegante Welt*, 18, September 1, 1915, 22.

36 See the keywords, "Feldgrau" [field gray] and "Camouflage," in Hirschfeld, Krumreich and Renz, eds., *Enzyklopädie Erster Weltkrieg*; further information and analysis on the subject can be found in Alison Matthews David, "Fashion's chameleons: Camouflage, 'conspicuousness,' and gendered display during World War I," in *The Places and Spaces of Fashion, 1800–207*, John Potvin, ed. (New York: Routledge, 2009), 89–107.

37 Hamburg, Museum für Kunst und Gewerbe, *Afternoon dress*, c. 1915–16, acc. no. MKG 1977.108; see figure 17 in Rasche, *Wardrobes in Wartime*.

38 For further information on the German perspective, see Barbara Mundt, ed., *Metropolen machen Mode. Haute Couture der Zwanziger Jahre*, 3rd, rev. edn, catalogue for an exhibition at the Staatliche Museen Preußischer Kulturbesitz (Berlin: Dietrich Reimer Verlag, 1989), 30–2. For the American Perspective, see Jacqueline Field, "Dyes, chemistry and clothing: The influence of World War I on fabrics, fashions and silk," *Dress* 28, 1, (2001): 77–91. For the French perspective, see Brachet-Champsaur, "De l'Odalisque de Poiret," 216–20.

39 Translated from "Die deutsche Modeschau in Bern," *Elegante Welt*, 19, September 12, 1917, 7.

40 Translated from Ola Alsen, "Das Straßenkleid 1918," *Elegante Welt*, 1, January 2, 1918, 11.

41 See Mundt, ed., *Metropolen machen Mode*; Birgit Haase, "'Metamorphose des Girl'—Tendenzen der Damenmode in der späten Weimarer Republik," in *Glamour! Das Girl wird feine Dame—Frauendarstellungen in der späten Weimarer Republik*, Verena Dollenmaier and Ursel Berger, eds., catalogue for an exhibition at the Georg Kolbe Museum, Berlin, February 17–May 12, 2008 (Leipzig: E. A. Seemann, 2008), 28–9.

References

Alsen, Ola. "Die Dame in Feldgrau." *Elegante Welt*, 46, November 18, 1914.
Alsen, Ola. "Farben der Zeit." *Elegante Welt*, 18, September 1, 1915.
Alsen, Ola. "Das Straßenkleid 1918." *Elegante Welt*, 1, January 2, 1918.
"Berlin als Modestadt." *Elegante Welt*, 3, February 2, 1916.
Brachet-Champsaur, Florence. "De l'odalisque de Poiret à la femme nouvelle de Chanel: Une victoire de la femme?" in Évelyne Morin-Rotureau, *Combats de femmes 1914–1918*. Paris: Autrement "Mémoires/Histoire," 2004.
Buxbaum, Gerda. *Mode aus Wien 1815–1938*. Wien: Residenz Verlag, 1986.
Chaumette, Xavier, Emmanuelle Montet, and Claude Fauque. *Le Tailleur. Un vêtement-message*. Paris: Syros-Alternatives, 1992.
Cunningham, Patricia. *Reforming Women's Fashion, 1850–1920: Politics, Health, and Art*. Kent, OH, and London: Kent State University Press, 2003.
Daniel, Ute. "Frauen." In *Enzyklopädie Erster Weltkrieg*, Gerhard Hirschfeld, Gerd Krumeich, and Irina Renz, eds., 116–34, 2nd rev. edn, Paderborn: Schöningh, 2004.
David, Alison Matthews. "Fashion's chameleons: Camouflage, 'conspicuousness,' and gendered display during World War I." In *The Places and Spaces of Fashion, 1800–2007*, John Potvin, ed., 89–107. New York: Routledge, 2009.
"Der Kampf um den weiten Rock," *Elegante Welt*, 19, September 15, 1915.
Deslandres, Yvonne. *Poiret—Paul Poiret, 1879–1944*. Paris: Éditions du regard, 1986.
"Die deutsche Modeschau in Bern," *Elegante Welt*, 19, September 12, 1917.
"Diskrete Indiskretionen." *Elegante Welt*, 10, May 12, 1915.
Field, Jacqueline. "Dyes, chemistry and clothing: The influence of World War I on fabrics, fashions and silk." *Dress* 28, 1, 2001: 77–91.
Guillemot, Maurice. "L'Esthétique de la mode." *Les Arts français*, 1916.
Haas-Heye, Otto. "Die Mode und diese Zeit. Bruchstücke aus einer Plauderei." In *Graphische Modeblätter*. Berlin: Graphik-Verl, 1916.
Haase, Birgit. "'Metamorphose des Girl'—Tendenzen der Damenmode in der späten Weimarer Republik." In *Glamour! Das Girl wird feine Dame—Frauendarstellungen in der späten Weimarer Republik*. Verena Dollenmeier and Ursel Berger, eds. 28–44. Leipzig: E. A. Seemann, 2008. Catalogue of an exhibition at the Georg Kolbe Museum, Berlin, February 17–May 12, 2008.
Haase, Birgit. "Modern ambivalence: Women's fashions during the First World War from the German perspective." In *Wardrobes in Wartime: Fashion and Fashion Images during the First World War 1914–1918*, Adelheid Rasche, ed., 18–29. Leipzig: E. A. Seemann, 2014. Catalogue of an exhibition at the Staatliche Museen, Berlin, September 25, 2014–January 18, 2015.
Hirschfeld, Gerhard, Gerd Krumreich and Irina Renz, eds. *Enzyklopädie Erster Weltkrieg*. 2nd rev. edn. Paderborn: Schöningh, 2004.
Hirschfeld, Magnus and Andreas Gaspar, eds. *Sittengeschichte des Ersten Weltkrieges*. Reprint of 2nd rev. edn. Frechen: Kiepenheuer, *c*. 1981.

Koda, Harold and Andrew Bolton. *Poiret*. New York, New Haven, CT, and London: Yale University Press, 2007. Catalogue for an exhibition in The Metropolitan Museum of Art, New York, May 9–August 5, 2007.

"'Le bal des crinolines' chez Mme la duchesse de Gramont." *Fémina* 322, June 15, 1914, supplement.

Marion. "Die Krinoline ist wieder da!" *Elgegante Welt*, 49, December, 1913.

Martin, Richard, and Harold Koda. *The Historical Mode: Fashion and Art in the 1980s*. New York: Rizzoli, 1989. Catalogue for an exhibition in the Fashion Institute of Technology, New York, November 1, 1989–January 27, 1990.

Morini, Enrica and Margherita Rosini, eds. *Le Donne, la moda, la guerra. Emancipazione femminile e moda durante la Prima guerra mondiale*. Roverto: Museo Storico Italiano della Guerra, 2003. Catalogue for an exhibition in Museo Storico Italiano della Guerra, Rovereto, December 13, 2003–March 14, 2004.

Müller, Siegfried, ed. *Kleider machen Politik. Zur Repräsentation von Nationalstaat und Politik durch Kleidung in Europa vom 18. bis 20. Jahrhundert*. Oldenburg: Isensee Verlag, 2002. Catalogue for an exhibition in the Landesmuseum, Oldenburg, September 7–November 24, 2002.

Mundt, Barbara, ed. *Metropolen machen Mode. Haute Couture der Zwanziger Jahre*, 3rd edn, rev. Berlin: Dietrich Reimer Verlag, 1989. Catalogue for an exhibition in the Kunstgewerbemuseum, Berlin, and the Staatliche Museen Preußischer Kulturbesitz.

Rasche, Adelheid. "Wiener Mode in Berlin, 1907 bis 1932." In *Intermezzo Berlin. Wiener in Berlin 1890–1933*. Berlin Kunstbibliothek, 1998. Catalogue for an exhibition in the Kunstbibliothek, Berlin, November 11, 1998–January 10, 1999.

Rasche, Adelheid. "Krieg und Kleider: Modegrafik zur Zeit des Ersten Weltkriegs." *Museumsjournal* 4 (2014): 45, available at: https://smart.smb.museum/export/downloadPM.php?id=3098 (accessed June 19, 2020).

Rasche, Adelheid. *Wardrobes in Wartime: Fashion and Fashion Images during the First World War 1914–1918*. Leipzig: E. A. Seemann, 2014. Catalogue for an exhibition in the Kunstbibliothek, Berlin, September 25, 2014–January 18, 2015.

Sander, Klara. *Die Mode im Spiegel des Krieges*. Essen: G. D. Baedeker, 1915.

Sgubin, Raffaella. "Women and work during the First World War: Aspects of clothing." In *Wardrobes in Wartime: Fashion and Fashion Images during the First World War 1914–1918*, Adelheid Rasche, ed. 38–45. Leipzig: E. A. Seemann, 2014. Catalogue for an exhibition in the Kunstbibliothek, Berlin, September 25, 2014–January 18, 2015.

"Special édition: 'Le Costume et la mode de 1914 à 1918.'" *Les Arts français*, 19, 1918.

"Tailor-made. Das ideale Gebrauchskleid." *Elegante Welt*, 2, January 22, 1914.

Troy, Nancy. "Paul Poiret's minaret style: Originality, reproduction and art in fashion." *Fashion Theory: The Journal of Dress, Body and Culture* 6, 2 (2002): 117–44.

Trübner, Alice. "Arabeske," in *Graphische Modeblätter*, ed. Otto Haas-Heye (Berlin: Graphik-Verl., 1916), unpaginated.

"Unter dem Roten Kreuz," *Elegante Welt*, 32, August 3, 1914, 4–7.

"Wiener Moden." *Elegante Welt*, 21, October 13, 1915.

Wilson, Elizabeth. "Fashion and modernity." In *Fashion and Modernity*, Christopher Breward and Caroline Evans, eds., 9–14 Oxford and New York: Berg, 2005.

5

Fashion in Belgium during the First World War and the case of Norine Couture

Nele Bernheim

What happens to civil life during wartime is a favorite subject of historians and commands major interest among the learned public. Our best source on the situation in Belgium during the First World War is Sophie De Schaepdrijver's acclaimed book *De Groote Oorlog: Het Koninkrijk België tijdens de Eerste Wereldoorlog* (The Great War: The Kingdom of Belgium During the Great War).[1] However, to date, there has been no research on the Belgian wartime luxury trade, let alone fashion. For most Belgian historians, fashion during this time of hardship was the last of people's preoccupations.

Of course, fashion historians know better.[2] The contrast between perception and reality rests on the cliché that survival and subsistence become the overriding concerns during war and that aesthetic life freezes—particularly the most "frivolous" of all aesthetic endeavors, fashion. Already in 1915, Paul-Gustave Van Hecke (1887–1967), a fashion luminary and the major protagonist of this story about Belgium, protested against the alleged neglect of fashion by the Flemish cultural scene during the war: "How is it possible that in a serious scientific newspaper such as this *De Vlaamsche Post*, there has not been any talk about fashion?"[3] Indeed, this paper asks, what of fashion in "Brave Little Belgium?"[4]

The historical context

The Belgian Belle Époque was an era of unprecedented capitalist expansion.[5] The most densely populated country in the world on the eve of the First World War, Belgium ranked fifth among the industrial powers.[6] The country's economy drew from the colony it set up in the Congo and from exports of railroads, metros, and tramways.[7] Antwerp's port (second only to New York's) thrived as the main gateway to Europe. Consequently, the *anciens* and *nouveaux riches* of Belgium enjoyed affluence and luxury. The country's economic wealth was reflected in its Art Nouveau treasures.

There were dark sides to Belgium's prosperity in this era of industrial high capitalism. That the average standard of living was lower than in neighboring countries is a measure of the degree of exploitation of the working class. But not only that. The Belgian bourgeois was affluent but indulged in luxury goods such as cars, telephones, perfumery, and haute couture much less than the well-to-do elsewhere in Europe.[8] By and large, the hard-working petty-bourgeois mentality had not been fundamentally changed by prosperity and modernity.[9] Belgium was suffused with subtle class distinctions. Apparel, for instance, did not so much denote taste or purchasing power, but rather the belonging to a "certain category" of people.[10] The *grande bourgeoisie* and the *petite bourgeoisie* ate, dressed, and leisured accordingly, and everybody made a point of staying within one's class.[11] To quote a contemporary Belgian fashion magazine: "One has to know how to choose and dress according to one's personality, according to one's rank."[12] The difference with the lower classes was enormous. The Belgian working class was among the most impoverished of Western Europe.[13]

On August 4, 1914, the German army marched into neutral Belgium. It overtook more than 90 percent of the country, pushing 200,000 Belgian soldiers to the far west. Hundreds of thousands of Belgians fled to the Netherlands, which remained neutral throughout the war, as well as to France and the United Kingdom.[14] Belgium now lived under German rule and would be locked in for fifty months. The Germans plundered Belgian industrial equipment. Due to the Allied blockade, imports of raw materials ceased and exports dwindled. Unemployment soared and reliance on charity increased. The next four years, Belgians would be dependent on the welfare of the Comité National de Secours et d'Alimentation (National Relief and Food Committee).[15] A major part of the relief effort's foodstuff came from the United States, where, after a highly mediatized campaign to support "the poor, heroic Belgians," the Commission for Relief in Belgium had been set up.[16]

The sociology of wartime life

The majority of the people relied on soup kitchens, where food would be distributed once a day. But the "better people," many of whom had become the "new poor," preferred starvation than be seen asking for support.[17] They could eat in "bourgeois food halls," behind closed curtains, or depend on organizations such as Charité Discrète (Discrete Charity), a group of young women of good breeding who delivered aid packages.[18] Most of these activities were coordinated by gentry and *bourgeoises*, who employed working-class women for the fieldwork.[19]

Unlike in the other belligerent countries, the Belgian women were not called to work in the war industry, which supplied the occupier—nor were Belgian men, for that matter.[20] A mere 20 percent of army-age men were fighting or in exile; the remainder were trapped inside the occupied country, together with the women.[21] Belgium was not like France, a "strange world wherein half of the adult male population had disappeared from daily life."[22] Belgian women were even encouraged to leave the labor market, in return for a small allowance, so as to ensure the scarce employment opportunities remaining went to men.[23] However, the Comité de la Dentelle (Lace Committee), one of the subcommittees of the Comité National (National Committee), subsidized schooling and encouraged skilled lacemakers to work from home.[24]

Opportunities for emancipation of women in Belgium were scarce.[25] However, to do their bit in dealing with the challenges of wartime, upper-class women concentrated on the so-called female tasks such as charity and nursing. Belgium's Queen Elisabeth, the Bavarian-German born spouse of "heroic" King Albert I, was a role model for these women. During the war, the Queen worked in the hospitals of De Panne, a town to the northeast of Dunkirk, France, where she was cast in a role of supreme caregiver.

To clothe the naked in the First World War

Working-class women, working in huge sewing workshops, were put to the task of modifying and mending the secondhand clothes provided by the Commission for Relief in Belgium.[26] The eminent Flemish author Karel Van de Woestijne (1878–1929), who from 1906 to 1920 was the correspondent in Belgium for the Dutch newspaper *Nieuwe Rotterdamsche Courant* (New Rotterdam Courant), was a keen observer of life during the occupation. Upon visiting a clothing distribution hall, he wrote this thoughtful vignette: "The heat from the stove causes the hundreds and hundreds of garments, orderly stacked on long tables, to sweat: the smell of wool and cotton; the smell of the poor seamstress rooms where these clothes were made; the smell of genteel and stoic poverty."[27]

Thanks to these initiatives, the working class, or "soup-goers," were spared rags, but, obviously, never dressed in fashion. There is evidence, however, that much of the upper classes were preoccupied with fashion. The English-speaking Brussels *bourgeoise*, Constance Ellis Graeffe wrote in her 1914 diary: "The life ... of most girls ... here in Brussels would be this. First of all, she thinks of her dress, her hat, shoes & hair, how to look interesting & what will be the next amusement she'll be able to get to. At any rate here you see many very smart modern model fashions."[28]

In the women's press in Belgium, much as that in the warring countries, women were encouraged to dress well, if only as a civic duty. For instance, *Les Jolies Modes* (The Pretty Fashions) urged: "Say, my sisters, let's make ourselves beautiful. ... Let us be the most attractive of springs' flowers. Let's also take

Figure 5.1 *Elvira De Baets sent photographs of herself in fashionable outfits to her fiancé, kept prisoner in Soltau, Germany, winter 1914. Courtesy Yves De Baets, Diest. Photo retouching Kaydesign bvba.*

out our pretty attires. Dress up, dress up, for we embody hope!"[29] Women of all classes did their best to look smart. An endearing example is Elvira De Baets, a young working-class woman from Ghent. Between 1914 and 1919, she sent photographs of herself in fashionable outfits to her fiancé, who was languishing as a prisoner of war in Germany (Figure 5.1).[30] Elvira would not have been the kind of woman to patronize couture houses, but she dressed in the fashionable garments that she could afford.

The example of Norine Couture

War or no war, some couture houses remained open in occupied Belgium and, to some extent, fashion was able to thrive. Proof of this is Norine Couture, the couture house run by Paul-Gustave Van Hecke and his companion Honorine Maria "Norine" Deschryver (1887–1977). Although both were of modest descent, they would become key figures in Belgium's avant-garde scene during the Roaring Twenties (Figure 5.2).[31]

In an interview in 1928, Van Hecke explained what led them to establish a couture business during the war:

> This was the situation: my wife was an industrious seamstress, I was a journalist, but obsessed with good taste and ... ambition ... We then noticed that the big couture houses in Brussels were tottering or plodding, by virtue of the fact that they were cut off from Paris and could not buy their models there anymore. The idea came to me to create models myself and to engage these powerful competitors in a handicap race ... We took off and triumphed immediately.[32]

Turning a difficulty into an opportunity epitomized the dashing and daring Van Hecke at his best. The trenches cut Belgium off from the lifeline of Paris couture, leaving room for something new. What he did not mention in the interview above, was that Brussels could still get its models from Berlin and Vienna, despite the war.

Figure 5.2 *Norine Deschryver and Paul-Gustave Van Hecke in their workshop, c. 1919. Courtesy Collection City of Antwerp, Letterenhuis.*

Fashion as defiance of wartime adversity

Born and bred in the middle class of Ghent, Van Hecke was a militant socialist from an early age. In the years before the war, he had become a man of the arts. He was a leading figure of the Flemish Expressionist art movement, the editor of several liberal literary journals, the founder of a Flemish theatre association and himself a playwright and actor. To earn a living, he took up journalism.[33]

Shortly after the outbreak of the war, Van Hecke settled in Brussels, where he joined the Flemish activist movement.[34] A generation of modernists would work for a renaissance of the Dutch language and Flemish culture, which they felt had been dishonored. *De Vlaamsche Post* (The Flemish Post), where Van Hecke worked as the Brussels correspondent from February 1915 to May 1916, was the daily newspaper of Jong Vlaanderen (Young Flanders), a radical faction in the Flemish activist movement.[35]

In his first contribution, Van Hecke drew a slightly idealistic image of the relatively normal life in the capital under German occupation: "Truly, there are moments—it is actually usually so—that we can barely see that the people of Brussels are 'burdened' by the governance or suffering from war conditions. . . . After all, above anything, they prefer to walk the streets fashionably or half-fashionably dressed and spend the bulk of their time in coffee houses and cinemas."[36] This was certainly a frivolous view on wartime life. The Allied blockade of the Central Powers and their conquered territories caused major shortages in imports, such as coffee. Van Hecke's "people" were evidently the privileged class; in pubs, they were possibly served beer aplenty, but probably no coffee or cocoa. He continued that the pride-driven inhabitants weren't all that displeased by the quality nor quantity of food and dry goods provided by the "foodcommittee." They were, however, mortified by the conspicuous stamps featuring on the garments distributed by this relief organization.

Some of Van Hecke's subsequent contributions to *De Vlaamsche Post* throw light on the situation of fashion in occupied Belgium. One of his next articles was dedicated to changes in fashion (as well as to pickled and smoked meat): "it is not true that the new trends in women's clothing come from Paris and Paris alone, and not also from Vienna and Berlin."[37] Even in a fashion column, Van Hecke managed to metaphorically sneer at the oppression of the Flemish under the French-speakers' yoke (and not under the Germans'). Describing the change from the constricting hobble skirt to the war crinoline, perceived as liberating, he continued: "Brussels, during the European War, no longer wanted to have anything to do with the 'entraves' [fetters], but declared itself open for free legs and free hips. Please understand the symbolic meaning of the opposition between the fettered and the free . . ."[38]

In May and June 1915, Van Hecke's column assumed the name of *Modekronijk* (Fashion Chronicle) and was signed "NORINE."[39] Within the history of Norine Couture, this denotes Van Hecke's first alliance with Norine Deschryver and probably served as a subtle advertisement for the couple's newly established, or soon to be established, couture house. About the fashionable woman dressed in the new war crinoline, Van Hecke wrote this rather callous and condescending comment: "We would be wrong to declare the women who launch the new [fashions] as insensitive to the current situation. We should forgive them for making a soup-goer step out of the way in order for her to pass with her wind-catching wide skirt."[40]

Of more interest to the fashion historian is what he wrote next:

> Where did this new fashion come from? Most would say: "Paris." The truth is that the leading "couturières" of Brussels, have their models from... Viennese fashion magazines, however, probably without being aware of it. Indeed, the many fashion magazines available here carry Parisian or Parisian-sounding titles: *Le Chic Parisien, Le Grand Tailleur de Paris, La Parisienne Élégante*, etc. Yet they are actually all printed in Vienna... The nice Parisian magazines: *Chiffons, Fémina, L'Art et la Mode* are at the moment not available at the bookstore over here. The few copies I was able to see don't show anything more than even wider skirts, almost as wide as a crinoline. However, I also saw these summer-styles in German fashion magazines such as *Die Dame, Elegante Welt*, etc.[41]

For Van Hecke, Vienna and Germany had nothing to envy from Paris.[42]

Karel Van de Woestijne also extolled women's ability to keep up with the current fashions and believed it attested to high spirits: "It can't be said that women take war so tragically that they would renounce showing off.... The woman who keeps dressing according to the demands of fashion is proof of counteracting discouragement."[43] In war, being fashionable was a defiance of adversity. Moreover, according to him, Brussels' women dressed "as ever before, in Parisian fashion."[44] He continued:

> For we still receive the Parisian fashion magazines. While it became well-nigh impossible, if not completely forbidden to get books that were published in France, the ladies have made it happen to get the special fashion literature across the borders, across the electric fences. I would not have believed it, had I not seen it with my own eyes. I myself have such an album in my hands, published by a French firm.... And the captions are translated in German.[45]

What Van de Woestijne probably saw—"without being aware of it"—was, as Van Hecke wrote in *De Vlaamsche Post*, a Viennese magazine, with a French title for the Belgian market.[46] *Le Goût à Paris*, instead of *Die Wienerin*, for instance, or *Le Chic Parisien* instead of *Wiener Mode Kunst*.[47] This was probably not a real tribute to Paris, but only a commercial gimmick to make use of the prestige of Paris to cater to a Belgian public. Ultimately, it was to cover for the fact that these magazines came from a German ally. One was not supposed to be seen with a magazine with things Viennese.

Belgian fashion magazines during the First World War

However, Belgium did have its own fashion magazines—all in French. There was the quite basic weekly magazine *La Mode 1915* (Fashion 1915), printed on low-quality paper, which featured a fashion column, readers' letters, and fashion sketches with captions.[48]

The fancier monthly *Les Jolies Modes* (The Pretty Fashions), was initially printed on high-quality paper, but as the war dragged on, its paper lost its gloss.[49] Besides a fashion column and sketches with descriptive captions and technical drawings, it also featured photographs of actresses. Both these magazines served as inspiration for seamstresses, both professional and amateur. They did not mention couture houses by name, nor did they feature advertisements.

The weekly *Modes Élégantes* (Elegant Fashions) seems to have been a little more upscale (Figure 5.3).[50] Aside from a fashion column, it also published handiwork patterns and advice from a *couturière*. Particularly striking in this magazine is the abundance of luxury-trade advertisements for beauty parlors, jewelers, and chocolate-makers, among others. But, then again, the magazine was short-lived. It ceased publication in 1916, as did *Élégances*.

Élégances: Grand Magazine de la Femme (Elegance: Grand Magazine for Women) was the most luxurious of them all.[51] It included a society section, called "Mondanités," which reported on events

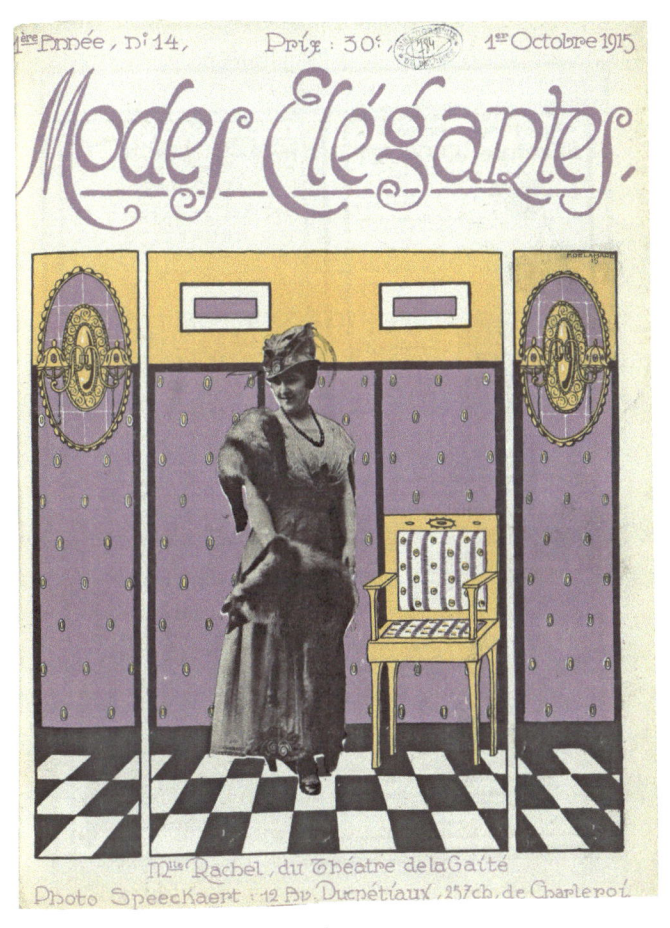

Figure 5.3 *The Belgian fashion magazine* Modes Élégantes, *October 1, 1915. Courtesy Royal Library of Belgium, Brussels.*

such as plays and musicals; the magazine also featured an abundance of fashion illustrations. It is the only magazine that mentioned a couture house by name in its captions: a certain *Maison Smeets*. These magazines must have represented a kind of Tantalus torture for most women, but were, seemingly, a normal part of life for the happy few.

The editor's column in *Élégances*' inaugural issue in December 1915 declared: "Above all, we felt that there was no need to remain dependent on foreign countries, which literally flood us with their illustrated magazines. We want to show that we can do as well, if not better …"[52] We find a similar statement in *Les Jolies Modes* of December 1916: "We want to show … that a Belgian house can publish a fashion journal that is more beautiful, richer, and cheaper than those arriving from abroad."[53] We can assume the editors had in mind the aforementioned German and Austrian publications, the only ones readily available on Belgium's newsstands. At any rate, Vienna, Berlin, let alone Paris, were never mentioned in the pages of any of these Belgian magazines. It is as if mere reference even only to the fashions of the warring powers was taboo.

The war was hardly ever mentioned, and then only allusively. This was in line with most international women's magazines of the time. *Élégances* concluded the introduction of its first issue by conveying its best wishes for the coming year to its readers: "May it be a new era of prosperity and happiness for them; it is our dearest wish."[54] The catastrophes of Verdun, the Somme, Passchendaele and two more years of war and hardships lay ahead…

Norine Couture: Removed from the carnage

We do not have official records of the founding of Norine Couture.[55] However, Van Hecke signed his fashion chronicles with "NORINE" as of May 1915; we can assume the house opened then or shortly thereafter. In November 1915, Van Hecke left *De Vlaamsche Post* and founded a Flemish theatre, Het Vlaamsch Toneel (The Flemish Theatre) in the Brussels venue Alhambra. Throughout the rest of the war years, he occasionally appeared in the Flemish activist movement but assumed a more moderate political stance and was more careful (writing under the pseudonym "PIK," for example).[56] In the spring of 1916, much to the displeasure of his activist friends, Van Hecke even briefly took on the directorship of the French-language theatre La Bonbonnière (The Candy Box).[57] And as befits a true *maison de couture* and its clientele, throughout its approximately thirty-seven years of existence, only French was spoken at Norine Couture.[58]

When Van Hecke's prewar years' friends returned from exile, they found "Gust Van Hecke … who almost became a rich man: *grand couturier*!"[59] Amidst and despite the hardships of war, Norine Couture must have thrived during the first years of its existence. Even so much so that, as Van Hecke stated: "Once the war was over, all we had to do was to establish ourselves on the

Avenue Louise in order to make a career with great pride and energy and become the leading house of Brussels."[60]

There is no archival documentation of Norine Couture's creations before 1919. However, considering Van Hecke's artistic past and the later modernist trajectory of the house during its ensuing heydays in the 1920s, Van Hecke and Norine were probably drawn to the designs of the Wiener Werkstätte and Berlin houses such as Alfred-Marie. With its avant-garde views on fashion, the latter stood somewhat apart from other Austrian and German houses.[61] Much as Alfred-Marie (which was inspired by prewar Parisian Paul Poiret) relied on artist Annie Offerdinger for its graphics, Norine Couture would later (equally inspired by prewar Poiret, and on par with Parisian contemporaries like Vionnet, Chanel, and Schiaparelli) collaborate with modern artists such as Frits Van den Berghe, Gustave Desmet, E.L.T. Mesens, and, mainly, René Magritte (Figure 5.4).

From the 1920s onwards, Norine Couture played with the latest aesthetics and incorporated avant-garde artistic imagery into many of its designs. For instance, Norine Couture's signature creation of the mid-twenties was the "*robe peinte*" (painted dress), undoubtedly hand-printed by René Magritte.[62]

Figure 5.4 *René Magritte, poster design for Norine, 1926. Private collection. Courtesy © Succession René Magritte, SABAM, Belgium, 2020.*

We also know of embroideries based on works by Raoul Dufy, Max Ernst, and Man Ray. Whether this already began during the war, we cannot say. Even during the Second World War, under the occupation of Nazi Germany, Norine Couture would continue to operate. However, Van Hecke was no Nazi-sympathizer or collaborator. In fact, on the eve of the war, he was a fervent opponent of National Socialism.[63] Van Hecke's leftist politics notwithstanding, the rather occupation-collaborationist women's magazine *Anne-Marie* published a spread on his couture house.[64]

Unanswered questions

This preliminary study of Norine Couture during the First World War still leaves open some important questions. Although Norine Couture was successful, did other Belgian couture houses go bankrupt during the war? Or, because Belgium had to become self-reliant for fashion, were there more start-ups like Norine Couture? Who were the houses' clients during the First World War? Who could afford couture? In 1915 alone, prices of mere fabric had increased 300 to 400 percent.[65] And if Norine Couture was as avant-garde during the war as it would prove to be later, was there a constituency for modernism? Was there already during the First World War anything like Norine Couture's later clientele of affluent bohemians? Were Norine Couture's clients the wives of people who economically profited from the war? Did the house at first dress Flemish activists' wives? German officers' wives? Their mistresses? Actresses? Did the "better people" still have the means to buy couture despite being hit by shortages?

Was Van Hecke a political opportunist? In 1916, when the war's outcome was still far from clear, Van Hecke tempered his involvement with Flemish activism and, in his own words "the *métier* of couturier did not leave me for a moment."[66] This move eventually served him well, because Flemish nationalist activism, even if only cultural, would be considered treasonous after the war. In due course, 312 Flemish activists were sentenced, including 37 to death (no one was ultimately executed) and 15 to life sentences. Many more were prosecuted.[67]

Thus, Van Hecke's professionally ambitious character seems to be the clue to his political coat-turning, as it were. Couture-business related considerations weighed much more than political precautions for this entrepreneur. Van Hecke was described by Karel Van de Woestijne and others as quite able to talk himself into anything, and therefore presumably also out of anything. Van de Woestijne wrote in 1917: "Gustaaf Van Hecke … is a young man, so convinced of his own irresistibility, that even stronger minds willingly grant him plenty … An arriviste of sorts without acknowledging it, he effortlessly lets himself be driven by all the means that will lead him to the success he never doubts."[68] However, this ambiguous praise also suggested that his intelligence and wit were at least as important to explain his success.

Conclusion: The beginning of Belgian fashion

From the beginning to the end, Norine Couture fervently proclaimed it was the only house making its own designs rather than copying Paris. After the war, Van Hecke no longer even mentioned the Viennese or Berlin fashions he had praised. In retrospect, the history of the now much celebrated Belgian avant-garde fashion began with Norine Couture.

However, if we believe Karel Van de Woestijne (slightly facetiously), Belgian avant-garde fashion may also have started in the streets of Belgium in 1918, as a side effect of shortages. Indeed, in July of that year, Van de Woestijne observed that, as a consequence of the confiscation of dress fabric, a new "gentlemen-aesthetic" had come about: "the aesthetic of the jackets turned inside out." He wrote:

> These days there is no Belgian male who doesn't walk around with his jacket turned inside out, which is not an unpleasant pastime. For the ladies, on the contrary, things are completely different. Apparently, it is very difficult to turn womenswear inside out. In contrast, it is very easy to cut dresses and suits out of bed sheets and even the covers of emptied mattresses. Immerse it in a jar with paint and you look as fresh as a rose, whilst we finally, free from Paris and even Vienna, are creating a real Belgian fashion.[69]

Reading this, contemporary fashion historians might recall the work of a more contemporary Belgian fashion house, founded in 1989: Maison Martin Margiela and its "deconstructivist" garments, turned inside out so as to reveal their construction.[70] Martin Margiela is known as one of the "first-generation" Belgian designers. Together with the so-called Antwerp Six—Walter Van Beirendonck, Ann Demeulemeester, Dries Van Noten, Dirk Van Saene, Marina Yee, and Dirk Bikkembergs—Margiela put Belgian fashion, known as avant-garde, conceptual, and subversive, on the map.[71] A Fall-Winter 1999–2000 Maison Martin Margiela duvet coat is one such example of upcycling—the process of reworking unusual materials into garments. One of the house's signature techniques is to cover garments with paint. As the garments are worn, the paint cracks, slowly revealing hidden colors and taking on new textures, showing the history of the piece.

In this account of fashion in Belgium during the First World War, we have encountered three assertions as to the beginnings of Belgian fashion. Indeed, Norine Couture can be considered the first genuine Belgian fashion house. However, Norine Couture never competed with its foreign counterparts, nor did it receive international recognition. In fact, Van Hecke and Norine probably never sought an international dimension. Obviously, Van de Woestijne's statement that Belgian fashion originated in the streets of Brussels in 1918 is not to be taken too seriously. The truth is, when Norine Couture closed its doors in 1952, it left a void in Belgian avant-garde fashion. There would be some unconnected and inconsequential surges of Belgian fashion design in the seventies and eighties, but it are the Antwerp Six and Margiela who, at the end of the 1980s are to be credited for Belgian fashion's ascent from obscurity to its persistent international prominence.

Notes

1 Sophie De Schaepdrijver, *De Groote Oorlog. Het Koninkrijk België tijdens de Eerste Wereldoorlog* (Antwerpen: Houtekiet, 2013).

2 As does De Schaepdrijver, who hadn't looked into the matter herself, but kindly reviewed this paper.

3 Paul-Gustave Van Hecke, "Binnenland: Brussel," *De Vlaamsche Post*, March 22, 1915.

4 This is how the initially neutral crossroads country was known worldwide after having been "raped" and overrun by the Kaiser's army in the late summer of 1914. When the Western Front stabilized for what would prove to be four years, only a tiny piece of the country behind the Yser river, with Ypres as its main town, remained Belgian.

5 De Schaepdrijver, *De Groote Oorlog*, 13.

6 Ibid.

7 Ibid., 14.

8 Ibid., 15.

9 Ibid.

10 Ibid.

11 Ibid.

12 Ninon, "Que sera la mode nouvelle?," *La Mode 1915* 20, 1, March 20, 1915, 5.

13 De Schaepdrijver, *De Groote Oorlog*, 19.

14 Ibid., 113.

15 Ibid., 116 and 118.

16 Ibid., 117.

17 Ibid., 124.

18 Ibid.

19 Geraldine Reymenants and Marysa Demoor, "Belgische vrouwen aangemoedigd niet te werken. Liefdadigheid: typisch vrouwelijk," in *De oorlogskranten: Een unieke collectie van oorspronkelijke dagbladen uit de Grote Oorlog 1914–1918*, Part 20 (Zellik: CEGESOMA, Centre for Historical Research and Documentation on War and Contemporary Society, 2014), 3.

20 Hans Boers, "'O subliem leger der Moeders!': Vrouwen in de Belgische oorlogskranten," in *De oorlogskranten*, Part 20, 2.

21 Compared to up to 54 percent in the UK, 78 in Italy, 85 in France, and 86 in Germany. Éliane Gubin, "Bespiegelingen over sekse en oorlog in België," *Jaarboek voor Vrouwengeschiedenis* 15 (1995): 35.

22 Françoise Thébaud, *La Femme au temps de la guerre de 14* (Paris: Stock, 1986), quoted by Gubin in ibid.

23 Reymenants and Demoor, "Belgische vrouwen aangemoedigd niet te werken," 3.

24 Gubin, "Bespiegelingen over sekse en oorlog in België," 37. See more on the so-called "war lace" in Marguerite Coppens' contribution to this book, Chapter 8.

25 It took even a second World War before Belgian women got the right to vote. Ibid.

26 Larry Zuckerman, *The Rape of Belgium: The Untold History of World War I* (New York: New York University Press, 2004), 142.

27 Karel Van de Woestijne, December 9, 1914, in Karel Van de Woestijne, *Verzameld journalistiek werk. Deel 7. Nieuwe Rotterdamsche Courant november 1913—maart 1915*, Ada Deprez, ed. (Gent: Cultureel Documentatiecentrum, 1991), 623.

28 Constance Graeffe, April 26, 1915, in *"We who are so cosmopolitan": The War Diary of Constance Graeffe, 1914–1915*, Sophie De Schaepdrijver, ed., Studies on World War One (Brussels: State Archives, 2014), 154.

29 "Chronique de la mode," *Les Jolies Modes,* no. 18, April 1916, 3.

30 From the genealogy website of the De Baets family, Waarschoot, see: http://www.debaets.be/yves/11-2.htm (accessed March 10, 2016).

31 For more on Norine Couture, see, e.g., Bernheim Nele, "Norine: Pioneer of the Belgian avant-garde (1915–1952)," in *The Belgians: An Unexpected Fashion Story*, Didier Vervaeren, ed. (Ostfildern: Hatje Cantz Verlag, 2015), 33–42.

32 Paul-Gustave Van Hecke quoted in Paul Kenis, "Paul Gustave Van Hecke of Van Letterkundige tot Couturier à la Mode," in *Den Gulden Winckel*, 12, December 20, 1928, 361.

33 Manu Van der Aa, "De activistische en andere avonturen van P.-G. Van Hecke tijdens de Eerste Wereldoorlog," in *Paul-Gustave Van Hecke (1887–1967)*, Manu van der Aa, Sjoerd van Faassen, Hans Renders, and Marc Somers, eds. (Antwerp: Garant, 2012), 35–41.

34 This branch of the Flemish Movement sprang from the occupation regime's *Flamenpolitik*, a policy designed to attract Flemings by favoring linguistic laws and creating Flemish institutions and Flemish media outlets. In short, the Flamenpolitik pretended to advance the cause of Flanders. But, in reality, the ultimate objective of this policy was the "independence" of Flanders as a German puppet state, preferably in a union with the Netherlands. An intermediary goal of this Flamenpolitik was to overturn the preeminence of French-speakers in Flanders, because French was the dominant language of the Belgian government and the upper classes of society, also in Flanders. Flanders is the northern Dutch-language half of Belgium. Brussels then was a genuine bilingual city, whereas today, Dutch-speakers are in minority.

35 Van der Aa, "De activistische," 41–8; Lodewijk Wils, *Onverfranst, Onverduitst? Flamenpolitik, activisme, frontbeweging* (Tielt: Pelckmans, Tielt), 80, 83–90, and 319–29.

36 Paul-Gustave Van Hecke, "Binnenland: Brussel," *De Vlaamsche Post*, February 22, 1915.

37 Paul-Gustave Van Hecke, "Binnenland: Brussel," *De Vlaamsche Post*, March 22, 1915.

38 Ibid. The fetters, or *entraves*, referred to the hobble skirt, which was fashionable from 1910–15.

39 Norine [Paul-Gustave Van Hecke], "Modekronijk: Inleiding tot het nieuwe," *De Vlaamsche Post*, May 23–4, 1915; "Modekronkijk: Weener- en Parijzermodellen," *De Vlaamsche Post*, June 21, 1915.

40 Norine, May 23–4, 1915.

41 Ibid. Note the choice for the feminine denomination of *couturières*, which was undoubtedly an allusion to Norine Couture.

42 For more on the subject of contemporary German and Austrian fashion, see Rasche, ed., *Wardrobes in Wartime: Fashion and Fashion Images during the First World War* (Leipzig: Seeman, 2014). Birgit Haase, chapter 4.

43 Karel Van de Woestijne, "XXVII," March 29, 1916, in Karel Van de Woestijne, *Verzameld journalistiek werk. Deel 9. Nieuwe Rotterdamsche Courant maart 1916—september 1919*, Ada Deprez, ed. (Gent: Cultureel Documentatiecentrum, 1992), 46.

44 Ibid.

45 Ibid.

46 Norine, Modekronkijk, May 23–24, 1915; Norine, "Modekronkijk," June 21, 1915.

47 Between 1915 and 1918, the Viennese copies of the magazine *Le Chic Parisien* (1898–1942) adopted the title *Wiener Modekunst,* while in Belgium, the magazine kept its original French-language title. The magazine's full quotation in Germany's *Zeitschriftendatenbank* (magazine database) is: *Le Chic parisien: Journal spécial pour modèles des Paris et Vienne* (1898–1942)—*Wiener Modekunst* (1915–1918) (Paris/Wien: Bachwitz).

48 *La Mode 1915*, Brussels, March 20, 1915–June 1915.

49 *Les Jolies Modes*, February 1912, no. 305, 1940. Initially entitled *Les Jolies Modes de Paris,* the magazine eventually, probably quite significantly, dropped "de Paris" from its title. Unfortunately, there is a lacuna between 1912 and 1915 in the Royal Library of Belgium's holdings which doesn't allow us to know when this occurred. We can however confirm that, from no. 66, March 1920 onwards, its original title was reinstated.

50 *Modes Élégantes*, Brussels, May 27, 1915–May 1, 1916.

51 *Élégances*, December 1915–April 1916.

52 Ibid., December 1915, 3.

53 *Les Jolies Modes*, December, 1916, 25. This concludes the notice—exceptionally also in Dutch—on the magazine's paper-quality decrease and subscription fee increase.

54 *Élégances*, Ibid.

55 The two sources that could have provided information revealed none. The first, the *Annuaire du commerce et de l'industrie de Belgique: Bruxelles et sa banlieue* (Annuary of Belgian Commerce and Industry: Brussels and its Suburbs), ceased publication during the war. As for the second, the official *Moniteur belge* (Belgian Monitor), published by the government in exile, did not contain any information about Belgium's trade at the time.

56 Used for his contributions in *Vlaamsch Leven* from August 25 to September 29, 1918.

57 33   Manu Van der Aa, "De activistische en andere avonturen van P.-G. Van Hecke tijdens de Eerste Wereldoorlog," in *Paul-Gustave Van Hecke (1887–1967)*, Manu van der Aa, Sjoerd van Faassen, Hans Renders, and Marc Somers, eds. (Antwerp: Garant, 2012), 35–41.

58 Information from testimony of Aline Goossens, seamstress at Norine Couture from c. 1941 to 1944, interviewed by the author, Brussels, April 10, 2011. Throughout the rest of his career, Van Hecke's writings would be both in Dutch and French.

59 Antwerp, Letterenhuis, Letter from André De Ridder to Paul Kenis, March 7, 1919.

60 Paul-Gustave Van Hecke quoted in Kenis, Ibid. The Avenue Louise was the most elegant avenue in Brussels at the time, radiating out from the inner city to the park of the Bois de La Cambre.

61 See Rasche, "The Berlin Alfred-Marie Fashion House: Otto Haas-Heye and Annie Offterdinger," in ibid. 118–37. Birgit Haase, chapter 4, p. 63.

62 "Norine crée des robes peintes," *Psyché: Le Miroir des belles choses*, May 1925, n.p.

63 This can be tracked through his articles in the social-democratic Flemish daily newspaper *Vooruit*, which he directed as editor-in-chief from 1938 to 1940.

64 "J'ai vu une grande maison de couture: Norine couture S.A.," *Anne-Marie*, May 24, 1942, 12–13.

65 Larry Zuckerman, *The Rape of Belgium: The Untold History of World War I* (New York: New York University Press, 2004), 165.

66 Kenis, (?) 362.

67 Michel Deckers, "De strafrechtelijk vervolging van het activisme. Deel III: De Omvang. Besluiten," *Wetenschappelijke Tijdingen* 62, 1 (January 2003): 22.

68 Karel Van de Woestijne and Herman Teirlinck, "De Leemen Torens: Vooroorlogse kroniek van twee steden," in *Verzameld werk van Karel van de Woestijne*, vol. 7 (Brussels: A. Manteau N.V., 1948), 560.

69 Karel Van de Woestijne, "Over het roest van stalen pennen," in Karel Van de Woestijne, *Verzameld journalistiek werk: Deel 9. Nieuwe Rotterdamsche Courant maart 1916–1919*, 317.

70 It was Bill Cunningham who first applied the term to fashion, after having seen Maison Martin Margiela's fashion show in March 1990. See Bill Cunningham, "The Collections," *Details*, March, 1990, 80.

71 See Karen Van Godtsenhoven, "The birth of Belgian avant-garde fashion: Breakthrough and careers of the Antwerp Six+1," in *The Belgians. An Unexpected Fashion Story*, 55–72.

References

Bernheim, Nele, "Norine: Pioneer of the Belgian avant-garde (1915–1952)." In The Belgians: An Unexpected Fashion Story, ed. Didier Vervaeren, 33–42. Ostfildern: Hatje Cantz Verlag, 2015.
Boers, Hans. "'O subliem leger der Moeders!': Vrouwen in de Belgische oorlogskranten." In *De oorlogskranten: Een unieke collectie van oorspronkelijke dagbladen uit de Grote Oorlog 1914–1918*. Vol. 20. Zellik: CEGESOMA, Centre for Historical Research and Documentation on War and Contemporary Society, 2014.
"Chronique de la mode." In *Les Jolies modes*, 18, April 1916.
Cunningham Bill. "The Collections." In *Details*, March, 1990.
De Baets family and genealogy website, Waarschoot. Available at: http://www.debaets.be/yves/11-2.htm (accessed March 10, 2016).
De Ridder, André. Manuscripts. The Letterenhuis: The Memory of Flemish Literature, Antwerp.
De Schaepdrijver, Sophie. *De Groote Oorlog: Het Koninkrijk België tijdens de Eerste Wereldoorlog*. Antwerp: Houtekiet, 2013.
De Schaepdrijver, Sophie and Mark De Geest. *Brave Little Belgium*. Four-part documentary (in Dutch) broadcasted by CANVAS. Available at: https://communicatie.canvas.be/brave-little-belgium (accessed June 28, 2020).
Deckers, Michel. "De strafrechtelijk vervolging van het activisme. Deel III: De Omvang." *Wetenschappelijke Tijdingen* 62, 1 (January 2003): 22–31.
Élégances. Brussels, December 1915–April 1916.
Goossens, Aline. Interview by author, Brussels, April 10, 2011.

Gubin, Éliane. "Bespiegelingen over sekse en oorlog in België." *Jaarboek voor Vrouwengeschiedenis* 15 (1995): 33–48.

"J'ai vue une grande maison de couture: Norine couture S.A." In *Anne-Marie*, May 24, 1942.

Kenis, Paul. "Paul Gustave Van Hecke of Van Letterkundige tot Couturier à la Mode." In *Den Gulden Winckel*, 12, December 20, 1928, 358–64.

La Mode 1915. Brussels, 20 March 1915–June 1915.

Le Chic Parisien: Journal spécial pour modèles des Paris et Vienne (1898–1942)—*Wiener Modekunst* (1915–1918). Paris and Vienna: Bachwitz.

Les Jolies Modes (de Paris), Brussels, 1 February 1912—no. 305, 1940.

Modes Élégantes. Brussels, 27 May 1915–1 May 1916.

Ninon. "Que sera la mode nouvelle?" In *La Mode 1915*, 1, March 20, 1915.

"Norine crée des robes peintes." In *Psyché: Le Miroir des belles choses*, May, 1925.

Norine [Paul-Gustave Van Hecke]. "Modekronijk: Inleiding tot het nieuwe." *De Vlaamsche Post*, May 23–24, 1915.

Norine [Paul-Gustave Van Hecke]. "Modekronkijk: Weener- en Parijzermodellen." *De Vlaamsche Post*, June 22, 1915.

Rasche, Adelheid, ed. *Wardrobes in Wartime 1914–1918: Fashion and Fashion Images during the First World War*. Leipzig: Seemann, 2014.

Reymenants Geraldine and Marysa Demoor. "De Belgische vrouwen aangemoedigd niet te werken. Liefdadigheid: typisch vrouwelijk." *De oorlogskranten: Een unieke collectie van oorspronkelijke dagbladen uit de Grote Oorlog 1914–1918*. Part 20. Zellik: CEGESOMA, Centre for Historical Research and Documentation on War and Contemporary Society, 2014.

Van Hecke, Paul-Gustave. "Binnenland: Brussel." *De Vlaamsche Post*, February 16, 1915.

Van Hecke, Paul-Gustave. "Binnenland: Brussel." *De Vlaamsche Post*, March 22, 1915.

Van de Woestijne, Karel. *Verzameld journalistiek werk: Deel 7. Nieuwe Rotterdamsche Courant november 1913–maart 1915*. Ada Deprez. Ghent, ed., Cultureel Documentatiecentrum: 1991.

Van de Woestijne, Karel. *Verzameld journalistiek werk. Deel 9. Nieuwe Rotterdamsche Courant maart 1916–september 1919*. Ada Deprez, ed. Ghent: Cultureel Documentatiecentrum, 1991.

Van de Woestijne, Karel and Herman Teirlinck. "De Leemen Torens: Vooroorlogse kroniek van twee steden." In *Verzameld werk van Karel van de Woestijne*. Vol. 7. Brussels: A. Manteau N.V., 1948.

Van der Aa, Manu. "De activistische en andere avonturen van P.-G. Van Hecke tijdens de Eerste Wereldoorlog." *Zacht Lawijd: Literair-historisch tijdschrift* 13, no. 3 (2014): 34–59.

Van Godtsenhoven, Karen. "The birth of Belgian avant-garde fashion: Breakthrough and careers of the Antwerp Six+1." In *The Belgians: An Unexpected Fashion Story*, ed. Didier Vervaeren, 55–72. Ostfildern: Hatje Cantz, 2015.

"*We who are so cosmopolitan*": *The War Diary of Constance Graeffe, 1914–1915*. Studies on World War One. Brussels: State Archives, 2014.

Wils, Lodewijk. *Onverfranst, Onverduitst?: Flamenpolitik, activisme, frontbeweging*. Tielt: Pelckmans, 2014.

Zuckerman, Larry. *The Rape of Belgium: The Untold History of World War I*. New York: New York University Press, 2004.

Part Two

The materiality of wartime fashion and textile industries

6

Dressed to quill

The origin and significance of the feathered showgirl in First World War Paris

Emily Brayshaw

Plumes and Paris

The fashions for women's large, elaborate hats trimmed with vast sprays of ostrich feathers began in the 1880s and coincided with the period of French history known as the Belle Époque, an era of affluence, security and gaiety that lasted from 1871 until the outbreak of the First World War in 1914.[1] The finest ostrich plumes were very expensive, but with at least fourteen varieties and countless grades available, women from all social backgrounds could purchase ostrich-feathered fashions.[2] In November 1903, for example, the Cawston Ostrich Farm in California offered American consumers plumes from $1.50 each and 1.5-yard long feather boas for $35 each.

While the Californian ostrich feather industry rose to capitalize on the high prices of raw South African plumes, feathered fashions emanated from Paris, not the United States. Indeed, by the 1890s, many wealthy American socialites traveled annually to Paris to order bespoke wardrobes from the new collections.[3] Parisian fashions were also the subject of countless international newspaper and magazine reports, which coincided with the phenomenon of famous actresses appearing on world stages wearing the latest French haute couture.[4] Consumers' knowledge of Parisian fashions, therefore, meant that ostrich feathers remained modish as long as France decreed them so.

France was a leading global consumer of raw ostrich feathers prior to 1914 and Paris, where the plumes were treated and readied for sale in extensive manufactories, crafted the world's finest trimmings.[5] The prolonged, ubiquitous popularity of plumed fashions during the Belle Époque meant that the Parisian feather industry was a significant economic force in France. However, the outbreak of the First World War in July 1914 was accompanied by a mood of austerity in French fashion and women needed utilitarian clothes for war work, which contributed to the decline in fashion of garments and hats trimmed with large ostrich plumes.[6] Thus, the global price of ostrich feathers crashed in the early winter of 1914.[7] Plumes, it seemed, were *passé*.

Laisse les Tomber!

Laisse les Tomber!, an opulent revue in two acts with fifty scenes, opened on December 12, 1917, at the Casino de Paris and starred the French music hall star Gaby Deslys (born Marie-Elise-Gabrielle Caire, 1881–1920) wearing towering ostrich feather headdresses made by Maison Lewis, a leading court and society milliner with workshops in Paris and London. The revue also featured more than 800 costumes designed by Canabate (dates unknown) and the great costume designer and poster artist, Charles Gesmar (1900–28), and executed by one of the Belle Époque's leading costumiers, Maison Pascaud of Paris. Deslys and her co-star, Harry Pilcer (1885–1961), danced to American ragtime. The press praised the show, writing, "The revue, 'Laissez les Tomber,' [*sic*] ... is a magnificent show ... The costumes are gorgeous, particularly for war time [*sic*]! The ladder scene has been introduced as the three colors (red, white, blue), and pleased immensely."[8] The ladder scene, which the New York theater publication *Variety* called "the most important tableaux,"[9] featured dozens of nude showgirls wearing large, feathered headdresses descending 30-foot ladders.[10] The revue's international and local audiences would have simultaneously associated the showgirls' red, white and blue feathers with the *tricolore* of the French flag (due to the French history of tying nationalism with commercial and musical culture) and with the British Union Jack.[11] Any Americans present would have associated it with their own flag; *Laisse les Tomber!* included the musical number, "Stars and Stripes" (1917).

Laisse les Tomber! also left an indelible impression on the avant-gardist, Jean Cocteau (1889–1963), who wrote:

> M. Pilcer ... and Mademoiselle Gaby Deslys, a great ventriloquist's doll with ... [an] ostrich-feathered gown, danced through this tornado of drum and rhythm ... The house was on its feet to applaud, roused from its torpor by this extraordinary turn, which is to the frenzy of Offenbach, as a tank is to an 1870s state carriage.[12]

Paris in 1917

Paris was in torpor in 1917. Workers, soldiers, cultural elites, and the fashion industry were despondent due to the war, poor working conditions, rationing, inflation, and the freezing winter of 1916–17.[13] The English journalist Helen (Pearl) Adam (1882–1957) wrote in her diary of life in Paris that the "deterioration of civilian morale" and that of the troops made itself felt in the spring of 1917.[14] The French expressed their dissatisfactions however they could, including industrial action, mutiny, sophisticated indifference, and by mocking German soldiers and civilians. On May 18, 1917, for example, 10,000 *midinettes* (dressmakers) from forty fashion houses in Paris went on strike; 5,000 female workers in the gunpowder factory of Toulouse went on strike for a week from June 13, 1917.[15] The *poilus* (French infantry) were also fed up and began a mutiny on April 17, 1917,[16] which by June included more than 40,000 soldiers who rejected the High Command's "mindless devotion to offensive at any cost".[17] This was in direct contrast with the image of tough, easy-going, jovial, scruffy *poilus* promoted by French propagandists in 1914.[18]

The avant-garde, cultural and intellectual elite of Paris too expressed its dissatisfaction with the war. Jean Cocteau's Futurist, one-act ballet, *Parade*, for example, dealt with the terror of war through its "cultivated apathy".[19] *Parade* premiered on May 18, 1917 and featured a score by French composer Erik Satie (1866–1925) and costumes and scenography designed by Pablo Picasso (1881–1973). It was performed by the Ballets Russes and represented a Parisian Sunday fair with a travelling theater that employed three music hall turns: a Chinese conjuror, an American girl, and a pair of acrobats. Many music halls typically employed acts outside the theater to entice potential audiences to the show.[20] Yet *Parade*'s costumes, music, and choreography were deliberately disjointed and distorted with the dancers becoming increasingly desperate and frantic, perhaps reflecting the conditions in Paris in 1917 and the horrors of war.

Parisian fashion designers and illustrators expressed their frustrations by mocking the Germans sartorially during the war years. Cartoons have always been a popular form of expression in France and during the war "an unexampled flood of cartoon and caricature poured from artists both celebrated and unknown."[21] Lou Taylor writes that, "The most successful cartoonists lampoon the circles they live amongst or close to".[22] Georges Kugelmann Benda (d. 1921), Leonetto Cappiello (1875–1942), and Georges Barbier (1882–1932), for example, were well positioned to mock restrictions placed on the Parisian fashion industry during the First World War. Cappiello was a prominent *fin-de-siècle* music-hall poster and advertising artist and caricaturist who produced covers for satirical journals, while Benda and Barbier produced illustrations for the highly influential fashion magazine, *La Gazette du Bon Ton*. Barbier was also a prominent costume designer. They, like many of their peers, however, also produced anti-German cartoons during the war for popular magazines, many of which mocked German approaches to fashion.

Such anti-German cartoons typically featured stout, tasteless, poorly dressed women, such as Cappiello's cover for *La Baïonnette,* on 20 January 1916 entitled *Les Gretchen* (The Gretchen).[23] A 1917 Benda sketch for the satirical magazine *La Baïonnette* entitled *Leur Theatre: La Grosse vedette* (Their Theater: The Big Star) shows a fat German performer wearing an outdated, ostrich feather-trimmed hat and a gown in a style from the early 1900s. The French term *la grosse vedette* implies a grotesque star past her prime. Such representations were antithetical to illustrations in the popular press by Cappiello, Benda, and Barbier of chic Parisian women and French music hall stars wearing elegant, ostrich-feathered fashions and costumes.

Parisian music halls

Music halls rose in France in the *fin de siècle* and incorporated sumptuous production values and interiors, lively music, and a brash aesthetic. They originated in England during the 1840s and the format was imported to the café-concert scene in Paris where the term "music hall" came to mean the theater itself and the type of entertainment held there.[24] Music hall programs of the Belle Époque predominantly featured *tours de chant* alternating with circus and ballet numbers and culminated in an "opulently staged *revue à grand spectacle*."[25] Paris's first *revue à grand spectacle* was performed at the Folies Bergère in 1887.[26] Music hall tickets ranged in cost from two to six francs in 1900, making them a "feasible entertainment venue for most of the French populace."[27] By 1914, music hall revues had become the focal point of an evening's entertainment for many Parisians.

Parisian music halls closed in August 1914 with the onset of the war, but reopened in December with a "stream of flag-waving revues" that glorified the Allied and French soldiers.[28] Despite their popularity with locals and visiting troops alike, however, the war took an economic and physical toll on the Parisian music halls, which were required to donate 15 percent of their takings to war-related charities.[29] *Variety* reported that Parisian music-hall attendances were also affected by curfews imposed in response to the threat of the *Parisgeschütz* (Paris gun), a long-range super-heavy field cannon the German army used to bombard Paris during the First World War.[30] The *Parisgeschütz* was designed to act as a psychological weapon against the French and the most vicious attacks were launched in March 1918, when more than 1,000 shells "fell on … Paris killing a total of 522 people and wounding 1,223."[31] Paul Duval (1880–1966), who became the director of the Folies Bergère in 1918, wrote that his music hall also took a hit during the attacks.[32]

The dissatisfaction with life in Paris in 1917 contributed to a social nostalgia for the security and affluence of the Belle Époque. Parisian music hall revues during the war expressed much of this nostalgia through their musical content, which included the hit song of 1917, "Quand Madelon" (1914), about a cheerful barmaid who serves *poilus* in her sunny rural tavern (Sweeney 2001: 255).[33]

The title of Deslys's revue scorned the threat of German bombardments by proclaiming, *Laisse les Tomber!*, which is often translated as "Let Them Fall!", but also literally translates as "Drop it!" or "Forget it!," which encouraged Parisians to rouse themselves from their torpor to attend the music halls.[34] *Laisse les Tomber!* also tapped into audiences' nostalgia for the Belle Époque, although not strictly through its musical content, which included many American ragtime numbers. Rather, the revue provided visual references to the movement, decadence, and ostrich feathered fashions of the Parisian Belle Époque, which were captured by Henri de Toulouse-Lautrec (1864–1901) in his work *La Troupe de Mademoiselle Eglantine* (Mademoiselle Eglantine's troupe) (1896). The poster shows the English dancer Jane Avril (1868–1943) and a female chorus line wearing large hats trimmed with ostrich plumes and performing the "cancan."

Sociopolitical and cultural context is important when people choose clothing that references the past. This is "particularly apparent in high design."[35] Cocteau's description of Deslys highlights her sartorial allusions to Belle Époque music halls through his mention of her ostrich feathers and his reference to composer Jacques Offenbach's (1819–80) music for the "cancan." Deslys herself, whose stage career had started around 1902, was also part of the Belle Époque's visual legacy. A famous actress, Deslys had used her exploits with wealthy, powerful lovers in the 1910s, such as King Manuel II of Portugal (1889–1932) and Harry Gordon Selfridge Sr. (1858–1947), the founder of Selfridge's department stores in the United Kingdom, alongside her jewelry, and displays of expensive fashion and feathers to fascinate her public.[36] Yet, Cocteau firmly situated Deslys in the Paris of 1917 with all of the subtlety of a military tank that ploughs through the old era, represented by an 1870s state carriage.

Le Retour des *plumes d'autruche*

Parisian nostalgia for the Belle Époque also meant that ostrich feathers did not become unfashionable during the war; rather they experienced a deliberate resurgence in use by French milliners and *couturiers* as modish trimmings. According to Steele, "[h]istorical revivalism is most often used as a tool to create a pervasive, and recognizable, environment for fashion that responds very pertinently to the times in which it is created."[37] An analysis of *Les Élégances des parisiennes* (the official monthly publication of the French fashion industry) from 1914 to 1918, for example, reveals that the industry pushed ostrich feathered fashions from April 1916 when it heralded *"Le Retour des plumes d'autruche"* (The return of ostrich feathers), noting that, "Ostrich feathers are coming back into fashion … Little tufts on the end of a long ostrich barb are straw-colored. We find borders of ostrich feathers on afternoon and evening gowns produced by the leading couturiers."[38]

Taylor cautions that fashion plates and magazines are idealized images, but in this context, they do provide strong evidence that Parisian fashions and music hall costumes used ostrich feathers during the war to signal frivolity and decadence to audiences starved of luxury and fantasy.[39] Barbier, for example, sketched a scene from the revue *Maousspoilpoil* (1916), *La Triomphe du Champagne* (The Triumph of Champagne), for *La Vie Parisienne* in 1916 that depicts the French music hall star Mlle Musidora (1889–1957) standing atop a champagne bottle wearing a large, foamy, straw-colored ostrich feathered headdress. Benda also drew Mlle Musidora as "Champagne" wearing the frothy ostrich-feathered headdress for a 1916 edition of *Fantasio*.[40] *La Vie parisienne* published an illustration by Barbier on November 11, 1916, entitled *Soldats de jadis* (Soldiers of Times Past), in which an early 1800s French Imperial Guard drum major and a contemporary young woman in fashionable dress, wearing hats trimmed with three large ostrich plumes, stand side by side. The caption reads, "*Le galant tambour-major de un* [sic] *concours de panaches*" (The gallant drum major in a contest of "panache"). "Panache" means "elegance" in French, but it also refers to a trimming that uses three large ostrich wing feathers.[41] Panache plumes were traditionally large, luxurious, and expensive and had historical ties to the sixteenth-century tournament wear of European noble houses, where they adorned the fighters' helmets.

An opinion piece in *Les Élégances Parisiennes* in February 1917, "Le Réveil de la Mode Parisienne" (The Rise of Paris Fashion), announced it was the duty of Paris's *modistes*, or female hatmakers, to renounce the austerity of previous seasons to make fashion, a core component of the French national economy, more palatable to global markets.[42] However, raw material and trimming shortages as well as the voluntary fabric restrictions agreed upon by the Syndicat de la Couture Parisienne in 1917 forced the Parisian fashion industry to produce the illusion of extravagance with very few materials and colors. For example, "woollen fabrics had risen to fearsome prices" and many colors were simply unavailable or very expensive in 1917 because "for two years no one had worn anything else, even when not in mourning, unless it was the very darkest blue or brown."[43] A note in the February 1917 edition of *Les Modes de Paris*, also pointed to necessity being the mother of invention: "*Une des caractéristiques de la saison sera la variété des tissus employés*" ("One of this season's features will be the use of a variety of fabrics").[44] The publication also promoted ostrich feathers as a trimming on mules.

Throughout 1917, therefore, the Parisian fashion industry, including milliners like Maison Lewis, used ostrich feathers to signal an apparent break from austerity, even though fashions did not reach the enormous proportions of women's Belle Époque picture hats with their vast ostrich plume sprays. For example, in March 1917 the *New York Herald* ran a catalogue for the American department store, Macy's, that contained an advertisement for hats manufactured in America but which copied Maison Lewis's latest styles. This included a small black and tan hat, which reflected the colors available for use in Paris, but which was trimmed with small ostrich plumes to lighten its mood. *The New York Times* also reported the trend, noting that the "revised popularity of ostrich feathers is a fashionable millinery trimming," and that the plumes were not subject to American anti-plumage laws.[45]

The influence of Paris on global fashion in 1917, even in the midst of a long and bloody war, remained strong enough to reach the Antipodes. *The West Australian*, for example, reported the trend of matching ostrich feather trims to the outfit as mandated in the April 1916 edition of *Les Élègances*, and the role of Parisian music hall fashions to signal light-heartedness:[46]

> In an exaggerated sort of way the theatres and reviews give us a foretaste of fashion, and, although one looks at first upon such displays as a huge joke, they help us to get accustomed to every freak of "La Mode," and to invest it with some association of gaiety, which is welcome in these times. The only thing is that the 1917 fashions seem curiously unsuited to economy and work.[47]

Meanwhile, the *New Zealand Herald* reported: "The uncurled ostrich feather is being used as trimming again. It rears itself in soft, straight fluffiness on tall, toques of crinoline, or fine straw. It . . . is sometimes turned into a sort of pompon, for one very smart milliner seems to like pompons this year."[48]

Finding feathers

There is sufficient evidence to suggest that the French fashion industry had ready, unrestricted access to cheap ostrich feathers that had been stockpiled and processed in Paris before the war. Prior to 1913, "Brokerage firms, feather wholesalers, and manufacturers in New York and London were stocking great quantities of feathers in anticipation of a rise in value."[49] Wholesalers in France also imported almost 146,371 lbs of unprocessed ostrich feathers in 1912 (mainly from London merchants), yet exported 5,810 lbs of processed ostrich feather trimmings.[50] This speculation and hoarding, however, proved unwise and the "ostrich feather trade in Paris during World War I was extremely bad."[51] Indeed, the number of ostriches and global imports of raw plumes declined during the war. The New York sales branch of a leading South African ostrich feather wholesale house reported a significant drop in the number of ostriches raised in South Africa from 776,268 at the end of 1913 to 399,010 in 1917.[52] London-based plume wholesalers were also so badly affected by the crash that ostrich farming became the butt of a joke in the English satire magazine, *Punch*, in 1917: "Imports of ostrich feathers to London have fallen from 33,000 lbs in 1915 to 182 lbs in 1917. Ostrich farmers, it appears, are on the verge of ruin as the result of their inability to obtain scissors and other suitable foodstuffs for the birds."[53]

In spite of the global crash, however, there were no restrictions on the use or supply of ostrich feathers in France.[54] Further, an analysis of ostrich-feather trimmings in photographs, news articles and illustrations in 1916 and 1917 indicates that existing plumes may have been repurposed. Four of the top ten fancy feather trimmings in the winter 1913 season were made from ostrich feathers.[55] Number ten resembles a trimming described in *Les Élégances* in April 1916, "little tufts on the end of a long ostrich barb." Number two, a larger chrysanthemum, resembles the ostrich feather "pompon"

Figure 6.1 Quelques fantasies typiques de la mode d'hiver 1913 *(Some trimmings typical of winter 1913 fashions). Lefèvre: 316 (1914). Credit: Robarts Library of Humanities and Social Sciences, University of Toronto, Canada.*

mentioned by the *New Zealand Herald* in 1917. This resurgence of pompons in fashion was a striking piece of French ingenuity and thrift in the face of austerity and rationing. Pompons are best made from offcuts produced when refining ostrich plumes, and thus inexpensive to produce.[56] Pompons also provided a material luxury of softness and signalled an almost incongruous levity in the face of war akin to the 'cultivated apathy' of Cocteau's *Parade* (Figure 6.1).

War work

Deslys's trademark feathered headpieces moved from the realm of fashionable hats to large, elaborate ostrich-plumed headdresses during the 1910s. Many of her headpieces were ordered from Maison Lewis, which prepared a "collection of astonishing hats" for her to wear in *Vera Violetta* (1911) in New York.[57] Deslys quickly became a symbol of the Allied Forces of France, Britain, and America and starred in productions and fundraising efforts in the UK and the during the war.[58] Maison Lewis continued to make Deslys's feathered headpieces throughout the 1910s including for her hit London show, *Suzette*, which opened on March 29, 1917 at the Globe Theatre and ran until October 1917.[59]

The USA entered the war on April 6, 1917, on the side of France and Britain against Germany, and Deslys celebrated by wearing an "Allied flags" costume in *Suzette* on April 20. *Variety* appreciated the sartorial significance of her cape with an ostrich feather border and headdress trimmed with ostrich plumes: "Great enthusiasm was manifested . . . when Gaby Deslys appeared in a costume representing the flags of the Allies, with a stupendous head-dress of red, white and blue, covered with stars."[60] *Punch* took Deslys's penchant for plumes and her support for the Allies one step further and published a cartoon on June 25, 1917 with the caption: "Mr. Punch's National Service for All. It is not implied that the above are at present out of War Work—but Mr. Punch is very anxious to see everybody's natural gifts employed to the best advantage."[61] Among the famous figures lampooned, including the author H. G. Wells (1866–1946) and the silent film star Charlie Chaplin (1889–1977), *Punch* presented Deslys displaying her design sketch for "The Gaby," an anti-shrapnel helmet shaped like a feathered headdress with protruding metal "plumes." Deslys's sartorial messages of support for the Allies were thus well-known prior to *Laisse les Tomber!* Her headdresses in *Suzette* also gave audiences a "foretaste" of *Laisse les Tomber!* and although Deslys's extravagant plumes seemed "unsuited to economy and work," they perfectly suited her important work as an actress who supported the French economy and devoted herself to fundraising and morale boosting during the war.

An ostrich in the hand . . .

The conditions of Deslys's return to the French stage reflected *Variety*'s 1917 claim that big stars were playing Paris for small salaries.[62] Léon Volterra (1881–1949) purchased the Casino de Paris in early 1917 as a rival to the Folies-Bergère and teamed with producer Jacques-Charles (dates unknown) to develop *Laisse les Tomber!* Deslys is believed to have owed Jacques-Charles a personal favor and therefore agreed to appear for a low salary and to pay for Pilcer's salary, her costumes, and the costumes of the showgirls in her scenes, many of whom had worked on *Suzette* in London.[63] Deslys also supervised the construction of her own costumes and those of her "girls." Despite this apparent generosity, however, Deslys was a shrewd businesswoman. In 1913, for example, she told the American press that:

> I have adapted from that old saying "A bird in the hand is worth two in the bush." I have written over my financial window: "Two per cent in the hand is worth seventeen per cent in the bush." I play safe . . . A true French woman, I believe that no sum is too small to save.[64]

A further measure of Deslys's business savvy is apparent in the three-year contract she negotiated in 1911 with American impresarios, the Shubert Brothers,[65] who guaranteed her $4,000 per week,[66] plus traveling expenses for her whole party.[67] Deslys, like many of her contemporaries, would have been aware of audiences' expectations that she appeared on stage wearing the latest French fashions, including feathered hats, to tempt women theatrergoers to her productions with displays of luxury and taste.[68] She also knew that these fashions were extremely expensive, with the American press reporting: "The costumes worn by Gaby Deslys at the Winter Garden in New York are said to have cost nearly $15,000 . . . For some of her gowns, she paid $1,000, while one . . . trimmed with Bird of Paradise feathers cost $3,000."[69]

It is, therefore, significant that Deslys injected her own cash, and stardom, into *Laisse les Tomber!* to boost the French economy and morale. An experienced actress, Deslys would have also been aware that massed feathers were visually spectacular on stage. Her involvement in the construction of her costumes suggests that she was aware of the cheap, ready supply of ostrich feathers in Paris in 1917. There is also strong evidence that Deslys re-wore and repurposed her feathers.

A photograph of Deslys in *A la Carte* (1913) by the London portrait studio Foulsham and Banfield, Ltd. shows her wearing a headdress trimmed with two large ostrich feather "barbs" that were fashionable in 1913 and in April 1916.[70] A portrait of Deslys taken in 1917 by the British photographer Emil Otto Hoppé (1878–1972), shows her wearing a headdress trimmed with eleven large ostrich feather barbs from *Suzette*.[71] This suggests that some of her plumes were recycled, while others were sourced from trimmings manufactured and stockpiled in Paris in 1913. Another photograph of Deslys by Foulsham and Banfield, published in the August 1917 pictorial "Gaby Plumes Herself" (publication unknown), shows her wearing another headdress from *Suzette* from which protrudes two long, horizontal sections of ostrich feathers and two large vertical plumes. A photograph of Deslys in *Laisse les Tomber!* by the Frenchman Albert Harlingue (1879–963) shows her wearing a headdress trimmed with large ostrich feathers protruding horizontally and vertically.[72] This appears to be a version of the headdress from the pictorial "Gaby Plumes Herself" that has been re-trimmed with *têtes*, which were also popular trimmings in 1913.[73] Harlingue's photograph demonstrates how Deslys enhanced the headdress's visual impact by teaming it with a gown featuring a tailpiece of long, uncurled ostrich feathers and a frontal fringe of Barbary plumes.

In early 1918, Cappiello produced a sketch of Deslys and Pilcer for *Fantasio* entitled *Pupazzi var Cappiello* (Cappiello's Italian Puppets), that demonstrated her thrift and her visual legacy of the Belle Époque (Figure 6.2).[74] Cappiello's illustration depicts Deslys wearing a large, dark ostrich feathered headdress which resembles one worn in *Suzette* and shows her dancing like the women in Lautrec's *La Troupe de Mademoiselle Eglantine* and like the ostrich-plumed "cancan" girl that Cappiello sketched for a 1899 cover of *Le Frou Frou*.[75] The dancing figure of Deslys in ostrich plumes evokes the joy and frivolity that were typical motifs expressed in Belle Époque poster art.

Figure 6.2 *Leonetto Cappiello, "Pupazzi var Cappiello," 1918.* Fantasio *(1918): 373. Courtesy the Author's Collection.*

The quick turnaround for Deslys and Pilcer between the end of *Suzette* and the opening of *Laisse les Tomber!* likely influenced the re-use of her headdresses. Nonetheless, this reuse, and the displays of massed ostrich plumes meant Deslys could create the opulence and luxury audiences associated with the *revues à grand spectacle* of the Parisian Belle Époque, while keeping to a tight budget amid strict rationing.

Conclusion and legacy

This chapter has discussed how Deslys's use of ostrich feathers on stage during the First World War deliberately coincided with the social and economic rationale for the resurgence of the plumes in French costume and fashion following the 1914 crash of the global ostrich feather market. Deslys's use of ostrich feathers *en masse* proved so visually arresting it was permanently adopted by the French music hall star Mistinguett (1875–1956) as her own trademark when she took over from Deslys in

Laisse les Tomber! in May 1918.[76] In addition, Gesmar, who had designed many of Deslys's costumes for the show, went on to design costumes for Mistinguett herself, after Deslys's death in 1920, ensuring the visual continuity of the aesthetic that led to the popular associations of showgirls with massed feathers that still persist around the world. Yet, this chapter's primary focus on the ostrich feather during the First World War as a complex sartorial symbol of thrift, ingenuity, and luxury consequently highlights the need for further analysis of the intersection of French revue costumes and fashion as social and economic responses to the war. Indeed, much has been written about the music of the French music halls during this era yet work on the costumes, which were an integral part of these spectacles, is often neglected.

International pressure on French fashion designers to produce collections that renounced the sober looks of 1914–15, combined with the unrestricted availability of cheap ostrich plumes in France during the war, influenced the trimming's resurgence in vogue in 1916. Deslys's ostensible lavishness was, therefore, typical of the innovation and thrift practised by the French fashion industry, which rejected the grimness of war by trimming the mantle of austerity with ostrich feathers. Parisians in 1917 articulated their dissatisfaction with the bleak realities of the war through strikes, mutinies, sophisticated indifference, and by mocking the Germans sartorially. It was in this environment that Deslys used her magnificent ostrich-feathered costumes to articulate her economic and moral support of France by evoking the visual landscape of the Belle Époque that Parisians yearned for. The ostrich plumes of *Laisse les Tomber!* celebrated French ingenuity, aesthetics, and extravagance, and sent the clear sartorial signal that France and her Allies would not bow to Germany.

Notes

1 Holmes and Tarr provide a broader discussion of the term Belle Époque in Diana Holmes and Carrie Tarr, *A Belle Époque? Women and Feminism in French Society and Culture 1890–1917* (Oxford: Berghahn Books, 2007), 1–2.

2 Sarah Abrevaya Stein, *Plumes: Ostrich Feathers, Jews, and a Lost World of Global Commerce* (New Haven, CT: Yale University Press, 2008), 21.

3 Marlis Schweitzer, *When Broadway was the Runway: Theatre, Fashion, and American Culture* (Philadelphia, PA: University of Pennsylvania Press, 2009), 132.

4 Ibid., 7, 8.

5 Abrevaya Stein, *Plumes*, 78.

6 The passage of anti-plumage legislation designed to protect rare birds around 1913 in the UK and US also contributed to the decline of the global ostrich feather market in 1914 as women became more aware of environmental issues and their demand for ornamental plumes decreased. Ibid., 24.

7 Ibid.

8 E. G. Kendrew, "In Paris," *Variety* 49, no. 6, January 4, 1918, 3.

9 "Casino Paris, reopens," *Variety* 49, no. 3, December 14, 1917, 59.

10 The term "nude" is used in revue parlance to indicate that the showgirl is topless. The nude showgirl generally wears tights, dancing shoes, a G-string, jewelry, body makeup, a headdress, and/or wig of some kind.

11 Nationalism had been, "well established in [French] commercial popular culture since the 1870s when a singer named Amiati had won fame wrapping herself in the Tricolor and singing 'La Marseillaise' in Paris music halls." Charles Rearick, *The French in Love and War: Popular Culture in the Era of the World Wars* (New Haven, CT: Yale University Press, 1997), 5.

12 Quoted in James Gardiner, *Gaby Deslys: A Fatal Attraction* (London: Sidgwick and Jackson, 1986), 152.

13 Helen (Pearl) Adam, *Paris Sees It Through: A Diary, 1914–1919* (London: Hodder and Stoughton, 1919), 107–32, provides a discussion of rationing in Paris and its social effects during the First World War. The French government could, "do little to keep down inflation, which soared over 400 percent between 1914 and 1919. Even if they had money, French families faced shortages in almost every category of consumable," Matthew F. Jordan, *Le Jazz: Jazz and French Cultural Identity* (Champaign, IL: University of Illinois, 2010), 47.

14 Helen (Pearl) Adam, *Paris Sees It Through*, 79.

15 Rod Kedward, *La Vie en blue: France and the French since 1900*, New Penguin History of France, 3 (London: Penguin Books, 2005), 150.

16 *Poilu* was the colloquial term for the French First World War infantryman. Although *poilus* were drawn from all strata of French society, the French media portrayed them as tough, scruffy, middle-aged smokers with facial hair. For example, the cover of the daily publication, *Excelsior*, 1706, July 12, 1915, featured the headline, "Le Poilu permissionnaire" ("The Soldier on Leave"), accompanied by a picture of a typically scruffy *poilu* walking next to a smartly dressed woman who is carrying a young child.

17 Kedward, *La Vie en blue*, 152.

18 Charles Rearick discusses the stereotype of the cheerful, singing *poilu* in *Paris Dreams, Paris Memories: The City and Its Mystique* (Palo Alto, CA: Stanford University Press, 2011), 5.

19 Daniel Albright, *Untwisting the Serpent: Modernism in Music, Literature, and Other Arts* (Chicago: University of Chicago Press, 2000), 197.

20 Albright, 189.

21 Helen Pearl Adam, *International Cartoons of the War* (New York: E.P. Dutton and Co., 1916), vi.

22 Lou Taylor, *The Study of Dress History* (Manchester: Manchester University Press, 2002), 141.

23 Gretchen was a common name for girls in Germany up to the 1950s and became a popular French slang term for a German woman. Benedikt Eppenberger, "*Eine Armee Gretchen*: Nazisploitation Made in Switzerland," in *Nazisploitation! The Nazi Image in Low-Brow Cinema and Culture*, Daniel H. Magilow, Elizabeth Bridges, and Kristen T. Vanderlugt, eds. (New York: Continuum International Publishing Group, 2012), 172.

24 Dave Russell, *Popular Music in England 1840–1914: A Social History* (Manchester: Manchester University Press, 1997), 73–104. The café concert was a form of popular entertainment during the Belle Époque. Cafés concerts were allowed to present one-act plays, operettas, and revues with a single set fixed to the floor. Many stage shows later evolved into, "rambling spectacles arranged in sumptuous tableaux, since the number of scenes (as opposed to the number of acts) was unrestricted." Stephen Moore Whiting, *Satie the Bohemian: From Cabaret to Concert Hall* (Clarendon: Oxford University Press, 1999), 22. It is possible that *Parade*'s single act may have been referencing the café concert format.

25 Steven Moore Whiting, *Satie the Bohemian: From Cabaret to Concert Hall* (Clarendon: Oxford University Press, 1999), 9.

26 Charles Castle, *The Folies Bergère* (New York: Franklin Watts, 1985), 27.

27 Matthew F. Jordan, *Le Jazz: Jazz and French Cultural Identity* (Champaign: University of Illinois Press, 2010), 19.

28 Rearick, *The French in Love and War*, 5.

29 Helen (Pearl) Adam, *Paris Sees It Through*, 39.

30 "The suspension of the subway and other means of urban transportation at the early hour of 10 p.m. . . . [in Paris] has played havoc with [attendances at] the amusement resorts," "In Paris," *Variety* 46, 9, April 27, 1917, 4.

31 Rearick, *Paris Dreams, Paris Memories*, 45.

32 Paul Duval, *The Folies Bergère*, Lucienne Hill, trans. (London: Methuen & Co. Ltd., 1955), 12.

33 Regina M. Sweeney, *Singing Our Way to Victory: French Cultural Politics and Music During the Great War* (Connecticut: Wesleyan University Press, 2001), 255.

34 While Rearick has argued that the true nostalgia for Belle Époque Paris and its glamorous nightclubs, restaurants, and music halls did not occur until the 1930s, his 1997 analysis of Parisian music hall and popular song does reveal that there was a strain of nostalgia operating in French society during the First World War for a prewar time that many remembered as "simpler." Rearick, *Paris Dreams, Paris Memories*, 3.

35 Valerie Steele, *The Berg Companion to Fashion* (Oxford: Berg, 2010), 420.

36 Gardiner, *Gaby Deslys*.

37 Steele, *The Berg Companion to Fashion*, 420.

38 "Nouvelles de la Mode," *Les Élégances parisiennes*, 1, April 7, 1917.

39 Taylor, *The Study of Dress History*, 136.

40 It is also possible that Benda and Barbier were deliberately evoking the mood of Lautrec's poster *La Troupe de Mademoiselle Eglantine*. Lautrec's poster, with its frothy, bubbly whites and yellows was, in turn, inspired by the artist Pierre Bonnard's (1867–1947) poster, *France-Champagne* (1891).

41 E. Lefèvre, *Le Commerce et l'industrie de la plume pour parure* (Paris: Chez l'Auteur, 1914), 254.

42 "Le Réveil de la mode Parisienne," *Les Élégances parisiennes*, 11, February 1917, 165.

43 Helen (Pearl) Adam, *Paris Sees It Through*, 127.

44 "La Mode et les modes," *Les Modes de Paris*, 170, February 1917, 12.

45 "As to ostrich feathers," *New York Times*, October 21, 1917.

46 "The modern note [on the tea frock] is represented by a triple row of curled ostrich feathers at the hem . . . White ostrich feathers are very plentiful just now, and if they are dyed to match the costumes successfully this decoration is sure of a prosperous career. . . . Ostrich feathers are to be in favour again in millinery, as they are in dress. I think that there is not a more becoming hat decoration," "Fashion notes by a Paris expert," *The West Australian*, May 8, 1917.

47 Ibid.

48 "Paris fashions," *New Zealand Herald* 54, 169, October 13, 1917, 4.

49 Abrevaya Stein, *Plumes*, 24.

50 Lefèvre, *Le Commerce et l'industrie*, 339.

51 Ibid., 79.

52 "Fewer South African ostriches," *New York Times*, April 22, 1917.

53 "Charivaria," *Punch, or the London Charivari* 153, November 28, 1917.

54 R. Pommereuil, *La Guerre Économique, 1914–1917: Legislation et réglementation douanières* (Paris: Poitiers Librairie administrative, 1917), 364.

55 Lefèvre, *Le Commerce et l'industrie*, 315, 316.

56 Ibid., 255.

57 Gardiner, *Gaby Deslys*, 54–5.

58 Deslys also had the gowns for all of her productions made in Paris during the war, including *The Rajah's Ruby* (1914) at the Palace in London and *Stop! Look! Listen!* (1915) at the Globe Theatre in New York.

59 *Suzette* ran for 256 shows, Gardiner, *Gaby Deslys*, 147.

60 "Gaby in flags: London, April 2," *Variety* 46, 9, April 4, 1917, 27.

61 "Mr. Punch's National Service for all," *Punch, or the London Charivari* 152, June 20, 1917, 27.

62 There was a "drought of acts in Paris" in 1917 and big stars were unable to demand their usual high salaries and consequently could expect engagements lasting only four to six weeks in Paris. "In Paris," *Variety* 46, 9, April 4, 1917, 27.

63 Gardiner, *Gaby Deslys*, 146.

64 Gaby Deslys, "A lesson in thrift by the witty French artiste who explains the folly of giving away anything you may need and the wisdom of holding on to everything you have," *Los Angeles Examiner*, April 6, 1913.

65 Lee Shubert (1871–1953) and Jacob J. Shubert (1879–1963) were two of New York's most influential theater owners, producers and directors in the early twentieth century.

66 This amounted to the equivalent of more than $100,000 per week in 2015.

67 Gardiner, *Gaby Deslys*, 53.

68 Many actresses in the late nineteenth and early twentieth centuries spent thousands of dollars each year on clothing and jewelry, and publicized that knowledge, to cement their positions within the profession, impress their fans and, "to prevent undesirable performers from gaining access to the stage," Schweitzer, *When Broadway was the Runway*, 100.

69 "Stage Clothes," *The Theatre* 20, 199, December 1914, 296.

70 Foulsham & Banfield, *Gaby Deslys (Marie-Elise Gabrielle Caire)*, published by Rotary Photographic Co. Ltd., bromide postcard print, early 1910s, NPG Ax160398, © National Portrait Gallery, London, at: http://www.npg.org.uk/collections/search/portrait-list.php?search=sp&sText=Ax160398&firstRun=true (accessed May 17, 2019).

71 "Passed by the Censor," *Harper's Bazaar*, July 1917.

72 *Gaby Deslys (1881–1920), chanteuse et meneuse de revues française, dans la revue "Laissez-les tomber"*, Casino de Paris, 1917. © Albert Harlingue / Roger-Viollet, at: http://www.parisenimages.fr/fr/galerie-collections/1239-15-gaby-deslys-1881-1920-chanteuse-meneuse-revues-francaise-revue-laissez-tomber-casino-paris-1917 (accessed March 5, 2015).

73 Lefèvre, *Le Commerce et L'Industrie*, 316.

74 The title of Cappiello's cartoon echoes Cocteau's description of Deslys as a "great ventriloquist's doll."

75 A cartoon published in April 1917 by the Irish artist Norman Morrow (1879–1917), "Gaby still wears those hats" in the London publication, *The Bystander*, includes a sketch of Pilcer performing "The Cold Water Rag." The cartoon also shows Deslys in various feathered headdresses, including one that resembles the headdress in Cappiello's cartoon. According to the official programme, Pilcer also performed "The Cold Water Rag" in *Laisse les Tomber!*

76 Mistinguett wore a large ostrich feathered headdress designed by the fashion and costume designer Romain de Tirtoff (1892–1990), better known as Erté, in the Orientalist fantasy *Gobette of Paris* (1917) that played at the Théâtre Fémina in Paris around the same time as *Laisse les Tomber!* Mistinguett's trademarks at that time, however, were her long legs and experience as an established Parisian performer, not expansive, ostrich-plumed headdresses.

References

Abrevaya Stein, Sarah. *Plumes: Ostrich Feathers, Jews, and a Lost World of Global Commerce.* New Haven, CT: Yale University Press, 2008.
Adam, Helen (Pearl). *International Cartoons of the War.* New York: E.P. Dutton and Co., 1916.
Adam, Helen (Pearl). *Paris Sees It Through: A Diary, 1914–1919.* London: Hodder and Stoughton, 1919.
Albright, Daniel. Untwisting the Serpent: Modernism in Music, Literature, and Other Arts, Chicago: University of Chicago Press, 2000.
"As to ostrich feathers." *New York Times*, October 21, 1917.
"Casino Paris, reopens." *Variety* 49, 3, December 14, 1917.
Castle, Charles. *The Folies Bergère.* New York: Franklin Watts, 1985.
"Charivaria." *Punch, or the London Charivari* 153, November 28, 1917.
Deslys, Gaby. "A lesson in thrift by the witty French artiste who explains the folly of giving away anything you may need and the wisdom of holding on to everything you have." *Los Angeles Examiner*, April 6, 1913.
Duval, Paul. *The Folies Bergère.* Lucienne Hill, trans. London: Methuen, 1955.
Eppenberger, Benedikt. "Eine Armee Gretchen: Nazisploitation Made in Switzerland." In *Nazisploitation! The Nazi Image in Low-Brow Cinema and Culture.* Daniel H. Magilow, Elizabeth Bridges, and Kirsten T. Vanderlugt, eds., 155–74. New York: Continuum International Publishing Group, 2012.
"Fashion notes by a Paris expert." *The West Australian*, May 8, 1917.
"Fewer South African ostriches." *New York Times*, April 22, 1917.
"Gaby in flags: London, April 2." *Variety* 46, 9, April 27, 1917.
Gardiner, James. *Gaby Deslys: A Fatal Attraction.* London: Sidgwick and Jackson, 1986.
Holmes, Diana and Carrie Tarr. *A Belle Epoque? Women and Feminism in French Society and Culture 1890–1917.* Oxford: Berghahn Books, 2007.
"In Paris." *Variety* 46, 9, 27 April, 1917.
Jordan, Matthew F. *Le Jazz: Jazz and French Cultural Identity.* Champaign, IL: University of Illinois, 2010.
Kedward, Rod. *La Vie en bleu: France and the French since 1900.* New Penguin History of France 3. London: Penguin Books, 2005.
Kendrew, E. G. "In Paris." *Variety* 49, 6, January 4, 1918.
"La Mode et les modes." *Les Modes de Paris*, 170, February, 1917.
"Le Poilu permissionnaire." *Excelsior*, 1706, July 12, 1915.

"Le Réveil de la mode parisienne." *Les Élégances parisiennes*, 11, February 1917.

Lefèvre, E. *Le Commerce et l'industrie de la plume pour Parure.* Paris: Chez l'Auteur, 1914.

Moore Whiting, Stephen. *Satie the Bohemian: From Cabaret to Concert Hall*. Clarendon: Oxford University Press, 1999.

Morrow, N. "Gaby still wears those hats." *The Bystander*, April, 1917.

"Mr. Punch's National Service for all." *Punch, or the London Charivari* 152, June 27, 1917.

"Nouvelles de la mode." *Les Élégances parisiennes*, 1, April 7, 1917.

"Paris fashions." *New Zealand Herald* 54, 169, October 13, 1917.

"Passed by the Censor." *Harper's Bazaar*, July, 1917.

Pommereuil, R. *La Guerre Économique, 1914–1917: Legislation et réglementation douanières.* Paris: Poitiers Librairie administrative, 1917.

Rearick, Charles. *The French in Love and War: Popular Culture in the Era of the World Wars.* New Haven, CT: Yale University Press, 1997.

Rearick, Charles. *Paris Dreams, Paris Memories: The City and Its Mystique,* Palo Alto, CA: Stanford University Press, 2011.

Russell, Dave. *Popular Music in England 1840–1914: A Social History*. Manchester: Manchester University Press, 1997.

Schweitzer, Marlis. *When Broadway was the Runway: Theatre, Fashion, and American Culture.* Philadelphia, PA: University of Pennsylvania Press, 2009.

"Stage clothes." *The Theatre* 20, 199, December 1914.

Steele, Valerie. *The Berg Companion to Fashion*. Oxford: Berg, 2010.

Taylor, Lou. *The Study of Dress History*. Manchester: Manchester University Press, 2002.

7

Between fashion and folk

Dress practices in Alsace during the First World War

Sara Hume

On November 22, 1918, the triumphant French forces entered Alsace following the German defeat. The victorious troops parading through the streets of Strasbourg were met with expressions of delirious joy from Alsatians. The festivities were documented in motion pictures, still photographs, postcards, posters, and countless illustrations (Figure 7.1). The girls, wearing enormous black bows, greeting the entering soldiers came to be the defining image of the day. The traditional costume of Alsace served as a symbol of the region, and in this enactment of Alsace's return to French control, the Alsatians received the French as their liberators.

The link in the popular imagination between the Alsatian traditional costume and loyalty to France deserves further consideration. Had the Germans prevailed after the First World War, would young Alsatian girls in traditional dress have flocked to meet the victorious German soldiers? In some ways, an embrace of Alsatian traditional dress might seem to be more consistent with German concepts of the nation than with the centralized vision of the nation embraced by France. However, a closer examination of dress practices in Alsace during the war reveals surprising differences between French and German strategies for securing loyalty and gaining military advantage: France focused on the symbolic power of the iconic image of women in traditional headbows; while Germany, which maintained political control of the region, deployed the clothing industry for its own war effort. The ways that Alsatians selected, produced, and wore their clothing represented a careful negotiation of the meanings imposed by the French and Germans.

To provide a little background about Alsace and its distinctive dress, it is important to understand Alsace's geographical situation right on the border between France and Germany. Its location put

Figure 7.1 *Henri Bacher, 22 Novembre 1918: L'Entrée glorieuse des troupes Françaises à Strasbourg, 1919.* Bibliothèque nationale et universitaire, Strasbourg, NIM23827.

Alsace in the center of the conflict between the two warring nations during the First World War. The region had long been disputed between the neighboring national powers. Between the seventeenth and the late nineteenth century, Alsace had been part of France. However, at the conclusion of the Franco-Prussian War in 1871, the newly unified German empire claimed Alsace as well as a portion of neighboring Lorraine. The loss of Alsace and Lorraine was a humiliating blow to France and was one of the grievances that fueled French hostility against Germany leading up to the First World War.

For Alsatians, the successive periods of rule by different national forces were deeply disruptive. The changes in political control of Alsace had created divided allegiances among the population. A significant number of Alsatians chose to retain French citizenship following German annexation in 1871 and hundreds of thousands moved to France.[1] This wave of emigration was primarily upper class: wealthy Alsatians who left a vacuum that was filled with a reciprocal wave of German immigrants into the region. By the time war broke out in 1914, an entire generation of Alsatians had grown up German. Young Alsatian men fought for Germany in the war. Despite the loyal service of Alsatians in wartime, soldiers from other parts of the German empire who were posted in Alsace during the war were highly suspicious of the allegiance of Alsatian civilians. Although the Alsatian dialect was a variation of German similar to that spoken elsewhere in southwestern Germany and in Switzerland, a significant proportion of the region's residents were bilingual. French was frequently the language of communication for the wealthier and better educated. Linguistic choices were often interpreted as indicators of political allegiance and were strongly restricted by occupying German forces during the war. At this time, by contrast, the French were less concerned with the German aspects of Alsatian culture because their contact with the region's residents was limited.

The traditional dress that developed during the course of the nineteenth century became another aspect of Alsatian culture that served as a marker of allegiance. Distinctive dress styles emerged as an expression of Alsace's dual culture at the border between the two nations. In contrast to the religious homogeneity of France, Alsace's demographics reflect a similar diversity of religious beliefs as in Germany.[2] The tensions between Catholics and Protestants found display in traditional dress that differentiated between the two confessions. The quintessential folk costume was actually the style of dress worn in the region around Strasbourg. Although different parts of Alsace had costumes that were quite different, this particular style came to represent Alsace in the popular imagination. The costume included a skirt of heavy wool and a small bodice or corselet with stomacher over a white blouse with a wide collar. The most prominent feature of the costume was the small cap adorned with an enormous bow. Young Catholic girls wore brightly colored bows, while young Protestant girls wore black bows. The original link between religious affiliation and these costumes depended on their being worn for pious occasions including weddings, first communions, and festivals such as Fête-Dieu. By the early twentieth century, the political tensions in the region became paramount, and the primary occasions for wearing folk dress shifted from religious festivities to political rallies.

Alsatians had worn traditional dress to political rallies well before the First World War. In fact, when Kaiser Wilhelm II (reign from 1888–1918) visited Strasbourg in 1877, he was greeted with a parade which included women dressed in their native *Tracht*.[3] The women were seated in a wagon decorated with garlands that was pulled by a team of draft horses. Illustrations of the procession closely resemble an earlier illustration of a wedding cortege in which the groom escorts his bride and her maids of honor on their way to the church.[4] Following the end of the First World War, women in rural Alsace filled very similar wagons festooned with garlands as they celebrated Liberation and the French victory.[5] This precedent might support the idea that traditional dress was a flexible symbol that simply stood for the region and could be deployed for whichever nation happened to be in power. However, by 1918, the French had largely appropriated the political symbolism of the Alsatian folk costume to serve their own agenda. While the rural parades after 1918 continued to maintain the traditional use of costume, urban parades, particularly in Strasbourg, had changed in response to French propaganda. The way Alsatians wore the costume and the form of the costumes themselves reflected the image of Alsatians in French posters and popular culture.

By the 1910s, traditional dress continued to be worn only in small pockets of rural Alsace, while most Alsatians wore fashionable clothing largely indistinguishable from their French or German neighbors. Once the war broke out, the Germans recognized the powerful hold that the French fashion industry had. The industry was an important sector of the economy, but just as importantly, it fostered a positive image of French culture. Even though Germany produced a substantial segment of the ready-to-wear clothing not only purchased in Germany but also exported abroad including to France, Germans had a reputation for lacking taste and style.[6] In Alsace, French influence over the fashion industry was especially widespread. Advertisements for clothing stores were written in French, even when they appeared in newspapers in which all of the editorial copy was written in German. Similarly, Alsatian fashion magazines such as *Album de Linge illustré* (Illustrated Album of Clothing) were given French titles even when the text was entirely in German. Shop owners assured their customers they were purchasing the latest Parisian models, even if the garments were actually made in Germany.[7]

Such examples of French domination of the fashion industry were the impetus behind the movement that emerged in Germany to promote an independent German fashion industry. The movement followed and drew inspiration from the better known efforts of the Deutscher Werkbund which promoted German industrial design more broadly. In a pamphlet that outlined the motivation and aims for the movement, Norbert Stern encouraged the German people to rise up against the "French fashion tyranny."[8] Alsatians joined this movement starting in early 1915, when those involved in the clothing and textile industries began organizing a working committee to promote their interests in the Chamber of Commerce in Strasbourg. The participants included men and women in the textile, lacemaking, tailoring and dressmaking trades as well as representatives of women's groups and trade organizations.[9] The chair of the committee, August Herborth, reported to the umbrella organization in Frankfurt, the Modebund.[10] The coordinated efforts of the fashion industry to both support their economic interests and also improve the quality of design produced across Germany reflected an increasing national cohesion. While the fashion industry in Paris benefited from its centralization and complete lack of competition from other French cities, Germany had several fashion centers including Berlin, Frankfurt, and Munich. During the early years of the war, the enmity with France drove Germans, including Alsatians, to pursue their common interest across the disparate German states. Traditional dress practices, which emphasized the distinctions among the German states, were completely disregarded in favor of a fashionable idea of national dress.

The push in Alsace to eliminate French influence on fashion fitted in with a larger crackdown on the use of French language in the widely bilingual region. Department stores in Strasbourg at the turn of the century bore names such as the Louvre and Bon Marché, which were obviously unacceptable under the wartime regime. A sampling of letterhead from the Louvre during the course of the war shows the progressive Germanification.[11] An example of the prewar letterhead from 1911 clearly shows that the operation was run in German as a GMBH (a limited liability company) with German signage despite its quintessentially French name. The letterhead for the same store in 1916 shows the renaming that occurred once the war started. The Kaufhaus Louvre became Kaufhaus Hoher Steg, a name derived from the business' street address. Along with the name change these letterheads show a shifting aesthetic, as the font became the Gothic style of German.

The efforts to eliminate the French elements of Alsatian culture served to increase tensions between German authorities and native Alsatians. While the renaming of stores and magazines was relatively innocuous, the enforcement of restrictions in the use of French led to detentions and denunciations that contributed to Alsatian resentment against German rule. As early as October 1914, the Alsatian artist Charles Spindler wrote in his journal:

> Par suite de toutes les mesures vexatoires qu'on leur impose, . . . les Alsaciens n'ont qu'un désir, c'est de voir les Allemands battus et humiliés. Ces derniers ont réussi, grâce à leur dictature, à annihiler ce que quarante-quatre ans d'administration civile avaient fait pour le rapprochement, et c'est en neuf semaines qu'on a obtenu ce magnifique résultat![12]

The suppression of the French language was indicative of the intolerance of Germans for Alsatian culture. The war led to an environment in which the tensions between the Germans and Alsatians escalated into open conflict.

A second major department store slated to open in Strasbourg in 1914 was originally known alternately as the Kaufhaus Modern or the Magasins Modernes. Unlike the older Kaufhaus Louvre, which had grown incrementally as several neighboring storefronts were subsumed into a larger single store, the Kaufhaus Modern was designed from scratch as a single coherent building. An advertisement from 1913 and the elevation from the building's architectural rendering show the modern appeal of this new edifice.[13] However, the outbreak of war prevented the store's grand opening, and instead the building was used as a warehouse for grain during the war years. The transformation of this department store, which symbolized modernity in urban design, into a storehouse for war materials is a fitting encapsulation of the tragic perversion of the First World War, wherein innovations of modern life were twisted into tools of destruction.

While the war effort took men away from jobs in rural Alsace, it provided opportunities for women in Strasbourg. By late September 1914, the Chamber of Commerce in Strasbourg established a municipal sewing studio, which employed women and girls to sew clothing and goods for the front.[14] The operation had the dual purpose of producing needed supplies for the military and providing employment for women whose husbands were on the front. The workshop was set up in a large hall that was outfitted with an array of electrical machines including sewing machines, irons, buttonhole machines and cutting machines. The workers made an array of products including bread bags, handkerchiefs, towels, neckties, helmet covers, tents, puttees, shirts, pants, and jackets. The wartime pressures led the municipal government to become involved in the industrial production of clothing, much to the protests of private enterprise who viewed this as competition. The government workshop took advantage of technological and organizational advancements to implement the sorts of high-volume production that were still not widespread in the region.

Despite the organization of these sewing workshops, the Germans suffered from a persistent lack of material goods. Much of the hardship that Alsatians faced under German rule during the war years was due to shortages. The German government in Alsace imposed rationing on civilian clothing which was overseen by an agency established to control clothing, the *Reichsbekleidungsstelle*. The agency demanded suppliers take careful inventories of their stocks and placed limits on purchasing and pricing of clothing for civilians.[15] By 1918, shortages had become so severe that the government could not find supplies to clothe workers in industries critical to the war effort. A call went out for civilians to donate their used clothing to meet the needs.[16] The German government also published posters that urged German citizens to donate their old clothing, uniforms and shoes. While the discourse at the beginning of the war focused on promoting the German fashion industry as a means of combating the admiration for French fashion, ultimately the reality of war made producing adequate supplies of clothing a matter of critical importance.

German interests in Alsace focused on clothing as a segment of the economy and as a good that was essential to the war effort. Germans concentrated on the political symbolism of fashionable dress to demonstrate their modernity and independence from French influence. Paradoxically, the French took a very different tack regarding clothing in Alsace by focusing on traditional dress. The use of the Alsatian woman or *Alsacienne* as an allegorical representation of the region put a face on the complicated political motivations for French participation in the First World War. Rather than abstract concepts such as self-determination and balance of power, the French were fighting to free the *Alsacienne* from her German captors and return her to the nation she loved.

One of the defining works which first established the model for French depictions of Alsatian women was the painter Jean-Jacques Henner's (1829–1905) 1871 piece *L'Alsace. Elle Attend*.[17] This painting shows a woman dressed all in black with a black headbow which has a small cockade affixed to it. The figure in mourning symbolizes the grief that Alsace felt at the break with France and the vigil she would keep until being returned to France. Henner was a native of Alsace, but he studied art in Paris, where he stayed after 1871, when he opted to remain French. Although the Alsatian woman in the painting wears the traditional *coiffe* and a black shawl, the dress she wears is actually closely in line with fashionable dress of the period. This painting established the headdress as the defining element that was sufficient to communicate Alsatianness. The addition of the cockade on the headbow became a typical element in the pro-French imagery. Although it had no part in Alsatian traditional dress, the cockade would later be adopted by Alsatian women when they wore the costume in political rallies.

Another Alsatian artist whose work helped shape the French understanding of both Alsace's traditional dress and its loyalty to France was Jean-Jacques Waltz (1873–1951), better known by his

Alsatian nickname "Hansi." Hansi was deeply anti-German and his work focused both on celebrating Alsace and on caricaturing Germans. In contrast to his treatment of Germans whom he depicted as unattractive, unfashionable, and humorless, he idealized the Alsatians who were portrayed as simple and pure (Figure 7.2). His work became popular in France following the publication of his satirical piece, *Professeur Knatschké* (1912), which also resulted in his arrest and imprisonment by German authorities. Much of Hansi's work was aimed at children, and he featured children wearing traditional dress as the central characters in his books. This extremely youthful *Alsacienne* emphasized the innocence and sweetness of Alsace.

While Alsatian artists such as Henner and Hansi were important in first incorporating traditional dress into images conveying political meaning, French artists continued to make use of the costume for their propaganda, often with far less regard for the resemblance to traditional dress practices. Countless postcards were produced immediately before and during the war and they depicted women dressed in Alsatian traditional dress.[18] It is clear that these photographs were of models dressed according to a French understanding of Alsatian traditional dress. The bow, which was the identifying feature of the costume, took on a variety of shapes that differed significantly from the Alsatian

Figure 7.2 *Hansi*, Pages d'Album, *c. 1915, Gravure no. 53/150. Musée Hansi, Colmar.*

originals. Many of these bows actually looked more like fashionable hats of the period than like Alsatian *coiffes*. The entire costumes in these images also took on a generically dirndl-like aspect rather than the style characteristic of Alsace. The very slim lines of some of these images strongly suggest that the models were wearing corsets. The resulting images corresponded more closely to fashionable ideals of the female form than the actual rural styles, which largely obscured the waist. In reshaping traditional styles into a sort of folk costume, the artists erased many of the aspects that made rural costumes appear foreign and rustic. The resulting styles were instead appealing and quaint.

By the 1910s, motion pictures provided another vehicle to carry propagandistic messages. In 1916, the French actress Réjane (Gabrielle Charlotte Réju, 1856–1920) pushed for the production of the film, *Alsace,* based on a play by the same name.[19] The plot centers on an Alsatian family loyal to France whose son marries the daughter of a German family who has immigrated to the region. The ultimate tragic death of the son occurs as a result of his loyalty to France. The mother, played by Réjane, is the incarnation of Alsace. She wears a theatrical costume intended to represent traditional dress, including the headbow. The costume in this instance, like those in other propaganda images, serves to connect the character to the region although the actress was Parisian and not Alsatian. Réjane's character has a climactic scene in which she sings a stirring rendition of *La Marseillaise.* This musical scene that appears in the movie poster closely echoes a common trope in propaganda posters that shows Alsatian women draped in the French flag (Figure 7.3).[20] The singing of the French national anthem was a particularly poignant act for Alsatians because the song had been composed in Strasbourg and attested to the important place Alsace held in French history.

The circulation of the postcards, movies and posters introduced the people of France to Alsace although most would not have had any direct contact with Alsatians. They would not have heard the Alsatian dialect, which was a form of German. The depictions did not emphasize the Alsatian cuisine with its sausage and sauerkraut or the architecture with the half-timbered houses so similar to German homes. Even more significantly the propaganda completely ignored the thousands of Alsatian men who wore the German uniform and fought for the Kaiser. The use of traditional dress as a symbolic representation of the region depended almost exclusively on the image of women. The resulting vision of Alsatianness was distinct enough to be recognizable but restricted to a framework that was palatable to the French public.

In her book on women in Alsace, Elizabeth Vlossak points out that the uses of the allegorical image played upon ideas of women's vulnerability and victimhood.[21] French propaganda from the First World War epitomized this characterization of Alsace as in need of protection and saving. The images generally diverged between those in which she is a beautiful woman and those in which she is an innocent young girl. The first type was very common in postcards and played upon a theme of romantic love. The military battle to reunite Alsace with France was reframed as a love story and many of these depictions established the allegory by showing Alsace as a young woman and France as a

Figure 7.3 *Leven and Lemonier,* Alsace interprété par Mme Réjane, *1916. Bibliothèque nationale et universitaire, Strasbourg, NIM18426.*

soldier. The postcards themselves were widely used as a means of communication between soldiers and their loved ones at home, thus serving as tangible tokens of love. The reimagining of the entire war itself as a romantic struggle for the heart of Alsace was a fitting theme for these postcards.

Depictions of the *Alsacienne* as a young girl generally began with the artwork of Hansi, but continued throughout the First World War and after. The focus on women and children in these allegorical scenes allowed evocations of Alsace in ways that rendered it safe. For France the danger of a strong regional identity for Alsace was the development of a separatist movement. At the end of the First World War, there actually was a strong risk of Alsatians fighting for independence rather than reunion with France. The cultivation of a distinctive Alsatian character thus had to be carefully balanced to ensure that it remained subordinate to the French nation.

Rather than a powerful symbol of independence, the *Alsacienne* was powerless and dependent. Both the portrayals of *Alsaciennes* as women and as young girls objectified them. In the case of the romantic heroines, they became a prize to be claimed by the French soldier. As for young girls, they were turned into dolls and given to French children. Such dolls dressed in regional dress date back to at least the mid-nineteenth century and became popular as souvenirs for tourists and collectible items for children. The dolls themselves even became the subject of propaganda posters such as one published by the Union Amicale d'Alsace Lorraine (Friendly Union of Alsace Lorraine) that encouraged French women to provide poor children with dolls of Alsace and Lorraine. The appeal of the youthful *Alsacienne* was clear as it bore a strong sentimental appeal and created a sympathetic image of Alsace.

Conclusion

The various tropes that were common in these propaganda images also made their way into celebrations at the end of the war. In the weeks following the armistice on November 11, 1918, the French troops moved into Alsace. Their arrival was planned in stages and carefully timed to allow the German forces to leave first. René Chambe, a captain of aviation was among the first wave of French soldiers to arrive in Alsace.[22] In describing his entry into the village of Niedernai, he recounted:

> Beaucoup de femmes ont revêtu le costume d'Alsacienne, sur leurs cheveux blonds le grand noeud noir. Pour la première fois depuis quarante-huit ans il s'étoile de la cocarde tricolore. C'est la vision de notre enfance, de notre adolescence, qui se réalise et s'anime sous nos yeux. Nous entrons tout vivants dans le rêve.[23]

While the welcome that Chambe received was spontaneous and unplanned, the festivities in Strasbourg were intentionally orchestrated to fit the French perception of Alsace that had been constructed in large part through postcards and posters. The arrival of troops into the regional capital was scheduled for November 22, 1918, allowing the city time to prepare the parade. A reception committee was formed with Auguste Braun as its secretary. Braun described the heated discussions that centered on whether young women dressed in traditional dress would be allowed to participate in the parades. Those who opposed the idea believed that it would be like a carnival; they argued that allowing girls from the city to dress up as peasants would be a "masquerade."[24] Ultimately the majority voted in favor of allowing costumes, and notices were posted throughout Strasbourg inviting young women interested in participating in costume to meet two days before the celebrations in order to receive instructions from the organizing committee. The notice, written in both French and Alsatian, further specified that the women had to be truly Alsatian and over the age of 16.[25] An estimated 800 Alsatian women showed up for the meeting, which ended with one particularly patriotic woman leading the crowd in singing "La Marseillaise."[26]

The scenes from the parade in Strasbourg were not only captured in photographs but were also filmed. The film footage shows women both parading along with the French soldiers and posing with them.[27] The costumes that these women wore revealed some modifications from the traditional costumes worn by rural villagers, particularly in the addition of the tricolor cockades. Like the French models in the postcards, these women would not have worn these costumes for any other occasion than this performance. The *mise en scène* of the victory parades was an enactment of the allegory in which Alsace receives her savior, France.

The forms of celebrations that marked the French victory were thus a direct result of a French interpretation of Alsatian culture. Such scenes would not have been enacted had Germany been victorious in part because of the different relationship established between German political power and Alsatian regional culture. Because Germany had long since consolidated political control of the region, Alsace did not evoke a powerful feeling of nostalgia and longing in the German imagination. As for the French, they were able to cultivate a favorable view of Alsatian distinctions as epitomized by the traditional dress because they did not have to deal with the frictions of accommodating Alsatians into their political system. In contrast, Germans were more concerned with the logistics of governing the region, which led to efforts to stamp out the lingering influence of French culture. Administering the border region where French culture still maintained a strong hold was made even more challenging by the difficulties that Germany was having as it suffered shortages in material and manpower as the First World War dragged on. The very effective use that the French made of Alsatian traditional dress in their propaganda did not have a parallel in German propaganda. Because Germany maintained political control of Alsace, the region did not serve as a rallying point for their soldiers and civilians. In fact, the Germans showed dangerously little regard for gaining or maintaining Alsatian loyalty. While the end of the war would have occurred as a welcome relief to the Alsatians regardless of the victor, the jubilant festivities that greeted the arrival of French troops into the region were a product both of French propaganda efforts and hardships faced under German rule during the war.

Notes

1 Elizabeth Vlossak, *Marianne or Germania? Nationalizing Women in Alsace, 1870–1946* (Oxford: Oxford University Press, 2010), 7.

2 Alfred Wahl, *Confession et comportement dans les campagnes d'Alsace et de Bade, 1871–1939: Catholiques, protestants et juifs: Démographie, dynamisme économique et social, vie de relation et attitude politique* (Strasbourg: Éditions COPRUR, 1980).

3 Bernhard Friedrich Wilhelm Rogge, *Kaiserbüchlein: 1797–1888. Zur Erinnerung an Kaiser Wilhelm den Grossen* (Bielefeld: Velhagen & Klasing, 1897), 63.

4 Illustration of "Intérieur d'une ferme du Kochersberg." Frédéric Théodore Piton, *Strasbourg illustré ou Panorama pittoresque, historique et statistique de Strasbourg et de ses environs: Promenades dans les faubourgs, déscription des environs* (Selbstverl, 1855), plate facing page 182.

5 Mairie de Geispolsheim, ed., *Geispolsheim: gare et village, une histoire*, Mémoire de vies (Strasbourg: Carré blanc, 2006), 41–3.

6 Irene Guenther, *Nazi Chic? Fashioning Women in the Third Reich* (Oxford and New York: Berg, 2004), 21–2.

7 "Die Umwandlung des Detailhandels im Reichslande, besonders in Strassburg, seit 1870 unter dem Einfluss der eingewanderten deutschen Kaufleute," *Strassburger Post*, January 7, 1894, 79 J 374, Archives départementales du Bas-Rhin.

8 Norbert Stern, *Die Weltpolitik der Weltmode* (Stuttgart and Berlin: Deutsche Verlags-Anstalt, 1915), 9.

9 "Textilgewerbe und deutsche Tracht," *Strassburger Post*, March 19, 1915, Strassburger Stadtnachrichten, 79 J 974, Archives départementales du Bas-Rhin.

10 "Protokollauszug der 1. Tagung des Modebund Frankfurt A. M.," June 20, 1915, 79 J 974, Archives départementales du Bas-Rhin.

11 "Magasin de Louvre (Kaufhaus Hoher Steg) letterhead," 1911–1916, 845 W 4 (Dossier de la police du bâtiment), Archives de Strasbourg.

12 Charles Spindler, *L'Alsace pendant la guerre* (Strasbourg: Treuttel & Würtz, 1925), 86–7.

13 Kaufhaus Modern advertisement, 5 MW 283 Archives de Strasbourg.

14 Dr. Emerich, "Der Städtische Nähbetrieb als Einrichtung der Kriegsfürsorge. Anlage zu dem Protokolle über die Sitzung des Gemenderats vom 4. Dezember 1914," December 4, 1914, 79 J 973, Archives départementales du Bas-Rhin.

15 "Bekanntmachung über Bezugsscheine—Bekanntmachung über die Regelung des Verkehrs mit Web-, Wirk- und Strickwaren für die bürgerliche Bevölkerung," June 10, 1916, 79 J 958, Archives départementales du Bas-Rhin.

16 "Sammlung von getragener Männerkleidung im ganzen Reiche," *Frankfurter Zeitung*, April 12, 1918, 79 J 959, Archives départementales du Bas-Rhin.

17 Jean-Jacques Henner, *L'Alsace. Elle Attend*, 1871, Oil on canvas, 60 cm x 30 cm, Paris, Musée Jean-Jacques Henner.

18 Among the sites online which post images of postcard collections are Tracy McFarlan, "Our Alsace-Lorraine Picture Postcard Collection," *Veritas Liberabit: Special Collections Student Blog* (blog), June 10, 2013, France, at (both sites accessed June 28, 2020): http://sites.lafayette.edu/specialcollections/2013/06/10/our-alsace-lorraine-picture-postcard-collection/ and "Cartes patriotiques guerre 14/18: Militaires," Forum et galerie de cartes postales anciennes de France, at: http://www.cparama.com/forum/cartes-patriotiques-guerre-14-18-t2799-20.html.

19 Odile Gozillon-Fronsacq, *Cinéma et Alsace: Stratégies Cinématographiques, 1896–1939* (Paris: Association française de recherche sur l'histoire du cinéma, 2003), 126–7.

20 Leven and Lemonier, *Alsace interprété par Mme Réjane*, 1916, colored lithograph, 1916, at: http://gallica.bnf.fr/ark:/12148/btv1b10209526q (accessed June 28, 2020).

21 Vlossak, *Marianne or Germania*, 190–3.

22 Captain Chambe's account is published in Jacques Granier, *Novembre 18 en Alsace, album du cinquantenaire* (Strasbourg: Éditions des "Dernières nouvelles de Strasbourg," 1969), 45–54.

23 Granier, *Novembre 18*, 51.

24 Ibid., 113.

25 *Avis important* (Imprimerie Alsacienne formerly G. Fischbach, Strasbourg, 1918), 502 Fi 56 Archives de Strasbourg.

26 Granier, *Novembre 18*, 114.

27 Office national de la radiodiffusion télévision française Strasbourg, "Déjà Une Caméra :11 Novembre 1918 à Strasbourg," Ina.fr, November 12, 1966, at: http://www.ina.fr/video/SXF02029218 (accessed June 26, 2020).

References

Avis important. Imprimerie Alsacienne formerly G. Fischbach, Strasbourg, 1918. 502 Fi 56, Archives de Strasbourg.

"Bekanntmachung über Bezugsscheine—Bekanntmachung über die Regelung des Verkehrs mit Web-, Wirk- und Strickwaren für die bürgerliche Bevölkerung." June 10, 1916. 79 J 958. Archives départementales du Bas-Rhin.

"Cartes patriotiques guerre 14/18: Militaires." Forum et galerie de cartes postales anciennes de France. Available at: http://www.cparama.com/forum/cartes-patriotiques-guerre-14-18-t2799-20.html (accessed February 8, 2015).

"Die Umwandlung des Detailhandels im Reichslande, besonders in Strassburg, seit 1870 unter dem Einfluss der eingewanderten deutschen Kaufleute." *Strassburger Post*, January 7, 1894. 79 J 374. Archives départementales du Bas-Rhin.

Emerich, Dr. "Der Städtische Nähbetrieb als Einrichtung der Kriegsfürsorge. Anlage zu dem Protokolle über die Sitzung des Gemenderats vom 4. Dezember 1914." December 4, 1914. 79 J 973. Archives départementales du Bas-Rhin.

Gozillon-Fronsacq, Odile. *Cinéma et Alsace: Stratégies Cinématographiques, 1896–1939*. Paris: Association française de recherche sur l'histoire du cinéma, 2003.

Granier, Jacques. *Novembre 18 en Alsace, album du cinquantenaire*. Strasbourg, Éditions des "Dernières nouvelles de Strasbourg," 1969.

Guenther, Irene. *Nazi Chic? Fashioning Women in the Third Reich*. Oxford and New York: Berg, 2004.

Henner, Jean-Jacques. *L'Alsace. Elle Attend*. 1871. Oil on canvas, 60 cm x 30 cm. Paris, Musée Jean-Jacques Henner.

Leven and Lemonier. *Alsace interprété par Mme Réjane*. 1916. Colored lithograph. Available at: http://gallica.bnf.fr/ark:/12148/btv1b10209526q (accessed June 28, 2020).

"Magasin de Louvre (Kaufhaus Hoher Steg) letterhead," 1911–1916. 845 W 4 (Dossier de la police du bâtiment). Archives de Strasbourg.

Mairie de Geispolsheim, ed. *Geispolsheim: gare et village, une histoire*. Mémoire de vies. Strasbourg: Carré blanc, 2006.

McFarlan, Tracy. "Our Alsace-Lorraine Picture Postcard Collection." *Veritas Liberabit: Special Collections Student Blog* (blog). Available at: http://sites.lafayette.edu/specialcollections/2013/06/10/our-alsace-lorraine-picture-postcard-collection/ (accessed June 28, 2020).

Office national de la radiodiffusion télévision française Strasbourg. "Déjà une caméra: 11 Novembre 1918 à Strasbourg." Ina.fr, November 12, 1966. Available at: http://www.ina.fr/video/SXF02029218 (accessed June 26, 2020).

Piton, Frédéric Théodore. *Strasbourg illustré ou Panorama pittoresque, historique et statistique de Strasbourg et de ses environs: Promenades dans les faubourgs, déscription des environs*. Strasbourg: printed by the author 1855.

"Protokollauszug der 1. Tagung des Modebund Frankfurt A. M.," June 20, 1915. 79 J 974. Archives départementales du Bas-Rhin.

Rogge, Bernhard Friedrich Wilhelm. *Kaiserbüchlein: 1797–1888. Zur Erinnerung an Kaiser Wilhelm den Grossen*. Bielefeld: Velhagen & Klasing, 1897.

"Sammlung von getragener Männerkleidung im ganzen Reiche." *Frankfurter Zeitung*. April 12, 1918. 79 J 959. Archives départementales du Bas-Rhin.

Spindler, Charles. *L'Alsace pendant la guerre*. Strasbourg: Treuttel & Würtz, 1925.

Stern, Norbert. *Die Weltpolitik der Weltmode*. Stuttgart and Berlin: Deutsche Verlags-Anstalt, 1915.

"Textilgewerbe und deutsche Tracht." *Strassburger Post*. March 19, 1915. Strassburger Stadtnachrichten. 79 J 974. Archives départementales du Bas-Rhin.

Vlossak, Elizabeth. *Marianne or Germania? Nationalizing Women in Alsace, 1870–1946*. Oxford: Oxford University Press, 2010.

Wahl, Alfred. *Confession et comportement dans les campagnes d'Alsace et de Bade, 1871–1939: Catholiques, protestants et juifs: Démographie, dynamisme économique et social, vie de relation et attitude politique*. Strasbourg: Éditions COPRUR, 1980.

8

The lace industry in France and Belgium during the First World War

Marguerite Coppens

While lace was still being produced manually in France and Belgium during the pre-war period, the practice had lost ground to mechanical production on the eve of the war. Around 1910, handmade lace had to depend on sales to the furniture industry rather than to fashion. The handmade lace industry—which was composed of women working by hand from their homes, in other words, all the economic and social handicaps of the time—was becoming old-fashioned and its survival cast in doubt. The social and moral context of the period played a determinant role in its continued survival during the war. The governments of France, which was *républicaine*, and Belgium, which was governed by the conservative Catholic party since 1884, both attempted various means to support manual production, but these efforts were not enough to keep the industry alive after the war.[1] The two countries adopted different approaches towards mechanical production. While Belgium never managed to develop a significant industry in mechanically produced lace, France did so with success.[2] In France, efforts were made to avoid casting mechanical production as an unworthy competitor; it was instead seen as a viable alternative, with each method suited to its own purposes.

Another major difference between the two countries can be seen in their respective approaches to compulsory education. In France, school education had been made mandatory in 1882; a consequence of this law was that lacemaking apprenticeships were delayed until the age of 14. As a result, the number of available lace makers was greatly reduced. The state was forced to address the situation, and the Engerand Act was enacted July 5, 1903. It again allowed early apprenticeships in lacemaking, albeit only in regions traditionally associated with the practice. In Belgium, the industry was unwilling to part with the so-called lacemaking "schools," which were in effect workshops taking advantage of cheap child labor. Compulsory education was not enacted until after the war.

The promotion of handmade lace in France and Belgium before the war

Proponents of handmade lace in both countries were aware that its benefits, as with most traditional crafts threatened by mechanical production, stemmed from this process of apprenticeship, which valorized the artisan's savoir faire. There was therefore much discussion about how to streamline production in order to train more profitable workers as well as how to train their "taste" so that they could make products that would compete against the machine-made alternatives. The Engerand Act allowed for the study of manual lacemaking in teacher-training colleges in the regions where lacemaking was traditionally practiced. In Belgium, it was through a private association, Les Amies de la dentelle (The Friends of Lace), that the study of lacemaking was introduced into teaching colleges.

Convincing buyers to pay the higher price for handmade lace was another challenge for its promoters. Advocates focused on the aesthetic quality of the lace, of course, but also reminded customers of the work involved in its production. Towards the end of the nineteenth century, various consumer leagues were created in France with the goal of helping the consumer understand the ethical implications behind the workers and industries producing their goods. They hoped to convince consumers to buy responsibly. Interest groups devoted to preserving handmaid lace took inspiration: La Dentelle de France (French Lace) was created in 1905 and Les Amies de la dentelle (Friends of Lace) in Belgium in 1910.[3] They fought to maintain employment—primarily in rural regions—and to ensure the "artistic excellence" of a "national" product. Their arguments had a moral component as well: lace making was work practiced by women in their own homes, allowing them to stay close to their children and maintain traditional domestic values. La Dentelle de France also encouraged the designers of haute couture to employ handmade lace in the fashion industry.[4] Both associations refrained from participating in direct commercial activity. The interest group fought on one hand to keep the apprenticeships and on the other to change the mindset of consumers, but avoided the root of the problem.

While these interest groups worked to support the long-standing tradition of apprenticeship, they did little to address another area of concern, which would put them at odds with the manufacturers: workers' remuneration. In their aim to make handmade lace competitive with machine production, they neglected the reality that the job would only remain viable for workers if wages were increased. The organization La Dentelle Belge (Belgian Lace), created in Brussels in 1911, sought salary increases for lace makers while also attempting to eliminate the intermediaries between workers and consumers, drawing the ire of lace production companies. Elisabeth of Bavaria, then Queen of Belgium, appears to have played a role in establishing the organization, which would resurface after the war under the name Coopérative dentellière (Lacemaking Cooperative).[5] In 1913, the Secrétariat général des Unions professionnelles féminines chrétiennes de Belgique (General Secretariat of the Belgian Christian Women's Trade Association) attempted to establish lacemaking unions, but the highly dispersed nature of the profession made the task difficult. The arrival of the war definitively halted their efforts.[6]

Lacemaking belongs to a long tradition of work conducted in the home—a topic that has recently been studied in depth, and which we cannot fully discuss here.[7] Suffice it to say that this type of work, highly decentralized and offering no legal protections, was especially susceptible to exploitation. The same held true for other sectors of the clothing industry, including lingerie production. Women, usually underpaid compared to their male counterparts, endured miserable conditions. This was a concern during the era, as well. Various studies were conducted on the industry between 1900 and the start of the war to investigate and exhibitions were mounted in order to sensitive the public to the problem as well.

The Belgian Ministry of Industry and Work ordered a series of investigations on work in the home, asking Pierre Verhaegan, of the Catholic Party, to lead the investigation on lace and tulle embroidery.[8] In 1911, he proposed a law regulating domestic industries. Socialist representative Camille Huysmans had already proposed a similar law in 1910, the same year that the International Congress on Work in the Home was held in Brussels. However, none of these efforts came to fruition. The ruling Catholic Party was unwilling to draft new legislation increasing public involvement in private enterprise. They were not willing to take a stance on the salaries either. They thought the women who wore the products should bear the responsibility for the conditions of fashion workers. While the Socialist Party denounced the abuses in these industries, the plight of female workers were, nevertheless, not a priority.

In addition, work in the home was especially difficult to regulate, as employees were not receiving hourly salaries. Opinions arguing against domestic lace production entirely were rare at the time (nobody wanted to admit that handmade lace could be easily copied by a machine), but Pierre Verhaegen, in his report, remarked that, "machine production is not only cheaper, it is also better ... we are wrong to believe that hand production achieves results impossible for the machine."[9] This position, however, failed to take into account the many women who relied on their income from lacemaking. Generally, lace production was a source of national pride that most were unwilling to challenge.

Belgium at war

In the years preceding the war, discussion of the lace industry had spread throughout the French and Belgian press, often inciting fervent debate on the "question dentellière" (lace question).[10] Although it is sometimes difficult today to fully comprehend how passionate people were about the subject, an understanding of the issue's importance in Belgian society allows us to better contextualize the industry's role during the war. Lace production remained a topic of national concern, even when seemingly more pressing matters were at play.

On August 4, 1914, Germany invaded Belgium, and the entire territory east of the Yser River soon fell under occupation. Unlike other countries, where women could mobilize to replace men in the workplace, Belgium's industrial sphere came to a standstill and the economy was paralyzed. The import of materials was halted, including the thread necessary for lace production. The fate of the Belgian people attracted international solidarity. The privately run relief organization Comité national de secours et d'alimentation (National Committee for Food and Relief) was created in September 1914, but it required international aid in order to appear credible for the German occupant. Neutral countries helped establish the Commission for Relief in Belgium (CRB, also known as the Belgian Relief), headed by future US President Herbert Hoover, which exported tons of food to be distributed among the famished citizens and helped sensibilize Americans to Belgium's plight April 1915, the Belgian Relief extended support to parts of France as well. The used flour sacks from aid efforts were recuperated and distributed to fashion schools, where they were either embroidered and sold as souvenirs or transformed into clothing. In a workshop in Charleroi, 30,000 sacks were converted into 15,000 shirts in the month of July 1916 alone.[11]

In addition to food aid, the Belgian Relief also distributed clothing and fabric. This was a necessity, as the price of fabric had already increased by 300–400 percent in 1915, thoroughly incapacitating the textile industry.[12] Fabric and garments had to be imported. The material was transported from the USA to Rotterdam before being directed towards Brussels. Patterns were cut and readied for assembly; 500 workers grouped them into bails and routed them towards various sub-branches. They would eventually make their way into the homes of workers in every province. A seamstress with children under her charge could expect to receive one bail of material to sew per week. Finished articles were returned to the Belgian Relief, who redistributed them. Thousands of unemployed workers thus were given work for a few days a week in return for a salary; rules capped the salary at 3 francs per week, or 6 francs for the month. Each Monday, women could work on their own clothing; each Tuesday, they repaired clothing brought to them by their village's poor.

The Belgian Wartime lace industry

The lace industry found itself incapacitated after hostilities began. It was unable to import the necessary raw materials or export the finished products. Due to the prestige of their position, however, lace makers received specific attention. The *Amies de la dentelle* were no longer able to operate independently and had to rely on the disciplined organization of the Comite national de secours et d'alimentation. But the war allowed the *Amies* to retain full control of the production.

Beginning August 8, 1914, only several days after Germany's invasion of Belgium, the Union patriotique des femmes Belges (Patriotic Union of Belgian Women) opened a placement office and a distribution service for home workers.[13] The Comité national de secours et d'alimentation, in turn, prioritized aid to this organization, granting them funds in support of lace production as early as September 5, 1914. On January 18, 1915, the Amies de la dentelle, now also subsidized by the Comité national, was renamed the Comité de la dentelle (Lace Committee). In March 15, the Comité national obliged the Union patriotique des femmes belges and the Comité de la dentelle to merge together under the name Aide et protection aux dentellières (Aid and Protection for Laceworkers). This merger was not without issues; the Union begrudgingly ceded its purview over true lace work, retaining control only over semi-handmade lace work (such as Luxeuil) and other related techniques, such filet lace.[14] The Amies, on the other hand, controlled distribution of materials to workers, choice of designs, and centralization of finished articles of bobbin and needle lace.[15]

The lace industry was significant enough that the importation of lace thread—once it became available again in early 1915—was regulated in the same way as food or clothing aid. Through an agreement with the Comité de la dentelle, thread was delivered to Belgium through England. The finished products were sent back to England, who then sold them to neutral countries. By May 1915, lace makers and apprentice workshops were once again in operation: 28,000 lacemakers received payment for their work, and 24 schools were subsidized.

Like the other garment workers subsidized by the Commission, lacemakers were limited to earning 3 francs per week. Before the war, that same worker would have earned an average of 1 franc per day, with no limit to the number of permissible workdays.[16] The allowance, then, was meager; it was acceptable only given the wartime circumstances. Ultimately, wartime lace production had no relation to the real needs of the market. These salary caps suited the prevailing ethos of the Commission, and of the era in general. Aid needed to reach the greatest number of the unemployed, yet it would be unthinkable to grant aid without work performed in return.[17] Labor, therefore, would have to be meted out evenly. We should also note that sewing and lacemaking were some of the few fields allotted to women amongst a broader series of public work programs intended solely for unemployed men.[18]

Propaganda efforts helped workers obtain additional funds. In 1916, the Commission arranged for American writer and journalist Charlotte Kellogg to spend 6 months in Belgium in order to testify to the difficulties confronting the Belgian people.[19] Her book *Women of Belgium Turning Tragedy to Triumph* was published in 1917. She would return to Belgium in January 1919, publishing *Bobbins of Belgium* in 1920.[20] Her writings, while somewhat intensified in their emotional tenor, give a very precise account of the situation at the time.

The invasion of Belgium had become an issue of international attention, the focal point of the developing war. Lace, in turn, represented the country's identity abroad, and became a useful motif in propaganda campaigns; the image of the lacemaker hunched over her cushion, surrounded by the ruins of her bombarded village, served as a recurring symbol. The *Amies* released these images as postcards, using them to attract buyers (Figure 8.1).

Lace's association with Belgium's martyrdom can also be seen in a number of lace productions that more directly showcase wartime iconography. These "war laces" often depicted symbols associated with the royal family, or banners and other emblems of the allied countries (Figs 8.2 and 8.3). The sales catalogs for the Comité de la dentelle, published beginning in summer 1915, offer parasols, fans, children's clothing, lingerie, and scarfs, all in very traditional styles (Figure 8.4). The prices are steep when compared with the weekly allocation of 3 francs for their creators: a decorative *volant* for the hem of a skirt, with a height of 15 cm, sold for 15 to 35 francs per meter; a 2.5 meter by 60 cm scarf from 75 to 3000 francs; and a fan leaf from 110 to 250 francs.

The Amies feared that the craft of lacemaking would be lost during wartime, and were determined to maintain production at any cost, regardless of any realistic assessment of the market. Lace, in truth,

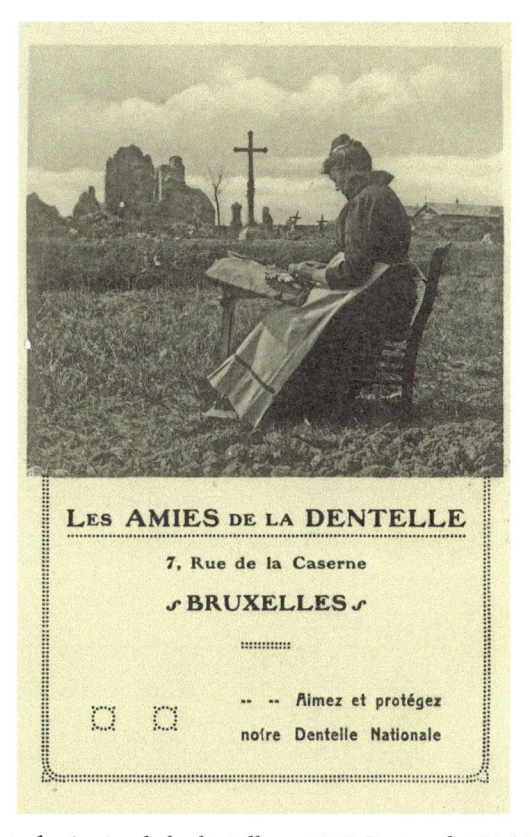

Figure 8.1 *Propaganda photo for* Amies de la dentelle, c. 1915. Postcard. *MA&H, Brussels. Copyright ACL.*

128　　　　　　　　　　*Fashion, Society, and the First World War*

Figure 8.2 *War Lace depicting the rooster, symbol of France.* Volant *in Malines lace (10 x 102 cm). MA&H, Brussels. Inv. D.1357.01. Copyright ACL.*

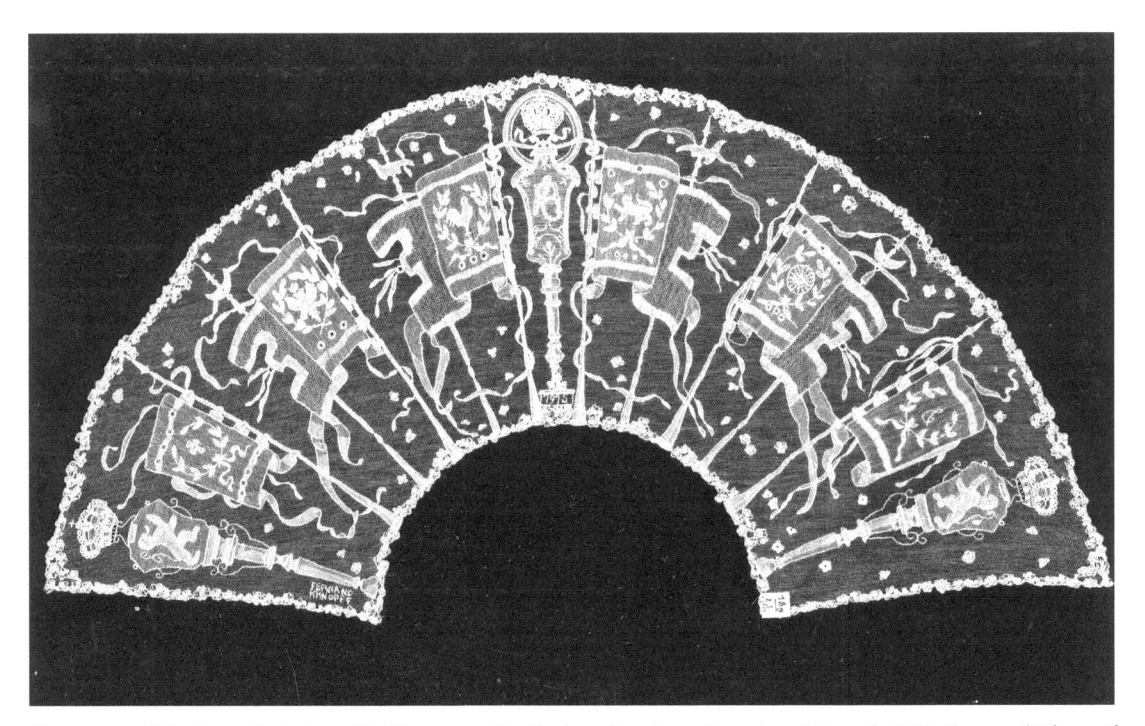

Figure 8.3 *War Lace depicting allies' banners. Needle-lace fan sheet. Dated and signed, 1915, Fernand Khnopff (24 x 50 cm). MA&H, Brussels, Inv.D.1361. Copyright ACL.*

did not fit in with the changes that had already been occurring in fashion since 1910. Proponents of lace believed that these changes were temporary, a mere ebb in the cyclic reordering of trends, and few opposing voices were raised at the time. However, when the US joined the war in 1917, it ceased sending aid to Belgium. The Comité received a credit which they were expected to reimburse through

Figure 8.4 *Paul Mussche, Comité de la dentelle, 1915, pl. 2. Catalogue of lace pieces offered for sale. MA&H, Brussels. Copyright ACL.*

the sale of lace products. Unfortunately, sales figures had never matched hopes. The Comité received 10,187,373 francs, of which only 1,200,000 was recovered through sales, a mere 11.8 percent. By the end of the war, the quantity of unsold stock was enormous. In 1918, production was stalled once again due to a complete shortage of thread.[21]

French lace during the war

The war had engendered entirely different circumstances in France, which, save for a select few territories, had not been occupied. The clothing industry never came to a halt, as in Belgium, but rather found itself attending to the demands of the military. As men were mobilized, women took their place in factories. Lacemaking did not attract much attention, being just one among many of the jobs in the clothing industry that could be performed in the home.

Before and during the war, aid for the poor and unemployed in Belgium was seen as a private affair. Even though government institutions did lend some support, the organizations coordinating relief in Belgium were all privately run. Matters were different in France, where the government drafted legislation in order to regulate salaries. The first country to institute a minimum wage for work performed at home had been Australia, in 1896. England's Trade Boards Act followed suit in 1909. Here, the law made no distinction between genders, and covered work performed in one's home or workshop, regulating wages either "hourly or per article."[22] It notably included regulations for the hand finishing of mechanically produced lace. France later took inspiration to enact similar measures.[23]

The French government's *Bulletin de L'Office du Travail* (Bulletin of the Work Office) commented on the 1902 Belgian investigation of lacemaking conducted by Verhaegen, but did not broach the topic of handmade lace in its own investigations on work performed in the home. Instead, the *Bulletin* mentioned three other investigations on lingerie, artificial flowers, and shoes.[24] We can surmise that lacemaking was not one of the Work Office's main preoccupations. Following these investigations, various, unsuccessful, bills were proposed in order to regulate work in the home, including a 1911 bill protecting female workers in the clothing industry. It was not until July 10, 1915 that this same bill became law, bolstered by the exceptional circumstances of the ongoing war. The new regulations remained limited in scope, applying only to women in the garment industry.[25] They did, however, extend to the fields of lingerie, hat making, hosiery, glove making, artificial flowers, lace, crochet, and embroidery. That these products—non-vital in times of war—were addressed through legislation shows that fashion remained a sensitive issue in France, even during the conflict. Interestingly, they covered both handmade lace and machine-made lace wherein part of the finishing work was completed in the home.

The law was not restricted by nationality, and it protected immigrants working in France as well as citizens. Significantly, the many Belgian lacemakers fleeing occupied Belgium would have been included. These legal protections also did nothing to limit the many private charitable actions organized for Belgian lacemaker refugees. Ateliers were soon set up for these women, such as that at Angers, where lacemaking tools such as frames and cushions were some of the first items created.

We cannot fully delve into the law's standards for salaries here, but suffice it to say they were detailed with rigor and precision. This made the regulations capable of being enforced, despite their complexity. The 1915 law was supplemented in 1922 and 1926; lacemaking for the furniture industry was added in 1922, as a number of lacemakers worked in both the furniture and clothing industries simultaneously, and it was often difficult to distinguish the labor performed for each.[26] The law was only expanded to include men in 1928. In Belgium, a similar law, applicable to both genders, was only issued in 1934, after first being proposed in 1910! After the First World War, however, the number of workers operating from home had declined, and by 1934, the number of lacemakers working by hand had become trivial.

Conclusion

France and Belgium faced very different circumstances during the war, but ultimately, neither country found a way to preserve the tradition of handmade lace. The war had irreversibly altered the cultural landscape, and the profession was fated to disappear for good. After the armistice, compulsory education was finally instituted in Belgium, putting an end to child labor and any semblance of competitive pricing for handmade lace. Moreover, education disrupted the apprenticeship process, and therefore the trade's method of self-perpetuation. In France, only a select few lacemaking methods that did not require a long apprenticeship survived, and then again only in disadvantaged areas, such as the department of Allier, a region in the center of France. The continued survival of the craft became an indicator of the underdevelopment of a region. Other more profitable careers began to open their doors to women. The lacemaking interest groups disappeared after the war as well. Their moral aim of keeping women in the domestic sphere had lost its potency now that working outside the home had become a necessity and reality during wartime.

As handmade lace disappeared from the fashion industry, machine-made lace took its turn in the spotlight, making its way into various designs in the newly fashionable Art Deco style. The war hastened the completion of a process originating as far back as the beginning of the nineteenth century. Handmade lace was already condemned the moment its machine-made counterpart first emerged, but it would take the turbulence of the First World War to impress the economic reality onto those holding on to tradition.

Notes

1 Marguerite Coppens, "Industrialization and the growth and decline of lacemaking from the late nineteenth to the early twentieth centuries: The evidence of the legislation on working from home," paper presented at Hertford College, Oxford, September 29, 2007.

2 The history of machine-made lace remains little studied. See Henri Hénon, *L'Industrie des tulles et dentelles mécaniques dans le Pas-de-Calais, 1815–1900* (Paris: Belin Frères, 1900); Léonce Bajart, *L'Industrie des tulles et dentelles en France: Son établissement dans le Cambrésis: L'Essor de Caudry* (Lille: S.I.L.I.C., 1953); Marguerite Coppens, "La Dentelle manuelle—la dentelle mécanique: Collaborations et rivalités," in *Art et Industrie. Les Arts décoratifs en Belgique au XIXe siècle*, Claire Leblanc, ed. (Brussels: MRAH, 2004), 86–93, paper presented at the Royal Museums for Art and History, Brussels, October 23–24, 2003.

3 The archives for the *Amies de la dentelle* are held at the Royal Museums of Art and History, Brussels.

4 *La Dentelle: Journal artistique, industriel et féminin* (April 1905): 1, (May–July 1905): 31, and (May–July 1906): 6.

5 Marguerite Coppens, *Les Dentelles royales* (Brussels: BBL, 1990), exhibition catalogue, 113–14; Edmond Rubens, "La Question dentellière," *La Femme belge* (1923).

6 Jeanne Elschot, "Aperçu sur la situation économique des ouvrières dentellières en Belgique," *La Femme belge: Revue de questions morales, sociales, littéraire, et artistique* 6/9, February 1923, 797–806.

7 See Colette Avrane, *Ouvrières à domicile: Le Combat pour un salaire minimum sous la Troisième République* (Rennes: Presses Universitaires de Rennes, 2013).

8 Pierre Verhaegen, *Les Industries à domicile en Belgique: La Dentelle et la broderie sur tulle*, vols 4 and 5, *Les Industries à domicile en Belgique* (Brussels: Lebègue, 1902); Pierre Verhaegen, *Travail à domicile et Sweating-System* (Brussels: Albert Dewit, 1912).

9 Verhaegen, *Travail à domicile et Sweating-System*, 7.

10 *La Question dentellière: essai de mise au point* (Brussels, 1912); G. Hector Quignon, *La Dentelle de Chantilly et la question dentellière* (Cayeux-sur-mer: P. Olivier, 1905).

11 Charlotte Kellogg, *Women of Belgium Turning Tragedy to Triumph* (New York: Funk & Wagnalls, 1917).

12 Ibid.

13 Jane Brigode, *Union patriotique des femmes belges*. Brussels: Report presented to the Comité national de secours et d'alimentation, August 8, 1914–February 28, 1915.

14 Coppens, *Les Dentelles royales*, 105–55.

15 The designs chosen by the *Amies de la dentelle* are conserved nearly in their entirety at the Royal Museums of Art and History in Brussels.

16 Charlotte Kellogg, *Bobbins of Belgium* (New York: Funk & Wagnalls, 1920), 44.

17 The allocation given to refugees by the French government without expectation of work in return was a novel and strongly criticized policy. Philippe Nivet, "Les réfugiées de guerre dans la société française (1914–1946)," *Histoire, économie et société* 2 (2004): 250.

18 Sophie de Schaepdrijver, "A civilian war effort: The Comité National de Secours et d'Alimentation in Occupied Belgium, 1914–1918," in *Remembering Herbert Hoover and the Commission for Relief in Belgium* (Brussels: Fondation Universitaire, 2007), 24–37.

19 Anton Goegebeur, "Charlotte Kellogg: Women of America and Belgium," (MA thesis, Katholieke Universiteit Leuven (KU Leuven), 2014).

20 Kellogg, *Bobbins of Belgium*.

21 Belgium, under German occupation, must have known of the German "Spitsen-Zentrale." See Coppens, "Les Dentelles royales," 119. This information was found in the Archives du Palais Royal, Albert et Elisabeth, Sécretariat No. 209.

22 *Bulletin de l'Office du travail*, vol. 17 (Paris: Office du Travail, 1910), 73; G. Duchene, *Les Progrès de la législation sur le salaire minimum* (Paris: M. Rivière & cie, 1918), 129–43.

23 Avrane, *Ouvrières à domicile*.

24 *Bulletin de l'Office du travail* (1903), 112, (1905), 311, and (1909), 1316–17.

25 Men receiving a salary inferior to the minimum amount set for women, while performing the same work, could sue their employer. *Bulletin de l'Office du travail*, (1915), 65.

26 Avrane, *Ouvrières à domicile*, 234.

References

Avrane, Colette. *Ouvrières à domicile: Le combat pour un salaire minimum sous la Troisième République*. Rennes: Presses Universitaires de Rennes, 2013.

Bajart, Léonce. *L'Industrie des tulles et dentelles en France: Son établissement dans le Cambrésis: L'Essor de Caudry*. Lille: S.I.L.I.C., 1953.

Brigode, Jane. *Union patriotique des femmes belges*. Brussels: Report presented to the Comité national de secours et d'alimentation, August 8, 1914–February 28, 1915.

Bulletin de l'Office du travail, vol. 17. Paris: Office du Travail, 1910,

Coppens, Marguerite. *Les Dentelles royales*. Brussels: BBL, 1990. Published in conjunction with an exhibition of the same title, September 19–November 4, 1990.

Coppens, Marguerite. "La Dentelle manuelle—la dentelle mécanique: Collaborations et rivalités." In *Art et Industrie. Les Arts décoratifs en Belgique au XIXe siècle*, Claire Leblanc, ed., 86–93. Brussels: MRAH, 2004, paper presented at the Royal Museums for Art and History, Brussels, October 23–24, 2003.

Coppens, Marguerite. "Industrialization and the growth and decline of lacemaking from the late nineteenth to the early twentieth centuries: The evidence of the legislation on working from home," paper presented at Hertford College, Oxford, September 29, 2007.

de Schaepdrijver, Sophie. "A civilian war effort: The Comité National de Secours et d'Alimentation in Occupied Belgium, 1914–1918." In *Remembering Herbert Hoover and the Commission for Relief in Belgium*, 24–37. Brussels: Fondation Universitaire, 2007.

Goegebeur, Anton. "Charlotte Kellogg: Women of America and Belgium." MA thesis, Katholieke Universiteit Leuven, 2014.

Hénon, Henri. *L'Industrie des tulles et dentelles mécaniques dans le Pas-de-Calais, 1815–1900* (Paris: Belin Frères, 1900);

Kellogg, Charlotte. *Women of Belgium Turning Tragedy to Triumph*. New York: Funk & Wagnalls, 1917.

Kellogg, Charlotte. *Bobbins of Belgium*. New York: Funk & Wagnalls, 1920.

La Dentelle: Journal artistique, industriel et féminin, 1905.

La Femme belge, 1923.

La Question dentellière: Essai de mise au point. Brussels: 1912.

Nivet, Philippe. "Les réfugiées de guerre dans la société française (1914–1946)." *Histoire, économie et société* 2 (2004): 250.

Quignon, Hector G. *La Dentelle de Chantilly et la question dentellière*. Cayeux-sur-mer: P. Olivier, 1905.

Verhaegen, Pierre. *Les Industries à domicile en Belgique: La Dentelle et la broderie sur tulle*, vols 4 and 5, *Les Industries à domicile en Belgique*. Brussels: Lebègue, 1902.

Verhaegen, Pierre. *Travail à domicile et Sweating-System*. Brussels: Albert Dewit, 1912.

9

Industrial and homemade clothing production in the Netherlands
A neutral country during the First World War

Marta Kargól

The centennial of the First World War in 2014 attracted a fair amount of attention in the Netherlands, perhaps surprisingly so, given that the country remained neutral throughout the war. The commemorative events provided an opportunity for scholars to discuss the Netherlands' role within the larger international conflict, as well as the political, economic, and social repercussions within the country. However, until recently, Dutch historiography has primarily focused on the political and economic effects of the war, without taking into account daily life during the conflict.[1] The question of clothing production and consumption in the Netherlands has never previously been examined. This article will attempt to fill that gap.

This paper will first contextualize clothing production in the Netherlands within the context of international and national events in order to grasp the problems that the industry faced during the war. Then it will examine the concept of Dutch fashion during the era, looking at foreign influences. Was the country able to develop a distinct national identity? Finally, the importance of homemade clothing will be addressed. Did the war have a direct impact on women's production habits? What of their renewed interest in needlework? Ultimately, this paper argues that the Netherlands offers a useful case study on the First World War's impact on clothing production and consumption in a neutral nation.

Much of the present research on the Netherlands' involvement in the First World War centers either on the country's neutrality and the measures taken to preserve this neutral position or on the presence of Belgian refugees in the country.[2] The state of daily life for Dutch women during the war has been less studied than other gender-related topics, such as women's voting rights or female espionage (as in the well-known case of Mata Hari).[3] Yet the lives and roles of women in countries that did go to war has been well researched.[4] Historians have broadly addressed women's dress and the difficulties in its production and distribution in England, for example, but the same attention has not been granted to the Netherlands.[5]

Dutch newspapers and women's magazines published during the war allow for a detailed study of women's daily dress. Newspapers such as *Algemeen Handelsblad of het Volk* (General Bulletin of the People) provide context on the political, economic, and social issues that affected manufacturing and framed daily life.[6] The women's magazines can be subdivided into two types: those that are fashion specific, such as *De Gracieuse* (The Gracious) and *Onze Kleeding* (Our Clothing), and general women's magazines such as *Vrouw en haar Huis* (The Woman and Her Home), intended for women of the middle or upper classes. Of these magazines, *De Gracieuse* had the widest impact; in 1904, it had a circulation of 22,000 copies.[7] In 1916, the magazine cost 30 cents for the standard issue and 45 cents for the luxury edition. *Onze Kleeding* was published by the Association of Trade Schools for the Betterment of Women and Children's Clothes (Vereeniging: Vakschool voor Verbeetering van Vrouwen—en Kinderkleding), which was founded in 1898.[8] The women's magazine *Vrouw en haar Huis* had a wider range of content than *De Gracieuse* and *Onze Kleeding*, covering topics ranging from culture and home improvement to women's voting rights. Generally, all of the magazines offered patterns for home clothing production. In 1916, *De Gracieuse* sold patterns for 5 cents apiece.[9] *De Vrouw en haar Huis*' prices varied depending on clothing type: a pattern for baby clothes costs 25 cents while one for one for a suit or coat cost 1 florin and 25 cents.[10] *De Vereeniging* sold patterns to members of the association at various price points.[11]

Daily life in the Netherlands during the war

Discussion of the war was at its most prevalent in these newspapers and women's magazines in 1914, 1917, and 1918. The war was mentioned less frequently between 1915 and 1917. After the first months, the panic surrounding the initial events wore off, and shortages and economic crisis didn't greatly affect the Netherlands until 1917.

An attitude of heightened anxiety predominated in the press at the start of the war. Writers were principally worried about the unviability of neutrality and the potential for economic decline. Two defining events consumed the attentions of the entire population: the mobilization of the armed forces, carried out in early August 1914, and the subsequent influx of thousands of Belgian refugees into the Netherlands.[12] Government aid from the Netherlands was often insufficient in meeting the needs of the displaced population and so civil society was asked to step in and help. Eventually, the feared economic crisis did arrive, reaching its peak in 1917 and 1918. Heightened submarine warfare in the North Sea had disrupted trade and Dutch neutrality had not eradicated commercial pressures from neighboring nations, notably England and Germany.[13] Neutrality was not only a privilege, it also created obligations at the international level. As of 1915, the Netherlands was no longer allowed to resell to Germany products purchased in England, or those made from English raw materials. This ban included clothing, textiles, and any product necessary for clothing manufacture. Germany, in turn, limited the number of their products which could be sold to the Netherlands, and began exporting quantities which were inadequate for the Dutch domestic market. The Netherlands was known for its production of colored cotton fabric, but this industry was particularly affected as Germany had a monopoly on the dyestuffs.[14]

Understanding the Netherlands' pre-war garment industry allows one to better contextualize the effects of the war. After 1800, the Dutch clothing and textile sectors experienced rapid growth.[15] Large factories proliferated in the eastern region of Twente and in the Brabant province, and the country became known for its high-quality cotton and wool textiles. The Netherlands maintained close trade relationships with multiple European countries as well as the United States. The Dutch imported hosiery and knitted goods from England, as well as fabric for the production of high-quality men's clothing. French imports included patterns for clothing production, fabric for women's clothing, furs, scarfs, shoes, and perfumes. From Germany, the Netherlands imported wool and cotton for the garment production, as well as stockings from Chemnitz and embroidery from Plauen. Belgium was a major provider of underclothes and lace. An article from *Algemeen Handelsblad* published in 1914 describes the nature of prewar clothing importation, but unfortunately does not provide quantities for the items mentioned.[16]

While the population was navigating the difficulties of the economic crisis and adjusting to the scarcity of products necessary for everyday life, Dutch society was experiencing another novel phenomenon: increasing calls for women's right to vote. The largest demonstration for voting rights took place in Amsterdam in 1916.[17] In 1919, after two decades of campaigning, voting rights were finally granted.[18] Demands for suffrage went hand in hand with the fight against poor living conditions. Women sought to ameliorate their personal circumstances, while concurrently addressing broader causes, such as international peace, for example.[19] Multiple demonstrations for improved economic conditions occurred during the war. Women also created petitions and engaged with local authorities. Their primary demands involved access to necessary goods, especially food.[20] The political and social aspects of women's lives became increasingly interdependent, as the demand for the right to vote joined a broader struggle that included the fights for better housing, access to medical care, and improved working conditions.[21] Women's movements drew from daily realities, and would continue to do so as they challenged the traditional domestic roles of the wife, mother, and housekeeper.

Many Dutch women began working during the war. Their situation was less fraught than that of women in neighboring countries at war. Since some Dutch men continued working as inactive reserves, women were not asked to work "masculine" jobs. Instead of working in factories, many women turned to help the needy—the poor, refugees, and soldiers.[22] Some entered the medical sector. A training course for nurses was instituted in Amsterdam at the beginning of the war. According to an article in *Onze Kleeding*, hundreds of women took part.[23] According to the association "Onze Kleeding," this course provided the occasion for women to point out the impracticality of the traditional nurse's uniforms, whose long straight skirts impeded movement, and prevented one from kneeling next to the wounded.[24] The magazine *De Gracieuse* proposed their own set of uniforms, which were nevertheless still characterized by narrow skirts and shirts. Yet, period photographs of Dutch nurses in the Red Cross show that uniforms would differ from the ones described, with designs that were much more ample and comfortable.[25]

Industrial clothing production

The press, and women's magazines in particular, expressed fears about potential economic troubles that the Netherlands could face from the very beginning of the war. But the real troubles would not appear for several years. Initially, Dutch factories had recourse to sufficient reserves of materials and the employees who had been mobilized into the army were quickly replaced by Belgian refugees.[26] At the start of the war, the situation was indeed favorable for many clothing manufacturers, as orders from the military bolstered sales.[27] Women's magazines encouraged women to dress themselves elegantly and to purchase new clothes, as this supported the national economy and employment numbers.[28] The national production of underclothes increased in 1916—what had previously been purchased from Germany was now produced in the Netherlands.[29] These early successes led the press to believe that Dutch production after the war's end would remain strong, and that the country would have the additional benefit of being less dependent on the importation of foreign goods.

Unfortunately, a production crisis emerged in the spring of 1916, with the press reporting that the price of fabric had increased to a significant degree.[30] Unemployment also began to rise sharply at this time. Throughout the course of the year, clothing of good quality became increasingly expensive, while affordable clothes became increasingly unattainable. The root cause was a shortage of fabric and other primary materials.[31] In August 1916, the newspaper *Het Volk* (The People) wrote:

> For some while now, a shortage of thread has become apparent. German factories send us nothing due to the ban on exports. Belgian factories are destroyed and otherwise non-operational, English factories produce very little. The clothing industry is constantly facing new difficulties. Companies and designers in need of thread know not where to turn.[32]

The situation became even more difficult in 1917 and 1918. Ongoing submarine warfare prevented commerce with much of Europe, as well as the United States and Asia, an important market for the Netherlands. Wool and cotton were notably in short supply. England, for example, which had still exported 60,000 lbs of cotton yarn to the Netherlands in 1915, halted supplies almost completely in 1917.[33] The price of European imports tripled. As a result, domestic production was severely curtailed, and as textile factories closed down in the eastern regions. Many lost employment—12,000 people lost their positions in the town of Enschede, for example.[34] Clothing became more expensive, with the price of shoes jumping from 6 or 7 florins to 15 in 1917.[35] The price of a men's suit, in that same year, reached 50 or 60 florins, from the expected 20 or 25.[36] These examples show that the price of clothing doubled.[37]

Poverty was becoming increasingly prevalent, and whilst food was the primary concern, the press also reported an enormous demand for clothing and shoes. The magazine *Het Volk* reported on the situation in Rotterdam: "The families of the unemployed are in dire need of clothing and shoes. Thousands of items are being delivered, but the situation is very urgent, as demand is still great."[38] In 1917 and 1918, charitable organizations in Utrecht delivered twice as many clothes to the needy as in the previous years.[39] The recipients lacked every kind of item, especially socks and shoes. To compensate, many turned to wearing military uniforms bought back from the soldiers.[40] The police also noted an uptick in clothing theft and confirmed that clothing had indeed become a highly sought-after commodity.[41]

Dutch fashion during the war

Dutch fashion was largely inspired by French fashion before the war, even though women's magazines occasionally criticized French couture for its lack of practicality. German fashion, itself influenced by Parisian couture, also played a part in inspiring Dutch fashion design.[42] Many articles in Dutch women's magazines continued to be devoted to French and German couture, even during the war. Yet, in the fall of 1916, the Dutch press revealed that the so-called French patterns sold in Germany and Austria were not in fact of French origin, but counterfeits derived from French fashion journals. The Dutch fashion magazine *De Fransche Modejournalen* (The French Fashion Magazine), recommended three veritable French publications to its readers: *Les Elégances Parisiennes*, *Le Tailleur*, and *La Blouse*.[43]

In the early days of the war, the women's journals frequently discussed the war's influence on fashion. Journalists—their names were often not attached to articles in this period—posed the question of whether it was still appropriate to be preoccupied with fashion during wartime. Many pointed to the new designs coming out of countries engaged in war, such as France, as proof that the matter remained important, despite the difficult circumstances.[44] In November 1914, *De Gracieuse* wrote:

The initial fear of the war has nevertheless subsided, and we can return to our daily lives with a measure of calm; we are once again able to appreciate simple domestic pleasures. For evening events with our soldiers, and for charity events, we feel the need for more sophisticated wardrobes.[45]

In 1914, the newspaper *Algemeen Handelsblad* published an article attributed to A.K. stating: "All are still operating: Worth and Paquin, Drécolle and Callot, Doucet and Bernard, and Besschoff-David [*sic*]. The great Parisian fashion houses are still turning out, as if by magic, their dresses and coats; they are still sending their ethereal tulle to all corners of the world."[46]

Deliveries of women's fashion in the Netherlands for the fall and winter seasons of 1914 arrived early, which spurred sales, and gave Dutch women reason to remain calm.[47] Many believed that fashion would become simpler in the following year, but this information came from England and not Paris, as the French designs had not yet arrived, and stores no longer imported from Germany.[48] Some of the silhouettes did change slightly—dresses, for example, became wider. Skirts gained in popularity, as they allowed one to mix and match with a variety of blouses and jackets (Figure 9.1).

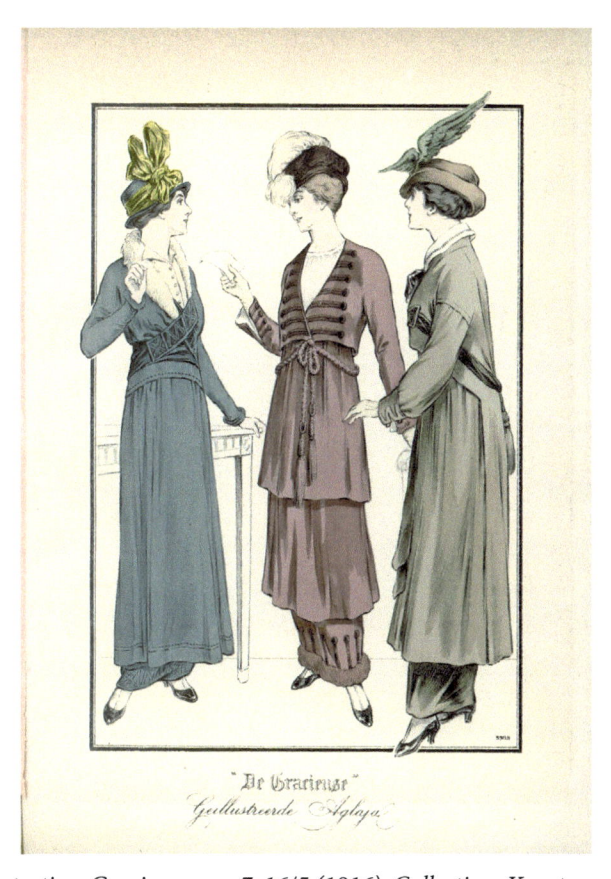

Figure 9.1 *Fashion illustration.* Gracieuse, *no. 7: 16/5 (1916). Collection: Kunstmuseum, Den Haag.*

In 1916, new, even larger skirts attracted much attention in the Dutch press. This fashion development appeared illogical to the Dutch: why design skirts requiring so much fabric when it was an expensive and scarce commodity?[49] The following year, skirts narrowed once again. Newspaper *Algemeen Handelsblad* confirmed that this was notably a Dutch phenomenon, seen as preferable for women in the Netherlands.[50] Simplicity became the standard, but international influences remained prominent (Figure 9.2).

Despite the crisis, new stores and fashion houses did emerge during the war. An English house designing men's clothing opened in The Hague in September 1915, and fashion house Peek & Cloppenburg followed suit in 1917.[51] That same year, the Amsterdam-based fashion house Hirsch organized a fashion show of Parisian and Viennese couture.[52] An author with the initials T.G.-B. wrote an article in *De Mode* on its subject: "Paris or Vienna!? . . . This show of Parisian and Viennese fashion forces us to compare the two, and it's no easy task to determine who comes out on top. We are currently quite dependent on foreign fashion."[53] This dependence was often mentioned in the context of the Netherlands' lack of a national fashion identity. In this same article, the author lamented the fact that

Figure 9.2 *Fashion illustration.* Gracieuse, no. 8: 16/3 (1915). Collection: Kunstmuseum, Den Haag.

no Dutch woman had attained success as a couturière. Dutch women were adept at creating clothes for themselves and their children, but none were able to carve out a professional career designing clothing.[54]

Domestic couture

Studying the production of clothes in individual households is always difficult—few sources provide adequate information on the popularity of the phenomenon. We can base some of our hypotheses on the number of magazines containing sewing and knitting patterns: there was indeed a larger demand for all types of patterns during the war.[55] Nevertheless, these figures do not indicate the total number of magazines sold, and while we can read into how closely the patterns followed the popular fashions at the time, we should not ignore the fact that each woman would have put her own personal touches on the designs, replicating them to varying degrees of faithfulness. Homemade clothing could be the result of stylistic trends or individual passion, but more often than not it arose as a necessity in times of crisis or economic difficulty. Eventually, homemade clothing in the Netherlands became a public affair, as women were urged to clothe soldiers and the needy.

The call to mobilize provided the Dutch with the war's first major disruption to daily life. Although the army provided clothing to soldiers, the uniforms were often severely damaged or incomplete. Soldiers were advised to pack their own underclothes.[56] As a result, women's magazines urged their readers to sew and knit warm underclothes for the men (Figure 9.3):

> As our soldiers stand watch out in the cold on the frontier, in order to preserve our neutrality, us women have a duty to make warm clothing for our husbands and our sons. Let us set to work, knitting assiduously, and appreciate this art which has somewhat fallen out of fashion.[57]

It is interesting that knitting was deemed "out of fashion". Knitting, it seems, had become seen as a slightly outdated practice at the dawn of the war, one that it was necessary to imbue with new value and purpose. After this call went out, thousands of socks were made and dispatched to the army. Dutch women made 35,000 balaclavas, called "bivakmutsen."[58] These efforts welcomed by the soldiers, and in total 60,000 of these face masks were sent out in the early months of the war[59] Women's magazines provided instructions and patterns for knitting caps, socks, gloves, and other clothing items (Figure 9.4).

Belgian refugees were also in need of warm clothing, as well as food and blankets. Many female Belgian refugees were employed in the fashion industry, and were recompensed with one item of clothing per week, as well as their salary.[60] A fashion school in Amsterdam organized a drive to help Belgian families; during their vacation, each student had to knit one sweater.[61]

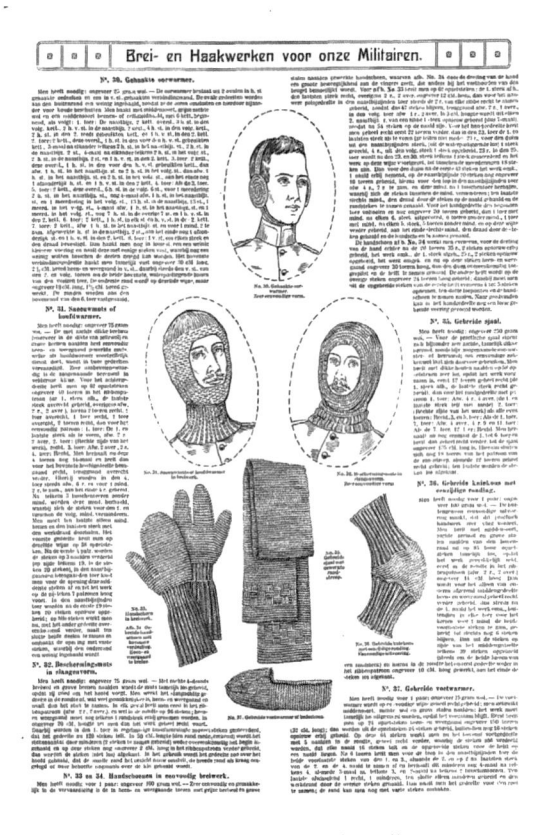

Figure 9.3 *Knitting for soldiers.* Gracieuse, no. 19: 13 (1914). Collection: Kunstmuseum, Den Haag.

These efforts were an undeniable boon to the popularity of needlework, and were accompanied by renewed interest from women in making their own clothes, in order to compensate for the rising cost of living.[62] Homemade clothing existed in the Netherlands prior to the war, and multiple magazines for patterns had been published since the latter half of the nineteenth century.[63] However, the homemade had become less popular at the end of the century, as industrial production was often cheaper and of higher quality, as evidenced by the following statement issued in the early months of the war:

Knitting stockings! Who did not learn that at school? Then, they invented a machine that could do the work more quickly. When factories began producing knitted goods that were shinier and straighter than the ones made by hand—when manufacturers were capable of producing an inexhaustible supply of cheap socks and stockings—we packed up the knitting needles that had been in our hands all day long. Schools stopped teaching the practice.[64]

The war brought the practice back in full. The resultant handmade clothes were simple and practical, and while they began as a product of necessity, they soon became fashionable, and even a

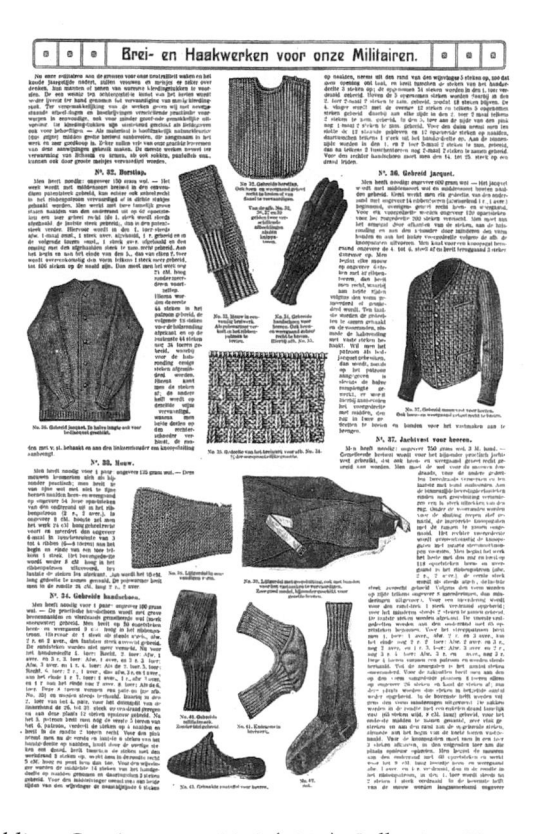

Figure 9.4 *Knitting for soldiers.* Gracieuse, no. 20: 9 (1917). Collection: Kunstmuseum, Den Haag.

symbol of elegance at times. As one journalist wrote in *De Gracieuze*, "In this time of war, knitting has once again become appreciated, not only for making clothes for soldiers, but also, in service of fashion. We now wear dresses that are shorter and wider, with white stockings that we make ourselves."[65] Women organized informal groups to knit together and to teach the practice to young girls. In an article published in 1915 in *Vrouw en haar Huis*, the journalist Geertruida Carelsen argued that handsewing was superior to machine work in certain instances, and called on women to repair their used and damaged clothing: "The needle is very useful for small reparations. Here and there, you can resew a small tear to prevent the hole from widening, disguise worn fabric with a small pleat, or connect two pieces that are too delicate for the machine."[66]

Generally, women's magazines devoted an increasing amount of space to the reparation and reuse of old clothing, as well as to advice on transforming cheap dresses into fashionable ones. The magazines also advised, especially after 1917, that due to a shortage of soap, women should avoid wearing light clothing in favor of darker fabric. They suggested that readers make their own fabric and clothing from the cotton that was available in stores, a method that was particularly popular with women in the countryside.[67] For work clothing, women's magazines presented a number of replicable designs which used embroidery and other forms of ornamentation: "These are hard times! Prices are high in every sector, we're continuously confronted with harsh realities, and it has become more practical to create all of the decorations for our clothes at home."[68] While embroidery was already popular in major magazines such as *Le Gracieuse* and *Vrouw en haar Huis* before the war, it soon gained even greater prominence as a practical solution for making simple clothes chic and elegant. It also happened to be in line with the fashions coming out of Paris, as houses such as Chanel, Doucet, and Premet, for instance, began featuring embroidery in their designs as well.

During this era, Dutch women, notably in the northern province of Friesland, still wore regional costumes with white lace Dutch bonnets. Due to supply problems, women began to knit their caps themselves—several examples are today conserved at the Fries Museum in Leeuwarden.[69] At the beginning of the war, *Onze Kleeding* wrote that one had to dress in a manner that was practical, simple, and sound.[70] In 1914, the association organized a number of exhibitions in Amsterdam, Rotterdam, Groningen, and Den Bosch to showcase and promote such simple designs. Women's interest in these exhibitions was substantial, confirming that the seeming fascination with home clothing production was not simply propaganda released through women's magazines, but a real response to the problems caused by the war.[71]

Conclusion

The state of industrial and home clothing production in the Netherlands during the First World War can only be understood in relation to the complex political, economic, and social phenomena that were reshaping the country. The war had a considerable effect on factory production and served as a test to the nation's self-sufficiency. From 1914 until 1916, the situation appeared advantageous for the Dutch economy, as trade with the neighboring British and German empires continued. After submarine warfare between these two parties heightened in the North Sea in 1917, trade became difficult and economic prospects dimmed. Poverty increased substantially, affecting factory workers, who were already economically vulnerable before the war.

While the country did not develop a veritable national identity in terms of its wardrobe, it did seek to emancipate itself from Parisian influences, as foreign fashion revealed itself to be poorly suited towards the country's new ways of life. Thus, clothing that was simple, practical, and easy to make by hand became recognized as typically Dutch. Nevertheless, after the war's end, Paris continued to dominate the Dutch market and sense of style.

The war caused an increase in homemade clothing production. Needlework was practiced before the war, but the conflict engendered it with new meaning; it was not only a practical response to shortages and economic difficulties, but soon became fashionable in its own right. It served as a social, communal practice, and as a sign of one's personal contribution to the war effort. While Dutch women were fighting for their voting rights and for improved living conditions, they were concurrently demonstrating that they were good mothers, wives, and citizens.

The situation in the Netherlands during the war was undoubtedly preferable to that in neighboring countries engaged in warfare. It might appear less exciting to study clothing production and living conditions in a country that remained neutral throughout the conflict, but as we delve deeper, we find nuances in the country's approach towards production that reveal much about its overall response to wartime.

Notes

1 The following works address the history of the Netherlands during the war: Paul Moeyes, Buitenschot: Nederland tijdens de Eerste Wereldoorlog 1914-1918 (Utrecht: Uitgeverij De Arbeiderspers, 2014); Eddy Schaafsma, ed., Onze Eerste Wereldoorlog: Van Aardappeloproer tot Mata Hari: Hoe Neutraal Nederland diep werd Geraakt door de Oorlog van 1914-1918 (Amsterdam: Reed Business Media, 2014); Wim Klinkert, ed., Nederland Neutraal: De Eerste Wereldoorlog 1914-1918 (Amsterdam, Uitgeverij Boom, 2014); Samuel Kruizinga, Overlegeconomie in Oorlogstijd: de Nederlandsche Overzee Trustmaatschappij en de Eerste Wereldoorlog (Zutphen: Walburg Pers, 2012); Wim Klinkert, Defending Neutrality: The Netherlands Prepares for War, 1900-1925 (Leiden: Brill, 2013); Martin Kraaijestein and Paul Schulten, eds., Wankel Evenwicht: Neutraal Nederland en de Eerste Wereldoorlog (Soesterberg: Aspekt, 2007); and Maartje Abbenhuis-Ash, The Art of Staying Neutral: The Netherlands in the First World War, 1914-1918 (Amsterdam: Amsterdam University Press, 2006).

2 Ismee Tames, "Oorlog voor onze Gedachten." Oorlog, Neutraliteit en Identiteit in het Nederlandse Publieke Debat, 1914-1918 (Hilversum: Uitgeverij Verloren, 2006); Martin Philip Bossenbroek, Geert Laporte, J. B. C. Kruishoop, Romain Van Eenoo, M. De Waele, and H. W. Von der Dunk, Vluchten voor de Groote Oorlog: Belgen in Nederland 1914-1918 (Amsterdam: De Bataafsche Leeuw, 1988); and Michael Amara, Vluchten voor de Oorlog: Belgische vluchtelingen 1914-1918 (Gent: Davidsfonds, 2004).

3 Hanneke Hoekstra, Het Hart van de Hatie: Morele Verontwaardiging en Politieke Verandering in Nederland 1870-1919 (Deventer: Kluwer, 2006).

4 Among others: Margaret Darrow, French Women and the First World War: War Stories of the Home Front (Oxford and New York: Bloomsbury Academic, 2000); Claire A. Culleton, Working-Class Culture, Women and Britain, 1914-1921 (London: Palgrave Macmillan, 2000); Erika A. Kuhlman, Petticoats and White Feathers: Gender Conformity, Race, the Progressive Peace Movement, and the Debate over War 1895-1919 (Westport, CT, and London: Greenwood Press, 1997); Susan R. Grayzel, Women and the First World War (London: Routledge, 2002); Arthur Marwick, Women at War, 1914-1918 (London: Fontana for the Imperial War Museum, 1977).

5 Lucy Adlington, Great War Fashion: Tales from the History Wardrobe (Stroud: History Press, 2014); ibid., Fashion: Women in World War One (Stroud: History Press, 2014); Barton Hacker and Margaret Vining, "Cutting a new pattern: Uniforms and women's mobilization for war 1854-1919," Textile History 41 (2010): 108-43.

6 The political and religious affiliations of each newspaper must be taken into account. Their biases force us to use prudence, but also allow us to observe reality reflected through various perspectives.

7 Christine Delhaye, *Door Consumptie tot Individu: Modebladen in Nederland 1880–1914* (Amsterdam: Amsterdam University Press, 2008), 14.

8 This organization also led courses in fashion design and production, and organized exhibitions to promote clothing that was practical and comfortable.

9 This cost only included mailing and administration. *De Gracieuse*, January 1, 1916, 1.

10 "Prijzen der Knippatronen," *De Vrouw en haar Huis*, 11, March, 1915, 372.

11 "Knippatronen," *Onze Kleeding*, 10, October 1, 1918, 67.

12 Dirk Starink, *De Jonge Jaren van de Luchtmacht: Het Luchtwapen in het Nederlandse Leger 1913–1939* (Amsterdam: Uitgeverij Boom, 2013), 90–1. It has been estimated that 1 million Belgian refugees arrived in the Netherlands at the start of the war: 500,000 in Brabant, 400,000–500,000 in Zeeland, and the rest in Limburg, see Amara, *Vluchten voor de Oorlog*, 13.

13 The organization *De Nederlandsche Overzee Trust Maatschappij* (The Dutch Overseas Trust Company, or NOT) was created in November 2014. This organization regulated commerce with neighboring countries and responded to their demands. It served as a means to ensure the Netherlands' political neutrality during the war.

14 "Een Gevaar voor de Textielindustrie," *Het Volk: Dagblad voor de arbeiderspartij*, November 13, 1914, 5.

15 Marjolein Morée and Marjan Schwegman, *Vrouwenarbeid in Nederland* (Rijswijk: Elmar 1981), 105.

16 "De Vrouw: De Mode in Oorlogstijd," *Algemeen Handelsblad*, September 28, 1914.

17 Hoekstra, *Het hart van de natie*, 168–77.

18 Remieg Aerts, Herman De Liagre Böhl, Piet De Rooy, and Henk Te Velde, *Land van Kleine Gebaren: Een Politieke Geschiedenis van Nederland 1780–1990* (Nijmegen: Sun 1999), 161–75.

19 The International Congress of Women organized a conference in The Hague on the subject of pacifism in 1915, which proved to be one of the most important events for the women's movement during the war. A report on the Congress was published in the magazine: "Indrukken van het Internationaal Congress van Vrouwen," *De Vrouw en haar Huis*, 2, June 1915, 52–7.

20 "De Vrouwen tegen de Duurte," *Het Volk: Dagblad voor de Arbeiderspartij*, September 17, 1915, 5 (a petition signed in Dordrecht); "De Vrouwen in Actie," *Algemene Nieuwsblad*, February 2, 1917, s. 9. (a delegation of women who met with the mayor of Leiden); "De Straat Betogingen," *Het Volk: Dagblad voor de Arbeiderspartij*, February 6, 1917, 5 (a demonstration of women in Rotterdam).

21 Hoekstra, *Het hart van de natie*, 177.

22 "Het Werk onzer Nederlandsche Vrouwen," *De Vrouw en haar huis*, 9, January, 1915, 294–6.

23 J. Stärcke, "Van Oorlog en Vrede en van Onpraktische Kleding," *Onze Kleeding*, 9, September 1, 1914, 135–6.

24 Ibid.

25 "*Geheugen van Nederland*," at: http://www.geheugenvannederland.nl/?/nl/items/SFA03:SFA022804910/&p=1&i=19&t=52&st=rode%20kruis%20eerste%20wereldoorlog&sc=%28cql.serverChoice%20all%20rode%20%20AND%20kruis%20%20AND%20eerste%20%20AND%20wereldoorlog%29/&wst=rode%20kruis%20eerste%20wereldoorlog (accessd June 26, 2020).

26 A. van Schelven, *Vereniging Het Nederlandsch Economisch-Historisch Archief, Textiel, Kleding-, Leder-, Schoen-e.a. Lederwaren Industrie: Een Geschiedenis en Bronnenoverzicht* (Amsterdam: NEHA, 1993), 26.

27 Friso Wielenga, *Nederland in de Twintigste Eeuw* (Amsterdam: Uitgeverij Boom, 2009), 74.

28 "De Oorlog en de Vrouwenkleding," *De Gracieuse*, 19, October 1, 1914–November 1, 1914, 4.

29 Ibid.

30 "De Huidige Toestand van Textiel-branche," *Middelburgsche Courant*, April 8, 1916, 3.

31 "Uit de Textiel-industrie," *Tilburgsche Courant*, February 6, 1917, 2.

32 "Het Oorlogsgevaar: Gebrek aan Naai-garen," *Het Volk: Dagblad voor de Arbeiderspartij*, August 22, 1916, 3.

33 "Nederland en de Oorlog: Export-Centrale," *Algemeen Handelsblad*, May 23, 1917, 5.

34 "Werkloosheid te Enschede," *Nieuwsblad van Friesland: Hepkema's Courant*, May 27, 1917, 1.

35 "Rubriek voor Vrouwen: Mode en Kleeding," *Nieuwsblad van het Noorden*, December 23, 1916, 17.

36 André Bauwens and Miranda Haak, *Bange Jaren: Zeeuws-Vlaanderen en de Eerste Wereldoorlog* (Heemkundige Kring West-Zeeuws-Vlaanderen 2014).

37 Ibid.

38 "Rotterdamsch Nieuws: De Dringende Behoefte aan Kleeding en Schoeisel," *Het Volk: Dagblad voor de Arbeiderspartij*, January 18, 1915, 6.

39 *Commissie tot Verstrekking Hoofdzakelijk van Kleeding en Dekking aan Minvermogenden en Algemene Vergaderingen 1908–1916*, Utrecht Archieven 727.30.

40 "Het Onbevoegd Dragen van Militaire Kleeding," *De Telegraaf*, June 13, 1919, 5.

41 "Diefstal," *Nieuwe Tilburgsche Courant*, June, 1917, 5; "Aangehouden," *Algemeen Handelsblad*, June 8, 1919, 2.

42 In the 1910s, the association Onze Kleeding collaborated with the German Movement for the Betterment of Women's Clothing (Deutscher Verband für Neue Frauenkleidung und Frauenkultur). "Het Herstellen van Waschbare Stoffen," *De Gracieuse*, 24, December 15, 1915, 1.

43 "Allerlei: De Fransche Modejournalen," *De Telegraaf*, December 13, 1916, 8.

44 "Onze Kleeding," *Algemeen Handelsblad*, November 13, 1914, 5.

45 "Nieuwe, Eenvoudige Wintermodes," *De Gracieuse*, 23, December 1, 1914, 1.

46 "De Vrouw: De Mode in Oorlogstijd," *Algemeen Handelsblad*, November 28, 1914, 3.

47 *Onze Kleeding*, *Algemeen Handelsblad*, November 13, 1914, p. 5.

48 Ibid. "De Vrouw: De Mode in Oorlogstijd," p. 3.

49 "Tegen de Wijde Rokken," *De Tijd: Godsdienstig-Staatkundig Dagblad*, March 23, 1916, 5; "De Vrouw: Tirannie van de Mode," *Algemeen Handelsblad*, May 13, 1916, 9.

50 "De Vrouw CXCVIII: De Mode," ibid., March 18, 1917, 18.

51 "Brieven uit de Hoofdstad," *Leeuwarder Courant*, April 7, 1917, 9.

52 On the subject of Hirsch & Cie: Femke Knoop, *Hirsch & Cie: Amsterdam (1882–1976): Haute Couture op het Leidseplein* (Hilversum: Uitgeverij Verloren, 2018).

53 "De Vrouw CXCVIII: De Mode," *Algemeen Handelsblad*, March 18, 1917, 18.

54 Ibid.

55 Frieda Sorber, "Homemade fashions: Fact or fiction?," *Living Fashion: Women's Daily Wear 1750–1950: From the Jacoba de Jonge Collection* (Tielt: Uitgeverij Lannoo, 2012), 123–35.

56 Moeyes, *Buitenschot*. s. 68–9.

57 "Brei- en Haakwerken voor onze Militairen," *De Gracieuse*, 19, October 1, 1914, 13.

58 "Bivakmutsen," *Algemeen Nieuwsblad*, December 4, 1914, 6.

59 The president of the commission organizing this effort was the Baron van Voorsttot Voorst-Cremes, a resident of Arnhem. "Voor de Militairen," *De Tijd: Godsdienstig-staatkundig Dagblad*, March 29, 1915, 1.

60 Bossenbroek, *Vluchten voor de Grote Oorlog*, 40.

61 Tweer-Westerman, J., "De Vakschool Commissie," *Onze Kleeding*, 4, April 1, 1915, 38.

62 Notably in short supply were energy, fuel, leather, fabric, thread, soap, and foodstuffs such as potatoes, flour, and meat. These products were very expensive, and either of poor quality or entirely unavailable.

63 Tweer-Westerman, "De Vakschool Commissie," 38.

64 E. M. Rogge, "Een Oud Handwerk in Eere Hersteld," *Vrouw en haar Huis*, 6, October 1914, 193.

65 "Met de Hand Gebreide Dames- en Kinder—Kousen met Open Patronen," *De Gracieuse*, 13, July 1, 1915, 3.

66 G. Carelsen, "De Naald," *Vrouw en haar Huis*, 11, March, 1915, 363.

67 "Zeepratsoen," *Onze Kleeding*, 4, April 1 1917, 45.

68 "De Vrouw CCXXIV: Borduursel," *Algemeen Handelsblad*, September 16, 1917, 5.

69 The author would like to thank Gieneke Arnolli, a restorer in the Fabric and Costumes Department of the Fries Museum in Leeuwarden, who generously shared her knowledge of Friesian dress and other important pieces in the museum.

70 "Onze Taak in de Naaste Toekomst," *Onze Kleeding*, 9, November 1, 1914, 1–2.

71 Tweer-Westerman, "De Vakschool Commissie," s. 38.

References

Abbenhuis-Ash, Maartje. *The Art of Sstaying Neutral: The Netherlands in the First World War 1914–1918*. Amsterdam: Amsterdam University Press, 2006.
Adlington, Lucy. *Fashion: Women in World War One*. Stroud: History Press, 2014.
Adlington, Lucy. *Great War Fashion: Tales from the History Wardrobe*. Stroud: History Press, 2014.
Aerts, Remieg, Herman De Liagre Böhl, Piet De Rooy, and Henk Te Velde. *Land van kleine gebaren. Een politieke geschiedenis van Nederland 1780–1990*. Nijmegen: Sun, 1999.
Algemeen Handelsblad, 1914–19.
Algemeen Nieuwsblad, 1914.
Amara, Michael. *Vluchten voor de oorlog. Belgische vluchtelingen 1914–1918*. Gent: Davidsfonds, 2004.
Bauwens, André and Haak Miranda. *Bange jaren. Zeeuws-Vlaanderen en de Eerste Wereldoorlog*. Heemkundige Kring West-Zeeuws-Vlaanderen, 2014.

Bossenbroek, Martin Philip, Geert Laporte, J. B. C. Kruishoop, Romain Van Eenoo, M. De Waele, and H. W. Von der Dunk. *Vluchten voor de Groote Oorlog. Belgen in Nederland 1914-1918*. Amsterdam: De Bataafsche Leeuw, 1988.
Commissie tot Verstrekking Hoofdzakelijk van Kleeding en Dekking aan Minvermogenen en Algemene Vergaderingen 1908-1916, Utrecht Archieven 727.30.
Culleton, Claire A. *Working-Class Culture, Women and Britain, 1914-1921*. London: Palgrave Macmillan, 2000.
Cunningham, Patricia A. *Reforming Women's Fashion, 1850-1920: Politics, Health and Art*. Kent, OH: Kent State University Press, 2003.
Darrow, Margaret H. *French Women and the First World War: War Stories of the Home Front*. Oxford and New York: Bloomsbury Academic, 2000.
De Gracieuse, 1914-16.
De Telegraaf, 1916-19.
De Tijd: Godsdienstig-Staatkundig Dagblad, 1915-16.
De Vrouw en haar Huis, 1914-15.
Delhaye, Christine. *Door consumptie tot individu: Modebladen in Nederland 1880-1914*. Amsterdam: Amsterdam University Press, 2008.
"Geheugen van Nederland." Available at: http://www.geheugenvannederland.nl/?/nl/items/SFA03:SFA022804910/&p=1&i=19&t=52&st=rode%20kruis%20eerste%20wereldoorlog&sc=%28cql.serverChoice%20all%20rode%20%20AND%20kruis%20%20AND%20eerste%20%20AND%20wereldoorlog%29/&wst=rode%20kruis%20eerste%20wereldoorlog (accessed June 26, 2020).
Grayzel, Susan R. *Women and the First World War*. London: Routledge, 2002.
Hacker, Barton and Vining Margeret. "Cutting a new pattern: uniforms and women's mobilization for war 1854-1919," *Textile History* 41 (2010): 10843.
Het Volk: Dagblad voor de Arbeiderspartij, 1914-16.
Hoekstra, Hanneke. *Het hart van de natie. Morele verontwaardiging en politieke verandering in Nederland 1870-1919*. Deventer: Kluwer, 2006.
Klinkert, Wim. *Defending Neutrality: The Netherlands Prepares for War, 1900-1925*. Leiden: Brill, 2013.
Klinkert, Wim, ed. *Nederland neutraal. De Eerste Wereldoorlog 1914-1918*. Amsterdam: Uitgeverij Boom, 2014.
Knoop, Femke. *Hirsch & Cie. Amsterdam (1882-1976). Haute couture op het Leidseplein*. Hilversum: Verloren, 2018.
Kraaijestein, Martin and Paul Schulten, eds. *Wankelevenwicht. Neutraal Nederland en de Eerste Wereldoorlog*. Soesterberg: Aspekt, 2007.
Kruizinga, Samuel. *Overlegeconomie in oorlogstijd. De Nederlandsche Overzee Trustmaatschappij en de Eerste Wereldoorlog*. Zutphen: Walburg Pers, 2012.
Kuhlman, Erika A. *Petticoats and White Feathers: Gender Conformity, Race, the Progressive Peace Movement, and the Debate over War, 1895-1919*. Westport, CT, and London: Greenwood Press, 1997.
Leeuwarder Courant, 1916.
Marwick, Arthur. *Women at War, 1914-1918*. London: Fontana for the Imperial War Museum, 1977.
Middelburgsche Courant, 1916.
Moeyes, Paul. *Buitenschot. Nederland tijdens de Eerste Wereldoorlog 1914-1918*. Utrecht: Uitgeverij De Arbeiderspers, 2014.
Morée, Marjolein and Marjan Schwegman. *Vrouwenarbeid in Nederland*. Rijswijk: Elmar, 1981.
Nieuwsblad van Friesland: Hepkema's Courant, 1917.
Nieuwsblad van het Noorden, 1916.
Onze Kleeding, 1914-18.
Schaafsma, Eddy, ed. *Onze Eerste Wereldoorlog. Van Aardappeloproer tot Mata Hari. Hoe neutraal Nederland diep werd geraakt door de oorlog van 1914-1918*. Amsterdam: Reed Business Media, 2014.
Schnitger, Carin and Goldhoorn Inge. *Reformkleding in Nederland*. Utrecht: Centraal Museum Utrecht, 1984.
Sorber, Frieda. "Homemade fashions: Fact or fiction?" *Living Fashion: Women's Daily Wear 1750-1950: From the Jacoba de Jonge Collection*. Tielt: Uitgeverij Lannoo, 2012.

Starink, Dirk. *De jonge jaren van de luchtmacht. Het luchtwapen in het Nederlandse leger 1913–1939*. Amsterdam: Uitgeverij Boom, 2013.

Tames, Ismee. *"Oorlog voor onze gedachten." Oorlog, neutraliteit en identiteit in het Nederlandse publieke debat, 1914–1918*. Hilversum: Uitgeverij Verloren, 2006.

Tilburgsche Courant, 1917.

van Schelven, A., *Textiel-, kleding-, leder-, schoen-e.a. lederwaren industrie. Een geschiedenis en bronnenoverzicht*. Amsterdam: NEHA, 1993.

Wielenga, Friso. *Nederland in de twintigste eeuw*. Amsterdam: Uitgeverij Boom, 2009.

10

Wartime fabrics in the historical archives of Como weavers and in the collections of the Fondazione Antonio Ratti

Margherita Rosina

The archives of Como manufacturers, which have never been studied before, and sample books held at the textile museum Museo Studio del Tessuto (MuST), which is part of the Fondazione Antonio Ratti (FAR), in Como, highlight how high-level Italian silk production never ceased during the war.[1] This essay focuses on silk fabrics, since they are the production of excellence of the Como district as well as the main field covered by Antonio Ratti's collecting practice.

The supremacy of France in the silk weaving trade remained undisputed for at least three centuries and was still unchallenged in the early twentieth century. By the start of the First World War, Italian silk mills were making good-quality products that could have, indeed, competed with those produced in Lyon. For what concerned woolen fabrics, though, Italy was still dependent on imports. The most authoritative women's magazine in Italy during the period of World War I, *Margherita*, reported in October 1914 that: "whilst our silk industry has made surprising progress, to the point of seriously competing with Lyon itself, the same cannot be said—at least not for the moment—of woollen fabrics. For these, the supremacy of France, Germany and Britain remains undisputed."[2]

Italian silk fabrics for clothing were produced mainly in the Como area, where many medium-sized manufactures were in a position to meet internal demand and attract orders from abroad. Historical texts on weaving in Como and orders found among the few extant paper documents held in private Como archives confirm this.[3] The biggest part of the work was carried out in the surrounding area, where families owned looms enabling them to work at home. On the eve of the First World War, firms like Bressi owned 250 handlooms and 25 Jacquards;[4] Casnati had 360 Jacquard looms that produced plain silks of the most varied qualities, had salespersons around the world, and won prizes at world exhibitions;[5] Rosasco employed about 500 people in the production of plain silks and linings;[6] and Luigi Taroni specialized in high fashion garments made with Brianza silk on mechanical as well as manual looms.[7]

In fact, the First World War was beneficial to silk manufacturers:

> Many of the looms of the world, which have heretofore given so much of their time to the weaving of beautiful stuffs for women to wear, are delegated to the sterner tasks of making uniform materials. Until now, the main business of weavers has been to dress women; men were clothed in what was left. Now men, the warriors of the world, must be clothed in such a way as to resist cold and wet, and women must be clothed in that which he does not need. This means a revolution in the making of textiles, and from this revolution, as with other revolutions, there will undoubtedly be many benefits. . . . Since man needs wool to keep him warm and dry, woman is requested—in fact she is in eminent danger of being summarily ordered—to wear silk.[8]

Wool was a raw material saved worldwide for soldiers at the front.[9] Silk became, out of necessity, one of the materials that could be most widely employed. This was particularly true towards the end of the war, *Margherita* also observed: "One of the principal consequences of the cornering of wool by the army has been the democratization of silk. Grownups and kids adopt it for dresses and cloaks, whilst wool is used only for trimmings."[10]

It is difficult to get a comprehensive view of wartime Como production as none of the manufacturers operating at that time and mentioned earlier are still active today. The surviving production archives covering those years are very few and incomplete. This makes it impossible to give an exhaustive account of what was being woven in the Como area or to make comparisons in terms of quality or quantity with the corresponding output in Lyon. The textile samples considered by this research only represent what can be dated with certainty from the period of the First World War, originating from the few sample books found.

The FISAC silk-mill wartime production

Among the silk mills operating in Como during the First World War, one of the most important was FISAC (Fabbriche Italiane di Seterie A. Clerici Sa). This firm was established in 1906, following the closure of Sas Braghenti Clerici & Co, which had been founded in 1890 and converted into Fabbriche Italiane di Seterie Clerici Braghenti & Co in 1902.[11] What remains today of the FISAC production archive is divided between Guarisco spa in Grandate, which took over the firm's premises at the time of its closure, and the Fondazione Antonio Ratti, which acquired a substantial number of its sample books. Since the corresponding paper documentation is unfortunately patchy, this material cannot be fully placed within its proper context.

FISAC's production consisted mainly of plain and figured fabrics for womenswear, in pure silk or in silk and cotton blends. These range from large floral patterns, in pastel shades or sharp color contrasts, to small brocaded motifs on taffetas. Numerous striped samples are also present; many of them feature a black-and-white contrast. This was one of the most fashionable trends of the 1910s, as witnessed by the journals and photographs of the era.[12]

It is difficult to say to what extent the war caused changes in production. There are no sensible differences between what was produced in the period between the beginning of the century and the outbreak of war and what can be gathered from the textile records of wartime years.

The FISAC color range between 1915 and 1918 continued to be just as extensive and rich with bright colors. This contradicts the news, as reported several times by the magazine *Margherita*, of a shortage of the dyes necessary to the textile industry. It also goes against the observations made by Jacqueline Field, who noticed a change in textile production in the United States due to a lack of dyes that had until then been imported from Germany.[13]

The Como silk industry does not appear to have been affected by this problem. The consumption of silk for women's fashion only represented a small section of the market since the articles made from this precious material were aimed for an elite market.[14] The amount of dyes required was therefore limited and could be found even under such exceptional circumstances as war. Nor does the war seem to be reflected in FISAC's output, which shows no hints of patriotism. Only the emphatic presence of black crêpe samples in different weights may, perhaps, be related to the veils worn by women in mourning, whose numbers dramatically increased during the conflict.

Parravicini & Co.

Another extant archive is that of the firm Parravicini & Co., now held by Industria Serica Taroni in Grandate. Parravicini had its headquarters in via Morazzone in Como. When Taroni was founded in 1921, it took over the Parravicini factory and also acquired its archives. Parravicini's earliest *contremarque* books date from 1913 and show that the firm's output was based on good-quality yarn-dyed silk in a broad color range, although most of its production remained confined to black and to neutral shades.

As in the case of FISAC, black and white striped samples often appear. The books cover all the war years, highlighting orders from Italy and abroad which show that trade was both brisk and international. In 1915, orders were placed by Ambrogio Spada, which had offices both at Lierna (Como) and in Buenos Aires; in February 1916, orders were placed by Aldermanbury & Co. of London; in November of that year, orders came from Baily & Huber, London, for miscellaneous pieces of *paillette glacé* in a wide variety of shades. Another London customer was Angel & Spiro, "Manufacturers and Silk Merchants," who bought numerous items in many color variants from Parravicini.

A careful examination of the surviving *contremarque* books clearly shows that Parravicini's production, which has unfortunately survived only in tiny samples, presented no particular wartime novelties. From 1913, however, heavy dark blue or black satins began to appear, characterized by highly particular selvedges, which sometimes were in nuanced colors or striped bands. In one or two cases, patriotic combinations were used in these selvedges during the war years, such as red, white, and green, or red, white, and blue, or black, yellow and red. Why devote so much work and so many precious dyes to a part of the fabric that is in reality normally cut while the garment is being made up, and is, in any case, not visible? A scholar of Como weaving, Pietro Pinchetti, writing at the end of the nineteenth century, defined selvedge as "the clue to the piece," by which he meant that selvedges were an indication of the yarn quality and weaver's ability, especially in the simpler fabrics.[15]

It has not been possible to find garments of the war period that were made with fabrics with selvedges like those by Parravicini. Yet, a brief mention from the magazine *Margherita* in 1915 does perhaps provide a clue in this respect: "attractive for informal wear is the blue marine serge with a high hem in small blue and wine-red stripes, to be used on the neck or waistcoat and for skirt pockets."[16] Could this have been the purpose of the striped selvedges? During the war, to display the colors of one's flag might have been an indirect way of supporting the soldiers at the front. Given Parravicini's international contacts, it is possible that similar textiles may have also been produced to meet foreign orders. A suit, cut in the manner of a military uniform, featured in the American magazine *The Dry Goods Reporter*, was decorated at the cuffs with a thin edge that appears to be tricolored.[17]

A 10 cm ribbon of Savoy-blue silk *gros*, crossed at the center by the red, white, and green stripes of the Italian flag, produced in 1917 and repeated in 1918, was certainly meant to be patriotic. We know that Parravicini occasionally produced a ribbon of these measurements, for Italy, other European countries, as well as for Argentina. A ribbon of this size could have served a military purpose, as trimmings for pennants, regimental insignia, or for the manufacture of patriotic cockades.

Fermo Fossati 1871

Not even in the tie sector, represented by the archives of Fermo Fossati 1871, another historic Como manufacturer, do any patriotic signs appear.[18] And, yet, this company had celebrated the 1911 war in Libya with ties decorated on the front side with the names of Italian victories or with miniature scenes depicting the conflict. And, in the 1930s, it paid homage to fascism with a line of ties glorifying the Duce.[19]

The weave patterns dating from between 1915 and 1918, and the related small samples of silk created, reflect a traditional production of polka-dotted and minute geometric motifs, interspersed with the occasional fine Paisley pattern in the first year (for Italy) of the war, without any reference to the war itself. The completeness of this archive, on the other hand, points to a drastic drop in production, which plummeted from more than one hundred new patterns per year of the prewar period, to approximately fifty for the period of 1916–18. The quality of the fabrics, too, deteriorated, with poorly beaten or opaque-looking silks. One of the causes of the lower output of ties may be identified with the very small number of civilians still around at the time. The war throughout Europe had put two generations of men into uniform, notably reducing the market.

French wartime silk production

The archives of the Fondazione Antonio Ratti hold a considerable number of sample albums of French silks, covering the years of the First World War. These are product samples, purchased by Antonio Ratti as a source of inspiration for his work. In the majority of cases, there are no paper documents to date them with certainty.

Among the more conspicuous items are the books of Chavent Père & Fils of Lyon, which cover an extraordinarily long period from the second half of the nineteenth century to the Second World War. These books contain textiles for womenswear, used by many important French couture houses, including Worth.[20] Despite the lack of reliable dating, the comparison with contemporary textiles shows that production was not conditioned by the conflict. During the war, Chavent continued create new, mostly floral, motifs.

The books of the Lyon firm Boisson & Fesquet, complete with explanatory notes on the dating and composition of its samples, are noticeable both for the completeness of their technical and industrial data, and for the attention paid to the subject of the war. Since the outbreak of the war, a small part of the firm's output included samples with the colors of the French flag. The emphasis on the patriotic theme is unique; it is not seen in the majority of samples of the same period kept in the archives of the Fondazione Antonio Ratti. From a technical point of view, striping is the simplest, fastest and most economical system of effectively evoking patriotic themes. It only requires the preparation of a warp with yarns of different colors to obtain an immediate decorative effect. The Boisson & Fesquet sample books contain veritable French *gros de tour* flags (similar to those seen in Parravicini's Como production), as well as lighter fabrics such as taffeta and *poult de soie* striped in red, white, and blue.

How were these fabrics used? Almost exclusively related to women's apparel, they may have been employed to make plain dresses, perhaps with the odd drapery, or in blouses and waistcoats worn underneath suits. An examination of the fashion magazines of the period, such as *Les Modes, Le Style parisien* and *Les Élégances parisiennes*, helps us imagine how patriotic silks were used in France.[21]

French red-white-blue colorways appear, but so do those of the flag of Belgium, the martyr nation which, despite its neutrality, was invaded by the Germans at the beginning of the war (Figure 10.1). The red, yellow, and black combination is not a random choice or one dictated by fashion; the sample book textually reproduces the wording "Sergé Belgique."[22] It is possible that during the war, the belts of women's dresses may have echoed the tricolor and have been made with fabrics similar to those presented, which celebrate the French and the Belgian flags, respectively (Figure 10.2). Ribbons on the same theme may have become patriotic trimmings on shirt collars.[23]

Another evidence of this wartime trend is represented by the "cartes de nuances" (hue cards), published twice a year by the Chambre Syndicale des Teinturiers (Association of Dyers) in Lyon. Kept in the Fondazione Antonio Ratti collection, the 52 folders cover, except for a few gaps, a period from 1906 to 1932.[24] These *cartes* were working tools for textile mills. Reproduced on every page—there were four to eight pages per book—were minute tufts of yarn-dyed organzine in six graduated shades for each color. They hint at passing color trends. Each color, besides having a numeric reference to the

Figure 10.1 *Lyon, Boisson & Fesquet, Sample of* Taffetas rayé, *1915. Fondazione Antonio Ratti, Como, LC. 1362, p.on 7542.*

Figure 10.2 *Lyon, Boisson & Fesquet, Sample of* Poult de soie rayé, *1914. Fondazione Antonio Ratti, Como, LC. 1362, p.on 7539.*

dye formula, also had a trade name evoking objects, flowers, places, or persons. In the case, for example, of the autumn 1914 *carte de nuances*, groups of skeins in lively tones are gathered under the name of Loie Fuller, the dancer who became famous spinning brightly colored veils as part of her performance.[25] The autumn 1916 edition, besides having fewer pages than usual, titled many of its colors with names closely linked to the war theme, such as "Miss Cawell" (*sic*), "Shrapnel," "Croix de Guerre," or "Lord Kitchener," after the British field marshal who, in June of that year, had perished in the North Sea on a cruiser sunk by the Germans.[26]

Ribbons

The items held in the FAR archive that most frequently refer to the First World War are ribbons: albums contain mostly French ribbons samples produced in the Saint-Étienne area. The wartime albums are the only ones containing explicit patriotic references, with stripes suggesting the colors of flags.

For items of this type, an important market—and one unaffected by fashion—was that of the orders of knighthood and military. These official decorations hung from wide, striped ribbons whose colors denoting their distinction. Heavier ribbons served to hold medals of merit and honors, as witnessed by a fragment kept in a miscellaneous album still bearing the specific words "Croix de Guerre."[27] Another album, also in the MuST archives, preserves other fragments of fabrics with the British flag, probably made for a specific British commission. Their quality and form suggest that they are thin strips to be cut to distinguish military uniforms.[28] Their usage was suggested by Nina Edwards, in her book *Dressed for War*, in which she has the following description:

> An eager English recruit, expecting that war will be a noble experience, finds that uniforms are initially unavailable, so he has to be satisfied with "just a square of card with the name of his regiment stamped on it, together with a bit of red white and blue ribbon attached, and such was sufficient to proclaim to the world at large that we were members of the British Army."[29]

Hats, too, were a way of stating one's patriotism. They had always been decorated with ribbons, but during the war they became expressions of love for one's country. In the FAR collections, there are fragments which refer to the war in their colors and decorative theme. For example, in the sample with a black background and two bands on either side with small tricolor seals, or in the sumptuous trimmings in brocaded satin decorated with the Gallic rooster, symbol of France.[30] A small part of the Boisson & Fesquet production of small textile flags may also probably be traced to this function,[31] as can be seen from two photographs published in *Les Modes* in 1917, illustrating two wide-brimmed hats with the base of the crown surrounded by wide tricolor ribbons.[32]

But above all, it was the patriotic cockades to be pinned onto jackets and hats that kept the ribbon-makers busy. An article published in the 1915 Christmas issue of *Les Modes* illustrates a competition for the creation of patriotic cockades, named after Mimi Pinson, the *grisette* and protagonist of a poem by Alfred de Musset. Entries came from leading Parisian fashion houses:

> Since the fashion shops and ateliers closed, the ones left unemployed have started making emblems for our buttonholes. The Allies supplied all the necessary colors with those of their flags. Fashioned by the women's skilled artists' fingers were firstly cockades, and then a gamut of fascinating feminine knick-knacks. From pin-cushions to garters, came a whole world of infinitely delicate, deliciously subtle coquettishness that never belied the fame of Paris. These works, which are almost works of art—were sold in aid of the wounded.[33]

The article features photographs of the stands mounted by the various couture houses, from that of Worth, decorated on its sides with long tricolor ribbons, to that of Chéruit, which presented rows of small multi-colored cockades in a riot of flags; Maison Callot Sœurs showed the Gallic rooster, symbol of France, standing out among festoons of cockades and charming hats decorated with patriotic ribbons. Another photo illustrated the creations of Paquin: a variety of cockades with original forms which, despite the black and white photograph, manage to convey the liveliness of these small objects. The competition was certainly a popular event, seeing that even the cover of *La Vie Parisienne* was dedicated to it, illustrated with a cockade-skirt in the colors of the French flag.[34]

Conclusion

To conclude, let us look at a ribbon of which unfortunately only a small portion remains (Figure 10.3). Represented in it, enclosed in a single circle divided into four parts, are the flags of the nations that were united as Allies at the outbreak of war: Britain, France, Belgium and Tsarist Russia.[35] The absence of the Italian flag next to those of the Allies dates it before May 24, 1915, when Italy entered the war.

It is technically a bravura piece, which, in a minute amount of space, manages to represent clearly the alliance between the four powers and the tragedy of war. It is a further demonstration of how, alas, war too can provide an interesting market opportunity.[36]

Figure 10.3 *Lyon (?), Fragment of ribbon,* Gros de Tour broché, *1914. Fondazione Antonio Ratti, Como, LC.316, p. 104.*

Notes

1. This essay originates from research first developed for an exhibition held in 2003 at the Museo della Guerra, a war museum in Rovereto, Italy. *Le donne la moda la guerra. Emancipazione femminile e moda durante la prima guerra mondiale*, Rovereto, Museo della Guerra, December 13, 2003–March 14, 2004, exhibition curated by Enrica Morini and Margherita Rosina. The text I wrote for the exhibition catalogue was based more on articles dedicated to textiles in Italian and international fashion magazines of that period than on the direct consultation of production archives. For the conference, "Fashion, Dress & Society during World War I," the sources of evidence for the research were broadened.

2. *Margherita*, October 1914.

3. Francesco Scardin, *L'Italia nei grandi esponenti della produzione*, vol. 1 *La Lombardia* (Milan: Capriolo & Massimino, 1912), 174–212.

4. Ibid., 176.

5. Ibid., 185.

6. Ibid., 180.

7. Ibid., 192.

8. "Patriotic fabrics to charm the New Mode," *Vogue*, March 15, 1918, 35–6.

9. "Save wool and serve the soldier," *Vogue*, February 1, 1918:

    At first the Government thought that the wool situation could be handled without restrictions, but recently it has placed wool under the control of the War Trade Board. Before this, however, the manufacturers and the makers of clothes had begun to conserve wool. To this end the men tailors are agreed that civilians shall sacrifice the flaps upon their coat pockets, the cuffs upon their trousers, and the belts upon their coats and overcoats. But when it comes to women the matter is much more difficult. . . . At a recent meeting in New York, the important makers of women's clothes agreed to use no more than four and one-half yards of material fifty-four inches wide in any suit or dress for spring and, if possible, to limit the quantity of material to three yards.

10. *Margherita*, June 1918.

11. Francina Chiara, "Indice documentario delle aziende," in *Seta. Il Novecento a Como*, Chiara Buss, ed. (Milano: Silvana Editoriale, 2001), 336.

12. *Les Modes*, February 1916, 15, "robe d'aprés-midi per Zimmermann"; *Margherita*, June 15, 1916.

13. Jacqueline Field, "Dyes, chemistry and clothing: The influence of World War I on fabrics, fashions and silk," *Dress* 28 (2001): 77–91.

14. Before the introduction of artificial and synthetic fibers, the ones most employed in clothing were wool, cotton, hemp, and linen; silk, a luxury fiber, only covered a small portion of the market.

15. Pietro Pinchetti (1838–1916) was a prominent professor at the Istituto Setificio, the training school in Como for workers in the silk industry. Pinchetti authored many publications on the techniques and history of silk-weaving, including a historical manual for weavers, c.f. Pietro Pinchetti, *Manuale del Tessitore* (Milan: Hoepli, 1907).

16. *Margherita*, October 15, 1915.

17. *The Dry Goods Reporter*, January 15, 1916, pl. XVI, at: http://babel.hathitrust.org/cgi/pt?id=uiug.30112106960112; view=1up;seq=109 (accessed August 20, 2020).

18 Francina Chiara, "Indice documentario delle aziende," 336.

19 Chiara Buss, ed., *Seta. Il Novecento a Como* (Milan: Silvana Editoriale, 2001), 206.

20 Margherita Rosina, ed., *Ritratti di signore. Tessuto moda e pittura tra Otto e Novecento* (Como: Fondazione Antonio Ratti, 2011), 30.

21 By way of example, cfr. *Les Modes*, February 1914, 15, "robe d'aprés-midi par Zimmermann"; April 1914, 16, "M.lle Lena Bruze du Théatre Impérial habillée par Parent Sœurs"; May 1914, 18, "Robe d'aprés midi par M. Marcel Regis"; *Le Style parisien*, 1915, figure 275, "Robe d'aprés-midi par Lanvin"; *Les Élégances parisiennes*, May 1916, figure 88 and 102, "Robes d'aprés-midi par Redfern."

22 Fondazione Antonio Ratti, LC. 123 and 1632, p. on 7603.

23 Adelheid Rasche, ed., *Wardrobes in Wartime, 1914–1918* (Berlin and Leipzig: Kunstbibliothek Staatliche Museen zu Berlin and E.A. Seemann Verlag, 2014), 90.

24 Chiara Buss, "Le 'Carte de Nuances' lionesi della Collezione Antonio Ratti," in *Seta e Colore* (Milan: Ratti s.p.a., 1997): 85–191.

25 FAR, MuST, LC. 892.

26 Edith Cavell (1865–1915) was a British nurse, based in Brussels, who was executed by the German forces in 1915. Cavell aided the escape of 200 British and French soldiers during the German occupation of Belgium. She was court martialed for war treason and sentenced to death, despite the numerous efforts of international governments and the press. Shrapnel is an anti-personnel shell containing a large number of bullets or metal objects, which are thrown in the air by an explosion. It was invented by the British general, Henry Shrapnel, in 1784. It was first used in 1808 by the British Army against the French Army, during the Battle of Vimeiro in Portugal, and was later extensively employed during the First and Second World War. FAR MuST, LC. 892.

27 FAR, MuST, LC. 135.

28 FAR, MuST, LC. 316, p. 110.

29 Nina Edwards, *Dressed for War: Uniform, Civilian Clothing and Trappings, 1914 to 1918* (London and New York: I.B. Tauris, 2015), 5.

30 FAR, MuST, LC. 316, p. 93; FAR, MuST, LC.144, p. 52.

31 FAR, MuST, LC. 1362, p.on 7532, indicated on the page as "Drapeau National."

32 *Les Modes*, 173, 1917, 16, "Chapeaux de ruban, par Claire et Marie Louise."

33 "Pendant la guerre: Les Parisiennes," *Les Modes*, Noël 1915, 2–5:

> Et, d'abord, rendons hommage à Mimi-Pinson. Musset avait chanté sa bravoure, il aurait bien d'autres raisons de faire son éloge aujourd'hui. Délassait le magasin de modes ou l'atelier, celles qui ne trouvaient plus à s'y employer se sont mises à fabriquer des emblèmes pour nos boutonnières. Les alliés leur fournirent, avec les couleurs de leurs drapeaux, toutes les nuances. De leur doigts artistes, elles chiffonnèrent des cocardes, d'abord, puis toutes sortes de charmants colifichets féminins. De la pelote à épingles aux jarretelles, c'est un ensemble de coquetterie infiniment délicate, délicieusement recherchée, qui ne fait point mentir le renom de Paris. Ces ouvrages, qui sont presque d'art, se vendirent au profit des blessés.

34 *La Vie parisienne* 49, December 4, 1915.

35 FAR, MuST, LC. 316, p. 104

36 My warmest thanks to the owners and to the archivists of the Como firms that still keep historical archives and who kindly allowed me to consult them for this research.

References

Buss, Chiara. "Le 'Carte de Nuances' lionesi della Collezione Antonio Ratti." In *Seta e Colore*, 85–191. Milan: Ratti s.p.a., 1997.
Buss, Chiara, ed. *Seta. Il Novecento a Como*. Milan: Silvana Editoriale, 2001.
Chiara, Francina. "Indice documentario delle aziende." In *Seta. Il Novecento a Como*, Chiara Buss, ed., 336. Milan: Silvana Editoriale, 2001.
Edwards, Nina. *Dressed for War: Uniform, Civilian Clothing and Trappings, 1914 to 1918*. London and New York: I.B. Tauris, 2015.
Field, Jacqueline. "Dyes, chemistry and clothing: The influence of World War I on fabrics, fashions and silk," *Dress* 28 (2001): 77–91.
Fondazione Antonio Ratti, LC. 123, 135, 144, 316, 892, 1362 and 1632; 7603.
La Vie parisienne 49, December 4, 1915.
Les Élégances parisiennes, May 1916
Les Modes, Noël 1915.
Les Modes, February 1916.
Les Modes 173, 1917.
Margherita, October, 1914.
Margherita, October 15, 1915.
Margherita, June 15, 1916.
Margherita, June, 1918.
Pinchetti, Pietro. *Manuale del Tessitore*. Milan: Hoepli, 1907.
Rasche, Adelheid, ed. *Wardrobes in Wartime, 1914–1918*. Berlin and Leipzig: Kunstbibliothek Staatliche Museen zu Berlin and E. A. Seemann Verlag, 2014.
Rosina, Margherita. "I tessuti di Guerra." In catalogue *Le donne la moda la guerra. Emancipazione femminile e moda durante la prima guerra mondiale*, Enrica Morini and Margherita Rosina, eds., 123–32. Rovereto: Museo Storico Italiano della Guerra, 2003.
Rosina, Margherita, ed. *Ritratti di signore. Tessuto moda e pittura tra Otto e Novecento*. Como: Fondazione Antonio Ratti, 2011.
Scardin, Francesco. *L'Italia nei grandi esponenti della produzione*, vol. 1 *La Lombardia*. Milan: Capriolo & Massimino, 1912.
The Dry Goods Reporter, January 15, 1916.
Vogue, February 1, 1918.
Vogue, March 15, 1918.

Part Three

Problematic uniforms: Male and female experiences and secondhand trade networks

11

"Breeched, booted, and cropped"

A dress historical analysis of the uniform worn by members of Britain's Women's Land Army, 1917–19

Amy de la Haye

In *War Memories of David Lloyd George*, the former British prime minister, 1916–22, evoked the Land Girl (as they were known and described themselves) thus, "Breeched, booted and cropped, she broke with startling effect upon the sleepy traditions of the English countryside."[1] His depiction of a dashing, somewhat dislocated, and solitary female figure is significant. Whereas many wartime service personnel were regularly viewed as part of an army *en masse*, members of the Women's Land Army (WLA) often worked alone or in small groups, occupying geographic and socially isolated, rural spaces. Furthermore, their uniformed bodies rendered them entirely conspicuous. The mostly natural palette of the textiles from which the uniform was made might have camouflaged with the natural hues of the countryside, but the sight of women wearing leather-belted, tailored "elephant ear" breeches did not.

Uniform formed part of the Land Girls' daily lives. It reshaped their bodies and identities and influenced how the public perceived them. This text analyses the design of WLA uniform, how it was worn, customized, and sometimes combined with luxurious personal garments, and the resulting implications.

Women, land workers, and war

From the late nineteenth century, the British countryside became steadily depopulated as agricultural workers were lured by new opportunities and higher wages offered in the towns and cities. Following the declaration of war, some 250,000 British men were redeployed from the land for war-related work. Lloyd George recorded how, "the military representatives cast covetous eyes on these sturdy sons of the soil and took every opportunity to slip them into khaki."[2] By 1914, the industry had fallen into decline and the British population (comprising some 36 million people, 27 million of whom lived in urban areas) were dependent upon imports for over 50 percent of food consumed.[3] It was imperative that the island nation became more self-sufficient and the role of women was to become critical.

In 1914, the Board of Agriculture formed The Women's National Land Service Corps (WNLSC), whose initial remit was to recruit and train two thousand, "educated women workers of the right type" to organize 40,000 "village women" to work on the land. WNLSC leaders, like those of the WLA that developed from it, unashamedly privileged educated, middle and upper-class women, like themselves, whom they believed would lead by example.[4] And, as volunteers had to be financially independent, working women were automatically excluded anyway.

From the outset, the WNLSC had to overcome ingrained attitudes within rural communities that farm work for women—other than traditional roles such as milking and feeding poultry—was degrading.[5] A lack of suitable working attire was also an obstacle. Boots, in particular, were considered so prohibitively expensive that the government made temporary arrangements with the Co-Operative Wholesale Society (CWS) to provide a five shillings discount for women who worked on the land for twenty-four or more hours a week. In turn, the women had to contend with skepticism about their abilities and hostility from workers who perceived their presence as a threat to jobs for men. Besides which, there was a prevailing optimism that the war would not last long and the status quo would soon return.

During 1915, as more men and horses were requisitioned, and supplies of fertilizer diminished (potash was previously imported from Germany and nitrates were redirected to make explosives) the employment of women became essential. That autumn, a Women's Branch of the Board of Agriculture, Food Production Department was formed with Miss (later Dame) Meriel L. Talbot (1866–1956) as Director. She divided women land workers into those who could undertake casual or part-time work, but could not leave their homes, and those who could provide full-time service and go wherever required. It was from this latter group that the WLA was subsequently formed.

Unsuitable clothing

Most urban dwelling WNLSC volunteers had scant, if any, experience of country life and they too lacked suitable utilitarian clothing. Attempts to introduce a regulation skirted outfit, via the CWS, proved unsuccessful, not least because of the thirty shillings price tag.[6] A former volunteer called Joe (the masculine was used as opposed to Jo) wrote in *The Landswoman*, the monthly journal for Land Girls, that:

> Farm-work meant—well—anything and the only idea we seemed to have about clothes suitable for farm-work was that the clothes must be *old*. Old skirts and blouses, tam'o'shanters and walking shoes. But some had visited Gamage's or some other shop where every need of a land-worker could be supplied. These arrived with shiny leggings, huge clogs, hats that looked like those of Boy Scouts and many other garments that they never used. The wealthy ones had visited Selfridges, and these had done the thing in style: silk skirts, smart corduroy breeches, brown leather leggings, elegant boots, sou'-westers for wet days, the latest thing in service gloves. Could they fail to be the admiration of us less fortunate ones?[7]

Joe noted that some rich women had arrived with the stated ambition of wearing breeches, but once achieved they became content to, "keep to fancy blouses and brooches, and saw nothing unfitting in finishing off with cashmere stockings and high-heeled shoes."[8] Although mostly well intentioned and hard-working, the Land Corps' representatives were often derided by farmers and agricultural workers as the "lilac sunbonnet brigade."[9] In turn, with only a badge and a green baize armlet featuring a red crown, to signify their patriotic allegiance, the women reported that they did not feel like "real" war workers (Figure 11.1).

The WLA: A uniformed force

National conscription for women was not introduced until 1917; Rowland Prothero (1851–1937) was appointed as Director of the Board of Agriculture that December. By this point, food supplies were critically low. The following month, the WLA was formed with Talbot as Director. In order to attract new recruits, at a time when competition for women's labor had become steep, WLA propaganda deftly extolled the restorative and redemptive qualities of the land (to the women) and their seemingly natural capacity to nurture (as opposed to destroy).

As the WLA was a paid and uniformed army, working women could now apply. The first Land Girls, just 7,000 selected from 40,000–50,000 applicants, were enrolled in March 1917. Demand for women's labor was great and Talbot rued that she was subsequently compelled to make a, "very wide

Figure 11.1 *Photographic portrait of member of Britain's Women's Land Army. The white overall the woman is wearing indicates that she was a dairy worker. Postcard, 1917–19. Orphan photograph. Collection: Amy de la Haye.*

appeal and bring in all and sundry."[10] Nonetheless, she stressed, "it was essential that only those who came up to a good standard in the matter of health and character should be accepted …"[11] New recruits could opt to work in Agriculture, Timber Cutting, or Forage (animal feed) and many undertook six-week training courses at a residential center. Souvenir photographs of newly qualified, pristinely uniformed, Land Girls record them as part of a collective. Thereafter they were dispersed to work the length and breadth of England and Wales (Scotland had its own WLA). Some resided in communal hostels, but many were sent to work and live with elderly couples, whose sons and workers had enlisted: the youngest were just 17 years old. When Nellie Owen went to work on a farm, she was accused of taking a man's job and driving him into the army.[12]

WLA uniform was manufactured under the auspices of the Army Clothing Department and issued by the training centers and County Secretaries. Many official WLA documents refer to outfits rather than uniforms. The service handbook included details of uniform allocation with tear-out receipts and application forms. Each Land Girl was ideally (it was not always available and the men's services were invariably privileged) allocated a head-to-toe uniform comprising two overalls, one hat, one pair of breeches, one pair of boots, one pair of canvas leggings, one jersey, one pair of clogs, and one mackintosh. When training and one month's satisfactory work had been undertaken they were issued with the following additional items: one overall, one pair of breeches, one pair of boots, one hat, and one pair of leggings. A third outfit, issued a year after enrolment was expected to last one year consisted of: three overalls, two hats, two pairs of boots, one pair of clogs, one pair of leggings, and one pair of canvas leggings. Land Girls who worked with "Motor Tractors"—outdoors and in all weathers—were entitled to additional items: one mackintosh, coat and trousers; two pairs of bib trousers, two dungaree coats, one motor cap, and a pair of gloves.[13]

Four pairs of breeches were supplied for two years' wear—two were made of cotton corduroy and two of a "thinner material for summer wear."[14] As with other services, hierarchies were made explicit. WLA Section Leaders wore a circular badge on the left lapel of their overall and an armlet with the word "Leader" to mark their rank. The Timber Corps wore an embroidered badge depicting a tree that was sewn on the left upper arm of their overall and a beret.

In *The Landswoman* article cited above, Joe recollected:

How we hailed the advent of the Land Army and its regulation outfit! How thankfully we discarded our make-shifts and dived into the white overalls, and stepped into the breeches, and fastened on the leggings! Even if their fit was not exactly tailor-made they seemed to give out a peculiar odour of utility and comfort![15]

Although women had already been recruited to work in agriculture and farming, as *The Landswoman* made explicit: "Until they did it in uniform it was not noticed."[16]

Uniform, survival, and material evidence

WLA uniform from both world wars is variously housed within museums dedicated to war, local history, and rural life. However, items from the First World War are very rare. The Imperial War Museum (IWM) houses some un-worn uniform items, which were collected contemporaneously. The IWM was founded in March 1917 to create a record of "everyone's experiences during the war—civilian and military—and to commemorate the sacrifices of all sections of society." The museum also houses print media pertaining to the WLA; paintings, drawings, and photographs (commissioned, professional, and personal) and, undertaken more latterly, oral testimony recordings, which have variously informed this research.

Once the women had completed their service, the Land Girls were mandated to return their uniform, which comprised government property. (There are exceptions: Mrs. M. Harrold, whose testimony is housed at the IWM, states that she was told she could retain her uniform when she left the WLA.) This partly explains why so few uniform garments from both wars, of the many tens of thousands manufactured, survive today and these are usually unworn. It is thus difficult to examine and explore garments that are imprinted with wear and have personal narratives. However, we can instead ponder the biography of the manufactured garment.

Cotton that was grown on the land, possibly picked in the US by American Land Girls, was shipped to Britain where it was woven into drill or corduroy and manufactured into multiple sized items of uniform. These were sent over land by train and road to various uniform depots for issue to Land Girls who, in turn, wore it to travel across the land and work upon it. Uniforms were not generously provided and were mostly worn out in the course of hard and dirty work. Any items that were returned that could be re-worn were re-issued. Otherwise they were sent to the Board of Trade, who sent it on to a depot in Dewsbury, West Yorkshire, where 3,000 women were employed to sort items for renovation, rags or those to be pulped for fertilizer. Like the changing of the seasons, these cotton and linen garments could be interpreted in the context of a cyclical process whereby they came from and were returned to the land.

One of the richest sources for researching the correct head-to-toe uniform and what was actually worn by the land girls on a day-to-day basis, are photographs taken by Horace W Nicholls (1867–1941) in his capacity as Home Front Official Photographer.[17] Satirical cartoons, commissioned by postcard companies and editors of journals such as *Punch* and *The Graphic*, are also insightful (Figure 11.2). These illustrations parody, affectionately and mercilessly, the Land Girls for wearing masculine-style uniform, whilst displaying stereotypically feminine responses to the rigors of country life and animal reproduction.

WLA uniform design

Whereas women working in services such as the Women's Police Service, Auxiliary Force, Emergency Corps and the navy (WRNS) wore a feminized, skirted, interpretation of masculine military uniform, WLA uniform was based upon occupational agricultural and gardening dress.

The closest precedent for WLA uniform this author has identified is the uniform worn by students attending a private horticultural school, established by Viscountess Frances Wolseley (1872–1936), in Glynde, Sussex, in 1902.[18] Her archive includes photographs of students wearing brimmed hats, similar to those worn by the Land Girls, shirts with ties and waist-tied cotton drill aprons, breeches and laced leather boots.

In an article called, "Concerning our uniform: A fashion article and short story," *The Landswoman* reported that:

Figure 11.2 *Satirical postcard, 1917–19. Collection: Amy de la Haye.*

One of the oldest of the War uniforms, and certainly the most significant is the smock and breeches of the land. It is almost more of a revolution that skirted women should honour gaited women, than that the conservative Army should share its greatcoat and A.S.C. badge with the weaker sex. It took a World-War to bring it about and this is its history.[19]

However, it is important to note that the traditional embroidered smock was replaced by a mass-produced khaki or white cotton overall. (Former Land Girl Margaret Brooks states in her testimony housed at the IWM that the buff colored overalls became white when washed multiple times.) This was significant in reframing farming as a modern industry. In her fictional narrative *A Land Girl's Love Story*, former Land Girl and author Berta Ruck mentions that they came in three sizes.[20] The design of these garments, that could be pulled in at the waist by self-fabric belts can be likened to daywear modes, such as the long, belted, jackets that formed part of contemporaneous tailored costumes and shorter jumper-blouses, also known as "blouse-coats," from 1917.

In contrast, the design of WLA breeches fell outside of fashions prevailing aesthetic and can be better likened to men's military and women's riding breeches. They were also unlike the trousers worn by other war working women, such as those in munitions, who wore softer and looser cotton drill trousers, beneath an overall. As Jennifer Craik has observed, uniforms signify order and discipline, and they are also fetishized and eroticized.[21] She writes that in contrast with men where there is, "a close fit between the attributes of normative *masculinity* as inscribed in uniform conduct and normative masculine roles and attributes. However, for women, there is a discrepancy between the gendered attributes of uniforms and normative *femininity*."[22]

At this time, only a few progressive women wore trousers in their daily lives. Although she never served as a working Land Girl, the aristocratic writer and gardener Vita Sackville-West (1892–1962) appropriated the style of the WLA uniform and breeches became associated with lesbian style. In her unpublished autobiography, she reminisced about the "transformative effect" she experienced when she first donned her, bespoke, breeches, "I had just got clothes like the women-on-the-land were wearing, and in the unaccustomed freedom of breeches and gaiters I went into wild spirits . . ."[23] In the following war Sackville-West was commissioned to write the official history of the WLA and served as a County Representative. She wore breeches for the rest of her life. As will be discussed below, not all women felt so comfortable wearing WLA uniform breeches.

Photographs, drawings and paintings of Land Girls working alongside local agricultural women workers show the latter wearing skirts and dresses. Such comparative analysis makes explicit just how very different the Land Girls looked. As single working women, living away from their families, wearing uniform that was interpreted as masculine, their behavior—as well as their dressed appearance—was scrutinized.

Uniform conduct

Whilst the Land Girls were not subject to military discipline, they were informed—in no uncertain terms—that they must conduct themselves in a manner that was considered by the organization to be exemplary at all times. Every recruit was told they must promise: "to respect the uniform and make it respected."[24] As *The Women's Land Army L.A.A.S. Handbook* exhorted:

> You are doing a man's work and so you are dressed rather like a man; but remember that just because you wear a smock and breeches you should take care to behave like an English girl who expects chivalry and respect from everyone she meets. Noisy or ugly behavior brings discredit, not only upon yourself, but upon the uniform, and the whole Women's Land Army.[25]

Precious and brief, their leisure time was also controlled: the Land Girls were forbidden to enter the bar of a public house, to smoke in public and were required to attend public worship. Of special interest in the context of this paper was the ruling that, "She should never wear the uniform after work without her overall, nor walk about with her hands in her breeches pockets." The wearing of different types of garments can alter posture and facilitate different gestures. In this instance, it would appear that the Land Girls were being warned to appear neither slovenly nor appropriate masculine demeanor. And, whilst they were doing a man's job, they should not forget that traditional binary gender hierarchies remained. As the Land Army Song made abundantly clear, "The men take the swords, And we must take the ploughs."[26]

Dissimilar responses

The intention of uniform can be different from the individual experience of wearing it, as can the reaction it provokes in others. And, some people felt that women war workers were wearing khaki unnecessarily when it was needed for the troops. In September 1917, *The Globe* published an article called "Khaki Girl," in which the writer protested: "it is almost unpatriotic for women to wear khaki. An armlet or badge should be quite enough to denote the women war-workers." There were also anxieties about the "mannish woman" war worker and the implications of this in peace time.

In June 1918, a writer for *The Queen* noted that perceptions of the Land Girls, from the farming community and broader public, had improved greatly following the introduction of uniform. She then observed:

> It is odd how much stronger a woman looks when she wears breeches and gaiters than she does in a Bond Street gown: and one can ask a woman in leggings to do things that one would not dream of requiring from a lady in georgette. How fortunate that the fancy for extremely short petticoats coincided with the venture into a longish tunic! As a matter of fact, I believe that many of the village women in their bundly skirts can put in as good a day's work as some of the Land Army girls, but they look neither as efficient nor as smart.[27]

The author, Margaret Heitland, noted that there was a need to replace men on the fields at a rate of 10,000 a month—5,000 milkers, 4,000 field workers and 1,000 carters.[28]

Compared to other women agricultural workers who wore long skirts the Land Girls certainly stood out. In her interview for the Imperial War Museum, Margaret A Brooks recalled how, attired in her new uniform, a woman in the street appraised her critically and then exclaimed "Hummph . . . neither a man nor a woman!"[29] Another interviewee Olive Croswell stated that:

> The people stared at us because we had breeches on, They'd never seen a girl in breeches and leggings before and mine were a pair of leather leggings which I thought was a great swank! Most of them wore puttees. . . . Yes we were treated very badly at first, but as they got used to us they were better . . .[30]

Olive worked from 6 a.m. until 10 p.m. She recalled, "There was no kindness, it was work and nothing else."[31] A press clipping housed in the archive of the Imperial War Museum states that some agricultural women who had originally looked "askance" at the breeches came to realise how much more functional they were than their own heavy skirts and started to ask for them.[32]

When a group of Land Girls marched into a small Northampton village to cut 2,000 fir trees for use in the mines, there was a veritable outcry. One resident recalled, "Just think of it: women in trousers! ... in this small English village where concepts of decency and modesty were pushed to their extreme limit, it gave rise to a veritable outburst of indignation."[33] Their uniform was decried as, "anything but feminine," even "shameful". Others recriminated, "If it can't be done by women in skirts let it be done by men."[34] When the land girls attended church wearing uniform, the villagers "indignation knew no bounds."[35] However, as the days passed and the Land Girls demonstrated the utmost professionalism, the villagers became less partisan.

Whilst some land girls felt empowered by their uniform, others felt it drew unwanted attention to them. Eva Marsh disliked intensely being seen wearing her uniform in public. She particularly loathed participating in recruitment rallies, which involved marching through urban streets, accompanied by modern tractors and hay balers, to the rousing music of a band, calling other women to join them on the land. Historian Bonnie White notes, "She was distressed by the spectacle surrounding the organization."[36] She enjoyed working on the land and proved capable but found the stress of performing as part of an army unbearable.

The Land Girls worked long hours undertaking work that was regularly grueling, sometimes harrowing, and invariably dirty. After work, they had to launder their uniforms, usually using small amounts of allocated cold water. They suffered with chilblains on their hands from cutting frosty vegetables by day and on their knees from wearing breeches that remained damp overnight. Some Land Girls also reported chaffing on their legs caused by unfinished internal seaming.[37]

Dress historians search for research that references their subject, but absence can also speak reams. Oral testimonies housed at the IWM do contain references to uniform, but not all do and some just mention the uniform in passing. Clearly, they were more critical to some women's experiences than others. Research undertaken on WLA uniform worn during the Second World War certainly reinforces this.[38]

Uniform and democracy

Uniform, when issued as regulation wear, is intended partly to generate democracy. In the spirit of patriotism, women from all social groups were seemingly mucking in together. However, elitist social attitudes within the WLA were never subsumed as the editorial of *The Landswoman* made explicit. A feature called, "Our cows" utilized anthropomorphic examples to stress that even on the land, the "natural" order of social distinction prevailed. "Our cows are ladies of both high and low degree. Wayward, gentle, hot tempered, submissive, homely, and beautiful, they are like every other mixed community of females." Whilst Polly was "rude and rough and greedy," Lady Betty was "quite above the status of the ordinary cow, both as regards birth, education, intellect, and social standing, and she wishes you to understand as much."[39]

Social status was rendered immediately visible by the wearing of bespoke or high-quality ready-made garments in place of, or combined with, standard issue uniform. The Cleveland Manufacturing Company (based at Fitzroy Square, London W1) regularly advertised "Land Outfits, Overalls, Blouses etc." in *The Landswoman*. Garments advertised in the August 1918 issue included the "coat smock," "a very smart Farm Overall with a tailor-made effect. It can be worn with the standard outfit." Offered in a choice of five different fabrics, the cheapest in "Amazon" cost 11/9; the most highly priced was "Munition Brown Jean" at 14/11. The design is similar to standard issue, whereas "The Yoke Smock" was smock-stitched and offered in the same fabrics and price range. "Tailor-cut breeches" cost 10/11 and a cambric shirt cost 6/11.[40] Exclusive London department store Harrods also placed an advertisement in this issue, offering breeches for 10/9 and a showerproof overall coat for 16/9. "Bedford breeches" for 15/9 ("Bedford cord" is a tough woven fabric similar to corduroy and worn for hunting).[41] A pair of good quality "Mayflowa war work boots" cost between 39/11 and seventy-five shillings.[42] By comparison, the Land Girls were paid twenty shillings a week and many paid eighteen shillings on board and lodgings.

The Landswoman "Exchange Column" advertised individual worn items and complete uniforms for sale. In March 1919, a "Board of Agriculture Uniform for Officers of the Women's Branch; nearly new, coat lined silk; large size £5"; "Wellington Boots, size seven, nearly new, 30s" and "Khaki overcoat, £3 or offer" were offered.[43] Wealthier Land Girls could thus purchase extra items which alleviated the burden of laundering garments that were often mud-laden; trying to dry them overnight and all too often wearing damp clothing early the next morning. It also facilitated more leisure time after a long day's work.

Awards of merit

The acquisition of awards of merit were perhaps more democratic than uniform accumulation. The Good Service Ribbon, equivalent of the Good Conduct Medal won by British soldiers, was awarded to Land Girls who had completed at least six months service and had no complaint brought against them—either on or off duty. Some 8,000 of these were awarded in the two-year duration of the WLA (Figure 11.3). These badges were shield-shaped and made of dark green cotton embroidered, in yellow and orange wool, with a crown motif above three rows of lettering: WLA, GS, and LAAS.

Figure 11.3 *Photographic postcard. A group of dairy workers (they wear white overalls) with their unit leader (front row, left); some wear arm bands, denoting a year of more work experience. Collection: Amy de la Haye.*

Most prestigious was the Distinguished Service Ribbon, which was often referred to as the "Victoria Cross of the Land," which was bestowed following, "an act of gallantry and devotion to duty against extraordinary odds."[44] In October 1919, the *Landswoman* commended Miss L. M. Fisher from East Sussex who received this:

> For great courage and presence of mind shown in saving a fellow-worker when attacked by a bull. The animal was loose in the stall when the cowman entered. He was about to chain the animal up when it knocked him down and began to gore him. Hearing his cry, Miss Fisher rushed in and, jumping the barrier, attacked the bull, kicking his nose. The bull backed from her kicks and the man was able to get up on the manger and attract the bull's attention whilst Miss Fisher made her escape![45]

Commitment was also rewarded. The Land Girls received a service armlet after thirty days work or 240 hours and a stripe for every six months worked. When four stripes were earned, they could be exchanged for a diamond shaped award.

Uniform, uniformity, and dissent

The word uniform is derived from the Latin *una* (one) form: its function is to reinforce the collective, rather than the individual. As the Land Girls were not subject to routine inspections, they had more leeway, than other service personnel, to adapt, for utilitarian and stylistic purposes, and personalize their uniforms. These practices caused considerable chagrin to WLA officials. After all, the rules of uniform transcend the individual garments and regalia: it is implicit that it should be worn unvaryingly—or *properly* (Figure 11.4).

In an article titled, "Woman & khaki: A distinctive touch desired," the *Newcastle Daily Journal* reported that, "The average woman loves a uniform, as long as it is not a uniform, for into the uniform she must always bring something that is her own, and distinctive and personal."[46]

Headwear was especially subject to individual expression. An article in *The Landswoman* called, "Concerning our uniform: A fashion article and short story," reported that:

Figure 11.4 *Studio portrait of a uniformed member of Britain's Women's Land Army, 1917–19. Orphan photograph. Collection: Amy de la Haye.*

Our hats showed great variety. There were shady summer-hats that would not stay on, in spite of ornamental hat-pins. There were hats begged from fathers or brothers. There were the Boy Scout kind and schoolday tam o'shanters; there were sun-bonnets, and coloured handkerchiefs. The great thing about our fashions was their variety—an entire lack of uniformity.[47]

As photographic evidence reveals, and conflicting with Lloyd George's memory of cropped hair, most women had shoulder length or longer hair. Headscarves added a touch of individuality, a dash of color and were eminently practical. A chalk and pencil drawing on paper by Randolph Schwabe called "In the Fields" depicts a land girl wearing a bright red head scarf and numerous official and personal photographs provide evidence that the land girls often donned a headscarf in place of the regulation brimmed felt hat.[48]

Horace Nicholls' photograph of two members of the Forestry Corps grinding an axe on a sharpening stone, shows one woman in regulation uniform.[49] The other wears a white embroidered voile blouse with her breeches and stylish, shaped, low-heeled boots are more conventionally feminine than the robust, front-lacing footwear that was standard issue. She also wears a wrist watch, which was a hard-to-come-by item that until the First World War was worn only by the military—civilians mostly wore fob watches.

Historians and book publishers have, in turn, expressed their own preferences for "non-uniform" uniform. Two key texts have as their chosen cover image, photographs of land girls wearing subverted uniform. Bonnie White's entirely rigorous history of the WLA in the First World War features as its cover image a photograph of a solitary land girl ploughing.[50] She is wearing—what was presumably considered more visually arresting than regulation uniform—a light-colored knitted jumper with a large collar, a rather flamboyant patterned tie and a dark-colored narrow waist belt. Her WLA overall is worn open and she wears regulation hat, breeches and boots. Similarly, the cover of the 2007 reprint of Nicola Tyrer's (1996) erudite history of the WLA in the Second World War shows two Land Girls wearing shorts made from breeches, which had presumably become worn out at the knees.[51] As broader photographic and surviving garment research reveals, this was not uncommon in spite of the fact that this explicitly contravened rules that forbade strictly any adaptation of government property.

Conclusion

In its two years' existence, the WLA recruited, often trained, and coordinated the placing of some 23,000 Land Girls.[52] (They were amongst the 113,000 extra women who worked on the land during war.)

The Land Girls were shaped by their wartime roles experientially and physically—many became physically stronger and enlarged their body frames. Certainly, the Land Girls who worked in the Second World War attribute their good health today to working on the land during the war and the impact it subsequently had upon their lives. However, rarely were their achievements and sacrifices recognized and even contemporaneously they were sometimes described as "Cinderellas of the Soil" and the organization as the "The Cinderella Force." Whilst they were not dressed in rags like their fairytale namesake, their uniform undoubtedly highlighted their difference. Sometimes, it commanded respect, but it also provoked ridicule and derision. Many Land Girls wore it with pride, for some it was barely noteworthy, and others intensely disliked the attention (of whatever sort) it attracted. In its issue of December 27, 1919, *The Queen* published an article titled, "The passing of Britain's Land Army," in which the writer H. P. Cummings rued: "The English country-side will certainly miss the picturesque figure of the land girl in her dust-colored breeches, her white overall and wide-brimmed hat."[53]

There was an increase of 822,000 tons of wheat and 619,000 tons of potatoes grown between 1917 and 1918. And, the numbers of women working on the land in England and Wales rose from 70,000 in 1911 to 230,000 in 1918. More and more families started to grow their own food: in 1918, there were more than 800,000 allotment gardens than before the war in 1918, each producing about a ton of food each.

Notes

1 David Lloyd George, *War Memories of David Lloyd George* (1933–1936), reprint (London: Odhams Press, 1938), 770.

2 Ibid., 772.

3 Bob Powell and Nigel Westacott, *The Women's Land Army* (Stroud: Sutton Publishing, 1997), 5.

4 *The Times*, July 1, 1916.

5 H. P. Cummings, "The passing of Britain's Land Army," *The Queen*, December 27, 1919.

6 Carol Twinch, *Women on the Land* (Cambridge: Lutterworth Press, 1990), 37.

7 *The Landswoman*, April, 1920, 74.

8 Ibid.

9 Lloyd George, *War Memories of David Lloyd George*, 772.

10 Meriel C. B. E. Talbot, "The Women's Land Army," *The Queen: The Lady's Newspaper*, February 15, 1919.

11 Ibid.

12 Imperial War Museum (IWM), London, "Leaves from organizing secretary's diary," October 19, 1917, 1.

13 *Women's Land Army L.A.A.S. Handbook* (1917), 13.

14 Ibid., 14.

15 *The Landswoman*, April, 1920, 74.

16 Ibid., November, 1918, 240.

17 See, for example, portraits of women in uniform at the IWM: Q30614, Q30622, Q30627, Q30352.

18 Wolseley had written two books: *In a College Garden* (London: John Murray, 1916) and *Women and the Land* (London: Chatto & Windus, 1916) and was subsequently appointed Organizing Secretary for the East Sussex branch of the WLA.

19 "Concerning our uniform: A fashion article and a short story," *The Landswoman*, November, 1918, 240.

20 Berta Ruck, *A Land Girl's Love Story* (New York: A.L. Burt Company, 1919), 116.

21 Jennifer Craik, *Uniform Exposed: From Conformity to Transgression* (Oxford: Berg, 2005), 3.

22 Ibid., 12–13.

23 Nigel Nicolson, *Portrait of a Marriage* (London: Phoenix, 1973), 15.

24 *Women's Land Army L.A.A.S. Handbook*, 6.

25 Ibid.

26 Ibid., 1.

27 Margaret Heirtland, *The Queen*, June 1918.

28 Ibid.

29 IWM, Interview, Reel 2.

30 IWM, Interview, Reel 1.

31 IWM, Interview 7482, Roll 1.

32 IWM, Press Cuttings, Women in Agriculture, Supplementary Material, 40/52: 2.

33 Maurice Thomas, *Do You Remember What Granny Told You about the Women's Land Army?*, T. Holmes, trans. (Abthorpe: R.J. Chapman, 1999), 12–13.

34 Ibid., 13.

35 Ibid., 15.

36 Bonnie White, *The Women's Land Army in First World War Britain* (Houndmills and New York: Palgrave Macmillan, 2014), 83.

37 Twitch, *Women on the Land*, 24.

38 See the exhibition and accompanying catalogue by Amy de la Haye, *The Land Girls: Cinderellas of the Soil* (Brighton: Royal Pavilion Libraries and Museums, 2009), catalogue of an exhibition at the Brighton Museum, Brighton, October 3, 2009–March 14, 2010.

39 "Our Cows," *The Landswoman*, January 1919, 1.

40 *The Landswoman*, August, 1918, inside cover.

41 Ibid., 174.

42 Ibid., 176.

43 Ibid., March, 1919, 74.

44 Ibid., October, 1919, 244.

45 Ibid.

46 IWM, Press Cuttings, n.p., "Women & khaki: A distinctive touch desired," *Newcastle Daily Journal*, November 1, 1919.

47 "Concerning our uniform," 240.

48 IWM, Art/WM ART 3923.

49 Ibid., Q30719.

50 White, *The Women's Land Army*. The image can be consulted at IWM, Q54607.

51 Nicola Tyrer, *They Fought in the Fields: The Woman's Land Army* (Stroud: History Press, 2008 [1996]).

52 Cummings, "The Passing of Britain's Land Army."

53 Ibid.

References

Clarke, Gill. *The Women's Land Army: A Portrait*. Bristol: Sansom & Company, 2008.
Countess Wolseley's Archive, Hove Central Library, East Sussex.
Craik, Jennifer. *Uniforms Exposed: From Conformity to Transgression*. Oxford: Berg, 2005.
Cummings, H. P. "The passing of Britain's Land Army," *The Queen*, 27 December, 1919.
de la Haye, Amy. *The Land Girls: Cinderellas of the Soil*. Brighton: Royal Pavilion Libraries and Museums, 2009.
    Catalogue of an exhibition at the Brighton Museum, Brighton, October 3, 2009–March 14, 2010.
Imperial War Museum, London.
King, Peter. *Women Rule the Plot*. London: Duckworth, 1999.
Lady Denman, Burrell Collection, Glasgow.
Lloyd George, David. *War Memories of David Lloyd George (1933–1936)*, reprint. London: Odhams Press, 1938.
Newcastle Daily Journal, 1919.
Nicolson, Nigel. *Portrait of a Marriage*. London: Phoenix, 1973.
Powell, Bob and Nigel Westacott. *The Women's Land Army*. Stroud: Sutton Publishing, 1997.
Ruck, Berta. *A Land Girl's Love Story*. New York: A.L. Burt Company, 1919.
Storey, Neil. R. and Molly Housego. *Women in the First World War*. Oxford: Shire Publications, 2010.
Talbot, Meriel. "The Women's Land Army," *The Queen: The Lady's Newspaper*, February 15, 1919.
The Landswoman.
The Times, 1916.
Thomas, Maurice. *Do You Remember What Granny Told You about the Women's Land Army*, T. Holmes, trans. Banbury and Abthorpe: R.J. Chapmann, 1999.
Twinch, Carol. *Women on the Land*. Cambridge: Lutterworth Press, 1990.
Tyrer, Nicola. *They Fought in the Fields: The Woman's Land Army*. Stroud: History Press, 2008 [1996].
White, Bonnie. *The Women's Land Army in First World War Britain*. Houndmills and New York: Palgrave Macmillan, 2014.
Wolseley, Frances. *In a College Garden*. London: John Murray, 1916.
Wolseley, Frances. *Women and the Land*. London: Chatto & Windus, 1916.
Women's Land Army L.A.A.S. Handbook 1917

12

The French home front in 1914–18
An investigation into female workwear
Jérémie Brucker

On August 1, 1915, a 39-year-old woman named Marguerite Durand began her work with the "Compagnie des Chemins de Fer de Paris à Lyon et à la Méditerranée," a French national railway service whose route ran from Paris to the Mediterranean coast, through the city of Lyon.[1] Following the death of her husband on May 27, 1915, Durand, a mother and homemaker, entered the workforce as a day worker from June 19 to July 27, 1915, and then began training to become a station master at the train station of Rillieux-la-Pape, a commune in the department of the Ain, to the north of Lyon.[2] No work uniform was provided for this position. Archives show that Durand received money from the company's welfare fund on two occasions: for the sum of 500 francs in 1915, and 250 francs in 1917. Her request for the latter sum, submitted on June 22, 1917, lists her annual compensation as 1,262.60 francs, which included her late husband's pension. After deducting rents and payments towards her own pension, her disposable annual income amounted to 98.50 francs. In her request, Durand wrote that she needed the funds in order to purchase clothing and shoes, items which she could not at the time afford.

Durand's story resembles those of the countless women who found themselves taking on administrative or factory jobs in order to replace the men on the front. The war initiated massive changes in the workplace, and while women were already a part of the workforce prior to mobilization, they often held menial positions requiring few qualifications.[3] This article addresses the realities of the women in the workplace during the First World War, examining the conditions of women working in predominantly male positions, as well as their new manners of dress. Closer examination of work attire allows us to understand how daily life played out against the backdrop of the war. Our interest lies especially with those women working with railroad companies, in factories, or in major administrations such as the postal services.

This article attempts to address a series of questions: were the new work clothes worn by women a visible, but temporary, manifestation of mass female wartime mobilization? Or did these clothes represent something more meaningful, particularly when they took on the character of "professional dress" associated with a specific profession?[4] Was female workwear a tool used to redefine the roles of women? Did these garments help entrench women in the working world? How did female wartime workwear highlight the restructuring of social and professional hierarchies? A number of period sources, from photographs to editorials, allow us to answer these questions.[5] Images and postcards depicting working women were prevalent during the war. Indeed, many were ordered by the Government in order to promote the war effort to the general public. Company archives, internal rulebooks, workplace inspection archives, and clothing catalogs add nuance to the era's popular media, which was often intended to uphold a culture of wartime solidarity.

Makeshift attire for a short war: Wearing ordinary, everyday clothes to work

Work attire has long been more than a mere aesthetic consideration in professions considered dangerous. In these jobs, physical protection is imperative. Questions on appropriate work dress for women in all kinds of jobs, dangerous or not, emerged at the very start of the First World War. Although it was believed that the war would end quickly, questions were still raised as to how to dress women who had not previously been working, or who were beginning jobs in fields formerly reserved for men.

In certain fields, women began to enter the workforce immediately. From the outset of the war, in the summer of 1914, women were encouraged to quickly replace men called away to war. They could do so wearing their usual clothing. René Viviani, President of the Council of Ministers, called for women to: "Stand, Women of France, young children, sons and daughters of the nation! Replace in the fields and the workplace those on the battlefield."[6] Factory doors began to open to women in the fall and early winter of 1914, after the farming women had completed the harvest, and after the supposed brevity of the war began to be called into question. The need to feed one's family, as well as the needs of the French economy, precipitated this transition. The government allocation for wives of mobilized men amounted to 1.25 francs per day in 1914, with an additional 50 centimes per child. A woman with no children would therefore receive an annual allowance of 456 francs. Yet, the average salary for her husband would have been 1,327 francs for a factory worker, or 1,400 for the starting salary of a Parisian postman.[7] Women needed to work in order to replace the salaries lost when their husbands were called to war.

Were the women pouring into the workforce able to purchase work attire for their new jobs? Department store catalogs from 1914 show only a limited selection of clothing for women. In a catalog specifically dedicated to work clothes, the French department store La Belle Jardinière featured a series of dark smocks, with or without pockets, in sturdy fabric with blue and white stripes, whose price ranged from 1.35 to 2.8 francs. Those same striped smocks in superior quality, with greater durability, cost between 5 and 7.75 francs. This was, in other words, one week's allocation for the wife of a soldier, or the equivalent of the monthly rent, 5 francs, for station-master Marguerite Durand.

Archival sources do not provide us the total number of women who were able to purchase their workwear from La Belle Jardinière, as the customer records were not preserved. But we know that these catalogues only provide a partial vision of the reality of what working women wore. Many women made workwear at home with the help of sewing machines. Prohibitive costs of readymade workwear, the presence of a lively secondhand market, and the popularity of repurposing used fabric all suggest that the clothing depicted in catalogs was worn by only a minority of workers. Most women used or modified clothes from their own wardrobe.

Providing work clothes for women was not a priority for manufacturers at the start of the war. And this despite the fact that women had been employed in metallurgical plants since the end of the nineteenth century. In 1911, 7.7 million women were recorded as working, with one quarter of them working in factory positions. But these changes in the workforce were rarely taken into account in the clothes marketed in the department store catalogs issued between 1900 and 1910. The 1914 catalog for the clothing manufacturer *Braillon*, which specialized in workwear, for example, featured only one version of a woman's smock in ecru canvas, as well as a sturdier rubberized smock at three times the price.[8]

The urgency of war, however, did lead to one major development from clothing manufacturers—the evolution of the nurse's uniform. In the 1914 edition of the *Belle Jardinière* catalog, the nurse's uniform is not depicted with the rest of the white canvas smocks, whose prices range from 4.5 to 5.5 francs. Rather, a separate page towards the end of the catalog is devoted to the "special uniform for the women of the Croix Rouge."[9] The catalog lists an ensemble made up of a blouse, a smock, a hairpiece, and a nurse's bag for the price of 13.05 francs—all the necessities for a front line nurse.

Workwear accommodations for temporary replacement workers

A decree on the work wardrobe had been issued in 1913, but its implementation was interrupted by the war.[10] Despite this, there were no popular calls to mandate dedicated work attire. The disorganization that accompanied the first three months of the war did not afford women the opportunity to put together attire specifically for work. Rather, they scrambled to find clothing that was suitable both for the physical demands of factory work and appropriate for domestic life. In the absence of work-provided or easily obtainable uniforms, women adapted their dress according to their circumstances. The few photographs and postcards from the era show women wearing a disparate array of outfits, with the smock and the blouse being the most commonly used garments for adapted workwear. In essence, the women entering the workforce in 1914—even those who took over traditionally masculine jobs—wore the same clothes as had women in the previous decade.

Workplace accommodations became a necessity as the war wore on. In factories, the traditionally masculine *surtout* (coverall) was prevalent. The coverall was a voluminous frock worn over one's clothes that offered protection from dirt or stains, albeit imperfectly, as the neck and wrist were left uncovered. It, nevertheless, protected the essentials, especially in munitions factories, and helped prevent women from bringing soiled, inflammable clothes back to the home. In their April 1914 catalog, Braillon offered several versions of the *pare-poussière* or duster, priced between 7 francs and 19 francs, the latter for the men's buttoned piece with pockets, resembling a trench coat.

Those in the service industry had to adapt as well, as male restaurant waiters and hosts were replaced by women. These men in these positions had been required to wear a specific uniform consisting of a black vest with nine pockets. The 1914 catalog for La Belle Jardinière lists such a black alpaca vest for 17.5 francs. At Braillon, a vest of similar quality in grosgrain fabric is listed for 18 francs. The café waiter's uniform was expensive—the ensemble of vest, jacket, shirt, dickey, tie, and even gloves could amount to a price of up to 52.55 francs.

Photographs taken in Parisian cafés soon after the start of the war show that service continued largely without men. Compromises in the work outfit were necessary, as no designated female uniform was being manufactured. Female servers replaced the male vest with a black blouse; in 1914, Braillon offered an example in black cotton twill, labeled as *grand teint* to indicate its color fast characteristics, even after a number of washes (Figure 12.1). The price ranged from 6.75 to 7.25 francs. The servant's apron, with pocket and bib, completed the uniform. It was through the black and white design of the outfit, rather than any one piece from the traditional male uniform, that female servers emulated their male counterparts and were thus able to denote their professional role. This temporary solution was typical for 1914. These ad hoc measures allowed women to dress appropriately for newly vacant positions.

Menswear for female replacement workers

As the war ground into the year 1915, the government renewed its call for women to take up jobs in military production factories, even certain skilled male workers were recalled from the front. The *remplaçantes*, or women who replaced men in previously male-only jobs, became "permanent" for the

Figure 12.1 *Women replacing male café waiters, 1914–18. Photograph by Maurice Louis Branger.* © Roger Viollet.

duration of the war. Yet the only items suitable for female factory workers featured in Braillon's 1915 catalog for workwear was a set of blouses—this despite the fact that women were increasingly operating machines that had previously been operated by men who wore special protective outfits.

Generally, civilian clothing production lagged, as demands for military attire had created a shortage of primary textiles and dyes. The adoption of "horizon blue" fabric, made using light and dark blue thread interwoven with white thread, alleviated some of the demands for indigo dye in the military. Yet, fabric supplies, in part imported from England, were primarily directed towards the army, and fabric reserved for civilians was limited.

Women, nevertheless, needed to be dressed. A government circular letter emitted on April 21, 1916 announced the establishment of the Comité du Travail Féminin (Committee for Female Labor), under the authority of Albert Thomas, Minister of Armaments. The Committee was formed to submit advice and propositions on working conditions for women.[11] That same year, on July 18, 1916, the Committee asked the Minister to ensure that industries provide workers appropriate work attire, and that they provide for the items' upkeep. This demand was upheld in a circular sent out by the state asking

Figure 12.2 *War-themed calendar, 1st year, August 1914–July 1915. Published in 1916. Photograph by E. Erfani. © Musée de l'Image, Épinal. © Kharbine-Tapabor.*

industries either to provide free protective clothing for workers, provide a suitable allowance, or withhold a portion of wages for that purpose. Albert Thomas called for industries to install small individual dressers in the cloakrooms in order for workers to store their clothes.[12] On September 18, 1916, the state-run *Bulletin des Usines de Guerre* (Bulletin on War Factories) announced that certain factories were already providing waterproof smocks or *surtouts* coveralls to the women charged with running machines, and that other factories in Paris would soon be following suit (Figure 12.2).

The *Bulletin* provided the following explanation for providing women with workwear: "through the performance of the varied tasks demanded by modern machinery, workers will be subjected to small droplets of oil projected into the air, which will cause rapid deterioration to civilian clothes if left are unprotected."[13]

Factories began to automate their production from the beginning of the nineteenth century onward. This technical progress resulted in the simplification and deskilling of certain tasks, which, in turn, allowed companies to increasingly hire women. The war amplified this trend. However, the uniforms most appropriate for this kind of work remained those fashioned for men. Both the *surtout* with buttons and the coverall were designed without any strings or loose fabric that could get caught in machinery. Yet, clothing manufacturers failed to take into account the shift towards a more feminine workforce—a number of catalogs from the era's providers of work clothing list only men's items, with no adjustments taking into account the female form. Women working dangerous positions often had to resort to menswear. A photograph taken in a foundry at the very end of 1914 shows two women out of the twelve depicted wearing men's coveralls. These women, engaged in grenade manufacturing, are spared the dangers of civilian clothes, but their garments are, nevertheless, ill-fitting.

Employers in less dangerous professions could avoid resorting to men's clothing, often by providing less stringent requirements for specific items. With the postal service, the postman's vest—a uniform often worn by the military veterans who frequently held the position—could not be worn by women.[14] The female postal worker instead wore a non-standardized black blouse. Accessories, such as the armband labeled "PTT" (the initials of post and telegraph service) and a cocarde worn on the cap helped transform daily dress into a makeshift uniform.

Sources show that while women did wear men's uniforms, the blouse and the *surtout* predominated. The *Bulletins des Usines de Guerre* suggests that many did not even wear real aprons or blouses; workers frequently made protective clothing out of a canvas bag attached at the waist. Nevertheless, in the popular imagination and in media depictions that circulated at front and in the rear, the image of the woman hiding her femininity by wearing men's uniforms was widespread.

Workwear and the "masculinization" of women

As the war continued to wear on, criticism emerged bemoaning the supposed masculinization of women—a fear stemming in part from the use of masculine dress in the workplace. Opposing voices that actually *supported* this masculinization were rare, but visible. The feminist Madeleine Pelletier, for instance, championed this change as a step to towards the equality of the sexes and saw the donning of pants as a political act.[15] Yet, clothing makers increasingly sought to create new work uniforms tailored specifically for women. A couturière who called herself "Madame Commard," installed on the Boulevard Magenta in Paris, designed a coverall called "la Françoise." On May 8, 1916, Commard wrote a letter heralding her product to Albert Thomas. The letter closes with the following statement: "The ideal scenario will be to have industries cover the costs to clothe their female workers." This sentiment was echoed by the Comité du Travail Féminin two months later. Their request was accompanied with their own laudatory tract on Commard's creation:

> For the woman in the workshop, engaged in production for the military, there is little that could be more ill-suited than the customary skirt and underskirt. The war, in fielding women into this line

of work, has created the need for clothing that reflects its daily realities. Men's pants are of little use, as they have no aesthetic appeal; with the garment we suggest, women will be able to retain the coquettish allure that is inherent to their femininity. "LA FRANÇOISE" is a one-piece garment with a skirt-culotte at the bottom, with the lower legs wrapped around the boots and held with a button. It is buttoned on the front, in the bodice, and the sleeve is buttoned and tightened at the wrist. The garment is closed between the legs, preventing the flow of dust. It is also fastened at the side, to the right of the pockets; the back contains a skirt flap that is buttoned underneath the belt, and can be folded down as needed.[16]

The "Françoise" was practical and functional, while still taking into account the female body. The couturière drew inspiration from pre-war fashion, notably a skirt-culotte that created a stir when first presented by the couture house Béchoff-David at the Auteuil racetrack in 1910–11. Commard informed her clients that the price of the "Françoise" was 12 francs when it was released in 1916, or the same price as the men's coveralls she also designed. The "Françoise" was less expensive than the men's coveralls for sale in the *Braillon* catalog in 1915.[17] That pair, in a high-quality blue longotte fabric (a sturdy plain weave cotton fabric) cost 50 francs. *Braillon*'s dusters cost between 28 and 55 francs. The Françoise was highly competitive with other work attire in the marketplace.

Commard's "Françoise" was the first feminine work garment patented during the war. The patent was filed May 16, 1916, by the tailor Léon Le Boucher and architect Henri François. The latter, whose family name surely inspired the name of the product, had his office at the same address as Commard. Other versions from different manufacturers followed shortly afterwards: the Femina, in August 1916, from the Parisian designer Léon Dulac; the Simplex coverall, patented by Le Boucher, working alone this time; and the Eureka, the factory work suit created by a couturier in Nance in April 1917.[18]

Unfortunately, no available information specifies the number of examples fabricated and sold. A photograph taken in 1917, however, allows us to confirm that this type of feminine coverall was indeed used. In one of the photo albums of automobile company Delahaye, entitled, "Collaboration of Women for the National Defense," a shot of workers in the process of stamping shell casings allows us to identify three such work suits—either the Françoise or a similar rendition.[19] At least six of the fourteen workers photographed are women, a number that corresponds with the ratio of women employed at the company at the end of 1916–42 percent (Figure 12.3).[20]

Commissioned by the state, the album's title reflects its intended purpose of upholding the war effort. Albert Thomas certainly wanted it to be known that the Comité du Travail Féminin was taking the demands and safety concerns of female workers seriously. The outfits depicted seem to show that Madame Commard's appeal had made inroads in the industry. But while the photographs may have been staged, they hint at a yet imperfect reality—the women's shoes are unprotected by wax coatings and are not entirely suited to the factory's conditions.

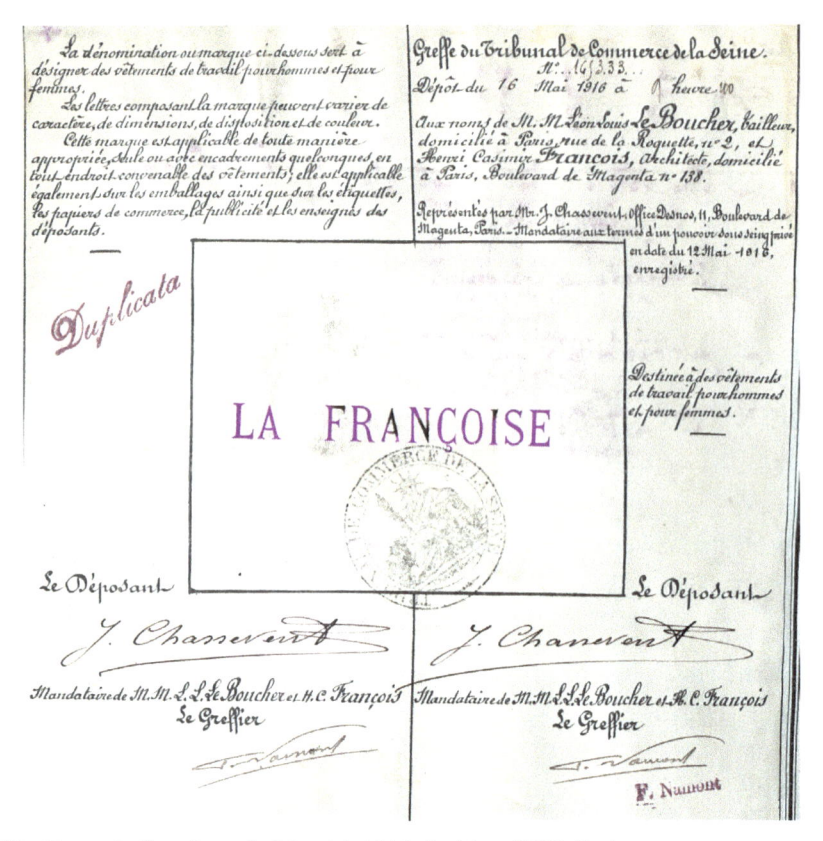

Figure 12.3 "La Françoise," trademark, May, 16, 1916. Archives INPI, Paris.

Female workwear: Between fantasy and reality

Did women's new work clothes allow them to fundamentally alter gender hierarchies and gain professional credibility, or did they merely serve to "reaffirm the immutability of the gender imbalance, standing in as a merely temporary solution," as historian Françoise Thébaud has claimed?[21] Several state institutions were created during the war to oversee the massive influx of women into the factory workforce, to varying degrees of success. The Comité du Travail Féminin (Committee for Female Labor) wrote propositions concerning work dress in 1916 and in 1917. The state released a circular on the subject of female workwear in August 1916, although the legal obligation to wear protective clothing was only regulated for those working with machines. A new school for factory superintendents, created May 1, 1917, played no role in ameliorating women's work dress after the designated superintendents took charge in 1918.

The principle labor unions operating during the war also did little to prioritize the question of work dress. Syndicates, or unions, were, in fact, largely hostile to the employment of women, and prior to the war, had seen them as undesired competitors to the male workforce. It was in this context that Alphonse Merrheim, head of the Fédération des Métaux (Federation of Metalworkers), declared on December 10, 1916, in Cherbourg: "The employment of women is a grave danger to the working class. When men return from the front, they will find it difficult to compete against these new workers, who will have acquired a certain level of ability, and will demand inferior salaries."[22] A number of women's unions existed in 1914, having first appeared in the early twentieth century, but they counted few members, totaling only 9 percent of all unionized workers. Women-led strikes, which were additionally supported by the main feminist organizations, mainly centered around the issues of salaries and time off during their husbands' military leave.

Our journalist and future station master Marguerite Durand, writing in the magazine *La Fronde* in August 1914, stated that feminist organizations would halt their demands for the duration of the war.[23] Although this ultimately proved not to be the case, prominent feminists mainly tried to help women who were victims of the war. They had little to say on the question of women's work dress, save through the intermediary of the Comité pour le Travail Féminin.[24] This lack of attention helps explain why, in the absence of measures taken by the state to ameliorate the work dress for mobilized women, a worker like Marguerite Durand would have needed to appeal to the company welfare fund to dress herself for work. The issue of female workwear was not a platform that feminists used to contest gender hierarchies during the First World War.

Throughout the war, a number of popular images imagined, invented, and reinvented the iconography of the feminine work dress, often representing it in ways that were impractical or even disparaging. Drawings by the illustrator Fabien Fabiano published in the satirical weekly magazine *La Baïonnette* in November 1915 are indicative of this collective state of mind at the start of the war. In Fabiano's cartoon, women's new work clothes are mocked. A female law enforcement officer is shown in a skirt that would have been considered extremely short for the era—an outfit that makes her position of authority untenable. The postal worker is also given a short skirt with high heels, which serves to eroticize her body. A cartoon such as this one, likely reassured men that the female workforce could only ever be a temporary measure.[25]

By 1917, representations of women in workwear had evolved. An illustration by Jean Villemot in the October 4, 1917, issue of *La Baïonnette*, which was dedicated to military production factories, shows a woman wearing blue coveralls identical to those of her male colleague (Figure 12.4). She holds herself like a man—leaning casually against the bar, glass in hand, with a cigarette dangling from the lips—as if this new outfit had managed to alter her body language and behavior as well. The dialogue between the two figures reads as follows: "And your man, what's he doing now?" The woman responds, "My man! He's busy back home! He's darning my silk stockings . . ." Indeed, many men were skeptical of female factory workers' new purchasing power, accusing them of buying luxury products such as silk stockings. *La Bataille syndicaliste* (The Syndicalist Battle), a morning daily published from

Figure 12.4 *Drawing by Jean Villemot, "Les Usines de guerre." La Baïonnette, no. 118, October 4, 1917.* © Kharbine-Tapabor.

Paris, and *La Voix des femmes* (The Women's Voice), a Parisian feminist newspaper, fought back against this tendency to disparage female workers for their perceived frivolous spending.[26]

Other typical depictions of working women included postcards sent to the front portraying female munitions workers. These women were elegant in appearance, shown wearing dresses, coveralls, blouses, or pants, which were still rare at the time. Additional markers of femininity such as clearly-defined silhouettes, polished boots with heels, makeup, and ambiguously seductive gazes completed the picture. These pictures exalted the female body, and the juxtaposition of the highly feminine against the industrial setting served as a source of amusement and perhaps comfort, reaffirming women's allure and social standing in the eyes of the soldiers. In another comedic poster from artist Guy Arnoux, made in 1916, a male military cook adopts a highly effeminate posture while stirring a pot—playing the homemaker, in a nod to the irony of the women at work back on the home front.[27] Yet, this image ignores the fact that in commercial kitchens women had not then earned the right to wear a chef's uniform, clothing which would remain exclusively male through the end of the war.

Illustrations of women at work proliferated, although many of them were exaggerated, either highlighting women's femininity or mocking their supposed masculinization. Existing misogynist clichés, dating from the nineteenth century, were reaffirmed during the war—men accused women, nurses for example, of working *in order* to wear the uniform. Wartime, for many, stood as a temporary moment of exception to the natural order of domesticity, and men found humor in emphasizing the comic incongruity of the woman at work.

Conclusion: An emancipatory trend in women's dress?

For some of the nearly 8 million women working during the First World War, the experience of working was entirely new, and often challenging. Many had to wear clothing that was not adequately adapted to their conditions. For the general public, it may have appeared like real changes were taking place—there were certainly visible signs of women at work, such as an armband with the acronym PTT stitched onto it for postal workers, or beginning in 1916, an armband with a grenade stitched onto for workers in military production factories. However, in truth, the hardships of the conflict did not allow designers and manufacturers the means to fully reinvent the female wardrobe for work.

At the time of demobilization, catalogs were offering several outfits that showed a distinct evolution in feminine apparel. In 1919, La Belle Jardinière offered a one-piece women's suit in blue twill, shown on a feminine figure with a *garçonne* hairstyle. But this evolution did not last—the suit disappeared from the catalog in 1920, as did the page devoted to nurse's uniforms in 1919, replaced by one for doctor's apparel. Only the women's smock persisted, offered from 1919—in gray, black, or chiné fabric—until 1923, when it was available in six different styles. The tailored female suit was still not sold in the pages of the catalogue.

While the emergence of a female professional wardrobe might have anchored the place of women in the workplace, few positions, if any, acquired lasting designated female workwear. The smock allowed women's work in factories to continue, in certain instances, but the menial nature of this position did not allow women to gain a foothold in other masculine professions, many of which required specific dress. For the most part, women were free to return to the home, while the smocks they had used could be repurposed for household work. Clothing manufacturers and company leadership were happy to maintain the dominant androcentric cultural and social order by preserving the codified system of dress. Nevertheless, certain changes were still visible. While female mail carriers were not granted any professional uniform, they remained on in the postal administration with one lasting victory—compensation for shoe purchases.

Notes

1. This article stems from the doctoral thesis "A history of professional dress in France since 1880," completed under the direction of Christine Bard, TEMOS-CNRS, Université d'Angers, and defended in December 2019. I wish to thank Christine Bard and Françoise Thébaud for their comments on this article.

2. Durand trained to be a "Chef de halte." The *halte* was an intermediary stop between the main *gares* or stations, usually accompanied by a small cottage and platform.

3. Françoise Thébaud, *Les Femmes au temps de la guerre de 14* (Paris: Payot, 2013); Sylvie Schweitzer, *Les Femmes ont toujours travaillé: Une histoire du travail des femmes aux XIXe et XXe siècles* (Paris: Odile Jacob, 2002).

4. For more on the distinction between ordinary work clothes and specific professional dress, see Jérémie Brucker, "Le Vêtement professionnel et l'inspection du travail, entre normes et pratiques," *Modes pratiques: Revue d'histoire du vêtement et de la mode* 1 (November 2015): 323–4.

5. For a more complete account of these sources, see ibid., "Le Vêtement professionnel féminin en 1914: Un Problème de guerre, une question de genre?" *TraverSCE* 17 (April 2015): 58–9.

6. René Viviani, Appel aux Femmes Françaises, August 6, 1914.

7. Chélini Michel-Pierre, *Les Salaires en France de 1944 à 1967* (Berne: Peter Lang, forthcoming).

8. Bibliothèque Forney, Paris, RES CC Theme of historical work clothes (1890–1957).

9. ANMT, Roubaix, 66 AQ 30, catalogue for *La Belle Jardinière*, 1914.

10. Jérémie Brucker, "Le Vêtement professionnel et l'inspection," 318–21.

11. Marie Llosa, "Le Travail des femmes dans les usines de guerre de la France méridionale (1914–1918)," *Annales du Midi* 120, 262 (2008): 205–17. Ten women were present in the Comité, which comprised 45 members and was presided over by radical senator Paul Strauss.

12. Ministère du travail et de la prévoyance sociale, *Bulletin de l'inspection du travail et de l'hygiène industrielle* 24 (Paris: Imprimerie Nationale, 1916): 80–1.

13. *Bulletins des usines de guerre*, September 18, 1916 (Le Creusot: Académie François Bourdon, digitized archives from the company Schneider, 1914–18).

14. Sébastien Richez, "La Poste dans le Calvados au XIXe siècle," (MA thesis, Caen, 1997), 63 and following pages.

15. Christine Bard, *Une Histoire politique du pantalon* (Paris: Le Seuil, 2010), 225–46.

16. Documents reproduced in Mathilde Dubesset, Françoise Thébaud, and Catherine Vincent, *Quand les Femmes entrent à l'usine: Les Ouvrières des usines de guerre de la Seine 1914–1918* (Paris: Université de Paris-VII, 1974), 147.

17. Bibliothèque Forney, Paris, RES CC, (1890–1957).

18. Ministère du Commerce, de l'Industrie, des Postes et des Télégraphes, *Bulletin Officiel de la Propriété Industrielle et Commerciale*, clothing brands published from January 1, 1914–December 31, 1918, Office National de la Propriété Industrielle, Paris, INPI Archives.

19. Published in Louis Le Roc'h-Morgère and Jean-François Grevet, *Les Munitionnettes: Les Femmes dans l'effort de guerre aux usines delahaye* (Roubaix: ANMT, 2016), 26.

20. Ibid., p. 7.

21 Thébaud, *Les Femmes au temps de la guerre.*

22 Cited in Le Roc'h Morgère and Grevet, *Les Munitionnettes*, 7.

23 Thébaud, *Les Femmes au temps de la guerre*, 35–6.

24 Florence Rochefort, "Les Féministes en guerre," in *Combats de Femmes 1914–1918. Les Femmes, pilier de l'effort de guerre*, Évelyne Morin-Rotureau, ed. (Paris: Autrement, 2004), 100.

25 "Les Remplaçantes," *La Baïonnette*, November 25, 1915.

26 See the April 14, 1917 of *La Bataille syndicaliste* and the October 18, 1918 edition of *La Voix des femmes*.

27 Guy Arnoux, *Le Parfait Cuisinier françois*, 1916, poster, Ville de Paris, Bibliothèque Forney.

References

Bard, Christine. *Une Histoire politique du pantalon.* Paris: Le Seuil, 2010.

Becker, Jean-Jacques. *La France en guerre, 1914–1918: Lla Grande mutation.* Bruxelles: Complexe, 1988.

Bette, Peggy, Amandine Le Ber, Nadège Schepens, Sébastien Richez, and Benjamin Thierry. "Les Postes dans la guerre, 1914–1918." *Les Cahiers pour l'histoire de la poste* 17 (rééd. du no. 3) (June 2014).

Brucker Jérémie. "Le vêtement professionnel féminin en 1914: un problème de guerre, une question de genre?" *TraverSCE* 17 (hors-série, April 2015): 58–71.

Brucker, Jérémie. "Le vêtement professionnel et l'inspection du travail, entre normes et pratiques." *Modes pratiques. Revue d'histoire du vêtement et de la mode* 1 (November 2015): 308–27.

Brucker, Jérémie. "Dressing the part. Professional clothing in France from 1880 to the present day." PhD thesis, TEMOS-CNRS, Université d'Angers, 2019.

Bulletins des usines de guerre, September 18, 1916. Le Creusot: Académie François Bourdon, digitized archives from the company Schneider, 1914–18.

Downs, Laura Lee. *L'Inégalité à la chaîne. La Distinction sexuée du travail dans l'industrie métallurgique en France et en Angleterre.* Paris: Albin Michel, 2002.

Dubesset, Mathilde, Françoise Thébaud, and Catherine Vincent. *Quand les femmes entrent à l'usine: Les Ouvrières des usines de guerre de la Seine 1914–1918.* Paris: Université de Paris-VII, 1974.

Dubesset, Mathilde, Françoise Thébaud, and Catherine Vincent. "Les munitionnettes de la Seine," *Cahiers du Mouvement social. 1914–1918. L'autre front* 2 (1977): 189–219.

La Bataille syndicaliste, April 14, 1917.

La Voix des femmes, October 18, 1918.

Le Roc'h Morgère, Louis and Jean-François Grevet. *Les Munitionnettes. Les Femmes dans l'effort de guerre aux usines Delahaye.* Roubaix: ANMT, 2016.

"Les Remplaçantes." *La Baïonnette*, November 25, 1915.

Llosa, Marie. "Le travail des femmes dans les usines de guerre de la France méridionale (1914–1918)," *Annales du Midi* 120, 262 (2008), 205–17.

Michel-Pierre, Chélini. *Les Salaires en France de 1944 à 1967.* Berne: Peter Lang, forthcoming.

Ministère du travail et de la prévoyance sociale. *Bulletin de l'inspection du travail et de l'hygiène industrielle* 24 (Paris: Imprimerie Nationale, 1916): 80–1.

Morin-Rotureau, Évelyne, ed. *Combats de femmes, 1914–1918. Les Femmes, pilier de l'effort de guerre.* Paris: Autrement, 2004.

Morin-Rotureau, Évelyne, ed. *Françaises en guerre (1914–1918).* Paris: Autrement, 2013.

Rennes, Juliette. *Femmes en métiers d'hommes, cartes postales 1890–1930*. Saint-Pourçain-Sur-Sioule: Bleu autour, 2013.

Richez, Sébastien. "La Poste dans le Calvados au XIXe siècle." MA thesis, Caen, 1997.

Rochefort, Florence. "Les Féministes en guerre." In *Combats de Femmes 1914–1918. Les Femmes, pilier de l'effort de guerre*, Évelyne Morin-Rotureau, ed., 100. Paris: Autrement, 2004.

Schweitzer, Sylvie. *Les Femmes ont toujours travaillé. Une histoire du travail des femmes aux XIXe et XXe siècles*. Paris: Odile Jacob, 2002.

Thébaud, Françoise. "La Grande Guerre. Le triomphe de la division sexuelle," in Georges Duby and Michelle Perrot, dir. *Histoire des femmes. Vol. 5: Le XXe siècle*, Michelle Perrot Duby, ed. Paris: Plon, 1992.

Thébaud, Françoise. *Les Femmes au temps de la guerre de 14*. Paris: Payot, 2013.

Viet, Vincent. "Le Droit du travail s'en va-t-en guerre (1914–1918)," *Revue française des affaires sociales* 1, 1 (2002): 155–67.

Viviani, René. Appel aux Femmes Françaises, August 6, 1914.

Woronoff, Denis. *La France industrielle. Gens des ateliers et des usines, 1890–1950*. Paris: Éditions du Chêne-Hachette Livre, 2003.

Zancarini-Fournel, Michelle. *Histoire des femmes en France, XIXe–XXe siècles*. Rennes: Presses Universitaires de Rennes, 2005.

13

Rushing to suit up

French aviation's adjustment to wartime uniforms, 1914–16

Guillaume de Syon

Upon arrival in October 1914 at the Saint-Cyr aviation field west of Paris where he had been affected, Sergeant Marchal was told that his infantry uniform was unacceptable: "Don't you know that aviation is part of the corps of engineers?"[1] He thus traded his red and blue regalia for the dark engineer's outfit. As he notes in his memoirs, "I did not think, militarily speaking, that I'd gained much in terms of looks, but I was now up to specs."[2] This remark reflects the challenges associated with the beginnings of French military aviation and its adjustment to war conditions, especially in terms of defining aviators' collective identity.

Vernacular memory and history have long tended to agree on the portrayal of the Great War military pilot as an undisciplined individual wearing a suit "whose elements are mostly unrelated to a military uniform."[3] While such a description bears an element of truth, its veracity is limited to appearances, for it overlooks important elements of early military aviation. Indeed, the adoption of a uniform fashion specific to aeronautics reflects in fact a search for identity through style, ritual, and distinctiveness. Taken together, they emphasize the different kind of combat French First World War pilots experienced for the very first time. Many collectors, military historians, and amateurs have extensively documented the evolution of the military aviation uniform.[4] Yet, when casting such fashion in both social and military contexts, Herbert Blumer's comments come to mind, whereby beneath the seeming anarchy lives a forward-looking structure: Fashion, whether military or civilian, is not the result of accident, but depends on both necessity and consumers' limited choices.[5]

This chapter considers the sociocultural aspect of a military tradition and its contribution to the fashion phenomenon in the Great War. The focus on French aeronautics is based on the circumstances affecting the beginning of hostilities in 1914. Although France, like other belligerent powers, had begun experimenting with less visible and more practical uniforms and equipment, it was not until 1915 that these were distributed to French troops, in contrast to other armies that had already adopted helmets and monotone uniforms.[6] Furthermore, aviation was a new weapon, the practice of which had yet to crystallize into any form of military tradition. There followed throughout the conflict an experimentation that covered not only flying techniques, but also the flyer's clothing. The interpretation of this process thus contributes to our understanding of a sociotechnical phenomenon.

The start of a tradition, 1911–14

A brief overview of the start of military aviators' uniforms is necessary, as it reflects the tensions associated with the transformation of aviation into a new weapon. Aeronautics was a heated subject at the French Assembly; it opposed the artillery and engineering branches of the service. Engineers came to incorporate aviation without, however, excluding the artillerymen who had demonstrated the value of aerial observation units.[7] Thus followed a dual tradition, whereby flyers wore the dark engineer's uniform. A newly created service, the corps of engineers attracted mostly members of the middle class and technical school graduates. The black color not only affirmed a bourgeois egalitarian military ideology, but reflected "parsimony, merit and hard work."[8]

However, aviation did not solely attract engineers before the Great War. Since there was no air force as such, it became acceptable to see flyers wearing either the uniform or at least the cap associated with their original realm of training. Even as standardization slowly occurred, the headpiece often stayed the same. The exception, as pioneer René Chambe recalls, was that aviation received a "distinctive color for its collar badges . . . orange ('tango' as specified in directives)."[9] Such a concession was in fact the result of an evolution begun in 1911, when another pioneer, Albert Étévé noted that aviator caps' golden pompons were "replaced with red plumes made of coq feathers."[10] Such disparity during the prewar period helps understand the individualist nature of the pilot. Even as they trained in the existing arms, the regulations in force did not easily match flight conditions.

Captain Louis Mazier added that officer pilots were required to carry the standard saber while in flight. However, when authorized to fly to another base or a distant city, they would leave the weapon on the ground as they considered it too dangerous (the size of the saber could damage the doped cloth fuselage of the plane). Consequently, they found themselves confined to quarters for "breaking sartorial regulations."[11] It took multiple protests and appeals from pilots to have the carrying of the saber replaced with a star sewn on the uniform's arm. Therefore, prior to the Great War, and independently of the Law of 1912 that acknowledged the nascent French air force, a symbolic separation of the aerial weapon from others had begun.[12] It appeared in the invention of badges, arm bands, and other insignia sewn on the black engineer's uniform.[13]

Wartime inspiration

The August 1914 mobilization did not modify the situation much, and even accentuated the odd mix of civilian and military pilots called to serve. The beginnings of trench warfare that fall affected a new change. For example, the dearth of textiles (many factories in northern France found themselves under German control) required the adoption of various uniform styles. This recast the aviator's identity. Whether beige velour with insignia sewn in a hurry or dark toned or black jackets, the message sent was that it was up to the flyers to figure something out.[14]

There followed a redevelopment of traditions that answered the double necessity of protecting oneself in operations all the while identifying oneself as an aviator on the ground and during leisure time. Thus, the introduction of the "horizon blue" uniform throughout the French army nonetheless kept the symbols specific to the air division. Since pilots and aerial observers were expected to carry the head piece of their original training arm, the mixes that followed became clear in many photographs whereby some pilots wore blue while others stuck with black (Figure 13.1).

Figure 13.1 *The mix of uniforms of this military class at the Avord training airfield reflects the variety of arms that contributed flyers to the nascent French Air Force. Traditionally, pilots adopted the dark engineer's uniform but kept the cap of their original unit. Some kept other parts of the uniform or had special ones made as there were no standard directives initially issued. Postcard from author's personal collection.*

General Fernand Hederer recalled decades later how his transfer from the navy to aviation training gave him a sense of freedom: Most aerial observers wore artillery uniforms, but the colonial infantry veterans kept their own style, while some former members of the cavalry still sported red pants and boots. Seeing such heterogeneity, the young officer ran off to Castel, a fashionable Paris couturier to have a uniform of his own design sewn up: a black belted vest with dark blue pants and boots.[15] Such confusion would prompt a belief that flyers were highly undisciplined. In fact, one should see in this disparity of dress an endeavor to adapt to conditions different from those at sea or on the ground. Indeed, it would eventually be combat gear that influenced uniforms, thus forging a peculiar fashion.

Accentuating difference: The flight suit

Jean Renoir's 1937 masterpiece movie, *The Grand Illusion*, follows the social interactions of a group of French prisoners of war. The start of the film presents an odd dialog. An airplane mechanic asks an aerial observer about to set off on a mission: "flight suit or goat skin?" to which the latter responds: "It doesn't matter, the flight suits stink and the goat skins lose their hair."[16] Indeed, flight suits, often made of canvas, would protect their wearer from the cold only when doubled, but their waterproof advantage also retained the wearer's sweat, and thus its smell. As for the notorious goat skin, its use dates back to the 1870 Franco-Prussian War, when its value as a shield against the cold was ably demonstrated.[17] Made of goat skin and sometimes doubled with sheepskin, its wearer could choose various sizes depending on how much warmth they sought. However, when poorly dried or exposed to humidity in altitude, it lost its hair, and its effectiveness. Its usage reflected the desperate need to adjust to new combat conditions. The adaptation of flyers to greater altitudes as well as night patrols created trouble in the granting of appropriate flight gear. Before the Great War, pilots known for their endurance flights such as Roland Garros or Adolphe Pégoud wore woolen sweaters, leather vests, and helmets and goggles comparable to those of early automobile drivers (Figure 13.2). Flights at the time were limited to day patrols in fair weather and at lower altitudes. As wartime demands on aviation became more specific and demanding, patrols came to last four to six hours on average. Describing the cold problem, a captain noted that "the most energetic pilot loses controls after 90 minutes."[18] Aerial observers, also freezing, had trouble taking notes or even operating the onboard camera. Commander Barrès, in charge of aviation supply in the fall of 1914 asked for the immediate study of a heating system, yet in the meantime squadron leaders had to order warm clothing on their own for their units.[19]

The lack of supply led to stunning exchanges between quartermasters and aviation units. Caught short, supply officers rushed the purchase of warm clothing in civilian stores, but had trouble finding the necessary numbers. The dearth of sufficient flight suits was such that pilots had to share them, or

Figure 13.2 *Pilot Adolphe Pégoud (1889–1915) sports a mix of clothing, combining leather pants with a leather coat over his military tunic in 1914, at the start of hostilities. Pégoud, who had first worked as a civilian pilot looping his airplane at air shows, was used to improvise his clothing choices. He became the first war ace, before his death in combat. Postcard from author's personal collection.*

even leave such clothing behind when transferring to another unit.[20] Ordered not to requisition too many raincoats reserved for the cavalry, or leather coats for truck drivers, squadron chiefs replied that both kinds were far too thin, and endeavored to explain how different operational conditions were between riders, drivers, and flyers. This amounted to obtaining a few dozen goat skins, balaclavas, sweaters, gloves, and lined shoes.[21] The delays in delivery forced many aviators to seek replacements on the home front. Aerial observer Louis Resal emphasized such needs in a letter to his sister:

> The silk balaclava I asked you for is not available in stores, but I think you could easily make one for me. By wearing a woolen balaclava and a silk one over, one gets good protection against the cold, since the silk one blocks the wind, while the other shields against the cold.[22]

As the war dragged on, its new dimensions complicated clothing discipline. Drivers operating on air bases, for example, were only entitled to infantry coats despite the fact that cavalry coats, reserved

Figure 13.3 *A postcard showing a typical reconnaissance crew wearing a combination of leather pants and fur coats or goat skins, c. 1915. Such improvisation was legion and came to influence the flyers' preference for an "anything goes" attitude in the air and on the ground. Postcard from author's personal collection.*

exclusively for riders, were better suited to drivers' activities. In another letter to his sister, Louis Resal mentions the need for a long scarf, an item that popular culture associates to this day with early aviation. Indeed, such an accessory not only protected one's face, but could be used to wipe goggles covered in engine oil. Yet, French authorities misunderstood such a need. In November 1914, Barrès sent an urgent message forbidding the use of such scarves, adding, "you may buy balaclavas instead."[23] In light of such supply difficulties, as well as evolving aerial combat conditions and the confusion surrounding needed equipment, aviators' own initiative is not surprising. Such a "takeover" was not so risky, for frontline inspections were relatively limited, but on the ground, conditions differed and saw a new elite endeavoring to affirm its own aviator identity (Figure 13.3).

A prestigious uniform?

Although flyers enjoyed regular rest periods in their mess halls between missions, patrolling conditions remained very difficult. Even though the relaxation time would have come across as paradise to the trench soldiers, few actually envied aviators: the fear of flying and of heights mixed with admiration for those who dared it. As a way to "decompress," flyers exhibited considerable fantasy in what they wore on their rest days. So long as the commanding officer showed patience about this particular practice, discipline in the unit was not an issue. As Lt. Marc notes in his memoirs, "the pilots who aren't bothered by petty officer harassment remain proper and disciplined."[24] Individualized clothing paralleled combat practices.

Such clothing fantasy further transformed pilot tradition and added to the myth that would crystallize with such aces as George Guynemer.[25] Other, less known, pilots also showed approach and illustrated the tension that arose between the need to control military aviation in a disciplined fashion, and that of supporting the initiative flyers showed in dealing with a new and poorly understood flying environment. In the air as on the ground, such deviation from standards both technical and sartorial gained acceptance, though it was not the first time this happened. In the nineteenth century, French officers were known to approach tailors and order uniforms that departed from the norm as a way of marking themselves apart from the rest of the troops.[26] One should thus speak of a social negotiation rather than a direct imposition when considering military aviators' uniforms.[27] War conditions as well as a public adulation for all people flying added to the individualism of pilots and aerial observers.[28]

The transformation of the pilot into a hero (even when he was not an ace with at least five aerial victories) encouraged many flyers on furlough to dress in a dandy way and break the rules in the hopes of being noticed and getting lucky. Bernard Mark has unearthed one such style of dressing: "a black tunic with a yellow belt; sky blue-striped salmon red britches."[29] While such fantasy worked well in salons and restaurants, any unfortunate encounter with a tradition-oriented officer could cause serious trouble. In February 1918, for example, fighter pilot Henry Aye de Slade was confined to quarters for a week for having sported in Paris "a kaki English coat, an open tunic, and a black regatta jacket."[30]

French ace Georges Guynemer did not experience such trouble. His sartorial choice, ironically, reflects some of the original traditions of the engineering corps. The ace liked the black uniform, but added to it an Anglo-Saxon style built around the "Sam Brown" belt around the waist with a strap over the shoulder. When he first used it in 1914, the thickness of the belt made him look ridiculous in light of his thin stature, yet two years later, his use of a longer jacket with large pockets helped him masculinize his style.[31] In so doing, Guynemer and others heralded the change of perception of the uniform and the body it enclosed. For all the variations in colors that subsided to the end of the Second World War, by 1916 the pilot fashion had found itself (Figure 13.4).

Conclusion: The end of individualism

Describing his joining the aerial observers in April 1917, Jean Dagullion notes in a journal entry that he and his comrades in arms received a kind of kit that included clothes needed for high

Figure 13.4 *By the end of the war, two air force uniforms existed, one light blue, worn by French top ace René Fonck at the victory parade on July 14, 1919, and the other dark blue (almost black), as shown here. Although Georges Guynemer had fewer confirmed combat kills (53) than Fonck (75), the former's death in 1917 became a kind of martyrdom and also contributed to a marked preference for a dark-blue uniform like the one he sports here. Postcard from author's personal collection.*

altitude operations.[32] Standardization was now in full swing in the field. The transformations of military production, operational tactics, and the need to grow the air force meant that the exploratory phase of uniform fashion was over. Even though fantasy in military dress continued to exist until the end of the conflict, aviators generally sported either the black color Guynemer so enjoyed until he was killed in action in 1917, or the pale blue variation other aces had chosen. René Fonck, the top-scoring French ace of the First World War, thus wore a powder blue uniform when bearing the flag down the Champs-Elysées when France celebrated its 1919 Bastille Day. This clearer identity, though much needed for what was then the biggest air force in the world, also heralded the end of a golden age in which escapism from the horrors of war was expressed in an improvised fashion that operators of a novel technological arm used to help them explore its newfound domain.

Notes

1 This chapter is based on the original presentation delivered at the Paris conference on Fashion in the Great War in December 2014, and on subsequent more advanced versions delivered at Albright College in April 2016 and at a luncheon lecture at the Royal Air Force Museum, Hendon, in November 2018. The author wishes to thank Dr. Nathalie Roseau for her support by granting him work space at the University of Paris-Est Marne-la-Vallée LATTS Center in 2018–19.
Marie-Catherine and Paul Villatoux, *L'Extraordinaire épopée du lieutenant Marchal* (Paris: Histoire et collections, 2013), 65–6.

2 Ibid.

3 Edmond Petit, *La Vie quotidienne dans l'aviation en France au début du XXème siècle* (Paris: Hachette, 1977), 126.

4 See the very detailed site "Le Musée de l'Air et de l'Espace," at: http://albindenis.free.fr/Site_escadrille/Equip_uniformes.htm (accessed March 2020).

5 Herbert Blumer, "Fashion: From class differentiation to collective selection," *Sociological Quarterly* 10, 3 (1969): 275–7.

6 Alexandre Rigal, "L'Uniforme militaire: La Production d'une identité collective," *Sociologies militaires*, November 13, 2011, at: http://sociomili.hypotheses.org/author/alexandrerigal (accessed December 2019).

7 Pascal Venesson, *Les Chevaliers de l'air* (Paris: Presse de Sciences Po, 1997), 49.

8 Dominique and François Gaulme, *Les Habits du pouvoir: Une histoire politique du vêtement masculin* (Paris: Flammarion, 2012), 162.

9 René Chambe, *Au Temps des carabines* (Paris: Flammarion, 1955), 21.

10 Albert Étévé, *La Victoire des cocardes* (Paris: Robert Laffont, 1970), 77.

11 Ibid., 95.

12 *Journal Officiel de la République française*, March 31, 1912, 3108.

13 Christian Benoit, "L'Aéronautique militaire à la conquête de son identité," in *La Grande guerre des aviateurs*, Gilles Aubagnac and Clémence Raynaud, eds. (Paris: Livres EMCC, 2014), 135–8.

14 See, for example, the photographs available at "Le Musée de l'Air et de l'Espace," at: http://centenaire.org/fr/tresors-darchives/fonds-publics/musees/archives/le-musee-de-lair-et-de-lespace (accessed May 2020).

15 Service historique de la défense (SHD), Vincennes, Oral History, No. 318, Fernand Hederer (1889–1984).

16 Jean Renoir, *La Grande illusion* (Réalisation d'Art Cinématographique, 1937).

17 "Variétés," *Les Modes parisiennes*, 1872, 221.

18 SHD, 1A 52/2, letter of Cpt. de Saint-Quentin, 2ème armée, November 20, 1914.

19 SHD, 1A 52/2, telegram of Cdr. Barrès to Army HQ, November 18, 1914.

20 SHD, 1A 52/2, "Equipement des avions 8/1914-7/1919," correspondence, October 1914–February 1915.

21 Ibid.

22 Jacques Resal and Pierre Allorant, *La Grande Guerre à tire d'ailes: Correspondance de deux frères dans l'aviation (1915–1918)* (Amiens: Encrage, 2014), 40.

23 SHD, 1A 52/2, "Vêtements chauds," telegram of Cdr. Barès to aviation units, November 4, 1914.

24 Jean Marcel Eugene Beraud-Villars (pseud. Lieutenant Marc), *Notes d'un pilote disparu (1916–1917)* (Paris: Hachette, 1918), 172.

25 *Guynemer: Un mythe, une histoire* (Paris: Service historique de l'Armée de l'air, 1997). Georges Guynemer (1894–1917) was the second-highest-scoring French fighter ace, with 54 victories during the First World War, and was a French national hero at the time of his death.

26 Alison Matthews David, "Decorated men: Fashioning the French soldier, 1852–1914," *Fashion Theory* 7, 1 (2003): 3–7.

27 A summary of this issue is found in Carrie Hertz, "The uniform: As material, as symbol, as negotiated object," *Midwestern Folklore* 32, 1–2 (2007): 43–56.

28 For an overview of the myth of the war ace, see Dominick Pisano, Thomas J. Dietz, Joanne M. Gernstein, and Karl S. Schneide, *Legend, Memory and the Great War in the Air* (Seattle, WA: University of Washington Press, 1992).

29 Bernard Marck, *Le Dernier vol de Guynemer* (Paris: Acropole, 1991), 77.

30 Noted in: http://lagrandeguerre.cultureforum.net/t51646p15-mon-aviateur-de-1914 (accessed December 2014).

31 Marck, *Le Dernier vol de Guynemer*, 35.

32 Jean Dagullion, *Le Sol est fait de nos morts: Carnets de guerre (1915–1918)* (Paris: Nouvelles éditions latines, 1987), 271–2.

References

24 février 2007, les aviateurs de 14-18." Available at: http://bleuhorizon.canalblog.com/archives/2007/02/24/4117538.html (accessed December 1, 2019).

Benoit, Christian. "L'Aéronautique militaire à la conquête de son identité," in *La Grande guerre des aviateurs*, Gilles Aubagnac and Clémence Raynaud, eds., 135–8. Paris: Livres EMCC, 2014.

Beraud-Villars, Jean Marcel Eugene (pseud. Lieutenant Marc). *Notes d'un pilote disparu (1916–1917)*. Paris: Hachette, 1918.

Blumer, Herbert. "Fashion: From class differentiation to collective selection." *Sociological Quarterly* 10, 3 (1969): 275–91.

Chambe, René. *Au Temps des carabines*. Paris: Flammarion, 1955.

Dagullion, Jean. *Le Sol est fait de nos morts: Carnets de guerre (1915–1918)*. Paris: Nouvelles éditions latines, 1987.

Etévé, Albert. *La Victoire des cocardes*. Paris: Robert Laffont, 1970.

Gaulme, Dominique and François. *Les Habits du pouvoir: Une histoire politique du vêtement masculin*. Paris: Flammarion, 2012.

Guynemer: Un mythe, une histoire. Paris: Service historique de l'armée de l'air, 1997.

Hertz, Carrie. "The uniform: As material, as Ssymbol, as negotiated object," *Midwestern Folklore* 32, 1–2 (2007): 43–56.

Journal Officiel de la République française, March 31, 1912, 3108.

"Les uniformes, équipements de vol." Available at: http://albindenis.free.fr/Site_escadrille/Equip_uniformes.htm (accessed March 2020).

"Le Musée de l'Air et de l'Espace." Available at: http://centenaire.org/fr/tresors-darchives/fonds-publics/musees/archives/le-musee-de-lair-et-de-lespace (accessed May 2020).

Marck, Bernard. *Le Dernier vol de Guynemer*. Paris: Acropole, 1991.

Matthews David, Alison. "Decorated men: Fashioning the French soldier, 1852–1914," *Fashion Theory* 7, 1 (2003): 3–37.

Petit, Edmond Peti. *La Vie quotidienne dans l'aviation en France au début du XXème siècle*. Paris: Hachette, 1977.

Pisano, Dominick, Thomas J. Dietz, Joanne M. Gernstein, and Karl S. Schneide. *Legend, Memory and the Great War in the Air*. Seattle, WA: University of Washington Press, 1992.

Renoir, Jean. *La Grande illusion*. Réalisation d'Art Cinématographique, 1937.

Resal, Jacques and Pierre Allorant. *La Grande Guerre à tire d'ailes: Correspondance de deux frères dans l'aviation (1915–1918)*. Amiens: Encrage, 2014.

Rigal, Alexandre. "L'Uniforme militaire: La production d'une identité collective." *Sociologies militaires*, November 13, 2011. Available at: http://sociomili.hypotheses.org/author/alexandrerigal (accessed December 2019).

Service historique de la défense (SHD), Vincennes, Oral History, No. 318, Fernand Hederer (1889–1984).

SHD, 1A 52/2, letter of Cpt. de Saint-Quentin, 2ème armée, November 20, 1914.

SHD, 1A 52/2, telegram of Cdr. Barrès to Army HQ, November 18, 1914.

SHD, 1A 52/2, "Équipement des avions 8/1914-7/1919", correspondence, October 1914–February 1915.

SHD, 1A 52/2, "Vêtements chauds," telegram of Cdr. Barès to aviation units, November 4, 1914.

"Uniformes. Equipements de vol." Available at: http://albindenis.free.fr/Site_escadrille/Equip_uniformes.htm (accessed December 2019).

"Variétés." *Les Modes parisiennes*, 1872, 221.

Venesson, Pascal. *Les chevaliers de l'air*. Paris: Presse de Sciences Po, 1997.

Villatoux, Marie-Catherine and Paul. *L'Extraordinaire épopée du lieutenant Marchal*. Paris: Histoire et collections, 2013.

14

The spoils of war

Use and transformations of secondhand uniforms during the First World War in France

Manuel Charpy

In March 1914, writer André Warnod (1885–1960) described a visit to a flea market in Bicêtre, a southern suburb of Paris, where he was able to observe *chiffoniers* at work. The *chiffoniers* were peripatetic ragpickers, or collectors of used clothing, who carried their finds on their backs, in baskets called *hottes*. Warnod was surprised to hear them discussing their business "going badly," with one man exclaiming, "It's the fault of their damned war . . . What are they bothering us with this nonsense for?" Warnod engaged with the men and a *chiffonier* explained, "Stores complain that they aren't selling because people aren't buying new things; so people don't want to give away their old clothes, which means that we are struggling . . ."[1] These were common complaints at the time, but not necessarily indicative of the reality. Although the secondhand market experienced major disruptions during the war, it generally saw a surge in activity, as used goods were in high demand. The market for used clothing had been a constant presence in French society since the beginning of the nineteenth century, and was especially common for the purchase of uniforms. But the war did, indeed, reconfigure the second hand market, changing how items were both sold and used.[2] From the damaged uniforms of soldiers killed at the front, to leftovers from factory production, to souvenirs and trophies from the battlefield, military clothing inevitably found its way into civil society—where it was repaired, transformed, and ultimately, imbued with new symbolic associations.

Repurposed uniforms and the secondhand Parisian markets

The market for old military uniforms was by no means new during the First World War. Throughout the nineteenth century, uniforms were an integral part of the continuously expanding secondhand market. In Paris, during the early 1800s, a vast, centralized market known as the Temple, capable of accommodating 1,880 vendors, replaced the older set of smaller, more widely dispersed markets. In the 1830s, the Temple was the largest secondhand market in the world, as well as the largest market for ready-made clothing in France. By 1847, 1,550 merchants were working there, including 864 with licenses.[3] Next to the Temple market proper stood a large rotunda which had been built in 1781, and was described in the mid-nineteenth century as "a gallery with forty-four arcades supported by Tuscan pillars, underneath which are laid out the rags, castoffs, hussar jackets, and sequined carnival and theatre garb of 44 clothing merchants, resellers, and *uniformiers*."[4] Jules Robert de Massy wrote of the outdoor market in 1862: "The Temple is always crowded. The throngs of buyers of all classes, whether frequent customers or first time visitors, help to explain the quantity and variety of the goods on display; the low prices ensure that items are sold quickly."[5] In 1865, a larger covered market hall was built at the site of the old Temple market which could now accommodate 2,000 merchants. To this remarkable figure, we can add yet more purveyors of used goods in Paris: a hundred or so stand-alone shops, and beginning in the 1880s, various new flea markets—at Bicêtre, Clignancourt, and Montreuil—where, as Warnod noted in 1914, "you can find everything, down to military cast offs."[6]

This immense market was not set up in the informal, chaotic manner frequently depicted in picaresque novels, with *chiffoniers* selling wares directly from their packs. Rather, it was a highly professional, organized affair. In 1847, the 864 licensed vendors employed 271 workers outside of their family circle, and 93 of them employed between 2 and 10 workers. The volume of goods exchanged and the degree of specialization point to a highly structured system of supply and distribution. While merchants by no means ignored the "bourgeois rags" the *chiffoniers* provided them, they received the majority of their clothes from avenues capable of centralizing larger quantities. The idea of clothing arriving from morgues captured the public imagination—contributing to the image of the "rags of misery" worn by those on the lowest rungs—but, in truth, this represented only a small portion of incoming items. Hospitals, on the other hand, were major contributors, and would regularly organize large sales of clothing, as did the customs administration and hospices.[7] Secondhand merchants sourced from almost every possible public and private institution—from boarding schools, for linens and uniforms, to auctions houses such as Mont-de-Piété or Drouot, which provided items from liquidations, stocks of damaged goods, and court auctions.[8] A government report from 1892 confirms, "Merchants buy principally from public sales or in bulk."[9]

One of the largest providers of clothing, however, was the military. Military uniforms were indeed the first clothes to be mass produced in fixed sizes, and this, along with frequent regime changes and redesigns, ensured that tens of thousands of uniforms were funneled into the commercial sphere.[10] During the Bourbon Restoration (1814–30), the government organized the auction of a great number of, "greatcoats, coats, waistcoats, canvas and wool trousers, shirts, boots, shoes, gators, police caps, epaulettes, haversacks etc."[11] Wholesalers bought, on average, 2,500 pieces per year. This phenomenon became even more prevalent after 1852, during the Second Empire (1852–70). Contracted manufacturers such as Dusautoy and Godillot received massive orders as wars and military expeditions grew in number.[12] The Empire, concerned with the appearance of its armies, augmented the frequency with which it renewed its uniforms. Shirts were renewed every six months and pants every year.

From the 1830s, the Temple market imported uniforms from all of Europe, as many countries preferred to export their outdated military dress. Once in the market, these uniforms entered the civil sphere. A dictionary of commerce released in 1861 noted that a uniform bought for 3 or 4 francs could be resold for between 7 and 10 francs after being "beaten, washed, ironed and, with the help of a mordant, colored on the seams and other areas which were lacking."[13] These retired military uniforms could also be remade into work jackets, shirts, "coachmen's jackets," or "ceremonial robes."[14] Consumers were eager to buy this former military garb, which was reputed to be relatively sturdy in its construction (Figure 14.1).

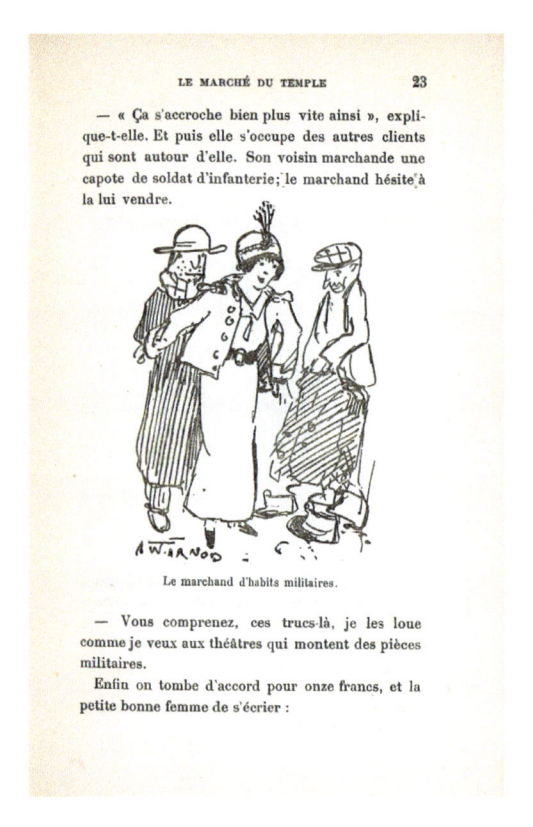

Figure 14.1 *"Le Marchand d'habits militaires" (The military clothing merchant). André Warnod,* La Brocante et les petits marchés de Paris *(Paris: Figuiere, March 1914), p. 23.*

A portion of the recycled uniforms sold in the Parisian clothing exchanges was sent to the countryside.[15] In 1857, a journalist for the *Figaro* remarked that, "almost all the shops post the following announcement: will send clothes to the provinces and abroad." The merchants thus developed a nationwide clientele. Giroult, for example, "did business with the municipal governments of every small commune in France, in order to inexpensively clothe the national guards" in secondhand uniforms.[16] A municipal report from 1892 stated that the secondhand merchants from all of France traveled to the Temple market to buy merchandise, which they "would go on to sell in all of the county fairs … everywhere where people are economical in their purchases."[17]

Goods from the markets could travel even further afield. In 1847, Felix Mornand commented that the Temple vendors "sent their surplus clothing to the Congo, Senegal, or the West Indies, where they delighted the black kings and dandies of Saint-Domingue or Barbados." Indeed, the numbers are astonishing. In 1859, the Temple exported over 800 metric tons of these "uniforms in varying states of repair, notably to the Antilles and Brazil," with the total number of items amounting to "the incredible figure of nearly 16 million."[18] Beginning in 1849, the new emperor of Haiti, Faustin I, clothed his army entirely from the Temple. A commerce guide from 1861 comments on the market's exports abroad: "A considerable quantity of these old uniforms are bought for export. This is how 200,000 national guard tunics were shipped to Saint Domingue and Brazil, all of them leftover from the events of December 2, in Paris alone, and this is how Soulouque's [Faustin I] guard of honor was equipped with the jackets of our Garde Mobile."[19]

The accounts for the French customs administration, published in *Tableau Général du Commerce*, established a category for secondhand clothing in 1834. In that year, 50 tons of secondhand clothes were exported. This number ballooned to 1,260 tons in 1854, and 1,838 in 1867. European nations and trading partners—especially those bordering France, including the Savoyard state and the Hanseatic League—absorbed over 60 percent of these exports. Russia, Latin America, and the Atlantic Coast of the USA took in an overall 10 percent. North Africa and Senegal began importing in the 1830s, and quantities rose rapidly, notably in Algeria, which, in 1860, collected 5 percent of total French exports. In 1886, the *Grande Encyclopédie* wrote: "International commerce has resulted in mountains of old pants and overcoats being sent overseas; if there is inadequate demand in France, the market abroad is guaranteed. Enormous bundles are boarded onto ships. The oceanic crossing is a voyage of rejuvenation for these threadbare items, which, under new skies, find a second life."

Repurposed uniforms, both refurbished or unaltered, predominated in these bundles departing from Paris or London, and this would remain true through the beginning of the twentieth century. By the start of the war in 1914, then, repurposed uniforms were a regular part of working class dress, not only in France, but also in its overseas territories—in the Antilles and Senegal since the 1860s, in Tahiti since the 1880s, and more generally, throughout the globe.

From waste to wardrobe

The war aggravated certain long-held fears about the proliferation of used clothing. Suspicions that secondhand clothes were vectors of disease had existed since the beginning of the nineteenth century. When cholera spread through France in 1832, many believed that the supposed miasmas arriving from India were carried by infected clothing. The authorities were especially concerned about the clothing circulating in and out of the Temple market, and in August 1831, forbade the import of "all old clothing items which are part of the second-hand market." These fears were heightened by popular tales of contagion in "exotic" locales such as Mauritius or the caravans of Mecca.[20] The cholera epidemic in 1884 reignited public concerns, resulting in the same import bans. In Paris, medical authorities observed a concentration of deaths on a street "running parallel to the Temple market, occupied in part by resellers of old clothing, which is rarely disinfected or even cleaned, as it almost always is in the market proper. These clothing items can carry not only cholera, but any number of contagious diseases."[21]

Preventative measures were quickly adopted across Europe, from the Austro-Hungarian Empire to the Kingdom of Denmark, the latter of which forbid "the importation of old linen, second-hand clothes or bedding, . . . rags, old wadding, carding wool and waste paper" from a number of locations, including Marseilles, Sicily, Egypt, Tonkin and Cochinchina, India, the Dutch East Indies, Red Sea ports, Brazil, Cuba, Haiti, and Puerto Rico.[22]

This association between secondhand clothing and disease continued during the Great War. Episodes of typhus, meningitis, measles, tuberculosis, and eventually the Spanish flu all provoked periodic measures to suspend the secondhand market or halt it entirely.[23] An enquiry by army hygienists singled out *chiffoniers* as carriers of disease, due to their being regularly covered in lice.[24] In 1916, the *Revue d'Hygiène et de Police Sanitaire* (Review of Hygiene and Police Sanitation) published an investigation on the "*Chiffonage* in Paris and its Suburbs," wherein the authors, all doctors, confused the roles of *chiffoniers* and secondhand merchants, tied the practice to the spread of measles, cholera, and pestilence, and called for their suspension. They proposed instituting new sorting plants such as those at Issy-les-Moulineaux, a southwestern suburb of Paris.[25] It was believed that these sorting plants could also help fill the gap left by the departure of much of the male workforce that made up the profession.

Mass purchases from hospitals and the army attracted a great deal of negative attention, often ignorant of the fact that the practice of steaming clothes to rid them of disease had been commonplace in the industry since the end of the nineteenth century. The greater visibility of the phenomenon in view of the ravages of war, however, led to public concern, with some equating the practice of selling secondhand clothes with stripping the remains from cadavers. In 1917, the Institut Pasteur de Tunis, in reference to the spread of disease, advised, "Old clothing, sold by peddlers, is all the more suspicious, as most of these clothes have come from the dead."[26]

Concerns over repurposed military clothes were not limited to hygiene; many were worried about the circulation of millions of unaccounted for uniforms, forgotten in the confusion of war. These could have potentially been used for deceptive enemy actions. Internal investigations were indeed alarming: on May 1, 1917, the army had lost track of over 8 million greatcoats, 13 million trousers, 21 million marching boots, 38 million shirts, and 20 million bandoliers.[27] Criminal impersonations using repurposed uniforms had long been considered a risk by the army and police departments, and restrictions on the free flow of army uniforms date back to the early 19th century. After 1802, merchants were mandated to carry a placard from the Paris police prefecture and keep a log that detailed "day by day, without a single omitted entry or error, the objects bought and sold."[28] Purchasing directly from soldiers was forbidden, and the police were attentive as well to other types of uniforms, including those of city officials and clerics.[29] Oddly, while the government under the July Monarchy (1830–48) organized large sales of uniforms, they also lifted the ban on purchases directly from military personnel in the years 1831, 1835, and 1841. By 1850, restrictions were reinstituted, with one military member confirming that "obsolete uniforms must be sold by the department of an auctioneer at public auctions, but before then, the buttons will have been taken off the breast of the tunics, and the cuffs of the sleeve cut off."[30]

Surveillance of the trade of uniforms was particularly pronounced in Algeria, where it was feared they could be appropriated by Algerian resistance fighters or bandits. In 1841, an order issued in Arabic and French forbid "the purchase of military uniforms and accessories," and punishment was severe: any person found with a uniform was issued a fine and two months in prison. Anybody who found an abandoned uniform had to immediately deliver it to the local authorities, or risk the same sanctions. The law increased the penalty if the uniform was found in the hands of a "reseller, secondhand merchant, innkeeper, landlord, restaurateur, or beverage salesman." The measures even extended to any secondhand merchant "recognized as having once possessed items of the type here listed," even if the "distinctive markers [have been removed] in order to hide the origins of the item, rendering it suitable for commerce."[31]

In 1857, military law reinforced these provisions against possession—including the suspected possession—of uniforms.[32] The city of Saint-Louis and the island of Gorée in Senegal were subject to similar scrutiny in the 1860s. The emergence of the secondhand market and the constant presence of French soldiers triggered close surveillance of auctions for "tunics, shakos, etc. . . . ," as well as heavy sanctions for those selling their uniforms directly (most commonly, members of the navy).[33] The volatility accompanying the First World War played into these ongoing fears. France was particularly worried about uniforms in Algeria and other colonies being diverted for criminal purposes or for political uprisings. Throughout the war, soldiers were required to carry a booklet detailing all of their issued items, a provision which complemented the measures already in place requiring merchants to keep records of goods. With direct sales from soldiers banned, there could at least be some regulation over military clothes' inevitable drift towards the sphere of commerce.[34]

The rags of war

These circumstances should have led to a rejection of the secondhand market—and especially, a rejection of clothing exchanges between the military and civilians. Instead, the second hand-market was embraced—although not without conflict. Heightened awareness of the spread of contagious diseases, disgust at the intimacy of sharing clothing with the unknown, and the idea that clothing was being stripped from the dead—all of these factors fed the negative public perception of secondhand clothing. At the same time, patriotism and popular support for the armed forces led to increased interest in clothing donation, including a resurgence of charitable clothing lockers in Protestant and Catholic churches.[35] The act of giving thus erased any prior disgust.

Charitable initiatives were launched, some of which were supported by the army (Figure 14.2). The autumn 1914 campaign "Knitting for the Soldier," which was led by newspaper l'*Écho de Paris*, encouraged women to knit and mend clothes and underclothes to send to the front. The operation was a success: in November, the *Écho*, along with a second newspaper, *L'Illustration*, claimed to have received 700,000 sweaters, 85,000 pairs of socks, and 80,000 shirts in one month alone, a significant portion of which were previously used.[36] The daily newspaper, in continuing to publish a record of gifts received for several months, replaced the unsavory nature of the secondhand with an aura of quotidian heroism (Figure 14.3).[37]

Figure 14.2 *"Le tricot du combattant" (The soldier's knit).* L'Illustration, *October 24, 1914.*

Figure 14.3 *Clothing distribution on the Front on the initiative of* La Revue hebdomadaire. La Revue hebdomadaire, *May 8, 1915.* © Manuel Charpy.

These charitable good works became common. The Franciscan Missionaries of Mary, a congregation of nuns who cared for the wounded during the war, called for donations for Christmas, specifically, "gifts of bedding, socks, and clothes, or gifts of coin."[38] The magazine *Le Foyer*, headed by the devoutly Catholic Henry Bordeaux, led its own initiative, "Clothes Against the Cold for the Soldiers" in September 1914, whose messaging proclaimed: "Each French man or woman can help our army: 1. In donating, without delay, flannel gilets or shirts, knitted vests, hunting vests, wool socks, and wool gloves; 2. In offering a monetary donation that can be used to purchase these items; 3. In employing the laborers who can work ceaselessly to produce these clothes." A large portion of the items received from this charitable drive—40,000 in several weeks—were secondhand clothes (Figure 14.4).

During this time of scarcity, the army continued to look for ways to reuse the piles of uniforms that had been abandoned, left on corpses, or damaged by military action and surgical intervention. Since the 1850s, the Bureau de l'Habillement (the administration office in charge of providing clothing to national employees) had been charged with recuperating lost or damaged items. They had also historically regulated resale to secondhand markets, determining the prices for "transformations"—

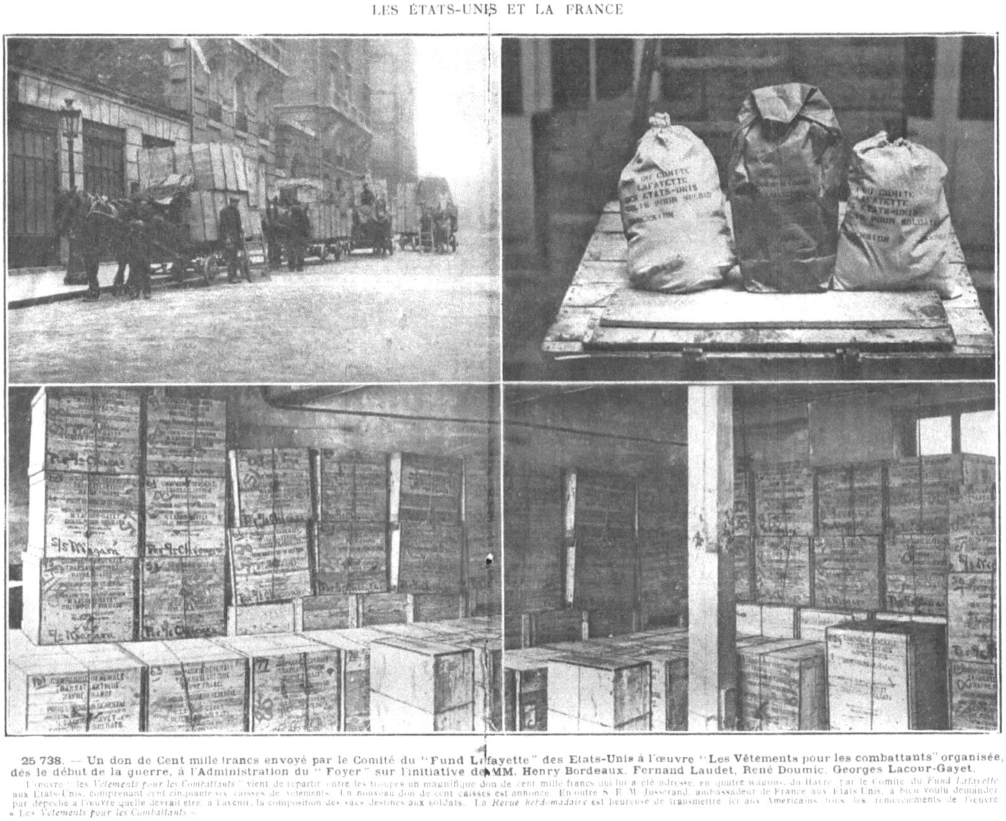

Figure 14.4 *The charity "Les Vêtements pour les combattants" (Clothing for soldiers). The Lafayette Committee Fund sent 156 boxes of clothing.* La Revue hebdomadaire, *March, 27, 1915. © Manuel Charpy.*

for example, the rate for converting military trousers into riding pants, or for turning a greatcoat into a jacket.[39] Each soldier was, however, supposed to take care of his own clothing. In 1915, a captain issued the instructions that: "All small repairs must be performed day by day by the soldier ... who must always carry thread of different colors, as well as buttons, laces, needles, and wax."[40] All damages outside of the individual's purview were the domain of the Bureau de l'Habillement.

Tailors would have been present in every camp during the war, but the army also continued to use *ateliers civiles* or civilian workshops to repair its uniforms, a practice that had been common since the 1850s. Previously, however, the army would have had recourse to workshops in the towns or markets it was passing through. During the war, the labor force of tailors and boot makers had been largely called to the front, leaving many smaller workshops incapable of operating.[41] The army turned to the immense mechanized factories—now run by a largely female workforce—which had adopted "the industrial organization of labor."[42] These factories continued producing new clothes, but now took on the role of the secondhand merchant as well, refurbishing greatcoats, jackets, shell jackets, trousers, or breeches. This work was costly and time consuming—seventeen hours of work were necessary for repairing a greatcoat and five-and-a-half for a pair of pants—but it allowed for economizing on the cost of fabric.[43] The practice of mending damaged clothing saw a resurgence among civilians as well. The Jesuit preacher Léonce de Grandmaison noted that, "a number of 'war trades' have emerged, not to mention all of the stores that 'mend' used goods (for example dyeing of faded clothing, refurbishment of old costumes, or invisible mending)."[44]

As the war drew on, even greater efforts were made to recuperate lost items. In October 1916, the *Figaro* called for the "creation of an army corps of *chiffoniers*." They justified the necessity of the position as follows:

> The task of the military *chiffonier* should be to collect, in service of the state, all that is left behind, lost, rotting, or burned in the wakes of the army's movements . . . The soldier complains of carrying too much weight, . . . so he throws his bothersome surplus by the side of the road, or leaves it in the camp. . . . We thus find in any area where soldiers have passed greatcoats, bedding, shoes, and mess kits; we find furniture and borrowed objects of all kinds in the abandoned houses of the neighboring village. This hodgepodge may appear picturesque on first glance; on deeper reflection, it is quite unfortunate. It is lost capital. . . . It is disorderly. *Chiffoniers* of the army, You will fill your baskets many times over![45]

The army had had trouble providing uniforms since the start of mobilization—recruits were initially asked to provide their own shoes—and was seeking to maximize its recovery of uniforms from the dead. Since the beginning of the war, rules had been set in place to ensure that damaged items were returned before new ones were sent. The regulations read as follows: "The corps must send back all unusable equipment to the *Entrepôts d'Effets d'Habillement* (Clothing Warehouse) . . . In principal, all delivery of new items should follow the receipt of those returned. . . . The officers in the camps must ensure the collection of all items left by the corps, and arrange for their return."[46] Unfortunately, this rule had been poorly observed, despite the bonuses offered for particularly zealous camps.

The issue first reached the national parliament in March 1916.[47] The figures from a set of reports in May 1917 reveal just how poorly recuperation efforts had played out: for the 12.2 million greatcoats sent to the army, only 4.1 million had been returned; out of 22.2 million pairs of pants, 7.4; for 29.2 million marching boots, 8.7; for 42.3 million shirts, 4.3.[48] The investigators pointed out that soldiers were not adept in the "methodical and careful gathering of all detritus, bedding, gear, or objects," and that "sudden, urgent departures" explained the fact that equipment in good condition was frequently abandoned. Poor returns were also explained "by the instability of the units, and the fatigue and preoccupation" of the soldiers. The reports arrive at the same conclusion, advocating for the creation of "teams of *chiffoniers*" to pick up objects left in camps as well as "by the roadside, in the trenches, or even on the battlefield." The 3,300 men proscribed for the role would be the oldest in the army reserve force or "those employed as *chiffoniers* in civilian life." The report continues: "There will be created within the Army's area of operation a specialized territorial service charged with collecting all of the military dress that is abandoned, for one reason or another, by the troops … All of the material collected will be sent to the *Entrepôts d'Effets d'Habillement* after brief sorting, without further handling." And while the report makes clear that there were already persons charged with collecting, "tinplate, bottles, bones, rags, horse skin, horsehair waste, equipment and gear," there would now be created new "Compagnies de Chiffoniers."[49] The uniforms that these *chiffoniers* collected, if overly damaged, would go on to rejoin the civilian secondhand market.

Souvenirs and surplus: The economy of leftovers

Mass mobilization on an unprecedented scale forced the military to confront the question of how to treat the uniforms of demobilized men. The Ministry of War had been concerned with the issue since at least the 1870s. At that time, the possibility of allowing men to keep their uniforms, in the manner of the National Guard, was considered. Army veterans were, after all, considered reservists, and this option also recognized the patriotic and almost corporeal attachment men developed with their uniforms. The newly established government of the Third Republic was worried about potential negative effects, however, and settled on a compromise: the Ministry announced in 1873 that demobilized "foot soldiers" could take with them "a pair of suspenders, a shirt, a cravat, a pair of canvas gators, and a pair of shoes." Furthermore, it was specified that, "these items must be, whenever possible, those in the poorest conditions that the men have as choices available to them," and that all other items must be "delivered, in a suitable state of cleanliness, to the army depot."[50]

The length of the First World War, as well as the sheer number of deaths and injuries, made the issue all the more apparent. Again, the army was worried that weapons or uniforms would fall into "suspicious hands." The administration thus called for strict checks, conducted with, "the utmost tact, especially when conducted with veterans whose motives could not possibly be called into doubt."[51] Nevertheless, soldiers continued to take small objects, uniforms, or even weapons as "souvenirs" of the war and reminders of their fallen brethren.

In February 1919, the Department of Mobilization attempted to clamp down on matters, issuing the following statement: "In an effort to punish theft of items belonging to the state by demobilized men, the Commander-in-Chief of the French Armies of the North and the East has proscribed the inspection of these men's luggage both at the departure of their unit and upon their entry into the grouping centers."[52] The army established "baggage checks on demobilized men," announcing that those "found with material belonging to the Army will be punished by law." The sheer number of demobilized men, however, made the task nearly impossible; and in the wake of the long war it was difficult to truly sanction men heading home with an errant bandolier, shirt, or greatcoat.

Authorities also noticed the emergence of another phenomenon; French soldiers were keeping German uniforms as "trophies," and conversely, civilians and British soldiers were collecting French military uniforms. The Ministry of War reminded citizens in June 1919 that material "taken from the enemy is the property of the state," but prying trophies from soldiers was a delicate matter, and the state had little means to enforce these provisions, especially for foreign items.[53] The explosion of the secondhand market only complicated the issue.

In 1919, British uniforms and even American uniforms—rare before the war—began pouring into European and Mediterranean markets, from Morocco to Anatolia.[54] The English army began reselling uniforms itself, first transforming them by dyeing them and altering their buttons.[55] Legislation in the United States facilitated matters there—while it was illegal to wear old uniforms, nothing prevented their purchase. Often unbeknownst to the army, factory rejects would enter into the market through the intermediary of contracted workshops in New York, Philadelphia, and Baltimore.[56]

From 1917 onward, the army itself sold uniforms outside the United States. In 1920, official estimates suggested that $500 million worth of American military material had been sold in France, half of which was from uniforms.[57] This allowed the army to rapidly rid itself of rejects and decommissioned uniforms. France soon adopted the American term "surplus" to describe the flourishing sector. Morocco, Algeria, and Tunisia became hubs for these surplus goods; secondhand merchants would buy goods from France or from American exporters and sell the items—modified to varying degrees— in the markets. In 1920, the *New York Times* was shocked to find in the markets of Algiers, "the olive drab blouses and overcoats that once belonged to the American Expeditionary Forces in France."[58] Although brick and mortar shops specializing in US military surplus would not be established in France until after the Second World War, American and French uniforms were being sold in markets and thrift stores from Morocco to Paris from 1917 onward.

Subversive uses

This flourishing market fed fears about criminal impersonations. Since the end of 1918, crimes committed by persons wearing French or American uniforms had multiplied. In January 1919, the *New York Times* published an article entitled, "Paris Apaches in Our Uniforms," which responded to incidents of American soldiers committing crimes in the French capital, claiming these as "existing nearly exclusively in the vivid imagination of sensational local newspapers."[59] Instead, these violent acts came from "Apaches of all nationalities dressed in American uniforms." This assertion was supported by evidence provided by the Paris Police Prefecture. While some part of the criminal population surely dressed in repurposed uniforms, stories such as these undoubtedly magnified fears.

Even beyond such impersonations, uniforms began taking on new meanings, gaining even greater symbolic significance among the general population. In the aftermath of the war, the uniform became a complex symbol evoking, depending on the context, either glory or trauma, order or mass-scale violence. Artists began to subvert the uniform's longstanding patriotic connotations. Use of the uniform for artistic purposes was not new. Throughout the eighteenth century, painters and other artists, especially theatre directors and "fairground spectacle performers," bought repurposed uniforms in order to "stage scenes of all of the European armies," of "every era."[60] During the early stages of wartime, in 1914, André Warnod described an exchange at the Temple in which a secondhand merchant was hesitant to sell a greatcoat, telling a client, "I can easily rent these things out to theaters staging military pieces."[61]

During the war, censorship prevented ambivalent depictions of the national uniform (although the cabaret Voltaire in Zurich staged such shows in 1916). But shortly after the war, pacifist and anti-military plays in Paris began depicting the uniform in a new light. Beginning in the 1920s, the "Phalange Artistique" made use of "makeshift sets" and "thrift store costumes," including uniforms.[62] In a 1924 theatrical staging of Henri Barbusse's pacifist novel *Le Feu*, the costumes, which stood out against relatively plain sets, were secondhand coats that had been used in the war by communist forces.[63] The views expressed in these pieces were not mainstream by any means, but they nevertheless represented a growing practice of using uniforms for anti-military or anarchist purposes.

This kind of subversive use of the uniform was not limited to the political sphere. Uniforms were also appropriated in homosexual circles in Paris and Berlin. While uniforms had been accessories to homoerotic fantasies before the war, notably in the case of the Navy, the war heightened these trends. Photographs of the "bal des folles" at Magic-City show gay attendees dressed as marines and soldiers.[64] The venue, fittingly, was a former amusement park near the Eiffel Tower in Paris which had been occupied by the army during the war. Gay iconography of the uniform managed to challenge both heterosexual gender norms and nationalist propriety.

The colonies were another place where uniforms could take on new meanings outside of their intended use. There, uniforms, which had been traded for natural goods and slaves since the eighteenth century, were used for displays of authority, or as status symbols and gifts. The Archbishop of Algiers made use of the uniform's seductive powers in 1884, when he gifted "the outfits of senators and ministers," bought from the Temple market, to King Muteesa I of Buganda.[65] In Africa, South America, and the West Indies, indigenous populations had taken a liking to military uniforms.

While Europeans commended themselves for imparting modesty upon local populations by having them wear western dress, travel narratives often mocked the efforts of "savages" incapable of mastering the proper use of the military wardrobe. The Count of Castlenau, for example, described an encounter in Brazil in the 1840s with a "sort of old monkey wearing a Portuguese officer's uniform."[66] This racist trope from Europeans reached a peak in the Americas with the rise of Faustin I of Haiti, who dressed his new army with uniforms from the Temple; the press delighted in their depictions of "*négriots* in uniform."[67] In Africa, the image of the native in uniform was common in both text and photographs (Figure 14.5).

From 1860 onwards, various kings became the subject of mockery, including Denis Rapontchombo of Gabon, whose wardrobe included embroidered uniforms, some of which were from the 18th century. In a travel narrative that was widely reprinted, including in France, Henry Morton Stanley described his encounter with the chief Ngufu Mpanda along the Congo River, describing him as, "a veritable Uncle Tom—in an English red military tunic, a brown felt hat, and ample cloth of check pattern around the lower portion of his body."[68] In *La Grande Encyclopédie*, Marcellin Berthelot states that: "the black kings adopt the uniforms of generals, prefects, and academics, or even the servant's livery."[69] At the end of the century, Belgian lawyer Pierre Verhaegen mocked the King of Tumba for wearing an "ancient uniform from the British army, with a faded red jacket" and sporting a "carabinier's hat straight out of Offenbach."[70]

Fig. 210. — Roitelet africain.

Figure 14.5 *Local leaders in European secondhand clothing. A common representation prewar, it disappeared with the involvement of Senegalese skirmishers. Colonel Henri-Nicolas Frey,* Côte occidentale d'Afrique: Vues, scènes, croquis *(Paris: Marpon et Flammarion, 1890). Drawing by Pierre-Georges Jeanniot.* © *Manuel Charpy.*

Until the 1880s, neither explorers nor colonial governments were particularly disturbed by these displays, particularly in the case of these subjugated kings. But use of uniforms soon spread within the local populations. In 1890, the Belgian friar Alexis Marie Gochet wrote: "The Western coast of Africa takes in an unimaginable quantity of old coats, worn frocks, outdated tailcoats, and obsolete tunics. The old red or blue uniforms of English or French soldiers take pride of place."[71] While the image of the king adorned in castoffs was still a source of amusement, the prevalence of native servants or merchants in elevated dress was more alarming. *L'Expansion Belge* wrote in 1910, "The blacks of Sierra Leone are even more unbearable than the ruling class of Dakar. They are all dressed in the latest fashions from Europe, and celebrate their Sundays by promenading in frock coats in 38° [Celsius] heat in the shade, in fine form." On the subject of the Congo, the Belgian Lieutenant General Baron De Witte noted in 1913:

> Today the indigenous people of Brazzaville are already overdressed, and come Sunday, those who possess multiple pairs of pants or multiple jackets will wear them one on top of the other, in order to show off their wealth. Many are eager to follow Parisian fashion, and having learned that Europeans would make fun of the negro's propensity for top hats, [...] most have given them up, and are seen today wearing elegant Panamas.[72]

These practices suggested a threat to colonial hierarchies, and colonial governments took notice, especially in Western and Central Africa. The French colonial government were cautious about contesting the uniforms of the Tirailleurs who had fought in the French army—even those who had been demobilized—but did survey the use of the uniforms closely.[73] Of particular concern was the anti-colonial movement in the Congo that formed around the religious figure and politician André Grenard Matsoua, who at one point, refused to remove his own uniform. Followers would wear military dress from the First World War, signaling their unwillingness to remain second class citizens. Colonial literature from 1920 to 1960 was rife with depictions of "negroes in their Sunday best," in uniforms bought from secondhand markets or retained by former Tirailleurs. These works range from *Tintin au Congo*—which ridiculed blacks in English uniforms with epaulettes—to André Gide's *Voyage au Congo*, which describe a Congolese chief "in a very long and very used frock coat, with a khaki helmet, khaki breeches, black leggings, and big hobnailed boots. The whole was indescribably ridiculous and ugly."[74] Even when these uniforms were worn by former Tirailleurs, they continued to appear to Europeans to be incongruous or even threatening.

Conclusion

While repurposed uniforms had been prevalent in civil society since the 1830s, both in France and throughout the world, the First World War ushered in major changes to the secondhand market. Old uniforms were widely seen as being carriers of disease, unceremoniously stripped from the dead. And yet, scarcity and the massive scale of the war pushed the military and the general population alike to recuperate, repair, transform, and resell countless uniforms. The governments of France, the United States, and England all made forays into the secondhand market, selling items such as shirts, breeches, and jackets, either domestically or abroad. Whereas the French uniform in many respects gained in symbolic power during the war as an emblem of nationalist valor, it also eventually became a tool for contesting that same power, especially after demobilization. Homosexuals, pacifists, anti-militarists, anti-colonialists, and other groups and individuals used the uniforms from the First World War to play against prescribed roles, often confronting the great nations that had ushered in the war in the first place.

Notes

1 André Warnod, *La Brocante et les petits marchés de Paris* (Paris: Figuiere, March 1914), 15–16.

2 See Manuel Charpy, "Formes et Échelles du commerce d'occasion au XIXe siècle: L'Exemple du vêtement à Paris," *Revue d'histoire du XIXe siècle* 24 (2002): 125–50.

3 Chambre de Commerce de Paris, *Statistique de l'industrie à Paris résultant de l'enquête faite par la chambre de commerce pour les années 1847–1848* (Paris: Guillaumin et Co., 1851), s.v. "Vêtements."

4 Félix Mornand, "Le Temple," *L'Illustration*, August 14, 1847.

5 Jules Robert de Massy, *Des Halles et des marchés et du commerce des objets à Paris et à Londres* (Paris: Imprimerie Impériale, 1862).

6 Archives Municipales de Saint-Ouen, AR/2706; Archives Départementales de Seine-Saint-Denis, DM6 3/3; Warnod, "Le Marché aux Puces" [Porte de Clignancourt], *La Brocante et les Petits Marchés de Paris*, 2.

7 For sources on hospitals, see Archives de l'Assistance Publique—Hôpitaux de Paris, Comptes Généraux des Hôpitaux et Hospices Civils, 2M/1-30 et APP, DB371, note from prefect Delessert, October 24, 1845. For information on the hospices, see Bibliothèque Historique de la Ville de Paris (BHVP), series Actualité/120, Comptoirs des Ventes.

8 Archives de Paris (AP), commercial correspondence from Blin, rue de la Corderie au Temple, DQ10; Groupe Archivale de Mont-de-Piété, boxes 13, 58, and 60—clothing represented 60 percent of objects sold mid-century, and, in 1883, the municipal institution still sold 110,000 clothing items per year; AP, auctioneers archival group; AP, Lycée Saint-Louis, letters from Blin Jeune, bulk secondhand sales, specializing and civilian and military items, rue de la Corderie au Temple and rue de Ménilmontant, 1904; letters of J. Landau and his sons, mass exportation of civil and military clothes to England, Africa, and the East Indies, with trading stations in Bombay, Durban, Johannesburg, Pretoria, and Lourenço-Marques, and agencies in Lahore, Kubachi, Calcutta, Madras, Beira, Inhambane, Madagascar, rue de Sévigné, 1907; Archives de la Préfecture de Police, Paris (APP), DB371, petition to prefect, March 12, 1842.

9 De Massy, *Des Halles et des marchés*.

10 Manuel Charpy, "Ajustements: Corps, vêtements à tailles Fixes et standards industriels au XIXe siècle," *Modes pratiques: Revue d'histoire du vêtement et de la mode* 1 (2015), "Normes et Transgressions," 96–127.

11 AP, DQ10/369 and 370.

12 See the expeditions in Crimea, Italy, Mexico, and Cochinchina, for instance.

13 *Dictionnaire universel théorique et pratique du commerce et de la navigation* (Paris: Guillaumin, 1859–61), s.v. "Vêtements confectionnés."

14 Albert Monnier, "Le Temple: Étude de Mœurs parisiennes," *Le Figaro*, March 15, 1857; Norbert Truquin recalled a mid-nineteenth-century tailor creating "ceremonial robes in repurposed military uniforms" in *Les Aventures d'un Prolétaire à Travers les Révolutions*, reprint (Paris: Maspéro, 1977 [1887]), 47.

15 We should add that the same was true for Petticoat Lane in London.

16 AP, 10 AZ 328.

17 *Rapport Présenté par M. Georges Villain au nom de la 2e commission sur diverses pétitions relatives au Marché du Temple* (Paris: Conseil Municipal de Paris, 1892), 151–7.

18 "Vêtements confectionnés," *Dictionnaire Universel*.

19 AP, D3R4/21, steward's letters, no. 2510 ff.

20 Augustin Fabre and Fortuné Chailan, *Histoire du choléra-morbus Asiatique: Depuis son départ des bords du Gange en 1817 jusques à l'invasion du Midi de la France en 1835* (Paris: Hivert et Marseille, Olive, 1835).

21 *Gazette Médicale de Paris*, December 13, 1884.

22 *London Gazette*, August 8 and June 9, 1889.

23 See municipal archives such as the Archives Municipal Île-et-Vilaine, which detail preventative measures for epidemics during 1914–19: 5 M 80–81 (diphtheria, meningitis, measles, scarlet fever ...), 4 M 86–87 (epidemics in schools), and 4 M 96–97 (cholera).

24 SHAT, GR 7 N 403, "Chiffonniers—Commission de récupération des effets d'habillement des armées," Typhus "amongst chiffonniers covered in lice," November 9, 1917 and January 22, 1918.

25 Robert Würtz and A. de Lauradour, "Le Chiffonnage à Paris et dans la banlieue en 1916," *Revue d'hygiène et de police sanitaire* 38 (1916): 416 and 430–3.

26 *Archives de l'Institut Pasteur de Tunis* 10 (1917): 115.

27 SHAT, GR 7 N 403, "Chiffonniers," 1917.

28 Ordinance of 4 Germinal year X (March 25, 1802).

29 Ordinance of November 25, 1812 regarding secondhand merchants; APP, DA52.

30 AP, D3R4/20. Letter 39, 1850.

31 E. Sautayra, *Législation de l'Algérie: Lois, ordonnances, décrets et arrêtés* (Paris: Maisonneuve, 1883), 255–6, s.v. "Effets Militaires, Mars 1841."

32 *Répertoire Méthodique et alphabétique de législation de doctrine et de jurisprudence en matière de droit civil commercial criminel administratif de droit des gens et de droit public jurisprudence générale* (Paris: Dalloz, 1869).

33 *Feuille Officielle du Sénégal et Dépendances,* 1860.

34 See *Le Livre du gradé d'artillerie ... Contenant toutes les matières nécessaires à l'exercice de leurs fonctions et conforme à tous les règlements parus jusqu'à ce jour ...* (Paris: Berger-Levrault, 1915), 837.

35 Jean-Luc Marais, *Histoire du Don en France de 1800 à 1939: Dons et legs charitables, pieux et philanthropiques* (Rennes: Presses Universitaires de Rennes, 1999).

36 "Le Tricot du combattant: L'Œuvre des lecteurs et des lectrices de *L'Écho de Paris*," *L'Écho de Paris*, November 9, 1914.

37 *L'Écho de Paris*, November 11, 1914.

38 Ibid., December 18, 1915.

39 SHAT, XAF 7, Imperial Guard, 1854–70.

40 Félix Chapuis, *L'Instruction théorique du cavalier par lui-même . . .* (Paris: 1915), 58.

41 *Bulletin du Ministère du travail et de la prévoyance sociale* (Paris: Berger-Levrault, 1916), 149.

42 SHAT, GR 7 N 403, "Chiffonniers," May 1917.

43 "Addition au tarif des confections, retouches et réparations des effets du service de l'habillement," *Bulletin Officiel des Ministères de la guerre*, June 10, 1918, 1966.

44 Léonce de Grandmaison, ed., *Impressions de Guerre de Prêtres Soldats* (Paris: Plon-Nourrit, 1916–1917), 332–3.

45 SHAT, press cutting, "Créons un Corps de Chiffonniers Militaires," October 9, 1916.

46 SHAT, GR 7 N 403, "Chiffonniers," and "Récupération des effets d'habillement dans la zone des armées: Rapport de la commission d'étude," May 7, 1917.

47 "Tabling of a report by M. Seydoux, conducted for the Commission de l'Armée, on the need for immediate discussion, and on the basis of the motion for a resolution by M. Brenier and several colleagues, attempting to organize the complete recuperation, on the front and in the rear, of all usable detritus and objects abandoned by the troops," March 1916.

48 SHAT, GR 7 N 403, "Chiffonniers—Commission de récupération des effets d'habillement des armées," "Récupération des effets d'habillement dans la zone des armées. Rapport de la Commission d'étude," May 7, 1917.

49 Ibid.

50 Ministère de la guerre, *Projet de règlement pour les services de petit équipement et de la masse individuelle dans les Corps de Troupe* (Paris: Imprimerie Nationale, 1873), art. 33.

51 SHAT, 7 N 175, EMA, 1914–1919, "Uniformes—Insignes;" Ministère de la guerre, "Commerce sur le front," June 1919.

52 SHAT, 7 N 175, EMA, 1914–1919, Bureau de l'Organisation et de la mobilisation de l'armée, "Uniformes—Insignes," February 14, 1919.

53 SHAT, 7 N 175, EMA, 1914–1919, Ministère de la guerre, "Uniformes—Insignes," June 17, 1919.

54 "The second-hand clothing market in Turkey," *Levant Trade Review* (1915): 418.

55 "Foreign trade notes," *Clothing Trade Journal* (November 1919): 81.

56 "Army uniform sale subject of inquiry," *New York Times*, August 1, 1918.

57 "Sales of army materials abroad," *Commercial and Financial Chronicle* 111–12 (1920): 1713.

58 Charles Divine, "After-the-war scenes in Algerian market towns," *New York Times*, February 8, 1920.

59 "Paris Apaches in our uniforms," *New York Times*, January 31, 1919.

60 BHVP, series Actualité/120, advertisement for Fortin, *c*. 1845; Cabinet des Estampes du Musée Carnavalet, advertisement for Jallais, 20, rue de Bruxelles, "Curiosities, antiques, weapons, military costumes for every era. Rentals for artists," *c*.1870.

61 Warnod, *La Brocante*, 23.

62 Léonor Delaunay, *La Scène bleue: Les Expériences théâtrales prolétariennes et révolutionnaires en France, de la Grande Guerre au front populaire* (Rennes: Presses universitaires de Rennes, 2011); André Palin, "Un Essai de théâtre populaire: La Phalange artistique," *La Révolution Prolétarienne*, 1926, private archives of Madeleine Palin.

63 Delaunay, *La Scène Bleue*; This performance was organized by the group "Art et Action," led by Louise Lara, pacifist and anarchist, and Édouard Autant. See also Paul Vaillant-Couturier, "Trois conscrits," *Trois conscrits, Le Monstre, Asie* (Paris: Bureau d'Éditions, 1929). For theatre during the war, see Chantal Meyer-Plantureux, ed., *Le Théâtre monte au front* (Paris: Éditions Complexe, 2008).

64 See photographs by Brassaï, as well as Farid Chenoune, "Leur Bal: Notes sur des photos de Magic-City, Bal des Tantes de l'entre-deux guerres," *Modes pratiques . . .*, 249–85; and Florence Tamagne, *Histoire de l'homosexualité en Europe: Berlin, Londres, Paris, 1919–1939* (Paris: Le Seuil, 2000).

65 The Archbishop had used the strategy of gifting outfits before: during a previous visit to North America, he had distributed Swiss parochial garments. *À l'Assaut des pays Nègres: Journal des missionnaires d'Alger dans l'Afrique Équatoriale* (Paris: À l'Œuvre des Écoles d'Orient, 1884), 18–19.

66 Francis de Castelanu, ed., *Expédition dans les parties centrales de l'Amérique du Sud, de Rio de Janeiro à Lima, et de Lima au Para*, vol. 1 (Paris: P. Bertrand, 1850), 351.

67 Monnier, "Le Temple."

68 Henry Morton Stanley, *Cinq années au Congo: 1879–1884*, Gérard Hardy, trans. (Paris: Dreyfous, 1885), 84–5.

69 "Fripier," *La Grande encyclopédie: Inventaire raisonné des sciences, des lettres et des arts* (Paris: Lamirault et Cie, 1886).

70 Pierre Verhaegen, *Au Congo: Impressions de voyage* (Gand: Siffer, 1898), 30–100; Lieutenant Lemaire, *Au Congo: Comment les Noirs travaillent* (Bruxelles: Bulens, 1895), 104–7.

71 Alexis Marie Gochet, *Le Congo Français illustré . . .* (Paris: Procure générale, 1890), 155ff.

72 (Baron) De Witte, *Les Deux Congos* (Paris: Plon 1913).

73 Marc Michel, *Les Africains et la Grande Guerre: L'Appel à l'Afrique (1914–1918)* (Paris: Karthala, 2003), 197ff.

74 "Tintin au Congo," *Petit Vingtième*, 1930–1; André Gide, *Voyage au Congo: Retour du Tchad* (Paris: Gallimard, 1927–8).

References

Archives

Archives de l'Assistance Publique, Hôpitaux de Paris, Comptes Généraux des Hôpitaux et Hospices Civils, 2M/1-30; DB371, note from prefect Delessert, October 24, 1845; DB371, petition to prefect, March 12, 1842; DA52.
Archives du Mont-de-Piété, boxes 13, 58, and 60. (SHAT), GR 7 N 403, "Chiffonniers—Commission de récupération des effets d'habillement des armées," November 9, 1917, and January 22, 1918; "Récupération des effets

d'habillement dans la zone des armées: Rapport de la commission d'étude," May 7, 1917; XAF 7, Imperial Guard, 1854–1870; press cutting, "Créons un Corps de chiffonniers militaires," October 9, 1916; 7 N 175, EMA, 1914–1919, "Uniformes—Insignes." Ministère de la Guerre, "Commerce sur le front," June 1919; Bureau de l'Organisation et de la mobilisation de l'armée, "Uniformes—Insignes," February 14, 1919.

Archives de Paris (AP), DQ10, commercial correspondence from Blin, rue de la Corderie au Temple; auctioneers archival group; Lycée Saint-Louis, letters from Blin Jeune, bulk secondhand sales, specializing and civilian and military items, rue de la Corderie au Temple and rue de Ménilmontant, 1904; letters of J. Landau and his sons, mass exportation of civil and military clothes to England, Africa, and the East Indies, with trading stations in Bombay, Durban, Johannesburg, Pretoria, and Lourenço-Marques, and agencies in Lahore, Kubachi, Calcutta, Madras, Beira, Inhambane, Madagascar, rue de Sévigné, 1907; DQ10/369 and 370; 10 AZ 328; D3R4/21, steward's letters, no. 2510 ff; D3R4/20. Letter 39, 1850.

Archives Départmentales of Seine-Saint-Denis, DM6 3/3.

Archives Municipal de Île-et-Villaine, 5 M 80–81; 4 M 86–87; 4 M 96–97.

Bibliothèque Historique de la Ville de Paris (BHVP), series Actualité/120, Comptoirs des Ventes; series Actualité/120, advertisement for Fortin, c. 1845.

Cabinet des Estampes du Musée Carnavalet, advertisement for Jallais, 20, rue de Bruxelles, "Curiosities, antiques, weapons, military costumes for every era. Rentals for artists," c. 1870.

Service historique de la Défense, boxes 13, 58, and 60.

Ordinance of 4 Germinal year X (March 25, 1802).

Ordinance of November 25, 1812 regarding secondhand merchants.

Secondary sources

À l'Assaut des Pays Nègres: Journal des missionnaires d'Alger dans l'Afrique Équatoriale. Paris: À l'Œuvre des Écoles d'Orient, 1884.

"Addition au tarif des confections, retouches et réparations des effets du service de l'habillement." *Bulletin Officiel des Ministères de la Guerre*, June 10, 1918.

Archives de l'Institut Pasteur de Tunis 10 (1917): 115.

"Army uniform sale subject of inquiry." *New York Times*, August 1, 1918.

Bulletin du Ministère du travail et de la prévoyance sociale. Paris: Berger-Levrault, 1916.

Castelanu, Francis de, ed. *Expédition dans les parties centrales de l'Amérique du Sud, de Rio de Janeiro à Lima, et de Lima au Para*, vol. 1. Paris: P. Bertrand, 1850.

Chambre de Commerce de Paris, *Statistique de l'industrie à Paris résultant de l'enquête faite par la chambre de commerce pour les années 1847–1848*. Paris: Guillaumin et Co., 1851.

Chapuis, Félix. *L'Instruction théorique du cavalier par lui-même, services et réglements militaires*. Paris: 1915.

Charpy, Manuel. "Ajustements: Corps, vêtements à tailles fixes et standards industriels au XIXe siècle." *Modes pratiques: Revue d'histoire du vêtement et de la mode: Normes et Transgressions* 1 (2015): 96–127.

Charpy, Manuel. "Formes et Échelles du commerce d'occasion au XIXe Siècle: L'Exemple du vêtement à Paris." *Revue d'histoire du XIXe siècle* 24 (2002): 125–50.

Chenoune, Farid. "Leur Bal: Notes sur des photos de Magic-City, Bal des Tantes de l'entre-deux guerres." *Modes pratiques: Revue d'histoire du vêtement et de la mode* 1 (2015): 249–85.

de Massy, Jules Robert. *Des Halles et des marchés et du commerce des objets à Paris et à Londres*. Paris: Imprimerie Impériale, 1862.

De Witte (Baron). *Les Deux Congos*. Paris: Plon 1913.

Delaunay, Léonor. *La Scène bleue: Les Expériences théâtrales prolétariennes et révolutionnaires en France, de la Grande Guerre au Front populaire*. Rennes: Presses universitaires de Rennes, 2011.

Dictionnaire universel théorique et pratique du commerce et de la mavigation. Paris: Guillaumin, 1859–61.

Divine, Charles. "After-the-war scenes in Algerian market towns." *New York Times*, February 8, 1920.
Fabre, Augustin and Fortuné Chailan. *Histoire du choléra-morbus Asiatique: Depuis son Départ des Bords du Gange en 1817 jusques à l'invasion du Midi de la France en 1835*. Paris: Hivert et Marseille, Olive, 1835.
Feuille Officielle du Sénégal et Dépendances, 1860.
"Foreign trade notes." *Clothing Trade Journal* (November 1919).
Gazette Médicale de Paris, December 13, 1884.
Gide, André. *Voyage au Congo—Retour du Tchad*. Paris: Gallimard, 1927–8.
Gochet, Alexis Marie. *Le Congo Français illustré . . .* Paris: Procure générale, 1890.
Grandmaison, Léonce de, ed. *Impressions de guerre de prêtres soldat*. Paris: Plon-Nourrit, 1916–17.
L'Écho de Paris, November 11, 1914.
L'Écho de Paris, December 18, 1915.
Le Livre du gradé d'artillerie a l'usage des élèves brigardiers, brigadiers et sous-officiers d'artillerie de campagne. Contenant toutes les matières nécessaires à l'exercice de leurs fonctions et conforme à tous les règlements parus jusqu'à ce jour. Paris: Berger-Levrault, 1915.
"Le Tricot du combattant: L'Œuvre des lecteurs et des lectrices de *L'Écho de Paris*." *L'Écho de Paris,* November 9, 1914.
Lieutenant Lemaire. *Au Congo: Comment les Noirs travaillent*. Bruxelles: Bulens, 1895.
London Gazette, August 8 and June 9, 1889.
Marais, Jean-Luc. *Histoire du Don en France de 1800 à 1939: Dons et legs charitables, pieux et philanthropiques*. Rennes: Presses Universitaires de Rennes, 1999.
Meyer-Plantureux, Chantal, ed. *Le Théâtre monte au front*. Paris: Éditions Complexe, 2008.
Michel, Marc. *Les Africains et la Grande Guerre: L'Appel à l'Afrique (1914–1918)*. Paris: Karthala, 2003.
Ministère de la Guerre. *Projet de Règlement pour les services de petit équipement et de la masse individuelle dans les Corps de Troupe*. Paris: Imprimerie Nationale, 1873.
Monnier, Albert. "Le Temple: Étude de Mœurs parisiennes." *Le Figaro*, March 15, 1857.
Mornand, Félix. "Le Temple." *L'Illustration*, August 14, 1847.
Palin, André. "Un Essai de Théâtre Populaire: La Phalange Artistique." *La Révolution Prolétarienne*, 1926 (private archives of Madeleine Palin).
"Paris Apaches in our uniforms." *New York Times*, January 31, 1919.
Rapport Présenté par M. Georges Villain au nom de la 2e commission sur diverses pétitions relatives au Marché du Temple. Paris: Conseil Municipal de Paris, 1892.
Répertoire Méthodique et alphabétique de législation de doctrine et de jurisprudence en matière de droit civil commercial criminel administratif de droit des gens et de droit public jurisprudence générale. Paris: Dalloz, 1869.
"Sales of Army materials abroad." *Commercial and Financial Chronicle* 111–12 (1920): 1713.
Sautayra, E. *Législation de l'Algérie: Lois, ordonnances, décrets et arrêtés*. Paris: Maisonneuve, 1883.
Stanley, Henry Morton. *Cinq années au Congo: 1879–1884*, Gérard Hardy, trans. Paris: Dreyfous, 1885.
Tamagne, Florence. *Histoire de l'homosexualité en Europe: Berlin, Londres, Paris, 1919–1939*. Paris: Le Seuil, 2000.
"The second-hand clothing market in Turkey." *Levant Trade Review* (1915).
"Tintin au Congo." *Petit Vingtième,* 1930–1.
Truquin, Norbert. *Les Aventures d'un prolétaire à Travers les revolutions*, reprint. Paris: Maspéro, 1977 [1887].
Vaillant-Couturier, Paul. *Trois conscrits, Le Monstre, Asie*. Paris: Bureau d'Éditions, 1929.
Verhaegen, Pierre. *Au Congo: Impressions de voyage*. Gand: Siffer, 1898.
Warnod, André. *La Brocante et les petits marchés de Paris*. Paris: Figuiere, March 1914.
Wurtz, Robert and A. de Lauradour, "Le Chiffonnage à Paris et dans la banlieue en 1916." *Revue d'hygiène et de police sanitaire* 38 (1916): 409–39.

Part Four

Fashion in print: Questions of national fashion and gender

15

The gentleman turned "enemy"
Men's fashion in the Hungarian press, 1914–18

Zsolt Mészáros

Conditions were by no means favorable for the men's clothing industry in Europe during the First World War. Trade was disrupted between the countries in the Central Empire (Germany, Austria-Hungary, Bulgaria, the Ottoman Empire), the Triple Entente (France, the United Kingdom, and Russia), and their allies (the United States, Italy, and Romania, among others). Textile industries were monopolized by various needs of the army and sales to the civil sphere declined all over Europe. Supply issues were further aggravated by shortages of raw materials such as wool and cotton and other necessary goods such as canvas.[1] Most significantly, a majority of workers and consumers were sent to the front. In the case of Austria-Hungary, partial mobilization was announced on July 25, 1914, with full mobilization following on July 31. Nevertheless, throughout the war, Hungarians wrote articles, drew fashion illustrations, took photographs, and produced advertisements that advocated for continued purchases of men's clothing and a renewal of the male wardrobe. The magazine *Szabó Otthon* (Home of the Tailor), primarily a trade journal, summarized the situation as such: "The First World War has provoked fundamental changes in all aspects of public life; male society cannot but be influenced by the war, even in matters of the wardrobe."[2]

Various studies written in the past twenty years have showcased the importance of consumption and dress in the construction of modern masculinity.[3] This article seeks to examine how the male civilian wardrobe changed during the First World War through a study of visual representations, military propaganda, and discourse in the fashion media. This analysis focuses on the case of the well-dressed upper-middle-class male in Hungary's capital, Budapest. Through a study of the often contradictory messaging on the masculine ideal, we aim to show the ways in which Hungarian and, more broadly, European fashion and public discourse were shaped by the extraordinary circumstances of the war.

There are relatively few sources from the era that cover the subject of men's fashion in depth and there were no periodicals devoted entirely to the topic published during the war. The magazine *Férfi Divat* (Men's Fashion) was the first and only Hungarian fashion journal targeted towards men published during the period of the Austro-Hungarian Dual Monarchy (1867–1918). Published between 1899 and 1908, it had ceased production when the war broke out. Leading up to 1914, newspapers and women's magazines would occasionally devote several paragraphs to men's dress, sometimes accompanied by illustrations. After the declaration of war, however, they no longer featured men's civilian clothes. They replaced the space reserved for a discussion on menswear with patterns for hats, mittens, scarves, socks, and the like that women could knit or crochet and send to the front.

The press began championing the military uniform, celebrating its "pike gray" tint, instead of talking about menswear.[4] Between 1914 and 1918, most general interest magazines stopped printing articles on men's fashion. Only the few active theatre journals, and certain other culture-oriented magazines (*Divat és Művészet, Színház és Divat, Színházi Élet, A Társaság*), continued to cover the subject, publishing photographs, illustrations, and advice on men's dress. Trade journals intended for tailors (*Szabó Otthon, Szabó Hírlap, Úri Szabók Divatlapja*) are another valuable source of information. Analysis of these last two sources—further complemented by information from French and Austrian magazines (*Le Carnet de la Semaine, Le Figaro, Le Gaulois, Le Pêle-Mêle, Le Temps, Neues Wiener Journal, Neuigkeits-Welt-Blatt, Reichspost*)—allows us an understanding of the practices and ideology associated with men's fashion in Hungary, and Europe more broadly, during the war.

Soldier versus civilian: Men's fashion discourse during wartime

One month after the war broke out, the satirical weekly magazine *Magyar Figaró* (Hungarian Figaro) published a front-page illustration depicting a soldier seated in a café and surrounded by women, while a finely dressed man sits alone in the background, seemingly distressed by the soldier's success. The caption for the drawing reads, "Today a wounded soldier is worth more than yesterday's dandy in good health"[5] (Figure 15.1). It is no surprise the uniform became associated with authentic masculinity following the declaration of mobilization; men's suits and civilian clothes were in turn associated with effeminacy and cowardice.[6] A patriotic distrust for fashion and luxury products arose in the public eye, and these suspicions extended more broadly to any form of non-essential consumption.[7] A similar attitude predominated in the French press as well. In 1916, the French illustrated satirical magazine *Le Carnet de la Semaine* published a poem by Jean Bastia (1878–1940) entitled, "Masculine Fashion," which bade farewell to the figure of the dandy:

> Despite your style,
> Your cravats and shined shoes
> I can assure you,
> That in Paris, your reign is over.[8]

In that same year, *Le Gaulois* criticized French tailors who advertised new menswear designs, claiming, "Real men's fashion, for two years now, has been the military uniform."[9]

In Hungary, this derisory attitude towards men's fashion softened somewhat after the first months of the war. *Magyar Figaró*, after mocking the dandy in August, published an article in November that noted that any indignation directed towards crowds in restaurants, theaters, and other venues for

Figure 15.1 *Cover illustration, "A nők kedvence" (The ladies' sweetheart), artist: Dezső Bér. Magyar Figaró (Hungarian Figaro) 32, 35 (August, 30, 1914).*

leisure was misplaced. "The capital of a victorious nation must not live like a town under siege," the writer stated.[10] Readers were advised that avarice (here meaning the unwillingness to spend) was a crime as dangerous as the spreading of false news, as both were capable of contributing to the nation's moral and financial distress. In addition, the magazine insisted that joyous civil life was beneficial for the relaxation of soldiers on leave—a strong, unified home front guaranteed a strong army, and thus, victory.

Certain Hungarian political figures shared this perspective, including Budapest mayor István Bárczy (1866–1943), who advocated in an article in 1916 for the necessity of fashion, entertainment, and consumption during wartime.[11] He considered these as necessary outlets, not only for the economy, but for morale as well. In Bárczy's words, soldiers would not want to come home only to find a valley of tears.[12] In many ways, Hungarian society responded to this call to participate in public life; the First World War coincided with a golden age of Hungarian theatre and cinema.[13]

Fashion was not paused for long in Budapest. "The arrival of the war in the summer of 1914 had an effect on men's fashion like that of the spring frost on the fruit tree ready to flower," wrote Béla Kolos Mangold (1859–1945) in 1916 in *Budapesti Hírlap*, one of the prominent Hungarian newspapers of the era.[14] Mangold was the former editor-in-chief of *Férfi Divat* and respected voice on fashion. His metaphor acknowledges that fashion did indeed face a period of dormancy in the early days of the war, as the public's attention turned towards the pike-gray uniform, but Mangold claims that this was soon followed by reemergence of interest in fashion on the part of non-combatants and soldiers on leave. While he gives no in-depth explanation for the shift in attention, another anonymous author pointed out that: "If one walks through the streets during the hour of the promenade, one happily notices that a number of well-dressed men with fine taste reside in Budapest."[15]

Hungarian tailors were, of course, in favor of this propagandist discourse which imbued commerce and fashion with a greater economic and patriotic significance. *Szabó Hírlap* (Tailor's Journal), the official magazine for multiple tailor's guilds, published an appeal to this effect in November 1914, under the title "Ne Takarékoskodjunk az Ipar Rovására" ("Don't Economize at the Expense of Industry"). According to the text, the drastic reduction in household clothing purchases emerged from a false, parsimonious patriotism, which ultimately weakened the country. The unnamed author recognized that reasonable financial limits should be adhered to, but argued that if an individual had money to spare, he also had a duty to purchase new clothing.[16] The call for continued spending carried on despite the difficulties tailors faced in producing clothing due to mobilization, elevated prices, and fabric shortages. This ethos of patriotic consumption can be seen in magazine *Magyar Iparművészet* (Hungarian Decorative Arts), which praised the new Austrian men's fashion magazine *Die Herrenwelt* (published 1916–17) for its emphasis on hygiene and the wardrobe, and their role in promoting good health, calm, and autonomy for the national fashion industry.[17]

The gentleman as enemy: Men's fashion vocabulary and the military propaganda

The countries in the Central Empire and the Triple Entente were engaged in a cultural battle in addition to their campaigns in the trenches throughout the war. An advertisement for the cosmetic company Dr. Jutassy demonstrates the extent of the nationalist fervor in Hungary: an illustration shows a soldier standing in front of a canon as it fires soaps into the air, with the text claiming that Dr. Jutassy clears away dangerous and ineffective French and English products (Figure 15.2).[18] The war had only been underway a few weeks when the Hungarian press began discussing the prospect of abandoning the French and English lexicon of the fashion industry in favor of native terms.

This emphasis on linguistic purification was not unique to Hungary. The French newspaper *Le Gaulois* reported on a 1915 conference held in Germany with the participation of the Central Bureau for German Fashion, the Berlin Chamber of Commerce, the Syndicate of Men's Fashion, the Syndical Union of Men's Tailors, and the Society for Purification of the German Language, as well as journalists and writers.[19] The parties discussed the possibility of finding German words for English and French terms such as *smoking, raglan, ulster, paletot, knickerbocker, breeches, escarpins, covert-coat, revers,*

Figure 15.2 *Advertisement for Dr. Jutassy's cosmetic brand,* Színházi Élet *(Theatrical Life)*. Színházi Élet 4, 12 (1915): II.

sweater, and *Norfolk*. Among the replacements agreed upon were *Abendjacke* (suit jacket), *Überzieher* (paletot), *Reithose* (breeches), *Sportwams* (sweater), and *Keilmantel* (raglan).[20]

No conference of this type was held in Hungary, but we can point to several similar initiatives. The Hungarian tailor's magazine *La Toilette* abandoned its French name in favor of a Hungarian one, *Úri Szabók Divatlapja* (Journal of Fashion for Tailors), in the fall of 1914, before announcing a boycott of enemy products, especially English fabrics. Certain other Hungarian magazines and stores nevertheless did continue to publish advertisements, articles, and catalogues with English and French words.

London was the capital of men's fashion in the nineteenth and twentieth centuries, with the figure of the *gentleman* representing the masculine ideal in Western fashion.[21] The war created new ideological repercussions for the perpetuation of this English ideal. The French magazine *Le Pêle-Mêle* continued to celebrate men's fashion from across the channel, praising the manner in which English tailors took inspiration from the war: "The craftsmen of Bond Street have not settled for a slavish imitation of the uniform, but instead draw practical inspiration from the military in the art of dress."[22] The article goes on to criticize the state of affairs in Paris, where designers simply imitate elements of the British uniform: "Every day, we see civilian men in the streets who have adopted the dolman or shell jacket, which imitate the bellows pockets that we see on the uniforms of the Tommies."[23]

The Hungarian press, on the other hand, began to position itself in opposition to English fashion.[24] Indeed, British fashion was labeled as immoral, and as such, its tailors no longer had the authority to proscribe rules of dress to the rest of Europe. In 1914, in an article for the Viennese newspaper *Neue Freie Presse* writer Raoul Auernheimer (1876–1948) announced the death of the "gentleman," a diagnosis confirmed by Hungarian journalist Olga Szende-Dárday (1878–1923).[25] The archetypal figure of continental elegance was now associated with the enemy. The countries of the Central Powers attempted to devise new ideals in its place. Auernheimer's solution was the *Ehrenmann* (literally, honorary man) while Szende-Dárday suggested the *kultúrember* (*Kulturmensch* or man of culture)—the latter figure, according to the journalist, intended to be cultivated, cosmopolitan, and emblematic of an international liberal vision.[26]

Questions rapidly emerged in Hungary over the course that men's fashion should take, especially in relation to the idea of a national stylistic autonomy. The Austrian catholic daily newspaper *Reichspost* defined fashion as a *Kulturfrage*, or a question of national culture: "Why must an Austrian soul fight from underneath a French outfit?"[27] Opinions were divided in Hungary regarding the adoption of a national style. Some defended the London styles, while others accused the English of having corrupted men's dress, claiming that Hungarian fashion would need to emancipate itself from foreign influence. According to *Szabó Otthon*, the interruption of trade with enemy countries made it necessary for Hungary to look for inspiration within its own borders. The trade bulletin insisted that wartime changes would stem from a new emphasis on the personal: the tastes of the tailor and the client would prevail over foreign trends regarding the cut.[28] Some parties attempted to adapt traditional Hungarian nobleman's garb for civilian use—these types of garments played a role in certain festivities involving the royal court, but did not find broader acceptance within the general population.[29]

Béla Kolos Mangold, for his part, expressed misgivings over English culture and its conception of the *gentleman*, yet did not feel that English stylistic influence could be eradicated from one day to the next. According to Mangold, the men's wardrobe would always be founded on English influences, and dressing oneself in this manner did not preclude one's patriotism.[30] In the fall of 1915, Mangold wrote in the magazine *A Társaság* (The Society) that English influence continued to prevail in the cut, color, and style of men's clothing in Hungary.[31] According to István Goreczky, a tailor in Budapest, truly independent Hungarian fashion could be seen in the streets; the beautiful clothes worn by pedestrians were no imitation of foreign styles, but rather bore the imprint of the individual. Goreczky criticized British dress, observing that, "with its heaviness, and with some of its lines, it amounts to a real caricature."[32] Nevertheless, the author admitted that men would surely return to following the London fashions after the war had ended.

While the opinions from journalists, intellectuals, and tailors on men's fashion were divided during the First World War, several commonalities remain: all writers shared a conflicted relationship with English fashion, emphasized local creation and production, and called for establishing new reference points and influences for men's dress. Ultimately, however, this ongoing ideological battle did not seem to strongly manifest itself in daily life. Photographs, fashion illustrations, and descriptions of clothing in the press show that men's dress in Hungary from 1914 to 1918 continued to follow the European standards, particularly those emanating from England.

The Hungarian menswear industry in crisis

On top of the ideological aversion to French and English fashion, the war also created logistical problems that isolated the Hungarian fashion and luxury sector from its European counterparts. The magazine *Divat és Művészet* (Fashion and Art) explained the three month delay of their August 1914 issue to readers by stating: "at the time of the declaration of war, there was no fashion."[33] The engravings that were due to arrive in Budapest from Paris for the fall-winter season were interrupted by the war, depriving the magazine of content. Although the magazine was eventually able to acquire the latest French designs from the United States (the article does not specify the details of this arrangement), they added designs created by the Budapest fashion houses Mme Berkovits and Mme Reiter. As the war drew on, designs from Austria, Germany, Hungary, and the United States replaced those from France and England in the press.

The manufacturing industry was faced with even graver difficulties, which were widely reported in the media at the time. These included the cancellation of credit for artisans, the military's takeover of most textile factories, and the departure of workers, artisans, and clients to the front.[34] Smaller companies were forced to close, and demand was overall greatly reduced. In addition, the army monopolized the use of railway lines and the postal service for the transportation of troops and munitions. Commercial packages were often late or lost entirely, resulting in disruptions which were especially pronounced for provincial tailors outside of the capital. The Austro-Hungarian military requisitioned textile companies in order to produce military clothing, and civilian production lagged. As a result, a number of textiles—notably wool, canvas, and cotton—were in shortage, with prices rising considerably.

In order to allow for a greater likelihood of orders arriving, suppliers recommended that tailors and other clients order two types of fabric—if one went missing, the second option could take its place.[35] Similar compromises were enacted for leather and fur. As the latter became increasingly expensive, suppliers advised tailors to use lambswool in its place for the linings of winter coats, rather than textile or plush fabric.[36] Throughout the war, businessmen and enterprises would continue to develop solutions to mitigate shortages—they searched for new sources of raw materials, used low-quality materials, or even experimented with new fabrics, such as those made from paper or synthetics.

The dress code in civil society: A change in masculine style

Although the war did introduce certain new clothing items to the civil sphere, it mainly reconfigured the functions and significance of those already in use. Suits became less formal, more practical and comfortable. A journalist for *Le Pêle-Mêle* wrote of men's fashion in 1916, "Current fashion draws above all from a utilitarian perspective."[37] Vests were worn less regularly, for example, while soft collars replaced the stiff collar.[38] Men preferred unstarched cuffs and shirt fronts as well, notably due to the increased cost in laundering and starching.[39] "The carnival has been all but over since 1914," declared French newspaper *Le Temps*, "The civilian's main duty is to remain quiet, and to dress himself simply."[40] Articles would often describe elegant men's dress as having lost its luster. The editor at *A Társaság* replied to a letter from a female reader as follows: "In this time of war, the rules of fashion have become more relaxed, and recently, a highly esteemed statesman was heard saying that the true gentleman today is not he who has the latest suit, but he whose suit is most worn. Looking down on someone for his dress is at the very least in poor taste."[41]

Generally, the rules around men's dress were relaxed. A columnist for *Le Temps* advised that especially luxurious formal wear was no longer appropriate given the political situation, before offering his intended solution: "At any hour day or night, no matter the circumstance or location, we are eager to see just one article of clothing, the most simple, the most unassuming and banal, the go-to for any invitation, the indefatigable *veston* (suit jacket)!"[42] The history of the suit jacket dates to the 1860s. Due to its comfort and practicality, it was previously worn as informal wear or for travel.[43] After 1914, its role evolved. French journalist, novelist, and playwright Régis Gignoux (1878–1931) devoted an article to the jacket in *Le Figaro*: "If our singers and poets hadn't already banded together in their taunting and humiliation of Wilhelm II, the kronprinz, Franz-Joseph, and his other accomplices, they would surely have bequeathed us a new song, The Victory of the *Veste*."[44] The author also provides an explanation for the jacket's newfound popularity at the Opéra de Paris, writing, "One now goes to the Opéra—as with other theaters in Paris—in one's 'informal wear,' because it is difficult to find transportation to go home only to change wardrobe, and because the spectacles these days are not soirées at the gala."[45] The Hungarian press remarked on this trend as well, noting the decline of the tail coat or frock coat as appropriate evening wear.[46] Hungarian writer Zsolt Harsányi (1887–1943) was less enthusiastic about the rise to prominence of the suit jacket, describing it as fit only for the "nouveau riche" and "uncivilized."[47]

Popular menswear also borrowed from sporting wear, hunting wear, and the military uniform—the effect of the latter can be seen in the use of breeches, or of coats and overcoats with raglan sleeves. Sándor Brachfeld, head of his own Hungarian fashion house for men, also identified military inspiration in the narrow fit for suits popular at the time.[48] The trench-coat gained prominence as well, adapted from its military origins for civilian use.[49] The top hat, on the other hand, lost ground as men turned increasingly towards the felt hat—although the former did retain its adherents, standing as a symbol of a more peaceful bygone era. One critic remarked, "The top hat suggests a certain timeless elegance, in a way the felt hat can never match."[50]

Indeed, the felt hat was overly casual, or even decadent, to some. In February 1918, the journalist Izidor Kálnoki (1863–1930), writing under the pseudonym Vulpes, published a sarcastic piece on the sorry state of masculine dress in the weekly *Az Érdekes Újság* (The Interesting Journal). Kálnoki remarked on the absence of top hats in the street, noting that pedestrians were sporting used and crumpled felt hats instead. The felt hat had an advantage, he thought, as a man "can carry it in his pocket as well as on his head, and thus he need not pay the price of the coat check."[51] Of the hats that had been made popular during the Belle Époque, men generally continued to favor the boater hat (called the Girardi hat in Austria-Hungary, after the famous Viennese actor Alexander Girardi) over the bowler, which was now seen as outdated (Figure 15.3): "The best hat makers of Oxford Street bear no regret in announcing that the hideous bowler has been relegated to the dustbin of history."[52] In previous years, the tweed cap had been popular mainly with young men, workers, and sportsmen, but photographs taken during the war show that had become more broadly adapted as daily informal wear.[53]

The colors of men's ensembles in Hungary were generally subdued, composed predominantly of shades of black, gray, brown, and blue. Sándor Brachfeld wrote, "Men's fashion has adapted to the seriousness of these somber times, avoiding any vivid coloring."[54] This diagnosis was seemingly also true for French fashion. *Le Pêle-Mêle* noticed a trend of kaki in Paris, finding that, "Some enthusiasts go so far as to wear shirts in the color."[55] In Hungary, bright colors were only permissible on handkerchiefs, ties, and socks. Popular patterns for fabrics included thick or thin stripes, checkers, or

Figure 15.3 *At the Budapest horse races, 1917. Photographer unknown. Foretpan/Magyar Bálint.*

small motifs.[56] Finally, beards and mustaches diminished in size. The poor hygiene in the trenches inspired the adoption of the new toothbrush moustache—a small moustache, shaved at the sides, extending from the nose to just above the upper lip.[57]

Conclusion

In conclusion, the Hungarian fashion sector was in poor condition at the end of the war. Its stocks had been exhausted and its workers were in short supply. Theatre magazines did not display any men's fashion in their pages in the period immediately after the war. In late 1918, the women's fashion magazine *Budapesti Bazár* went so far as to show its readers how to transform men's frocks and evening suits into women's coats and dresses.[58] Yet, while it may seem as if men's fashion, eclipsed by the ongoing war, stood at a standstill from 1914 to 1918, this did not turn out to be the case. Civilian fashion during the era was continuously evolving. Menswear was shaped by economic and cultural forces, including nationalist propaganda. It adapted to the vagaries of wartime industrial production, and was ultimately subject to the whims of individual taste. While the uniform certainly dominated public attention during the period, men's daily dress was an active participant in the era's ideological discourse on wartime solidarity, public life, and the masculine ideal.

Notes

1 In prewar Hungary, 1 kg of greasy wool cost 1.50–1.80 Krone, but this figure tripled to 5–6 Krone during the war. "A Posztóárakról" (On the price of wool), *Szabó Otthon* (Home of the Tailor), May 1, 1915, 3–4.

2 "A Jövő Divatja" (The fashion of the future), *Szabó Otthon* (Home of the Tailor), May 1, 1915, 4.

3 See, for example, Farid Chenoune, *Des Modes et des hommes: Deux siècles d'élégance masculine* (Paris: Flammarion, 1993); George L. Mosse, *L'Image de l'homme: L'Invention de la virilité moderne*, Michèle Hechter, trans. (Paris: Abbeville, 1997); Christopher Breward, *The Hidden Consumer: Masculinities, Fashion and City Life 1860–1914* (Manchester and New York: Manchester University Press, 1999); Brent Shannon, *The Cut of His Coat: Men, Dress, and Consumer Culture in Britain, 1860–1914* (Athens, OH: Ohio University Press, 2006); Laura Ugolini, *Men and Menswear: Sartorial Consumption in Britain 1880–1939* (Aldershot and Burlington, VT: Ashgate, 2007); Anne-Marie Sohn, *"Sois un homme!" La Construction de la masculinité au XIXe siècle* (Paris: Seuil, 2009).

4 The color of the military uniform during the Dual Monarchy was labeled in Austria as *feldgrau* (field-gray), and in Hungary as *csukaszürke* (pike-gray).

5 "A Nők Kedvence" (A sweetheart to the ladies), *Magyar Figaró* (Hungarian Figaro), August 30, 1914, 1, cover.

6 See Luc Capdevila, François Rouquet, Fabrice Virgili, and Danièle Voldman, *Sexes, Genre et Guerres (France, 1914–1945)* (Paris: Payot & Rivages, 2010), 111–12.

7 Ugolini, *Men and Menswear*, 71–98.

8 Jean Bastia, "La Mode masculine," *Le Carnet de la semaine*, November 12, 1916, 3.

9 "Ça et la," *Le Gaulois*, September 20, 1916, 3.

10 "Szép, Háborús Élet" (The godlife during war), *Magyar Figaró* (Hungarian Figaro), November 29, 1914, 4.

11 István Bárczy, "Színház, Divat, Háború" (Theatre, fashion, war), *Színház és Divat* (Theatre and Fashion), August 20, 1916, 1–2.

12 Ibid., 1.

13 On the Hungarian home front, see Joseph Held, "Culture in Hungary during World War I," in *European Culture in the Great War: The Arts, Entertainment and Propaganda, 1914–1918*, Aviel Roshwald and Richard Stites, eds. (Cambridge: Cambridge University Press, 1999), 176–9. For European context on the same subject, see Jay Winter and Jean-Louis Robert, eds., *Capital Cities at War: Paris, London, Berlin 1914–1919*, (Cambridge: Cambridge University Press, 1997).

14 "A Háborús Divatról" (On wartime fashion), *Budapesti Hírlap* (Budapest Journal), July 30, 1916, 22.

15 "Akik még Öltözködnek" (Those who still dress up), *Szabó Hírlap* (Tailor's Journal), July 1, 1916, 7.

16 "Ne Takarékoskodjunk az Ipar Rovására" (Don't economize at the expense of industry). *Szabó Hírlap* (Tailor's Journal), November 1, 1914, 8.

17 "A Férfidivat Esztétikája" (The aesthetic of men's fashion), *Magyar Iparművészet* (Hungarian Decorative Arts) 19, 3 (1916): 120, 129.

18 *Színházi Élet* (Theatrical Life) 4, 12 (1915): II.

19 "Ça et la," *Le Gaulois*, June 23, 1915, 2. This conference was widely reported on in the German, Austrian, Hungarian, and French media at the time.

20 "Das Fremdwort in der Herrenmode," *Neues Wiener Journal*, June 19, 1915, 9–10. We know of several other previous proposed words: *Abendanzug* (smoking), *Strassenanzug* (sacco), *Schultermantel* (raglan). "Deutsche Ramen in der Herrenmode," *Neuigkeits-Welt-Blatt*, March 4, 1915, 14.

21 Chenoune, *Des Modes et des Hommes*, 9.

22 "La Mode et la guerre," *Le Pêle-Mêle*, September 3, 1916, 2.

23 Ibid.

24 See Joëlle Beurier, "Frères Ennemis en images: Cultures de guerre en miroir? Presses illustrées Franco-Allemandes et cultures de guerre, 1914–1918," *20/21: Siècles: Cahiers du Centre Pierre Francastel* 4 (Winter 2006–7): 77–88; Eberhard Demm, "L'Image de l'ennemi dans la propagande Allemande et Alliée pendant la Première Guerre mondiale," in *Le Barbare: Images Phobiques et Réflexions sur l'Altérité dans la Culture Européenne*, Jean Schillinger and Philippe Alexandre, eds. (Bern: Peter Lang, 2008), 249–66.

25 Raoul Auernheimer, "Gentlemans Ende," *Neue Freie Presse*, November 14, 1914, 1–3; Olga Szende-Dárday, "A Gentleman Utóda" (The successor to the gentleman), *A Társaság* (The Society), January 14, 1915, 2. This article also appeared in German: Olga Szende-Dárday, "Gentlemans Nachfolger," *Sport & Salon*, January 23, 1915, 10.

26 On the German constructions of the gentleman, see Johannes Bilstein, "Deutsche Gentlemen—Deutsche Helden: Nationale Männlichkeitskonstruktionen 1900–1915," in *Erziehung, Bildung, und Geschlecht. Männlichkeiten im Fokus der Gender-Studies*, Meike Sophia Baader, Johannes Bilstein, and Toni Tholen, eds. (Wiesbaden: VS Verlag für Sozialwissenschaften, 2012), 41–60.

27 "Eine Kulturfrage," *Reichspost*, March 13, 1915, 2.

28 "A Jövő Divatja," 4–5. Ideas similar to this had already been circulating in the discourse on men's fashion.

29 See Katalin F. Dózsa, *Pictures of the Last Coronation in Hungary*, exhibition catalogue (Budapest: Budapest Historical Museum, 1996); Katalin F. Dózsa, "How the Hungarian national costume evolved," in *The Imperial Style: Fashions of the Habsburg Era*, exhibition catalogue (New York: Metropolitan Museum of Art–Rizzoli, 1980), 75–88.

30 Béla Kolos Mangold, "Az Új Év Férfidivatja" (Men's fashion in the New Year), *Szabó Hírlap* (Tailor's Journal), January 1, 1915, 6.

31 Béla Kolos Mangold, "Férfidivat" (Men's fashion), *A Társaság* (The Society), September 30, 1915, 15.

32 István Goreczky, "A Háború Hatása a Divatra" (The influence of the war on fashion), *Szabó Hírlap* (Tailor's Journal), June 15, 1918, 4.

33 "Olvasóinkhoz!" (To our Readers!), *Divat és Művészet* (Fashion and Art) 4, 8 (1914): 14.

34 See Capdevila et al., *Sexes, genre et guerres*, 50–1.

35 Szerkesztőség, "Áruinség:—Árudrágulás" (Shortage of commodities:—Price hike), *Úri Szabók Divatlapja* (Journal of Fashion for Tailors) / La Toilette, November 1914, 2; Announcement from supplier Adolf Krausz, *Úri Szabók Divatlapja* (Journal of Fashion for Tailors) / La Toilette, June–August, 1915, 4.

36 "Szőrmeáruk: Figyelmeztetés!" (Furs: Notice!), *Úri Szabók Divatlapja* (Journal of Fashion for Tailors) / *La Toilette*, September–October, 1914, 2.

37 "La Mode et la guerre," 2.

38 Cecil Willett Cunnington and Phillis Cunnington, *The History of Underclothes* (London: Michael Joseph, 1951), 222.

39 "A Háborús Divatról," 22.

40 "Une Mode Indésirable," *Le Temps*, March 27, 1916, 3.

41 "Szerkesztői Üzenetek" (Editorial messages), *A Társaság* (The Society), June 2, 1918, 353.

42 J. B., "Modes Masculines," *Le Temps*, January 26, 1916, 1.

43 Ingrid Loschek, *Mode im 20. Jahrhundert: Eine Kulturgeschichte unserer Zeit* (München: Bruckmann, 1978), 44.

44 Régis Gignoux, "En Veston," *Le Figaro*, November 6, 1916, 1.

45 Ibid.

46 Sándor Brachfeld, "Uri Divat" [Men's fashion], *A Társaság* (The Society), November 5, 1916, 874.

47 Zsolt Harsányi, "Úri Divat és Női Divat a Molnár-Premieren" (Men's fashion and women's fashion in the Molnar Premiere), *A Társaság* (The Society), December 2, 1917, 748.

48 "A Háborús Divatról," 22.

49 Jane Tynan, "Military dress and men's outdoor leisurewear: Burberry's trench coat in First World War Britain," *Journal of Design History* 24, 2 (2011): 139–56.

50 J. B., "Modes Masculines," 1.

51 (Izidor Kálnoki) Vulpes, "Úri Divat" (Men's fashion), *Az Érdekes Újság* (The Interesting Journal), February 7, 1918, 17.

52 "La Mode et la guerre," 2.

53 See the Hungarian digital archive Fortepan, which presents a collection of twentieth-century amateur photographs.

54 Brachfeld, "Uri Divat," 874.

55 "La Mode et la guerre," 2.

56 Katalin F. Dózsa, *Letűnt Idők, Eltűnt Divatok 1867–1945* (Budapest: Gondolat, 1989), 215–18.

57 Richard Corson, *Fashions in Hair: The First Five Thousand Years*, reprint (London: Peter Owen, 1966 [1965]), 575.

58 "Két női kabát egy Ferenc József-kabátból és egy frakkból!" (Two women's coats, one Franz Joseph/redingote, one tailcoat), *Budapesti Bazár* (Budapest Bazaar), October 18, 1918, 5.

References

"A Férfidivat Esztétikája" (The aesthetics of men's fashion). *Magyar Iparművészet* (Hungarian Decorative Arts) 19, 3 (1916): 120, 129.
"A Háborús Divatról" (On wartime fashion). *Budapesti Hírlap* (Budapest Journal), July 30, 1916, 22.
"A Jövő Divatja" (The fashion of the future). *Szabó Otthon* (Home of the Tailor), May 1, 1915, 4–5.

"A Nők Kedvence" (A sweetheart to the ladies), *Magyar Figaró* (Hungarian Figaro), August 30, 1914, 1.
"A Posztóárakról" (On the price of canvas). *Szabó Otthon* (Home of the Tailor), May 1, 1915, 3–4.
"Akik Még Öltözködnek (Those who still dress up). *Szabó Hírlap* (Tailor's Journal), July 1, 1916, 7–8.
Announcement from supplier Adolf Krausz. *Úri Szabók Divatlapja* (Journal of Fashion for Tailors) / La Toilette, June–August 1915, 4.
Auernheimer, Raoul. "Gentlemans Ende." *Neue Freie Presse*, November 14, 1914, 1–3.
Bárczy, István. "Színház, Divat, Háború" (Theatre, fashion, war). *Színház és Divat* (Theatre and Fashion), August 20, 1916, 1–2.
Bastia, Jean. "La Mode masculine." *Le Carnet de la semaine*, November 12, 1916, 3.
Beurier, Joëlle. "Frères ennemis en images: Cultures de guerre en miroir? Presses illustrées Franco-Allemandes et cultures de guerre, 1914–1918." *20/21. Siècles: Cahiers du Centre Pierre Francastel* 4 (Winter 2006-7): 77–88.
Bilstein, Johannes. "Deutsche Gentlemen—Deutsche Helden: Nationale Männlichkeitskonstruktionen 1900-1915." In *Erziehung, Bildung, und Geschlecht. Männlichkeiten im Fokus der Gender-Studies*, Meike Sophia Baader, Johannes Bilstein, and Toni Tholen, eds., 41–60. Wiesbaden: VS Verlag für Sozialwissenschaften, 2012.
Brachfeld, Sándor. "Uri Divat" (Men's fashion). *A Társaság* (The Society), November 5, 1916, 874.
Breward, Christopher. *The Hidden Consumer: Masculinities, Fashion and City Life 1860–1914*. Manchester and New York: Manchester University Press, 1999.
"Ça et la." *Le Gaulois*, June 23, 1915, 2.
"Ça et la." *Le Gaulois*, September 20, 1916, 3.
Capdevila, Luc, François Rouquet, Fabrice Virgili, and Danièle Voldman. *Sexes, genre et guerres (France, 1914–1945)*. Paris: Payot & Rivages, 2010.
Chenoune, Farid. *Des Modes et des hommes: Deux siècles d'élégance masculine*. Paris: Flammarion, 1993.
Corson, Richard. *Fashions in Hair: The First Five Thousand Years*, reprint. London: Peter Owen, 1966 [1965].
Cunnington, Cecil Willett and Phillis Cunnington. *The History of Underclothes*. London: Michael Joseph, 1951.
"Das Fremdwort in der Herrenmode." *Neues Wiener Journal*, June 19, 1915, 9–10.
Demm, Eberhard. "L'Image de l'ennemi dans la propagande Allemande et Alliée pendant la Première Guerre Mondiale." In *Le Barbare: Images phobiques et réflexions sur l'altérité dans la culture Européenne*, Jean Schillinger and Philippe Alexandre, eds., 249–66. Bern: Peter Lang, 2008.
"Deutsche Ramen in der Herrenmode." *Neuigkeits-Welt-Blatt*, March 4, 1915, 14.
Dózsa, Katalin F. "How the Hungarian national costume evolved." In exhibition catalogue, *The Imperial Style: Fashions of the Habsburg Era*, 75–88. New York: Metropolitan Museum of Art–Rizzoli, 1980.
Dózsa, Katalin F. *Letűnt Idők, Eltűnt Divatok 1867–1945*. Budapest: Gondolat, 1989.
"Eine Kulturfrage." *Reichspost*, March 13, 1915, 1–2.
Gignoux, Régis. "En Veston." *Le Figaro*, November 6, 1916, 1.
Goreczky, István. "A Háború Hatása a Divatra" (The influence of the war on fashion). *Szabó Hírlap* (Tailor's Journal), June 15, 1918, 2–5.
Harsányi, Zsolt. "Úri Divat és Női Divat a Molnár-Premieren" (Men's fashion and women's fashion in the Molnar Premiere). *A Társaság* (The Society), December 2, 1917, 747–9.
Held, Joseph. "Culture in Hungary during World War I." In *European Culture in the Great War: The Arts, Entertainment and Propaganda, 1914–1918*, Aviel Roshwald and Richard Stites, eds., 176–92. Cambridge: Cambridge University Press, 1999.
J. B. "Modes masculines." *Le Temps*, January 26, 1916, 1.
"Két női kabát egy Ferenc József-kabátból és egy frakkból!" (Two women's coats, one Franz Joseph/redingote, one tailcoat). *Budapesti Bazár* (Budapest Bazaar), October 18, 1918, 5.
"La Mode et la guerre." *Le Pêle-Mêle*, September 3, 1916, 2.
Loschek, Ingrid. *Mode im 20. Jahrhundert: Eine Kulturgeschichte unserer Zeit*. München: Bruckmann, 1978.
Mangold, Béla Kolos. "Az Új Év Férfidivatja" (Men's fashion in the New Year). *Szabó Hírlap* (Tailor's Journal), January 1, 1915, 6–7.

Mangold, Béla Kolos. "Férfidivat" (Men's fashion). *A Társaság* (The Society), September 30, 1915, 15.

Mosse, George L. *L'Image de l'homme: L'Invention de la virilité moderne*. Michèle Hechter, trans. Paris: Abbeville, 1997.

"Ne Takarékoskodjunk az Ipar Rovására" (Don't economize at the expense of industry). *Szabó Hírlap* (Tailor's Journal), November 1, 1914, 8.

"Olvasóinkhoz!" (To our readers!). *Divat és Művészet* (Fashion and Art) 4, 8 (1914): 14.

Shannon, Brent. *The Cut of His Coat: Men, Dress, and Consumer Culture in Britain, 1860–1914*. Athens, OH: Ohio University Press, 2006.

Sohn, Anne-Marie. *"Sois un homme!" La Construction de la masculinité au XIXe siècle*. Paris: Seuil, 2009.

Szende-Dárday, Olga. "A Gentleman Utóda" (The successor to the gentleman). *A Társaság* (The Society), January 14, 1915, 2.

Szende-Dárday, Olga. "Gentlemans Nachfolger." *Sport & Salon*, January 23, 1915, 10.

"Szép, Háborús Élet" (The good life during wartime). *Magyar Figaró* (Hungarian Figaro), November 29, 1914, 4.

"Szerkesztői Üzenetek" (Editorial messages). *A Társaság* (The Society), June 2, 1918, 353.

Szerkesztőség. "Áruinség:—Árudrágulás" (Shortage of commodities:—Price hike). *Úri Szabók Divatlapja* (Journal of Fashion for Tailors) / La Toilette, November 1914, 2–3.

Színházi Élet (Theatrical Life) 4, 12 (1915): II.

"Szőrmeáruk: Figyelmeztetés!" (Furs: Notice!). *Úri Szabók Divatlapja* (Journal of Fashion for Tailors) / La Toilette, September–October, 1914, 2.

Tynan, Jane. "Military dress and men's outdoor leisurewear: Burberry's trench coat in First World War Britain." *Journal of Design History* 24, 2 (2011): 139–56.

Ugolini, Laura. *Men and Menswear: Sartorial Consumption in Britain 1880–1939*. Aldershot and Burlington, VT: Ashgate, 2007.

"Une Mode indésirable." *Le Temps*, March 27, 1916, 3.

Vulpes (Kálnoki, Izidor). "Úri Divat" (Men's fashion). *Az Érdekes Újság* (The Interesting Journal), February 7, 1918, 17.

Winter, Jay and Jean-Louis Robert, eds. *Capital Cities at War: Paris, London, Berlin 1914–1919*. Cambridge: Cambridge University Press, 1997.

16

The politics of fashion

German fashion writings in times of war

Burcu Dogramaci

In 1915, the second year of the First World War, German intellectuals and artists believed in a near victory. This was reflected in their writing and their art, which tried to convince their contemporaries of the necessity of war. Architect and theorist Hermann Muthesius (1861–1927) used Otto von Bismarck's quote, "Let us put Germany in the saddle—it already knows how to ride," as the heading for his 1915 political pamphlet *Die Zukunft der deutschen Form* (The Future of German Form), shown in Figure 16.1.[1] He had his reasons for borrowing from Bismarck: in a speech before the North German Parliament on March 11, 1867, the then Prussian Prime Minister and President of the North German Confederation had vehemently opposed those who were concerned that Germany, unified under Prussian leadership, would not a be viable state. This statement was intended to support the future success of the undertaking.[2]

At the time Muthesius wrote this pamphlet, the Wilhelmine Empire was economically and culturally isolated from its enemies, France and England. Exchanges with Paris, the leading city of fashion, had stopped; the import of new designs from other countries had ceased almost entirely.[3] The pamphlet expressed an absolute belief in the perseverance of German design and saw the war as an opportunity. Muthesius, the chief ideologue of the Deutscher Werkbund (German Association of Craftsmen), encouraged the autonomy of German styling in all areas of design, but he was also particularly interested in liberating German fashion from the dominance of Parisian fashion production.

The aim of the Deutscher Werkbund, formed with the involvement of the architects Peter Behrens (1868–1940) and Josef Hoffmann (1870–1956) in 1907, was "gute Form" (good form) through the collaboration of art, industry, and craft.[4] Their goal, from the very beginning, was to strengthen the

Figure 16.1 *Pamphlet cover, Hermann Muthesius,* Die Zukunft der deutschen Form *(The Future of German Form) (Stuttgart and Berlin: Deutsche Verlags-Anstalt, 1915). Photo: author's personal collection.*

reputation and status of German goods on the global market. Creating an international network was of utmost importance.[5] The outbreak of the First World War in 1914 had led to a vitalization of German national thought in the field of design and its theoretical underpinning. War, and its consequences, determined the yearbooks of the Deutscher Werkbund in regards to subject matter: *Deutsche Form im Kriegsjahr* (German Form in War Years) was published in 1915 and *Kriegergräber im Felde und Daheim* (War Graves Afield and at Home) in 1916–17.

Well-known designers and authors such as Hermann Muthesius, Friedrich Naumann, Fritz Stahl, and Walter Riezler were proponents of a German style, the constitution of which was to be as independent of international impacts as possible. In this understanding, style or form—as molded material or matter—is tied to a nation and cultural sphere.[6] Books such as *Der deutsche Stil* (German Style), published by Naumann in 1915, or *Der Deutsche nach dem Kriege* (The German after the War), published by Muthesius in 1915, called for the aesthetic and economic autonomy of German style. (Figure 16.2). German fashion production, in particular, stood at the centre of a debate about the autonomy of a national style; countless essays and pamphlets propagated its independence from France.

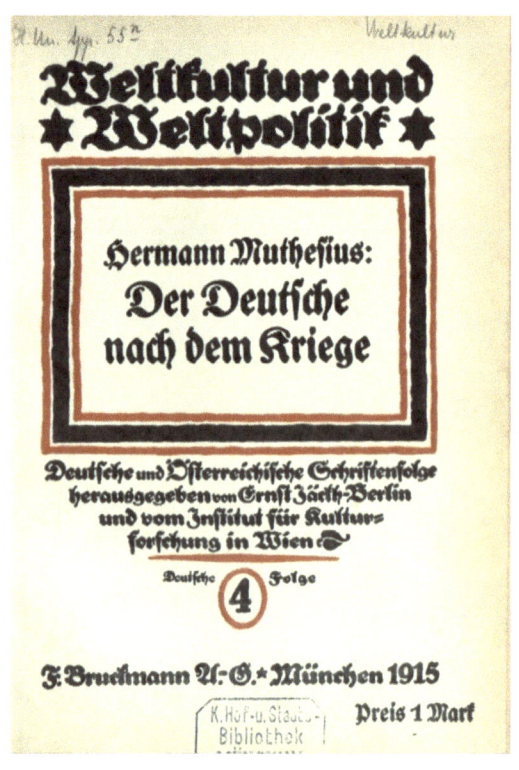

Figure 16.2 *Book cover, Hermann Muthesius,* Der Deutsche nach dem Kriege *(The German after the War) (München: F. Bruckmann, 1915). Photo: author's personal collection.*

In 1915, Muthesius promoted the creation of an independent fashion industry in Germany. The Deutscher Werkbund inaugurated a committee to support the efforts of establishing this German fashion industry, which was to be independent from Paris. Mathesisus's defiant attitude towards French fashion was supported by other writers. In his 1915 publication *Die Weltpolitik der Weltmode* (The Global Politics of Global Fashion), Norbert Stern wrote about Berlin as a new global fashion capital and emphasized the political potential of fashion (Figure 16.3). According to Stern, the new, German, national fashion industry would include not only the independent design of clothes in Germany, but other materials as well. Instead of French silk, which, due to the war, had become rare, hand-woven linen fabrics had become the national material of the time. With the *Kriegskrinoline* (war crinoline) silhouette, fashion designers and authors endeavored to refer back to a genuinely German era: the German Biedermeier period of the nineteenth century.

This essay incorporates a reading of, until now, lesser-known writings by Hermann Muthesius, Norbert Stern, and the German visual artist Rudolf Bosselt (1871–1928) from the beginnings of the First World War. Fashion caricatures will be analyzed as well in order to see how an argument was raised *against* French fashion and *in favor* of German fashion: What should a national German fashion

Figure 16.3 *Book cover, Norbert Stern,* Die Weltpolitik der Weltmode *(Global Politics of Global Fashion) (Stuttgart and Berlin: Deutsche Verlagsanstalt, 1915). Photo: author's personal collection.*

look like, and how should it differ in terms of design and material from the fashion of the neighboring enemy country? Which historical references were developed, for example, to situate German fashion in a cultural-historical context?

Against the primacy of French fashion, in favour of German design

In 1915, Muthesius published an article titled "Deutsche Mode" (German Fashion) in the journal *Der Kunstwart*. In it, he described how the outbreak of war had broken the monopoly of the Paris fashion industry and that the time for an independent, creative fashion industry in Germany had arrived. In this article, as well as in subsequent publications, Muthesius argued in favour of a German fashion and against a French one. The problem, as he diagnosed it, was careless German adaptation or imitation of Parisian models, which he attributed to underdeveloped self-confidence. Muthesisus accused German clothing designers of being unable to recognize their talent for invention:

> In Germany, namely, the adoption of that which is foreign has become habit. Over the course of the nineteenth century, the French model was replaced by that of the English in some areas, for example, in men's clothing. However, it never occurred to anyone that there was an alternative to copying the model of the more favoured neighbouring people.... It has always been characteristic of the Germans to willingly acknowledge that which is foreign and to even value it more than that which is their own.[7]

He continued:

> Even today, however, the strange, rather unbelievable state of affairs persists that Berlin is the leading manufacturing site in the world—certainly of coats—and occupies a dominant market position, without raising claim to intellectual authorship. Before the war, garment manufacturers from Berlin spent part of their lives in railroad cars, travelling to and from Paris, to gather ideas. After the war, however, this will, by necessity, change.[8]

Muthesius explained in great detail how, before the war broke out, fashion designers would make their way to Paris every February to purchase the carefully guarded new fashions, which would then be replicated upon return to their home countries.[9] For Muthesius, the war served as a wake-up call. Severed trade relations offered Germany an opportunity to gain artistic and economic independence:

> The fashion industry alone had remained disregarded [by the emancipation movement of German art and culture] until the beginning of the war. Here, independence from Paris and London seemed inevitable. The necessity to help oneself had an extremely healing effect and also resulted in Germany being entirely capable of seeing to its own affairs.[10]

"War has now changed everything. Paris is closed to us; it couldn't give us any models or ideas, even if we wanted them," Muthesius wrote.[11] In *Krieg und deutsche Mode* (War and German Fashion), published in 1915, Rudolf Bosselt expressed a similar idea:

> External events have determined and encouraged the time to push back against the French [fashion] dictatorship, at which we would have arrived at some point sooner or later. Paris is closed to us; the newly released fashions, apparently even via neutral countries, unobtainable. We are on our own. Now is the moment to test and assert our own strength—a better one will not come around again.[12]

In 1915, this belief in the "future of fashion through the war" was still characteristic of the interpretation of the war as a cathartic, stimulating event for national cultural production.[13]

If the propensity for German designers to copy Parisian styles as a result of a lack of self-confidence was bemoaned, the opposite was also felt to be true. This was particularly the case for Parisian fashion designer Paul Poiret (1879–1944), who Bosselt and Muthesius felt plagiarized German and Austrian reform dresses in his designs. According to Bosselt, Poiret availed himself of the creations of the Wiener Werkstätte.[14] Muthesius also characterized Poiret as a brazen copyist, who marketed that which was foreign as his own:

> But it is very telling ... that it was a Frenchman, Poiret, however, who zealously drew from these German impulses, which he recognized as being extraordinarily valuable, and from them created a "new genre," as it is known in clothing design jargon. This was then introduced to our dear public as the 'newest Parisian creation' with great pomp and on dainty young Parisian models (awkwardly referred to by the Germans with the Frenchified German word *Mannequin*).[15]

Interesting here are the ambivalent connotations of adaptation and appropriation. While the German fashion designers' act of copying was explained by false modesty and a lack of self-confidence (thereby transferring the "blame" to the dominating Parisian paragon), the act of emulation exposed the French "plagiarizers" as honorless forgers.

Reflections on originality, authorship, and uniqueness have shaped the cultural and artistic discourse of the early twentieth century. Erwin Panofsky's *Kopie oder Fälschung—Ein Beitrag zur Kritik einiger Zeichnungen aus der Werkstatt Michelangelos* (Copy or Forgery: A Critique of Several Drawings from Michelangelo's Workshop, 1928) and Max J. Friedlaender's *Echt und unecht—Aus den Erfahrungen des Kunstkenners* (Genuine and Counterfeit: Experiences of a Connoisseur, published in 1929 and translated in 1930) can be read alongside the positions introduced here in the context of German fashion production.[16] As Muthesius's statements exemplify, there was also a desire for a national fashion jargon: models were no longer to be referred to as mannequins but as *Modellmädchen* (mannequins).

National materials and clothing lines: Germany's construction of its own fashion history

The promotion of a new national fashion industry included more than just the independent design of new dresses in Germany. In the months after the outbreak of the war, the Deutsche Werkbund established a committee to create an independent German fashion industry. This committee called for all fabrics and materials to be manufactured in Germany and for the exclusive use of German terminology. Artists were to be involved throughout the entire production process; not only in the design of fashion lines but also in the creation of fabrics, laces, embellishments, buttons, and the like.[17]

In wartime texts on German fashion, artists were urged to help valorize German fashion production. Since the mass-production of clothing was thought to lack potential for innovation, the future of German fashion lay in the fashion workshops, which were to produce handmade and artistically valuable couture.[18] Authors such as Norbert Stern drew connections between these workshops and the medieval guilds during the golden age of German art. "What a rich artistic world was created by artisan craftwork in the days of Dürer!," Stern wrote.[19] The idea of a valorization of craftsmanship in reaction to the mechanical mass-production of objects had already been spurred by the Arts and Crafts movement of the nineteenth century and would also set the tone for the Bauhaus art school in post-war Weimar.[20] German fashion theorists during the First World War, however, linked the need for autonomy in national fashion production and the demand for qualitatively sophisticated products with a German art historical tradition. The reform dress of the turn of the century was rejected because it did not succeed in spreading beyond artistic circles and had not asserted itself on the international fashion market.[21]

German fashion critics, designers, and even the Reichsausschuss für deutsche Form (Reich Committee for German Form) advocated for alternative materials. Using domestic, handwoven linens was supported, partly for patriotic reasons.[22] Investing in flax cultivation was encouraged in order to obtain the raw materials needed for weaving linen, which also became fundamentally important in supplying the troops with clothing and textiles.[23] Silk, an imported good, was also replaced by an artificial version, which was already being successfully produced by German factories even before the outbreak of the war.[24] Since artificial silk was made of cellulose, thus of native fibers, it could even be considered—unlike the "French" silk—a domestic or national product.[25]

In terms of silhouette, a connection was sought to a genuinely German or Austrian era. The popular war crinoline, or *Kriegskrinoline*, for example, offered women more freedom of leg movement. The skirts were wider and shorter than before and were supported by two to three petticoats. Within fashion history, the crinoline silhouette was associated with the early nineteenth century. In fashion writing, references were made between the war crinoline and the German Biedermeier period, as well as the "Alt-Wiener Zeit," a nostalgic, fin-de-siècle representation of Vienna.[26] In doing so, writers situated the *Kriegskrinoline* within the country's own German-speaking cultural and fashion history, despite the fact that in the mid-nineteenth century as well as in its Rococo days, the crinoline had been claimed as a French invention.

The war crinoline, however, was not only worn in Germany. Caricatures attest to the fact that, during the war years, it also defined silhouettes in France and England.[27] However, like Gothic art—which, depending on one's point of view, can be claimed as either a genuinely French, English, or German stylistic era—the war crinoline was also regarded as a national phenomenon.[28] Nevertheless, as the war progressed, and in light of the tense economic situation, this patriotically connoted fashion found itself in the government's crosshairs. In 1916, in a petition addressed to the Ministry of War, the Verband für Deutsche Frauenkleidung und Frauenkultur (German Association for New Female Dress and Female Culture) demanded a ban on the production and wearing of skirts that exceeded three metres width.[29]

Fashion and politics

In the writings of German authors, fashion, art, and politics were argumentatively debated on the same level. The desire to monopolize fashion production in German became an indication of a wider hunger for political power. Muthesius emphasized this parallel succinctly: "Here, one is reminded of the monopoly position held by French fashion. It is hardly necessary to emphasize what this kind of power means to a people, what it means to have the whole world at your command, to mentally rule the world in this way."[30] Ultimately, the autonomy of German fashion production was not merely a question of economic sovereignty in wartimes but a moral matter in opposition to the "dictatorship of Parisian fashion."[31] Complete independence from their enemy in war was understood as an expression of love for the fatherland; this pertained not only to the import of dress designs from France but also to the production of German clothing, which was not to be dependent upon anything imported from abroad. "Creating a new fashion in Berlin using foreign materials during the war would mean supporting our enemies at the cost of our fatherland," Bosselt warned.[32]

Norbert Stern's book *Die Weltpolitik der Weltmode*, also published in 1915, inextricably linked fashion with politics. Stern hailed Berlin as the new fashion capital of the world and emphasized the political potential of fashion as "ideas of a political nature turned fabric."[33] Tracing France's monopoly in the production of couture back to the reign of Louis XIV, Stern interpreted fashion as a representative of history.[34] The many publications from 1915 that wrote in favor of a German fashion and against a French one pitted Berlin against Paris and projected the conflict on the battlefields onto a battle in the fashion world. Ultimately, these authors hoped to rewrite German fashion history.

Societies and associations were established that brought together fashion producers, distributors, and artists in an effort to contribute to this redefinition of a national fashion. Examples include the Verband für inländische Mode (Association for Domestic Fashion), founded in 1914 and presided over by Mechtilde Christiane Marie Gräfin von und zu Arco-Zinneberg (also known as the author Mechtilde Lichnowsky), as well as the Verband der Damenmode und ihrer Industrie (Association of Women's fashion and Its Industry), which was established in 1916 and had 1,500 members, from fabric manufacturers to clothing companies. In 1918, this Association hosted a fashion week in Berlin to present German fashion to an international audience.[35]

Conclusion

The *tabula rasa* of the war served as a catalyst for helping stimulate an internationally influential branch of the German economy. For authors such as Muthesius, Stahl, and Bosselt, war and fashion were interwoven global events. In this respect, it is striking that nearly all the major pamphlets in support of a German fashion date back to the year 1915. At that point, the German Empire, with its victory at the Battle of Tannenberg (August 26–30, 1914) and costly, yet successful, offensive on the Eastern Front, was still confident it would win the war. Later, as material battles, static front lines in the West, and radical losses in the East made the chances of a speedy victory seem slight at best, initiatives for a future for German fashion faded into the background. Terms such as "reason" and "frugality" became far more closely connected to fashion in Germany.[36]

Muthesius, Bosselt, and Stern attempted to link the German fashion of the future with the war, as it was the war that made possible a separation from Paris fashion. Ideologizing fashion for national purposes, however, neglected a central element. The authors hardly mentioned anything as to the form and style of a future German fashion, which was to become the nation's own fashion. This was to remain the task of future fashion designers and their partners in the business sector. Although Fritz Stahl did try to link functionality, practicality, and modernity with an explicitly German design sensibility in *Deutsche Form* (Stahl saw this in the products of the Deutscher Werkbund), what this could mean exactly for German form in fashion, however, ultimately remained unspecified.[37] Thus, the object of argument, namely German fashion, remained unclear. It was defined primarily through its opposition to unpopular French fashion, which was seen as wasteful, luxurious, and at times, even dictatorial.

Notes

1 "Setzen wir Deutschland in den Sattel, reiten wird es schon können," Hermann Muthesius, *Die Zukunft der deutschen Form* (Stuttgart and Berlin: Deutsche Verlags-Anstalt, 1915), 5. Bismarck, as the originator of this motto, however, remains unnamed. It is highly probable, though, that, at the time, the quote and its provenance were widely known. In his essay, "Deutsche Mode und Ähnliches" (German fashion and the like), Max Osborn also drew on Bismarck and ended his remarks with the words: "If we proceed this cautiously and carefully and at once unerringly, we may, with confidence, modify the famous words of the founder of the Reich and say: 'Let us put German fashion in the saddle—it already knows how to ride!'" (Wenn wir so bedacht und behutsam und zielsicher zugleich vorgehen, dürfen wir getrost ein berühmtes Wort des Reichsgründers abwandeln und sagen: "Setzen wir die deutsche Mode nur in den Sattel—reiten wird sie schon können!"), see Max Osborn, "Deutsche Mode und Ähnliches," in *Kriegs-Almanach. Velhagen und Klasings Kriegs-Almanach* (Berlin and Bielefeld: Velhagen und Klasing, 1915), 25.

2 See Horst Kohl, *Die Reden des Ministerpräsidenten und Bundeskanzlers Grafen von Bismarck im Preußischen Landtage und Reichstage des Norddeutschen Bundes: 1866–1868* (Stuttgart: Cotta'sche Buchhandlung, 1892), 184.

3 Alexandra Smetana, "Von der orientalisierenden Mode des Paul Poiret zur 'Kriegskrinoline': Plakate und Werbung für Mode in Wien vor dem und im Ersten Weltkrieg," *In Samt und Seide: Textilien und Texte zur Kulturgeschichte der Mode, Biblos: Beiträge zu Buch, Bibliothek und Schrift* 61, 1 (2012): 114.

4 In 1908, Friedrich Naumann formulated the following as a programmatic goal: "The forms of the machine age should be artistically saturated, both the forms of the best modern factory as well as the forms of the best design

of our buildings and their contents." (Es sollen die Formen des Maschinenzeitalters künstlerisch durchsättigt werden, sowohl die Formen des besten modernen Betriebes, wie die Formen der besten Gestaltung unserer Gebäude und ihres Inhaltes.) Friedrich Naumann, *Deutsche Gewerbekunst: Eine Arbeit über die Organisation des deutschen Werkbundes* (Berlin: Buchverlag der "Hilfe," 1908), 5.

5   This internationalization was expressed in the establishment of Werkbund-like organizations in other countries as well, which then sent delegations to the Werkbund exposition in Cologne, for example, in 1914. See Gustav Barcas von Hartmann and Wend Fischer, "Zur Geschichte des Deutschen Werkbundes," in *Zwischen Kunst und Industrie: Der Deutsche Werkbund,* catalogue (Munich: Die Neue Sammlung. Staatliches Museum für angewandte Kunst, 1975), 18.

6   Fundamental to the concept of form is the lexical meaning, which, at the time, already applied: "In fact, form is the opposite of material and refers to that which is made out of the material, the shape that it is given. Matter takes on shape and form." (Form ist überhaupt der gegensatz zum stoffe und bezeichnet das, was aus ihm gemacht wird, die gestalt, die ihm gegeben wird. die sache gewinnt gestalt und form.) Jacob and Wilhelm Grimm, *Deutsches Wörterbuch*, vol. 3 (Leipzig: Hirzel, 1862), 1898.

7   "Und namentlich in Deutschland wurde die Übernahme von Fremden zur Gewohnheit. Das französische Vorbild wurde im Laufe des 19. Jahrhunderts auf einigen Gebieten, so in der Männerkleidung, durch das englische ersetzt. Aber nie kam jemand auf den Gedanken, daß es etwas anderes zu tun gäbe, als das Vorbild der begünstigteren Nachbarvölker nachzuahmen ... Es ist stets die Eigenschaft der Deutschen gewesen, das Fremde willig anzuerkennen, ja es unter Umständen höher einzuschätzen als das Heimische." Muthesius, *Die Zukunft der deutschen Form*, 13–14.

8   "In der deutschen Konfektion liegt aber auch heute noch der merkwürdige, eigentlich unglaubliche Zustand vor, daß Berlin der Hauptfabrikationsplatz der ganzen Welt ist, ja, wie in Mänteln, eine durchaus beherrschende Stellung einnimmt, ohne den Anspruch auf geistige Urheberschaft zu erheben. Die Berliner Konfektionäre brachten vor dem Kriege einen Teil ihres Lebens in den Eisenbahnzügen nach und von Paris zu, um ihre Anregungen von dort zu holen. Das wird allerdings nach dem Kriege gezwungenermaßen anders werden." See Hermann Muthesius, *Der Deutsche nach dem Kriege* (München: F. Bruckmann, 1915), 25–6.

9   See ibid., "Deutsche Mode," *Kunstwart und Kulturwart* 29, 12 (1915): 205; ibid., "Der Krieg und die deutsche Modeindustrie," *Die Woche* 17, 11 (1915): 363.

10 "Nur das Gebiet der Modeindustrie war bis zum Kriege noch unberücksichtigt geblieben [von der Emanzipationsbewegung deutscher Kunst und Kultur, A/N]. Hier schien die Abhängigkeit von Paris und London unabwendbar. Die Notwendigkeit, sich selbst zu helfen, hat höchst heilsam gewirkt und auch hier das Ergebnis gebracht, daß Deutschland durchaus fähig ist, seine Angelegenheiten selbst zu besorgen." Muthesius, *Die Zukunft der deutschen Form*, 19.

11 "Der Krieg hat jetzt alles geändert. Paris ist für uns abgeschlossen, es könnte uns keine Modelle und keine Anregungen mehr geben, selbst wenn wir sie haben wollten." Muthesius, "Deutsche Mode," 206.

12 "Äußere Ereignisse haben den Zeitpunkt für den Vorstoß gegen die französische Diktatur [Modediktatur], zu dem wir einmal doch gekommen wären, bestimmt und begünstigten ihn. Paris ist uns verschlossen, die auszugebende neue Mode, wohl auch durch den Umweg über neutrale Länder, nicht erreichbar. Wir sind auf uns angewiesen. Jetzt ist der Augenblick für die Erprobung und Durchsetzung der eigenen Kraft, so günstig kehrt er nicht wieder." Rudolf Bosselt, *Krieg und deutsche Mode*, Dürerbund, 140. Flugschrift zur Ausdruckskultur (Munich: Callwey, 1915), 7.

13 "Zukunft der Mode durch den Krieg," ibid., 1.

14 "Well, the Viennese have had considerable success with, in particular, the greatest French tailor, Poiret, and we know just how inspired Poiret was especially by Vienna." (Nun, die Wiener haben gerade bei dem größten französischen Schneiderkünstler, Poiret, entscheidenden Erfolg gehabt, und wir wissen, wieviel Anregungen sich Poiret gerade aus Wien geholt hat.) Ibid., 20.

15 "Es ist nun aber höchst bezeichnend . . . daß aber ein Franzose, Poiret, diese von ihm als außerordentlich wertvoll erkannten deutschen Anregungen mit Eifer aufgegriffen und einen Pariser 'neuen Genre', wie es im Konfektionsjargon heißt, daraus entwickelt hat. Dieser wurde dann unserem lieben Publikum als die 'neueste Pariser Kreation' mit allem Pomp und auf niedlichen Pariser Modellmädchen (von den Deutschen krampfhaft mit dem französierten deutschen Worte Mannequin bezeichnet) vorgeführt," Muthesius, "Deutsche Mode," 208. Poiret did, in fact, purchase clothing materials from the Wiener Werkstätte during his stay in Vienna in 1911. See Angela Völker, *Die Stoffe der Wiener Werkstätte 1910–1932* (Vienna: Brandstätter 2004), 47.

16 For more on the topic of originality in the applied arts, see Carsten Jöhnk, "Notizen zum Wandel des Original-Begriffs in der Kunst," in *Wa(h)re Originale: Das Original in der angewandten Kunst*, catalogue (Bremen: Bremer Landesmuseum für Kunst und Kulturgeschichte, Focke-Museum, 1999), 12–18.

17 Bosselt, *Krieg und deutsche Mode*, 15–17.

18 Norbert Stern, *Die Weltpolitik der Weltmode* (Stuttgart and Berlin: Deutsche Verlagsanstalt, 1915), 34.

19 "Welch eine reiche Kunstwelt schuf uns das Kunsthandwerk zu Dürers Zeiten!" ibid., 39.

20 In a letter from 1919, Walter Gropius, founding director of the Bauhaus in Weimar writes: "I would like to create a working group in the Weimar school corporation—in keeping with the times, of course—similar to the *Bauhütten* [masons' lodges A/N] they had in the middle ages, in which artists and craftsmen of all ranks gathered to work together." (Ich möchte in dem Weimarer Schulunternehmen eine ähnliche Arbeitsgemeinschaft—natürlich der veränderten Zeit entsprechend—erzielen, wie sie im Mittelalter die Bauhütten hatten, in denen sich Künstler und Handwerker aller Grade zu gemeinsamer Arbeit zusammenfanden.) Walter Gropius, "Letter to Arnold Paulssen, 3/3/1919," in Volker Wahl, *Das Staatliche Bauhaus in Weimar: Dokumente zur Geschichte des Instituts 1919–1926* (Cologne, Weimar, and Vienna: Böhlau, 2009), 65. For references to a medieval craftsmanship and the Arts and Crafts movement's criticism of the industrial production of furniture, see Alan Crawford, "United Kingdom: Origins and first flowering," in *The Art & Crafts Movement in Europe & America: Design for the Modern World*, Wendy Kaplan, ed. (London: Thames and Hudson, 2004), 21–2.

21 See, e.g., Muthesius, "Der Krieg und die deutsche Modeindustrie," 364.

22 See Werner Faulstich, "Einführung: Die politischen und wirtschaftlichen Rahmendaten—mit Ausblicken auf Philosophie, Sportkultur und Mode," in *Kulturgeschichte des 20. Jahrhunderts: Das Zweite Jahrzehnt*, Werner Faulstich, ed. (Munich: Wilhelm Fink, 2007), 17.

23 Cf. Hugo Glafey, *Krieg und Textilindustrie*, Krieg und Volkswirtschaft, 8 (Berlin: Leonhard Simion NF, 1915), 16–19.

24 Cf. R. O. Herzog, ed., *Technologie der Textilfasern: Kunstseide*, vol. 7 (Berlin: Julius Springer, 1927), 340.

25 On the textile industry in wartime, see Sigrid and Wolfgang Jacobeit, *Illustrierte Alltags- und Sozialgeschichte Deutschlands 1900–1945* (Munster: Westfälisches Dampfboot, 1995), 294.

26 See Smetana, "Von der orientalisierenden," 115–16, which refers to a review of a 1916 Viennese fashion show in the journal *Sport und Salon* (11/11/1916), in which it reads: "In general, the style presented, originally from the year 1830, was one that died out with wide, coquettishly swaying skirts, with hoops that extravagantly swing in every

direction, furbelows and ruffles, simply arranged bodices enveloped by the hint of a lace fichu … it was a style reminiscent of the beautiful bygone days of Vienna, a time when things were infinitely more peaceful and calmer than they are today at the style's reappearance." (Im allgemeinen war ein Stil, anno 1830 vertreten, der in weiten, kokett wippenden Röcken ausklang, mit Reifen, die sich pretiös nach allen Seiten schwingen, Falbeln und Rüschen, Taillen in einfachem Arrangement, umwallt von dem Duft eines Spitzenfichus … es war ein Stil, der an die schöne Alt-Wiener Zeit gemahnte, in der es unendlich viel friedlicher und ruhiger zuging, als bei seiner heutigen Wiederkehr.)

27 See the examples in Friedrich Wendel, *Die Mode in der Karikatur* (Dresden: Paul Aretz, 1928), 260–72. Birgit Haase regards war crinoline as a combination of retrogression and an orientation to the present and, in adaptation of the cultural scholar Elizabeth Wilson's thesis, defines this ambivalence as characteristic of the modern era. Birgit Haase, "Moderne Ambivalenz: Damenmode im Ersten Weltkrieg aus deutscher Perspektive," in *Krieg und Kleider: Mode und Grafik zur Zeit des Ersten Weltkrieges 1914–1918*, cat. (Berlin: Kunstbibliothek, Staatliche Museen zu Berlin, 2014), 25; see also Elizabeth Wilson, "Fashion and modernity," in *Fashion and Modernity*, Christopher Breward and Caroline Evans, eds. (Oxford and New York: Berg, 2005), 9–14.

28 On the usurpation of the Gothic style as a national one, see, for example: Karl Scheffler, *Der Geist der Gotik* (Leipzig: Insel, 1917) and Gerhard Renda, "'Nun schauen wir euch anders an': Studien zur Gotikrezeption im deutschen Expressionismus" (PhD dissertation, Erlangen-Nuremberg, 1990), 60–2. Gebhardt traces Germany's enthusiasm for the Gothic style in the early twentieth century back to Goethe's essay "Von deutscher Baukunst" (On German architecture) (1773). See Volker Gebhardt, *Das Deutsche in der deutschen Kunst* (Cologne: DuMont, 2004), 106–9.

29 The association's petition is reproduced in Daniela Richter-Wittenfeld, *Die Arbeit des Verbandes für Deutsche Frauenkleidung und Frauenkultur auf dem Gebiet der Frauenkleidung von 1896 bis 1935, Schriftenreihe Schriften zur Kulturwissenschaft* 64 (Hamburg: Dr. Kovač, 2006), 398.

30 "Hier sei an die Monopolstellung der französischen Mode erinnert. Es bedarf kaum der besonderen Hervorhebung, was eine solche Macht für ein Volk bedeutet, was es heißt, den Taktstock über die Welt zu schwingen, die Welt in dieser Weise geistig zu regieren." Muthesius, *Die Zukunft der deutschen Form*, 25.

31 "Pariser Modediktatur." Fritz Stahl (Sigfried Lilienthal), *Deutsche Form: Die Eigenwerdung der deutschen Modeindustrie eine nationale und wirtschaftliche Notwendigkeit*, Flugschriften des Deutschen Werkbundes (Berlin: Ernst Wasmuth, 1915), 13.

32 "Während des Krieges eine neue Mode mit ausländischen Zutaten in Berlin schaffen, hieße unsere Feinde auf Kosten unseres Vaterlandes unterstützen." Bosselt, *Krieg und deutsche Mode*, 17.

33 "Stoff gewordene Ideen … politischer Natur," Stern, *Die Weltpolitik der Weltmode*, 10.

34 See also the chapter "Krieg und Moden" in Norbert Stern, *Mode* und *Kultur*, vol. 2 (Dresden: Klemm & Weiß, 1915), 119–221, here, in particular, 212.

35 Cf. Jacobeit, *Illustrierte Alltags*, 291–292.

36 Adelheid Rasche refers to the article "Ernste Modegedanken" (Serious thoughts on fashion) in the journal *Elegante Welt* from April 1918, in which precisely these terms are used. Adelheid Rasche, "Einführung," in *Krieg und Kleider 1914–1918: Mode und Grafik zur Zeit des Ersten Weltkrieges*, cat. (Berlin: Kunstbibliothek, Staatliche Museen zu Berlin, 2014), 10–12. The hardship of the times is expressed in the paper dresses and paper undergarments produced in the final years of the war. Jacobeit, *Illustrierte Alltags*, 294.

37 Stahl (Sigfried Lilienthal), *Deutsche Form*, 31–2.

References

Bosselt, Rudolf. *Krieg und deutsche Mode*. Dürerbund, 140. Flugschrift zur Ausdruckskultur. Munich: Callwey, 1915.

Crawford, Alan. "United Kingdom: Origins and first Flowering." In *The Art & Crafts Movement in Europe & America: Design for the Modern World*, Wendy Kaplan, ed., 20–66. London: Thames and Hudson, 2004.

Faulstich, Werner. "Einführung: Die politischen und wirtschaftlichen Rahmendaten—mit Ausblicken auf Philosophie, Sportkultur und Mode." In *Kulturgeschichte des 20. Jahrhunderts: Das Zweite Jahrzehnt*, Werner Faulstich, ed., 7–20. Munich: Wilhelm Fink, 2007.

Gebhardt, Volker. *Das Deutsche in der deutschen Kunst*. Cologne: DuMont, 2004.

Glafey, Hugo. *Krieg und Textilindustrie*. Krieg und Volkswirtschaft, 8. Berlin: Leonhard Simion NF, 1915.

Grimm, Jacob, and Wilhelm. *Deutsches Wörterbuch*, vol. 3. Leipzig: Hirzel, 1862.

Haase, Birgit. "Moderne Ambivalenz: Damenmode im Ersten Weltkrieg aus deutscher Perspektive." In *Krieg und Kleider: Mode und Grafik zur Zeit des Ersten Weltkrieges 1914–1918*, Catalogue, 18–29. Berlin: Kunstbibliothek, Staatliche Museen zu Berlin, 2014.

Herzog, R. O., ed. *Technologie der Textilfasern*, vol. 7: *Kunstseide*. Berlin: Julius Springer, 1927.

Jacobeit, Sigrid and Wolfgang. *Illustrierte Alltags- und Sozialgeschichte Deutschlands 1900–1945*. Munster: Westfälisches Dampfboot, 1995.

Jöhnk, Carsten. "Notizen zum Wandel des Original-Begriffs in der Kunst." In *Wa(h)re Originale: Das Original in der angewandten Kunst*. Catalogue, 12–18. Bremen: Bremer Landesmuseum für Kunst und Kulturgeschichte, Focke-Museum, 1999.

Kohl, Horst. *Die Reden des Ministerpräsidenten und Bundeskanzlers Grafen von Bismarck im Preußischen Landtage und Reichstage des Norddeutschen Bundes: 1866–1868*. Stuttgart: Cotta'sche Buchhandlung, 1892.

Muthesius, Hermann. *Der Deutsche nach dem Kriege*. München: F. Bruckmann, 1915.

Muthesius, Hermann. "Der Krieg und die deutsche Modeindustrie." *Die Woche* 17, 11 (1915): 363–5.

Muthesius, Hermann. "Deutsche Mode." *Kunstwart und Kulturwart* 29, 12 (1915): 205–8.

Muthesius, Hermann. *Die Zukunft der deutschen Form*. Stuttgart and Berlin: Deutsche Verlags-Anstalt, 1915.

Naumann, Friedrich. *Deutsche Gewerbekunst: Eine Arbeit über die Organisation des deutschen Werkbundes*. Berlin: Buchverlag der "Hilfe," 1908.

Osborn, Max. "Deutsche Mode und Ähnliches." In *Kriegs-Almanach: Velhagen und Klasings Kriegs-Almanach*, 17–25. Berlin and Bielefeld: Velhagen und Klasing, 1915.

Rasche, Adelheid. "Einführung ." In *Krieg und Kleider 1914–1918: Mode und Grafik zur Zeit des Ersten Weltkrieges*. Catalogue, 8–17. Berlin: Kunstbibliothek, Staatliche Museen zu Berlin, 2014.

Renda, Gerhard. "'Nun schauen wir euch anders an': Studien zur Gotikrezeption im deutschen Expressionismus." University dissertation, Erlangen-Nuremberg, 1990.

Richter-Wittenfeld, Daniela. *Die Arbeit des Verbandes für Deutsche Frauenkleidung und Frauenkultur auf dem Gebiet der Frauenkleidung von 1896 bis 1935*. Schriftenreihe Schriften zur Kulturwissenschaft. Hamburg: Dr. Kovač, 2006.

Scheffler, Karl. *Der Geist der Gotik*. Leipzig: Insel, 1917.

Smetana, Alexandra. "Von der orientalisierenden Mode des Paul Poiret zur 'Kriegskrinoline': Plakate und Werbung für Mode in Wien vor dem und im Ersten Weltkrieg," *In Samt und Seide: Textilien und Texte zur Kulturgeschichte der Mode, Biblos: Beiträge zu Buch, Bibliothek und Schrift* 61, no. 1 (2012): 114.

Stahl, Fritz (Sigfried Lilienthal). *Deutsche Form: Die Eigenwerdung der deutschen Modeindustrie eine nationale und wirtschaftliche Notwendigkeit*. Flugschriften des Deutschen Werkbundes. Berlin: Ernst Wasmuth, 1915.

Stern, Norbert. *Die Weltpolitik der Weltmode*. Stuttgart and Berlin: Deutsche Verlagsanstalt, 1915.

Stern, Norbert. *Mode und Kultur*, vol. 2. Dresden: Klemm & Weiß, 1915.

Völker, Angela. *Die Stoffe der Wiener Werkstätte 1910–1932*. Wien: Brandstätter, 2004.

von Hartmann, G. B. and Wend Fischer. "Zur Geschichte des Deutschen Werkbundes." In *Zwischen Kunst und Industrie: Der Deutsche Werkbund*. Catalogue, 15–21. Munich: Die Neue Sammlung. Staatliches Museum für angewandte Kunst, 1975.

Wahl, Volker. *Das Staatliche Bauhaus in Weimar: Dokumente zur Geschichte des Instituts 1919-1926*. Cologne, Weimar, and Vienna: Böhlau, 2009.

Wendel, Friedrich. *Die Mode in der Karikatur*. Dresden: Paul Aretz, 1928.

Wilson, Elizabeth. "Fashion and modernity." In *Fashion and Modernity*, Christopher Breward and Caroline Evans, eds., 9–14. Oxford and New York: Berg, 2005.

17

The Italian fashion magazine Margherita

The war, women, and the call for a "Moda Italiana," 1914–18

Enrica Morini

After Italy joined the First World War on May 24, 1915, Italian women endured the conflict like most women in the countries at war: many made clothing for the soldiers at the front, worked in shelters for refugees, or became nurses with the Italian Red Cross. Yet others joined the postal service, worked in munitions factories, or worked as business leaders, train conductors, and farmers. Yet, neither the war nor this widespread participation in the workplace distracted entirely from the question of fashion. The Italian clothing industry remained in operation for the duration of the war, and the subject of women's dress continued to interest many. Recent Italian historiography has examined some aspects of women's lives during the war, but the subject of fashion has so far not been addressed, thus omitting a major aspect of feminine culture during a trying period in Italian history.[1]

Fashion magazines are an important means to study the professional and daily lives of women in all of the countries at war during the period. The fashion magazine *Margherita* is of particular interest when studying the lives of Italian women during the First World War. Founded in 1878 by the publisher Treves, *Margherita* was the most prominent and prestigious women's magazine in Italy at the start of the war. It was aimed at an audience of the wealthy and upper bourgeoisie and, like most women's magazines, had large sections devoted to culture and fashion.[2] It also, however, had an additional section entitled "Women's Life" that showcased news articles and opinion pieces, covered women's rights, and published contributions from prominent Italian women such as the poet Amalia Guglielminetti (1881–1941), the suffragette Elena Lucifero, the writer and journalist Matilde Serao

(1856–1927), and the writer and art critic Margherita Sarfatti (1880–1941). According to *Margherita*'s director, Virginia Treves Tedeschi (1849–1916; Tedeschi directed *Margherita* from 1878 until her death), the magazine's articles were moderate in their tone, but nevertheless gradually familiarized readers with "a new image of the woman, one who is socially engaged, stakes her claim in the workspace, and demands equal rights as men."[3] The magazine was intended for the type of woman who wanted access to the latest fashions and embroidery patterns, but who also desired information and opinions on the world at large. During this era, that meant, especially, discussion about the war.

This approach differentiated *Margherita* from the other fashion magazines published in Milan up until 1915 (at which point, most of them halted production due to paper shortages).[4] Most of these magazines, including *Il Bazar* or *Il Monitore della Moda*, had previously adopted stances towards women's roles that were too conservative to allow for increased coverage of political issues and women's movements after 1914. These magazines, as well as others such as *La Novità*, *La Moda Illustrata*, and *La Gran Moda* were devoted almost entirely to images of the latest fashions and needlework patterns.

Between 1914 and 1918, *Margherita* adopted a unique approach towards women's fashion, becoming even more politically and socially engaged. Beginning in the fall of 1914, the magazine served as the mouthpiece for a movement aiming to replace the influence of French fashion with a true "Moda Italiana," a distinctly Italian fashion. This project, which united fashion houses, hat makers, and textile makers, was supported by intellectuals and feminists such as Teresita Guazzaroni and Amelia Rosselli (1870–1954). This call for a new national fashion was, in fact, an old idea that resurfaced regularly in the Italian industry under different guises.

After 1861, the patriotism surrounding the unification of Italy had provided an initial impetus for a discussion on national fashion. In the early twentieth century, the Milanese couturière Rosa Genoni promoted female Italian fashion and gave the movement syndicalist and feminist aims.[5] In 1914, a more concrete cause proved to be the motivating force for this third call: the war had resulted in the closing of the Parisian fashion houses, taking away the usual reference points for their Italian counterparts. In order to continue operating, the Italian houses needed new designs to show their clients. Wanting to change the entire *modus operandi* of Italian fashion, the designers felt that they could generate their own trends instead of merely replicating those arriving from Paris. During the conflict, *Margherita* not only informed the Italian bourgeoisie on the war and social issues, but also gave voice to this nationalist call for an Italian fashion.

Margherita's writers on the war and women

When the war broke out in 1914, the editorial board of *Margherita* adopted a pacifist stance, arguing in favor of neutrality. They justified their position in various editorials written by the magazine's staff, and by publishing the contributions of famous writers of the era such as Sofia Bisi Albini, Amalia Guglielminetti, and Dora Melegari.[6] These articles had a unified message: the war would mark the end of European culture as previously known, and would cause irreparable damage to the progressive ideals long advanced by politicians, philosophers, educators, and other European thinkers. On October 1, 1914, the Marquise of Villalba wrote:

> If so many centuries of civilization are to be lost in such a short lapse of time, if all of the progress that has been painstakingly carved out is to be erased due to the capriciousness of a few, then let us forget about the great ideas, let us throw out the sublime concept of universal peace that we have so long debated and hoped for, and let us return to the darkness and ignorance of ancient times.[7]

In her editorial, the Marquise decried the horror of the thousands of needless deaths already occurring, with young being men sent to fight the enemy "solely because they speak a different language, and have their coats and pants in a different color."[8] Neutrality was seen as the only reasonable solution.

Nevertheless, on May 24, 1915, Italy declared war on Austria. *Margherita* was obliged to accept the political reality of the situation and change the tone of their articles. While not exactly celebratory, the writers did try to explain to their readers the patriotic motives forcing Italy into the conflict. In multiple articles, Buon Genio (likely the *nom de plume* of Virginia Treves Tedeschi) attempted to justify the war by making reference to "Italian-ness," a "liberating war," and a "holy crusade," while advocating for the liberation of Trento and Trieste.[9] Despite the rhetoric, however, the magazine never devoted a cover to the war, and only once published a full page image of a wounded officer.[10]

Margherita treated the war from the point of view of women, sharing with its readers a sense of optimism tempered by anxiety. From early on, the magazine followed the progress of women working in the Italian Red Cross as well as those working in what have been previously considered as traditionally male jobs. The magazine gave news of women's activities in Belgium, England, France, Germany, and Austria; it even expressed trepidation over the political transformations of England's suffragettes, who, in the spirit of patriotism, made themselves subservient to men, their former "adversaries."[11] The writers reported on the early initiatives of Italian women's committees, such as they classes they created to teach women how to become typists or telegraph operators, to make military clothing, or to handle weapons.[12] Buon Genio wrote in praise of women's resilience:

> Up until now, we've witnessed the natural determination of German women, the calm of the English women, and the charm of French women, even in times of war. But we can tell you today that the Italian woman is not only intelligent and good of heart: she is strong.[13]

Of course, *Margherita* was appealing primarily to its readership of women in the upper bourgeoisie. They called on their readers to make and donate goods necessary to protect soldiers from the cold (the first freezes occurred in the summer of 1915), including furs, wool clothing, socks, and even mess kits.[14] The magazine often published patterns that allowed women to make such clothing at home.[15]

Margherita's calls for aid and engagement with the war effort increased as women continued to mobilize, and so too did the magazine's celebrations of their achievements.[16] In 1916, the magazine reported on the women-led distribution centers for sorting mail between soldiers and their families.[17] Reporters often focused on Milan and the efforts of Milanese women. Between 1915 and 1916, *Margherita* published a number of photographs of working women in Milan; the women are photographed working in day care centers, canteens, collection centers, and in the fashion industry (in the couture, hosiery, and fur sectors).[18] Yet, these celebratory depictions of the workplace did not prevent the magazine from covering the more painful aspects of wartime that women were subjected to. As Buon Genio wrote, "the anguish of waiting, the constant anxiety at the thought of threat facing husbands, brothers, and children, fears of being deprived of support, the cruel solitude made ever more excruciating by the absence of news . . . these fears eat away at women . . . terribly . . . cruelly."[19]

Nevertheless, a feeling began to take root among women of the educated classes—both in Italy and abroad—that the war was ushering in a shift in the traditional social roles for women. In *Margherita*'s analysis of an article by Tony d'Ulmès (Berthe Rey) published in *La Revue Hebdomadaire*, the writer remarked that "especially in France," women who had fought tooth and nail several years prior to receive the same rights and work the same positions as men, now had the opportunity to put their intelligence to task.[20] On March 15, 1916, Buon Genio wrote, "Women have definitively made their claim during this war!"[21] Theirs was a conquest that needed to be defended and consolidated. In 1917, *Margherita* published an article from French journal *La Renaissance* "on the situation of women after the war," and, in the following months, an article appeared advising women "to remain vigilant about the future."[22]

But the magazine, by this time, had already stopped reporting on women's issues and politics to the degree they had in the previous years. Virginia Treves Tedeschi died on July 7, 1916, and the new director, Amelia Brizzi Ramazzotti, greatly reduced the sections devoted to the women and the war. The "Women's Life" section became a short column, and the war eventually disappeared from the magazine's pages entirely—it was not even mentioned in order to explain the suspension of publication from November 1917 to February 1918 due to Italy's defeat in the battle of Caporetto, which lasted from October 24 until November 12, 1917.

Margherita and the call for an Italian fashion

Margherita was a fashion magazine above all else, and for Italian women, fashion was Paris. The news that the war had forced the closure of most Parisian fashion houses, and that there would be no fall fashion line to serve as guidance, was greatly discouraging. The images of Paris "without fashion" and of the windows of the great department stores, "the Galeries Lafayette, Grands Magasins du Louvre, and Printemps lined with uniforms, sweaters, blankets, and camping gear," as described by Guido Angeli in 1915, signified the end of business as usual.[23]

Yet, in 1915, Italy was not yet at war, and life continued normally, or at least relatively so. Women would soon be clamoring for fall clothing, and the garment sector was still extremely important economically, not least because it employed a great many workers, both in industrial and artisanal production. The sudden disappearance of Parisian design influence posed a problem that needed to be resolved quickly in order to avoid losing sales for the upcoming fall and winter collections.

For fashion magazines the absence of new designs from Paris was a significant setback as well. While magazines had previously mainly relayed Parisian styles, creating slight variations on occasion, they were now tasked with being creative forces in their own right, generating trends using designs that could be found in Italian stores. The industry was in need of solutions. For the artwork in its pages, *Margherita* called for "the collaboration of distinguished artists, specialists in feminine elegance" in order to obtain "designs expressly created for . . . the magazine."[24] But this was easier said than done, as Italian illustrators were used to working with Parisian styles as well, and were not, strictly speaking, true designers.

More promising was the news that the most prominent Italian fashion houses had obtained some early winter designs from Paris, as well as some additional pieces which had been arriving from "North America . . . since the summer."[25] According to *Margherita*, these might have offered a partial solution—from these two sources, they claimed, "the imaginations of couturiers will be able to draw innumerable variations."[26] But it was soon recognized that, "designs arriving from Paris and America were rare."[27] The second remaining option was to draw from, "the remnants of summer's styles," reworking summer designs into autumnal variations.[28] Looking at the designs published in *Margherita* during the war, one has the impression that this was the path most often followed. In any case, these two solutions could only be temporary. Italian couturiers knew that more drastic measures would be required after January, and they would need to "present entirely new pieces, either by creating new styles, or by repeating those of the past."[29]

The most radical solution voiced during the fall of 1914 was to create a new Italian fashion.[30] Initially this objective might have arisen out of Italian couturiers' simple need to show that they "knew perfectly well how to create designs," but it soon took on a nationalist significance.[31] As previously stated, this concept of a "Moda Italiana" was not new in 1914. Indeed, as recently as 1910, the idea had gained some ground amongst couturiers, intellectuals, aesthetes, and certain members of high society for a short period of time.[32] Paris's preoccupation with the war and Italy's neutrality offered the perfect opportunity for the idea to come to fruition—not only as a temporary solution during a period of economic desperation, the designers hoped, but with the goal of a new, sustainable autonomy after the war's end.

In a long article published in November 1914, *Margherita* journalist Teresita Guazzaroni exalted Italy's potential, praising the country's fine taste, evidenced by its tradition of artistry and its wonderful, "fabrics, silks, laces—the most beautiful in the world—and exquisite embroideries."[33] The main problem would be the absence of the appropriate skilled labor force, but the war, soon enough, provided a solution to this predicament as well. A number of Italian workers in the great Parisian houses had returned to their home country after finding themselves out of work.[34] Guazzaroni's impassioned piece offered convincing rhetoric, but underestimated the difficulties of such a project. *Margherita* only mentioned that the initiative would require, "a number of branches of the industry" that Italy did not yet possess, and that France had "powerful means at its disposal, with no equal in the world."[35]

Italian houses launching themselves feverishly into the production of new designs in the fall of 1914. It is difficult to know if this was out of a true desire to create a national Italian fashion, or merely a means to retain their clients. In any case, dressmakers, hat makers, and fabric stores set in search of young designers capable of generating ideas for a winter collection that would not make one "miss what Paris was unable to offer."[36] In October, the Proprietary Association of Couture Workshops for Women published a circular announcing that the new designs were ready and that the main workshops of Milan, Turin, and Genoa had organized charity events to present their winter collections.[37] In Milan, the Association organized, "a grandiose spectacle of art and charity complete with tableaux vivants," at the Teatro Lirico, one of the city's preeminent venues.[38] *Margherita* supported these displays by publishing an issue with images that were solely "copied from the new designs created by the greatest [Italian] fashion houses," proudly announcing that the magazine was "entirely conceived and made by Italians."[39]

Italian women, on the other hand, did not share the same fervor, and were not enamored with the results. As observed by the journalist Amelia Rosselli, the same type of woman who would have "gone mad with impatience if the couturier was delayed with her new dress by a single day, could now be seen wearing that old dress with a knowing grace and charm. Was it not supremely elegant, given that Paris could no longer dress us, to show that we would not dress ourselves at all?"[40] The efforts of Italian dressmakers and hat makers were met by the public only with, "words of praise, not backed up by sales."[41] The Italian industry would surely have been able to better rally for the following season, but this did not prove to be necessary—Parisian fashion returned in the spring of 1915. In April, *Margherita* published a photograph of a French design as its cover, and the project of an Italian fashion was soon forgotten.[42] In truth, some of the efforts had always been half-hearted. On October 15, 1915, Donna Vanna had noticed that the new Parisian designs sold by an important Milanese atelier were each bestowed with the name of an Italian politician: "Thus we see the new path of the Italian Fashion!," she commented ironically.[43]

The attentions granted to Italian fashion in the winter of 1914 were not entirely futile. The idea that Italy would find its voice in the international sphere was at the root of *Margherita*'s own transformation.

On May 1, 1916, the magazine was published in a completely redesigned form. The editorial board explained that they intended to create a magazine that was able to "rival the very best foreign publications in its artistry and refined tastes."[44] New connections were established with Paris, facilitated by the fact that France and Italy were now allies, and the magazine began publishing haute couture designs photographed by French photographers Félix, Talbot, and Manuel Frères.

The most visible change could be seen with the magazine's illustrations. The events of fall 1914 had pushed *Margherita* to reach out not only to new fashion illustrators, but to new artists from the graphic arts and fine arts. The new *Margherita* was thus able to present the works of a talented crop of Italian artists, capable of elevating their subject matter. Some of them were already of some renown, such as Marcello Dudovich and Luigi Bompard; others were promising young talents, such as Aroldo Bonzagni, Augusto Camerini or Golia (Eugenio Colmo).[45] Their art had a strong influence on other illustrators: Mario Cappelletti and Mario Cherubini, who had already been working with *Margherita* for a number of years, altered their typical style to suit the magazine's new direction, for instance. The few fashion journals still being published in Paris, such as *Le Style Parisien*, were surely a strong influence on these illustrators as well.

Although this new project only lasted several months, from May 1 to August 1, 1916, it would have lasting effects. The magazine never abandoned this impulse to seek talented and original artists for its illustrations, or to engage with fashion in a professional manner, as did the great international journals. It is no surprise that the images reprinted or imitated in *Margherita* in 1917 were from *Les Élégances Parisiennes* and *Vogue*.[46]

Margherita was continuously readapting to the changes brought on by the war, and to the new ways of thinking of the women of the Italian bourgeoisie. The stance taken during the first years of the war—as promoted by Virginia Treves Tedeschi—favoring the emancipation of the Italian fashion industry did not outlast the director's death. After Amelia Brizzi Ramazzotti succeeded her, and even more so after a new publisher took over from Treves in 1917, the magazine modernized, becoming a more specialized and refined fashion magazine. This decision was seemingly made in accordance with the demands of the times, but it proved insufficient in the long term. In 1921, the long history of *Margherita* came to an end. The publisher decided to merge with *Il Secolo delle Signore* to create a new magazine, *La Parisienne Élégante* (and subsequently *La Femme Parisienne*), which made its final appearance in 1922.[47]

Conclusion

As for the "Moda Italiana," the project never came to fruition during the First World War, but heightened interest in Italian fashion was not without consequences. After the war, certain magazines began promoting the idea of a national fashion. This concept eventually became one of the aims of the fascist regime.[48] For the professional sector, the urgent demand for self-sufficiency during the war, while brief, forced a moment of reflection on foreign dependence. Many came to believe that in the coming years they would need to more directly question their role within the international sphere. The effects of this sentiment would play out over the course of the next decade.[49]

Notes

1 See Stefania Bartoloni, *Italiane alla Guerra: l'Assistenza ai Feriti 1915-1918* (Venezia: Marsilio, 2003); Barbara Curli, *Italiane al lavoro (1914-1920)* (Venice: Marsilio, 2001); Beatrice Pisa, "Una Azienda di Stato a Domicilio: La Confezione di Indumenti Militari durante la Grande Guerra," *Storia Contemporanea* 6 (1989): 953-1006.

2 *Margherita* was quite expensive. In 1878, an annual subscription cost 24 lire, while that of *L'Eleganza*, a more popular fashion magazine from the same publisher, Treves, cost 6 lire. See Silvia Franchini, *Editori, Lettrici e Stampa di Moda: Giornali di Moda e di Famiglia a Milano dal Corriere delle Dame agli Editori dell'Italia Unita* (Milan: Franco Angeli, 2002), 292-7.

3 Federica Serva, "Margherita," in Rita Carrarini and Michele Giordano, eds., *Bibliografia dei Periodici Femminili Lombardi: 1786-1945* (Milan: Istituto Lombardo per la Storia del Movimento di Liberazione in Italia, Bibliografica, 1993), 225.

4 As noted in 1881 by Eugenio Torelli Violler, fashion journals were "a Milanese specialty." Eugenio Torelli Violler, "Movimento Librario," *Mediolanum*, vol. 3 (Milan: Valalrdi, 1881), 342.

5 Rita Carrarini, "La Stampa di Moda dall'Unità a Oggi," in *La Moda: Storia d'Italia. Annali 19*, Carlo Marco Belfanti and Fabio Giusberti, eds. (Turin: Einaudi, 2003), 809-10; Rosa Genoni, "Per una Moda Italiana," *Vita Femminile Italiana*, June 1908, 666-7; Enrica Morini, *Interazioni fra arte e moda. Boldini, Poiret, Genoni* (Milan: Mimesis, 2020).

6 "La Quindicina di 'Vita femminile': Le Nostre Scrittrici e la Guerra," *Margherita*, November 1, 1914, 339-40; R., "La Vita Femminile: Le Nostre Scrittrici e la Guerra," ibid., November 15, 1914, 358-9.

7 Marchesa di Villalba, "Corriere Mondano: Le Chiacchiere della Marchesa," ibid., October 1, 1914, 306.

8 Ibid.

9 Buon Genio, "Trieste per Sempre Riunita all'Italia," ibid., September 1, 1915, 274-5; ibid., "Al Soldato che Parte: Le Donne Italiane," ibid., October 1, 1915, 210; ibid., "Ai Soldati Partenti," ibid., December 1, 1915, 374.

10 "Ufficiale Ferito," ibid., July 15, 1916, 225-6.

11 R., "Le Donne e la Guerra," ibid., October 1, 1914, 307-10; "La Giornata Odierna delle Parigine," ibid., November 15, 1914, 352; "La Vita Femminile: Le Donne e la Guerra: L'Eroismo e l'Attività delle Donne Francesi," ibid., January 1, 1914, 7; "La Vita Femminile: Le Donne Inglese e Tedesche Lavorano Senza Tregua," ibid., August 15, 1915, 251-2; "Vita Femminile: La Mobilitazione delle Donne," ibid., October 15, 1915, 326; "La Vita Femminile: Femminismo in Tempo di Guerra," ibid., November 15, 1914, 354; "La Vita Femminile: La Redenzione delle Suffragette," ibid., December 15, 1914, 396.

12 See Stefania Bartoloni, "L'Associazionismo Femminile nella Prima Guerra Mondiale e la Mobilitazione per l'Assistenza Civile e la Propaganda," in *Donna lombarda*, Ada Gigli Marchetti and Nanda Torcellan, eds. (Milan: Franco Angeli, 1992), 65-91; Beatrice Pisa, "La Mobilitazione Civile e Politica delle Italiane nella Grande Guerra," *Giornale di Storia Contemporanea* 2 (December, 2001): 79-103.

13 Buon Genio, "Al Soldato che Parte: Le Donne Italiane," *Margherita*, October 1, 1915, 210.

14 Donna Vanna, "Corriere della Moda," ibid., August 15, 1915, 250; ibid., "Corriere della Moda," ibid., December 1, 1915, 366. ibid., "Corriere della Moda," ibid., September 15, 1915, 266; "La vita Femminile: Iniziative Femminili Milanesi," ibid., October 1, 1915, 310; "Vita Femminile: Un'altra Trovata contro il Freddo," ibid., November 1, 1915, 335. G. T., "Vita Femminile: Lo 'Scaldarancio,'" ibid., September 15, 1915, 267.

15 C. Bona, "Pagina di Lavori Pratici: Passamontagna, Fascia e Sottocorpetto," ibid., November 15, 1915, 356; "Passamontagna a Visiera con Doppia Pettorina," ibid., December 1, 1915, 366.

16 "Vita Femminile: Il Coraggio di due Signorine," ibid., September 1, 1915, 267; "Il Lavoro Femminile," ibid., July 15, 1916, 237; "Vita Femminile: La Casa Famiglia per le Orfane," ibid., October 15, 1916, n.p.; "La Vita Femminile: Iniziative Benefiche Natalizie," ibid., January 1, 1917, 8; "La Vita Femminile: La Prima Scuola di Munizionamento Femminile è Inaugurata," ibid., January 15, 1917, 30; "Vita Femminile: L'On. Boselli Esalta l'Opera della Donna nella Guerra," ibid., February 15, 1917, 60; "La Vita Femminile: La Mobilitazione Volontaria delle Donne Italiane" ibid., March 1, 1917, 72; "La Vita Femminile: Le Donne Italiane nell'Agricoltura," ibid., June 1917, 12; "La Vita Femminile: Infermiere della Croce Rossa Decorate," ibid., August 1917, 14; "La Vita Femminile: Un'imponente Riunione Femminile per la Guerra," ibid., April 1918: 22; "La Vita Femminile: Il Diritto di Voto delle Donne," *Margherita*, June 1916: 16; "Una Signora Decorata al Valore," ibid., July 1918, 18. See Curli, *Italiane al Lavoro*; Bartoloni, "L'Associazionismo Femminile"; Pisa, "La Mobilitazione Civile e Politica."

17 The "Ufficio per Notizie alle Famiglie dei Militari di Terra e di Mare" was founded in June 1915 by a group of women from Bologna, under the direction of Countess Lina Cavazza Bianconcini. See Elisa Erioli, "L'Ufficio per Notizie alle Famiglie dei Militari': Una Grande Storia di Volontariato Femminile Bolognese," *Bollettino del Museo del Risorgimento* 1 (2005): 75–89. Donna Vanna, "Intorno all'Operosità Femminile durante la Guerra," ibid., March 15, 1916, 93-4; "Un anno di Lavoro all'Ufficio Notizie," ibid., July 15, 1916, 22.

18 "Lavori Femminili in Tempo di Guerra," ibid., January 1, 1916, 6-7; "Lavori Femminili in Tempo di Guerra," ibid., January 15, 1916, 23; "Lavori Femminili in Tempo di Guerra," ibid., February 15, 1916, 39; "Lavori Femminili in Tempo di Guerra," ibid., March 1, 1916, 76; Donna Vanna, "Intorno all'Operosità Femminile durante la Guerra," ibid., March 15, 1916, 93-4.

19 Buon Genio, "La Donna è la più Duramente Colpita," ibid., October 15, 1915, 327.

20 "Per ottenere gli stessi diritti degli uomini, per accedere agli stessi impieghi," Tony D'Ulmes, "Vita Femminile: La Mobilitazione delle Donne," ibid., October 15, 1915, 326. Phrase translated into Italian from Tony D'Ulmes, "La Mobilisation des Femmes," *La Revue Hebdomadaire*, August 7, 1915, 76.

21 Buon Genio, "Voci di Pace," *Margherita*, May 15, 1916, 94.

22 "La Vita Femminile: La Situazione della Donna dopo la Guerra," ibid., April 15, 1917, 127; "La Vita Femminile: A Proposito di Femminismo," ibid., May 12, 1917.

23 Rosa, "Parigi Senza Mode," ibid., January 1, 1915, 3.

24 Donna Vanna, "Corriere della Moda," ibid., September 15, 1914, 282.

25 "Since June, several major fashion houses have obtained some winter designs," Donna Vanna, "Corriere della Moda," ibid., October 1, 1914, 298. "Note d'Attualità: La Moda e la Guerra," ibid., October 15, 1914, 315.

26 Ibid.

27 G. T., "La Moda in Tempo di Guerra: Esposizioni e Concorsi," ibid., November 1, 1914, 334.

28 "Note d'Attualità: La Moda e la Guerra."

29 G. T., "La moda in tempo di guerra."

30 "Note d'Attualità: La Moda e la Guerra."

31 Ibid.

32 Aurora Fiorentini, "L'Ornamento di Pura Arte Italiana: La Moda di Rosa Genoni," in *Abiti in Festa: L'Ornamento e la Sartoria Italiana* (Firenze: Sillabe, 1996): 41–59; Morini, *Interazioni fra arte e moda. Boldini, Poiret, Genoni*.

33 "Il Regno della Moda in Tempo di Guerra," Margherita, November 1, 1914, 334.

34 Ibid.

35 Donna Vanna, "Corriere della Moda," ibid., October 15, 1914, 314; "Il Regno della Moda in Tempo di Guerra."

36 Donna Vanna, "Corriere della Moda," ibid., October 15, 1914.

37 G. T., "La Moda in Tempo di Guerra."

38 Ibid.; "'Festa a Bordo,' uno dei Quadri delle 'Sorelle Testa' nei 'Quadri Viventi della Moda Attuale,' al Teatro Lirico di Milano," ibid., December 15, 1914, n.p.

39 "Alle nostre Lettrici," ibid., November 15, 1914, 346.

40 "Note d'Attualità: I Piccoli Doveri," ibid., January 15, 1915, 24.

41 Ibid.

42 "Abbigliamento di taffetà verde azzurro con ricami di tinta più scura. Fot. Henry (*sic*) Manuel, Parigi," ibid., April 15, 1915.

43 Donna Vanna, "Corriere della moda," ibid., October 15, 1915, 318.

44 "*Margherita* si Rinnova," ibid., May 1, 1916, 134.

45 See Roberto Curci, ed., *Marcello Dudovich: Oltre il Manisfesto* (Milan: Charta, 2002); Giovanni Granzotto, *Marcello Dudovich, 1878–1962* (Brescia: Corbelli, 2004); Cf. Mario Quesada, *Luigi Bompard: 1879–1953* (Rome: Emporio Floreale, 1983); Marina Pescatori, *Vagabondaggi di una matita: Luigi Bompard* (Rome: Gm, 2004). See also Guilio Carlo Argan, *Aroldo Bonzagni* (Ferrara: Arstudio, 1987); cf. Roberto Della Torre, *Invito al Cinema: Le Origini del Manifesto Cinematografico Italiano (1895–1930)* (Milan: EDUCatt Università Cattolica, 2014); cf. Antonio Faeti, *Guardare le Figure: Gli Illustratori Italiani dei Libri per l'Infanzia* (Turin: Einaudi, 1972); *Le Ceramiche Lenci, gli Artisti, i Secessionisti* (Milan: Sugarco, 1982).

46 In the July and October 1917 issues, *Margherita* published a great number of drawings copied or bought from *Les Élégances parisiennes*. The cover of the September 1917 issue is modified from a drawing published in the Parisian journal in May. Giuliana, "Corriere della Moda," *Margherita*, February 1, 1917, 74–5; "Storia del Ventaglio," ibid., March 1, 1917, 4.

47 *Corriere delle Signore* was a "journal of fashion and literature" founded in 1897 by publisher Treves and directed by Virginia Treves Tedeschi. It was bought by the Società Editoriale Italiana in 1917 and changed its title to *Il Secolo delle Signore*. Carrarini, "Corriere delle Signore," in *Bibliografia dei Periodici Femminili Lombardi: 1786–1945*, Rita Carrarini and Michele Giordano, eds. (Milan: Istituto Lombardo per la Storia del Movimento di Liberazione in Italia, Bibliografica, 1993), 80–2.

48 Grazietta Butazzi, ed., *1922–1943: Vent'anni di Moda Italiana: Proposta per un Museo della Moda a Milano* (Florence: Centro Di, 1980).

49 Roberta Orsi Landini, "Alle Origini della Grande Moda Italiana: Maria Monaci Gallenga," in *Moda Femminile tra le Due Guerre*, Caterina Chiarelli, ed. (Livorno: Sillabe, 2000), 30–41; Margherita Rosina and Francina Chiara, *Guido Ravasi il Signore della Seta* (Como: Il Nodo, 2008).

References

Argan, Giulio Carlo. *Aroldo Bonzagni*. Ferrara: Arstudio, 1987.
Bartoloni, Stefania. "L'Associazionismo Femminile nella Prima Guerra Mondiale e la Mobilitazione per l'Assistenza Civile e la Propaganda," in *Donna lombarda (1860-1945)*, Ada Gigli Marchetti and Nanda Torcellan, eds., 65–91. Milan: Franco Angeli, 1992.
Bartoloni, Stefania. *Italiane alla Guerra: L'Assistenza ai Feriti 1915-1918*. Venice: Marsilio, 2003.
Butazzi, Grazietta, ed. *1922-1943: Vent'anni di Moda Italiana: Proposta per un Museo della Moda a Milano*. Florence: Centro Di, 1980.
Carrarini, Rita. "Corriere delle Signore," in *Bibliografia dei Periodici Femminili Lombardi: 1786-1945*, Rita Carrarini and Michele Giordano, eds., 80–2. Milan: Istituto Lombardo per la Storia del Movimento di Liberazione in Italia, Bibliografica, 1993.
Carrarini, Rita. "La Stampa di Moda dall'Unità a Oggi," in *La Moda: Storia d'Italia. Annali 19*, Carlo Marco Belfanti and Fabio Giusberti, eds., 797–834. Turin: Einaudi, 2003.
Carrarini, Rita and Michele Giordano, eds. *Bibliografia dei Periodici Femminili Lombardi: 1786-1945*. Milan: Istituto Lombardo per la Storia del Movimento di Liberazione in Italia, Bibliografica, 1993.
Curci, Roberto, ed. *Marcello Dudovich: Oltre il Manifesto*. Milan: Charta, 2002.
Curli, Barbara. *Italiane al Lavoro (1914-1920)*. Venice: Marsilio, 2001.
D'Ulmes, Tony. "La Mobilisation des femmes," *La Revue hebdomadaire*, August 7, 1915, 73–83.
Della Torre, Roberto. *Invito al Cinema: Le Origini del Manifesto Cinematografico Italiano (1895-1930)*. Milan: EDUCatt Università Cattolica, 2014.
Erioli, Elisa. "L' 'Ufficio per Notizie alle Famiglie dei Militari': Una Grande Storia di Volontariato Femminile Bolognese." *Bollettino del Museo del Risorgimento* 1 (2005): 75–89.
Faeti, Antonio. *Guardare le Figure: Gli Illustratori Italiani dei Libri per l'Infanzia*. Turin: Einaudi, 1972.
Fiorentini, Aurora. "L'Ornamento di Pura Arte Italiana: La Moda di Rosa Genoni." In *Abiti in Festa: L'Ornamento e la Sartoria Italiana*, 41–59. Florence: Sillabe, 1996.
Franchini, Silvia. *Editori, Lettrici e Stampa di Moda: Giornali di Moda e di Famiglia a Milano dal Corriere delle Dame agli Editori dell'Italia Unita*. Milan: Franco Angeli, 2002.
Genoni, Rosa "Per una Moda Italiana." *Vita Femminile Italiana* (June 1908): 666–77.
Granzotto, Giovanni. *Marcello Dudovich 1878-1962*. Brescia: Corbelli, 2004.
Le Ceramiche Lenci: Gli Artisti-I Secessionisti. Milan: Sugarco, 1982.
Margherita, 1914–18.
Morini, Enrica. *Interazioni fra arte e moda. Boldini, Poiret, Genoni*. Milan: Mimesis 2020.
Orsi Landini, Roberta. "Alle Origini della Grande Moda Italiana: Maria Monaci Gallenga." In *Moda Femminile tra le Due Guerre*, Caterina Chiarelli, ed., 30–41. Livorno: Sillabe, 2000.
Pescatori, Marina. *Vagabondaggi di una Matita: Luigi Bompard*. Rome: Gm., 2004.
Pisa, Beatrice. "Una Azienda di Stato a Domicilio: La Confezione di Indumenti Militari durante la Grande Guerra." *Storia Contemporanea* 6 (1989): 953–1006.
Pisa, Beatrice. "La Mobilitazione Civile e Politica delle Italiane nella Grande Guerra." *Giornale di Storia Contemporanea* 2 (December 2001): 79–103.
Quesada, Mario, ed. *Luigi Bompard: 1879-1953*. Rome: Emporio Floreale, 1983.

Rosina, Margherita and Francina Chiara, eds. *Guido Ravasi il Signore della Seta*. Como: Il Nodo, 2008.

Serva, Federica. "Margherita." In *Bibliografia dei Periodici Femminili Lombardi: 1786–1945*, Rita Carrarini and Michele Giordano, eds., 225. Milan: Istituto Lombardo per la Storia del Movimento di Liberazione in Italia, Bibliografica, 1993.

Torelli Violler, Eugenio. "Movimento Librario." In *Mediolanum*, vol. 3, 341–61. Milan: Vallardi, 1881.

18

Le Flambeau's *fashion discourse during the First World War*
Towards a retrograde femininity?
Nigel Lezama

Le Flambeau: Grand Magazine de Luxe Hebdomadaire (The Torch: Weekly Luxury Magazine) was a short-lived Parisian magazine published between May 1915 and January 1916, with a primarily middle-class readership. The magazine sold for 75 centimes an issue, or 32 francs for a yearly subscription. The magazine was a subsidiary of *Le Matin*, one of the major newspapers of the era with a circulation of 1.62 million copies in 1916.[1] *Le Flambeau*'s editorial mission was to herald France's imminent victory in the First World War, while celebrating the country's cultural heritage and military triumphs.

We need look no further than the front cover of the first issue to see how the magazine cultivated an image of nationalist valor (Figure 18.1). The Latinized typography—with the "u" of *Flambeau* stylized in the Latin "v" shape—established a lineage with the historical past, a reassuring connection with tradition. The image of the torch, the eponymous *flambeau,* decorated with oak leaves and an acorn employed well-worn heraldic symbols. Wind blows the torch's flame to the east, in the direction of the French front line, representing, no doubt, the magazine's intention of shedding light on the French army's exploits. The introductory text inside the issue continued this appeal to the past, listing a series of pivotal moments in French history in a comparison with the ongoing conflict.[2] The body of the magazine consisted of short works of fiction, articles and stories from the war, and images of French soldiers in the field.

A brief section devoted to fashion was hidden near the end of the magazine. The column took up just a single page in the first issue, as if it were an afterthought in a magazine that was primarily concerned with upholding nationalist sentiment.[3] Nevertheless, the section grew in size issue by issue, eventually filling three or four pages, extending to the end of the magazine. What, then, did this conservative magazine, whose aesthetics leaned towards historicism, have to say on the subject of women's fashion during the war?[4] Although fashion was clearly a secondary concern in *Le Flambeau*, never spilling out from its designated section into the rest of the magazine, it was addressed. What role, then, did the *Flambeau*'s discourse on female fashion play in the context of a deadly and bloody war?

The fashion section of *Le Flambeau* was penned by three successive writers, each of whom offered her own distinct voice and conception of wartime fashion. Louise Faure-Favier (1870–1961) was at the helm of the column in the first issues (Figure 18.2). She wrote primarily for a wealthy audience. Her texts covered the new social and aesthetic constraints imposed by the war and modern life. After three months, Camille Duguet (dates unknown) took charge. Duguet was known for her fashion writing in *Le Figaro, La Nouvelle Mode,* and *Chiffons.* Duguet's column, newly titled "Propositions on Fashion," analyzed stylistic trends with greater specificity than Faure-Favier's, but was somewhat narrower in scope.[5] Finally, Jeanne Tournier (dates unknown), of whom little is today known, took over the column. Tournier instituted a new focus on practicality, targeting a readership of more

Figure 18.1 *Cover of* Le Flambeau*'s first issue, May 29, 1915. gallica.bnf.fr/Bibliothèque Nationale de France (BnF).*

Figure 18.2 *Louise Faure-Favier's first fashion column*, Le Flambeau, *May 29, 1915. gallica.bnf.fr/BnF.*

modest means. As a whole, *Le Flambeau*'s fashion discourse was relatively elitist, with few direct appeals to the working class, although economic consideration gained more focus as the war drew on. Yet, certain undercurrents of the ongoing social changes sometimes came to the fore amidst the magazine's conservatism, complicating matters. Women gradually gained new freedoms during the war, not only in terms of dress—with the abandonment of the corset and a move towards less ornate, restrictive fashions—but also in terms of social mores, as women moved to fill the economic and professional void left by the men on the front lines. The fashion writing in *Le Flambeau* responded to these changes, playing against them at times, in an effort to alleviate social anxiety over women's entry into public life.

The war and fashion: The columns of Louise Faure-Favier

The very first column dedicated to women's dress, which was published in the first issue of *Le Flambeau*, was titled "Fashion in 1915." It began with a statement that separated fashion from the political climate surrounding it: "While everything has more or less come to a halt for this nation, fashion continues its natural evolution, insouciant, floating above the fray."[6] According to Faure-Favier, (masculine) public life had come to a standstill during the crisis, while fashion—in her usage, solely the domain of the woman—was undergoing a "veritable revolution." Was Faure-Favier suggesting that fashion, in a state of constant flux, was being insensitive towards the sociopolitical realities of the time? The article did— as its title suggests—evoke the tensions created as women's fashion navigated wartime. Indeed, Faure-Favier elevated fashion to the level of political news: "Despite the war, fashion has decreed a small revolution."[7] The militarist language ("decree," "revolution") removed fashion from the private sphere, and accorded it a role in public discourse. Faure-Favier extended the military symbolism to the body as well: "The docile female body submits to the new decree of sovereign fashion."[8]

The military lexicon, and the rhetoric of the submissive female body, were not innocent. During the war, there was little tolerance for supposedly defiant women. The historian Françoise Navet-Bouron has written about how women's speech was subject to rigorous censure during the war, as the press sought to maintain civil order, prevent demoralization, and limit discussion of pacifism.[9] Navet-Bouron found that, "Throughout the war, four main themes emerge as the subjects of censure: women on strike are by far the most frequently targeted, followed by female spies, and victims of German atrocities. Finally, expressions of grief by mothers and widows were limited."[10] In this period, women's errant activity in the public sphere was considered destabilizing to the social order; men were experiencing horrors at the front, and so publicizing women's fashion and luxury was a sensitive endeavor. By using the rhetoric of the subjugated female body, Faure-Favier preempted any possible recrimination for turning public attention to a seemingly frivolous matter during such perilous times.

In the second issue of *Le Flambeau*, from June 6, 1915, Faure-Favier continued her rhetoric surrounding the subjugated female body, claiming, "Here, perhaps, we see signs of the coming peace? Feminine dress is demilitarizing itself."[11] She again championed feminine docility by making this so-called "demilitarized" fashion a sign of contemporary womanhood: "Thus, the wardrobe is feminizing itself. It is now pure grace and simplicity. It suits the new communal spirit we share, the urge to be more *woman*, in the best possible sense, that is to say, increasingly gentle, tender, collected, and wise."[12] Masculine accessories, she claimed, were no longer in style: "As to the policeman's cap, it is now worn solely by female tramway conductors."[13] Faure-Favier paid no other mention to work dress in this article, which privileged the clothing of the wealthy.

Faure-Favier's positioning of women's dress served two ideological functions. In focusing solely on the clothing of the wealthy, she devalued the dress adopted by women entering the workplace: it was no longer desirable, to her, for women's fashion to draw inspiration from the male uniform.[14] Work dress, and analogously, the working woman, were rendered *démodé* in the writer's texts. Women's forays into the working world were circumscribed by their inherent femininity. Second, the fact that Faure-Favier reduced the new aesthetics of women's fashion to a mere symbol of the oncoming peace reinforced the women's ornamental role. In these columns, the fashionable woman was reassuringly passive; she was prepared to abandon the jobs that had been intended solely for men as soon as the war was over.

Feminism and fashion

Faure-Favier did make one reference to feminism while introducing another stylistic trend in a later article: "Someone once wrote: feminism will triumph only when women have pockets."[15] This mention of feminism, while lighthearted, marked another step into the ideological debate over the role of women in public life.[16] The column linked this lack of pockets to the traditional requirement for women to have a guardian:

> Indeed, women—until recently—have not played a role in many of life's major events, unable to carry contracts or proof of identity, mainly due to their lack of a place to put them. For the little bags we've carried have never been able to hold anything that was not frivolous.[17]

The inferior status of women was a symptom of inadequate clothing to allow for their enfranchisement, as well as a result of their inherent frivolity. According to Faure-Faiver, it was thanks to the war—and to the arrival of pockets—that women seemed to have found a degree of independence:

> Then came the war. From one day to the next, frivolous women were transformed into breadwinners, factory overseers, and heads of enterprise. Oh, the complications that met these women forced to travel alone, weighed down with important papers, safe passages, money! Finally, pockets were imposed upon nurses.[18]

This argument, teasing out the relationships between the war, fashion, and women's liberation, reduced female emancipation to a material condition, and perhaps even a trend, as fleeting as the season's fashion, and capable of being replaced just as quickly. This line of thought becomes all the more apparent when read in concert with Faure-Favier's previous criticism of the out-of-style militarist or masculine trends of working women. The subtext was that after the war, the need for pockets would disappear, and with them, so, too, would women from public life.

The historian Françoise Thébaud has chronicled the deliberate attempts made in the post-war period to restore pre-war gender roles and reinstate the equilibrium upset by the dominant public presence of women.[19] Between 1914 to 1918, she claims, "gender identities were disrupted, but . . . the post-war period saw a painstaking restoration of the former relations between men and women. Declaring peace also meant rebuilding this endangered equilibrium."[20] Faure-Favier's feminism was ultimately undermined by her own discourse. She applauded women's new social engagement, relating it to masculinized dress;

but this participation in the public sphere, dependent as it is on current trends, would only be relevant during wartime. What need would there be for pockets when the men had returned?

These texts should be taken with a grain of salt. Fashion writing has always been characterized by a certain performativity, drawing from a combination of the author's voice, discourse on class, and commercial considerations. Faure-Favier, the woman, likely held more serious beliefs on the status of the feminine sex; Faure-Favier, the writer, however, projected the lighthearted spirit demanded of fashion discourse in the media. According to her, the woman *was* what she wore—the "frivolous" contents of her handbag typified her own frivolity. This view was in accordance with the belief that the emergence of women in society happened at the expense of men. Women had gained no rights or self-determination; economic agency had simply been imposed upon them, just as "pockets were *imposed upon* nurses" [author's emphasis].

It was not unusual, at the time, for prejudice against women to be revealed through blinkered discussion of their dress. In 1910, in his dissection of the "Parisienne," the writer Octave Uzanne (1851–1931) built his argument around women's sportswear: "All sports become, for the contemporary Parisienne, rather than a true physical vocation, a pretext for dressing up: remove the riding habit, bid adieu to the horse. Take away the designated clothes for female motorists, bikers, aeronauts, hunters, and fencers, and women's sports will swiftly follow suit."[21] For Uzanne, women's increasing participation in public life was reduced to a mere byproduct of their natural inclination towards dress. In a similar vein, discussion of women's emancipation often revolved around their clothes. Appropriation of male dress was one of the first demands of the early feminists in the mid-nineteenth century. At the first National Women's Rights Convention, held in Worcester, Massachusetts in 1850, a letter from the French writer Helene Marie Weber was discussed, in which she stated that "In ten years' time, male attire will be generally worn by the women of most civilized countries."[22]

The sporting woman: Camille Duguet as columnist

When Camille Duguet took over the fashion section of *Le Flambeau*, she began appealing to a new ideal reader: the modern woman who exercised her new freedoms through sports and through her dress. "Golf and tennis have found favor with Parisian women, who travel to Fontainebleau," she advised, "For these activities, one dresses simply, while retaining that little bit of *allure*."[23] In this article, Duguet did not shy away from the criticisms lobbied by Uzanne several years prior that fashionabilty was the main concern for women, as they adopted new and modern behaviours (Figure 18.3). Women had a duty to preserve their femininity: "Sporting dress must not masculinize women. Any clothing that takes away from her natural charm is quite regrettable, and should not under any circumstances be tolerated."[24]

Figure 18.3 *Camille Duguet's fashion column,* Le Flambeau, *August 28, 1915. gallica.bnf.fr/BnF.*

In introducing the idea of "masculinization," Duguet's text positioned itself in relation to two phenomena that had emerged in the era's discourse on women and their bodies: it made reference to the debate surrounding the effects of physical activity on women's health, and addressed male anxieties over the new roles and behaviors of modern women. In the late nineteenth century, the medical field had issued contradictory arguments on the value of exercise for the female body; one view held that exercise was a means to strengthen the female body for the perpetuation of the sex, while others claimed that exercise denatured women's bodies.[25] This era also saw increased anxieties over shifting moral codes and changes in women's roles in the public sphere. These concerns were drastically heightened after male mobilization in 1914.

Talk of women's emancipation induced widespread apprehension and was considered a threat to the social order. As historian Jean-Yves Le Naour has written of women's new roles in the work force, "Women's increasing presence in the industrial sphere, especially in positions previously reserved for the stronger sex, was a destabilizing force, and this virilization of women led to growing sentiments of frustration and emasculation."[26] The illustrated women's magazine *La Vie heureuse* (The Happy Life) specified the magazine's position on "the proper feminism," in its September 1910 issue, describing it as "feminism that makes women virile, giving them strength, but does not masculinize, which would be a disgrace."[27] Within this context, Duguet's language preempted accusations of "masculinization" by aligning itself with a social order that assured familiarity and stability amidst the chaotic sociopolitical circumstances.

Duguet's emphasis on preserving femininity, and on ensuring a certain continuity in matters of both gender and aesthetics, can be compared with a tendency in her writing to appeal to nostalgia.[28] In her October column celebrating the fashion of 1915, she describes a winter dress adorned with fur, whose sleeves "extend from lower shoulder, which is, in turn, beautifully molded by the fabric of the bodice, which, in its delicate roundness, recalls the graceful style of 1830."[29] Another dress with a long skirt decorated with zibeline seems to have "escaped from a page of the *Journal des Dames et des Demoiselles*, now made new again."[30] That date of 1830 along with the mention of the *Journal des Dames et des Demoiselles* (Journals of Ladies and Young Women), founded in 1833, evoke a period in the nineteenth century seen as the apogee of Parisian elegance. Duguet was harking back to a time before the colorful extravagance of courtesans in the Second Empire, or the decadence of the fin de siècle, periods in which the roles and expectations for women became more loosely defined (Figure 18.4).

Figure 18.4 *Camille Duguet's fashion column,* Le Flambeau, *October 9, 1915. gallica.bnf.fr/BnF.*

However, this valorization of the past (and of its less ambiguous gender roles) is complicated by other anachronistic references. In the same article, Duguet described a winter outfit which was crowned by "a small hat with a receding profile, enveloped by Chantilly lace, which manages to remind us of the pretty women of the *Éducation Sentimentale* (Sentimental Education)."[31] Duguet made a second reference to Gustave Flaubert's bildungsroman in another hat description from the same article: "We see yet more reminders of this era in the original bonnet, seen above. It is in pleated satin, crowned with a velour ribbon. This is exactly how Flaubert's Rosanette preferred them."[32] Duguet was more precise with her second allusion: she is referring to the promiscuous courtesan in the *Éducation sentimentale* (Sentimental Education), a novel that covers the Revolution of 1848, another turbulent period in French history. This evocation of the turbulence and questionable morality in Flaubert's novel stands at odds with Duguet's usual emphasis on social order and stability. It appears almost as if allowing this Flaubertian discourse into her column were a lapse on the author's part—one that nevertheless proves enlightening, testifying to the destabilizing role of fashion during times of political conflict.

During the war, fashion and feminine luxury became issues with which men could valorize or denigrate femininity in equal measure. On the one hand, the fashion and luxury sectors were a source of national pride, and the Parisian woman stood as a figurehead of French charm and industriousness. The phenomenon of the *Mimi Pinsons*—fashion workers who mobilized in order to craft cockades and other items for the war effort—is one example of the heroism associated with the industry.[33] On the other hand, Parisian women were also subject to recrimination for their material obsessions: "How many women, after becoming head of the family, have we seen blinded by gold and silver, throwing caution to the wind in order to dress themselves in the latest finery," wrote a certain Germain Balard in his war journal.[34] Another soldier by the name of Fernand revealed his dispirited resignation when, in a letter to his brother dated August 1917, he wrote, "Back in Paris, I've noticed that on the home front, people have become resigned to the war. I've seen women showing off their bare arms, eager to be seen. It's a sad thing, we're dropping like flies, women are laughing, and the children forget."[35] In this climate of ambivalence, where women's fashion was simultaneously glorified and the object of suspicion, the references to fashion under the July Monarchy and to the women in *L'Éducation Sentimentale* seem to rely on nostalgia to diffuse anxieties over the shifting social and moral order during wartime.

Jeanne Tournier and the containment of women's bodies and behavior

The third columnist for *Le Flambeau*, Jeanne Tournier, adopted a more populist tone in her articles than her predecessors (Figure 18.5). Or at least, this appears to be the case on first reading. In the opening lines of her first column, "How to Make a Fashionable Dress at Home," she stated her intentions of appealing to an entirely new demographic: "This advice is not meant for those privileged with fortune, who, in order to dress elegantly, need only to order several gowns from a renowned couturier. It is meant for those of us—many in number, these days—who dream of wearing the latest styles while spending very little."[36] The article provided a pattern so that readers could sew their own dress. A more inclusive format was apparent from the very first column. Tournier's language seemed to limit its praise for luxury and ostentation—increasingly seen as offensive in light of the suffering on the front. On this note, she advised, "By deciding which fabric to use, and which decorations to add on, the dress can be made more or less luxurious depending on one's intentions."[37] She offered the choice to customize, and even *mitigate* one's display of luxury. The column's new title, "A Little Elegance" or, in certain issues, "A Little Practical Elegance," was indicative of this shift. It seems as if the editorial board of *Flambeau* made a conscious decision to target a different type of reader. One of Tournier's columns from several weeks later began with an admission intended as sympathetic commiseration with readers: "Those of us who are unable to spend a considerable sum on our wardrobe, especially in times like these, have often, in these past few months, resented couturiers and fashion."[38]

Figure 18.5 *Jeanne Tournier's first fashion column,* Le Flambeau, *November 13, 1915. gallica.bnf.fr/BnF.*

Nevertheless, these columns have the same tendency to correct female actions and behavior. Tournier, continuing with her economic pragmatism, advised, "We have moved on from the time when we could walk into the couturier to buy 'a simple suit' and leave, several hours later, realizing to our great surprise that we have ordered four or five dresses."[39] This preoccupation with feminine excess was not a phenomenon that was unique to the Great War. Since the end of the eighteenth century—and with increasing prevalence in the nineteenth century—luxury, and its associated traits of femininity and effeminacy, had become subject to suspicion, and these sentiments reached a peak during the war.[40] Tournier continued, "We have now become more reasonable, and I truly hope that the wise habits we have adopted during the war rid us permanently of our taste for exaggerated spending."[41] The war had become a regulating force acting on women's behavior.

Moreover, while Tournier's language was populist, nevertheless, it retained its appeals to the ruling class; she addressed those who *had the means* for exaggerated spending in the first place—or at least, did so in the past. Ultimately, "A Little Practical Elegance" didn't truly establish a new lower-class readership, but rather added a new layer of corrective discourse which turned the existing *bourgeoise* readership into its own regulatory instrument. Women were compelled to limit their taste for luxury in light of the wartime crisis. Like its predecessors, the column casts a blind eye to the role working-class women played in the fashion industry and in constructing fashion discourse, turning it into a locus of nationalist pride, as Patricia Tilburg has argued in her discussion of *Mimi Pinson*.[42]

Conclusion

French gender dynamics were reconfigured during the First World War. With women's new roles in the public sphere came new expectations and methods of control, often variants of those handed down from the nineteenth century. Analyzing *Le Flambeau*'s fashion column—and the distinct perspectives of its three columnists—allows us to see these tensions at play. During this time of national crisis, when the masculine presence in society was severely reduced, women were left to fill the void while navigating often contradictory standards. While *Le Flambeau* was open to various new practices and roles for women, and eventually introduced dialogue that was more inclusive towards the working class (at least on the surface level), it, nevertheless, did not encourage broader social engagement or feminist thought. Closer inspection of the texts of each of our three columnists reveals tendencies that run counter to any claims of openness towards female emancipation.

Furthermore, various passages reveal a need to corral feminine behavior in an effort to limit the moral or social disorder that women were deemed capable of fostering. Faure-Favier began the magazine's foray into fashion with a column that brought women's dress out of the private sphere, discussing it within the context of public life. In order to emphasize the importance of daily dress, she invoked feminism at one point; however, she did not manage to grant women autonomy in her texts, neither politically nor in relation to their own wardrobe. Duguet's perspective covered a new array of feminine activities, including engagement in sports, but these sympathies with modernity were limited by a denunciation of any accompanying masculinization. In addition, her nostalgic tendencies—centered around the period of the July Monarchy—muddy her embrace of the modern woman. The final columnist, Tournier, did, indeed, initiate a more democratic approach towards fashion, but integrated a corrective lens that condemned exaggerated feminine luxury while simultaneously clouding her connection with the lower classes.

We can thus conclude that the process of situating women's expected roles and behaviors within their socio-political milieu was a major preoccupation in the discourse stemming from *Le Flambeau*'s fashion column. The trope of the woman as an anxiety-producing figure seeped through even amidst attempts at liberalism and openness. This ambivalence also obscured the presence of the working class in the discussion, despite concessions made later in the magazine's run. The First World War threw masculinity into crisis, and it was therefore inevitable that, in turn, femininity would come under scrutiny. In these circumstances, fashion—as the public expression of the feminine world—would need to accord itself with the dominant ideologies of the times. As such, the discursive construction of the magazine's female reader favored a retrograde and circumscribed femininity.

Notes

1 *Le Matin* was owned by Maurice Bunau-Varilla (1856–1944), a French press magnate. See Gabrielle Cadier-Rey, "Le Club des Quatre de la Glorieuse Époque," at: https://p6.storage.canalblog.com/69/28/1046708/91144123.pdf (accessed July 26, 2020).

2 In the first issue, for example, the introductory text draws a comparison between France's current situation and a number of momentous events in French history, in order to contextualize the magazine's editorial purpose:

> The France of Henry IV, of Louis XIV, of the Encyclopédistes, of the Revolution, and of the Empire is today the France of the Republic. It is one and the same. It has always taken pride in being industrious and confident in times of sorrow, enterprising and ingenious amidst war, resolute and tenacious in the face of peril; it has fostered creation during great trials, given birth during times of despair: how could we give up these traditional virtues when we can already see the aurora of victory alight on the horizon, and when our cause has become that of all of humanity? "Le Flambeau," *Le Flambeau*, 1, May 29, 1915.

3 The nationalism of *Le Matin* reached its peak during the First World War, with its editorial stance later turning towards "anti-parliamentarism and anticommunism, veering towards the far right," and eventually landing at collaborationism during the Second World War (cf. "Historique des Titres de Presses Numérisés," at: https://p7.storage.canalblog.com/78/35/1046708/98477633.pdf accessed July 26, 2020).

4 In general, the fashion press suffered during the First World War and a number of journals ceased publication. *Le Salon de la Mode*, *Le Bel Écho de la Mode,* and *Le Journal des Dames et des Modes*, for example, all stopped in 1914.

La Gazette du Bon Ton, a more cutting-edge magazine, halted production during the war, save for one special wartime edition in the summer of 1915—intended, in part, to uphold French fashion internationally. Suffice it to say, the fashion press had extra incentive to fall in line with the dominant political preoccupations of the time. Valerie Steele covers this period of "revolution" in fashion in her germinal work, *Paris Fashion: A Cultural History*, 2nd edn (Oxford: Berg, 1998). According to Steele, a number of the innovations considered as originating during the war in reality stemmed from the prewar modernist movement. She cites as examples: the evolution from corset to the girdle, the v-neck blouse, and the "war crinoline," with its wider, shorter skirts. Cf. Steele, "Fashion Revolution," in *Paris Fashion*, 219–43.

5 Each of Faure-Favier's articles bears a unique title, some of which are lyrical or amusingly glib, such as "The bag is dead: Long live the pocket!" Louise Faure-Favier, "Le Sac est mort: vive la poche!" *Le Flambeau*, 4, June 19, 1915.

6 One of the ways in which writings on fashion aligned themselves with political realities was by situating themselves within a broader historical context. Titles such as "Fashion in 1915" (or 1916, etc.) became a leitmotif in the discourse on fashion during the Great War. This historical contextualization served as a tool to give greater weight to the arguments expressed therein. Louise Faure-Favier, "La Mode en 1915," *Le Flambeau*, 1, May 29, 1915.

7 Ibid.

8 Ibid.

9 Françoise Navet-Bouron, "La Censure et la femme pendant la Première Guerre Mondiale," *Guerres Mondiales et Conflits Contemporains* 198 (2000), 43–51, at: http://www.jstor.org/stable/2573z675 (accessed June 15, 2019).

10 Ibid., 43.

11 Louise Faure-Favier, "Une Robe légère, un chapeau de bergère," *Le Flambeau*, 2, June 5, 1915.

12 Ibid.

13 Ibid.

14 The uniform has a long history dating back to the eighteenth century as a garment used to discipline the male body. The use of uniforms in the Prussian military launched a practice that spread to all of the European royal courts, and shortly, the civil sphere as well, introducing a social code that reinforced the phallocentrism of modern society (cf. Elizabeth Hackspiel-Mikosch, "Uniforms and the creation of ideal masculinity," in *The Men's Fashion Reader*, Peter McNeil and Vicki Karaminas, eds. (Oxford: Berg, 2009), 117–129. With this in mind, the distancing of feminine fashion from military inspirations can be read as a response to the anxiety produced by the increasing presence of women in public forums.

15 Faure-Favier, "Le Sac est mort!"

16 Anxieties regarding the roles of women in public and private forums began to mount in the late nineteenth century, and women's new roles were often discussed or condemned by way of their appearance and dress. In his reporting on the Congrès Féministe de Paris in 1896, for example, a journalist for the *Figaro* commented that, "In such assemblies, the eyes must do more work than the ears, such that the success of an orator will be judged primarily by the sheen of her fabric and the slimness of her waist—desirable qualities, no doubt, but little indicative of sharp intelligence or fine judgement." ("Leur Congés," *Le Figaro*, April 12, 1896). The appearance of the woman and her role in society were so enmeshed that the former risked eclipsing the latter. When Faure-Favier integrates feminism into her descriptions of fashion, she enters into a discussion that had long been brewing, reaching its peak during the First World War due to women's entry into the workplace.

17 Faure-Favier, "Le Sac est mort!"

18 Ibid.

19 Françoise Thébaud, "Penser la guerre à partir des femmes et du genre: L'Exemple de la Grande Guerre," *Astérion* 2 (2004), at: http://asterion.revues.org/103 (accessed June 15, 2019).

20 Ibid., § 7.

21 Octave Uzanne, *Parisiennes de ce temps en leurs divers milieux, états etconditions: Études pour servir à l'histoire des femmes, de la société, de la galanterie française, des Moeurs contemporaines et de l'égoïsme masculine* (Paris: Mercure de France, 1910), 334–5.

22 Cited in Michel Erlich, "Transgressions corporelles et vestimentaires," *Le Vêtement: Colloque de Cerisy*, Frédéric Monneyron, ed. (Paris: L'Harmattan, 2001), 62.

23 Camille Duguet, "Propos sur la mode," *Le Flambeau*, 14, August 28, 1915.

24 Ibid.

25 See Anaïs Bohuon, "La Pratique physique et sportive féminine à l'Aube du XXe siècle: Moyen technique de maintien d'une définition normative des corps, l'exemple de la menstruation," *Gesnerus* 70, 1 (2013), 111–26.

26 Jean-Yves Le Naour, "'Il faut sauver notre pantalon:' La Première Guerre Mondiale et le sentiment masculin d'inversion du rapport de domination," *Cahiers d'Histoire: Revue d'histoire critique* 84 (2001): § 11, at: http://chrhc.revues.org/1866 (accessed June 15, 2019).

27 Cited in Guillaume Pinson, "La Femme masculinisée dans la presse française de la Belle Époque," *Clio: Histoire, femmes, et sociétés* 30 (2009), §14, at: http://clio.revues.org/9471 (accessed June 15, 2019).

28 Nostalgia, of course, was not a new occurrence in the fashion press. The prolific Vicomtesse de Renneville (1811–90), for example, a fashion writer for multiple magazines during the Second Empire, including *Le Moniteur de la Mode*, *Le Bon Ton*, *Journal de Modes*, *Littérature et Beaux-arts*, and *Le Figaro*, often made reference to figures of the Ancien Régime in order to emphasize the elegance of new trends. This phenomenon continues today, as journals write about the elegance of the dandy or the casual charm of the early-twentieth-century *bohème*. We find here what Walter Benjamin attributed to fashion as "the eternal recurrence of the new." Nevertheless, the fact that Duguet so privileged this return to the past during a time of great modernism and experimentation in women's fashion—exemplified by Poiret's creations or the drawings of Paul Iribe—signifies a politically minded will to valorize a certain traditional and conservative current in fashion.

29 Camille Duguet, "Propos sur la mode," *Le Flambeau*, 21, October 16, 1915.

30 Ibid.

31 Ibid., "Propos sur la mode," *Le Flambeau*, 20, October 9, 1915.

32 Ibid.

33 I am here beholden to Patricia Tilburg, who, in her fascinating article, "Mimi Pinson goes to war: Taste, class, and gender in France, 1900–18," *Gender & History* 23, 1 (April 2011): 92–110, sheds light on the unsung history of these workers, who supported the nation through their work during the war.

34 Cited in Le Naour, "'Il Faut sauver notre pantalon,'" § 11.

35 Jean-Claude Auriol, *Mémoires de papier: Correspondance des poilus de la Grande Guerre* (Paris: Tirésias, 2005), 150.

36 Jeanne Tournier, "Comment on fait soi-même une robe à la mode," *Le Flambeau*, 25, November 13, 1915.

37 Ibid.

38 Jeanne Tournier, "Un Peu d'élégance pratique," *Le Flambeau*, 26, November 20, 1915.

39 Ibid., "Un Peu d'élégance," *Le Flambeau*, 25, November 13, 1915.

40 The associations between luxury and the effeminization of society (and other similar recriminations) occurring in the political and economic discourse at the end of the eighteenth century and throughout the nineteenth century are covered by David Kuchta in his excellent book, *The Three-Piece Suit and Modern Masculinity* (Berkeley and Los Angeles, CA, and London: University of California Press, 2002). This book holds Britain as its primary focus, but in reproducing the opinions of the great political and economic thinkers of the time, demonstrates the impact of this phenomenon throughout Europe.

41 Tournier, "Un Peu d'élégance."

42 Tilburg explains in her article, "Mimi Pinson goes to war."

References

Auriol, Jean-Claude, *Mémoires de Papier: Correspondance des Poilus de la Grande Guerre*. Paris: Tirésias, 2005.

Bohuon, Anaïs. "La Pratique physique et sportive féminine à l'Aube du XXe siècle: Moyen technique de maintien d'une définition normative des corps, l'exemple de la menstruation." *Gesnerus* 70, 1 (2013): 111–26.

Boulongne, Yves-Pierre. "Pierre de Coubertin et le sport féminin." Available at: http://library.la84.org/OlympicInformationCenter/RevueOlympique/2000/orfXXVI31/ORFXXVI31za.pdf (accessed June 15, 2019).

Cadier-Rey, Gabrielle. "Le Club des Quatre de la Glorieuse Époque." Available at: https://p6.storage.canalblog.com/69/28/1046708/91144123.pdf (accessed July 26, 2020).

Duguet, Camille. "Propos sur la mode." *Le Flambeau*, 14, April 28, 1915.

Duguet, Camille. "Propos sur la mode." *Le Flambeau*, 20, October 9, 1915.

Duguet, Camille. "Propos sur la mode." *Le Flambeau*, 21, October 16, 1915.

Erlich, Michel. "Transgressions corporelles et vestimentaires." In *Le Vêtement: Colloque de Cerisy*, Frédéric Monneyron, ed., 43–67. Paris: L'Harmattan, 2001.

Faure-Favier, Louise. "La Mode en 1915." *Le Flambeau*, 1, May 29, 1915.

Faure-Favier, Louise. "Une Robe légère, un chapeau de bergère." *Le Flambeau*, 2, June 5, 1915.

Faure-Favier, Louise. "Le Sac est mort: Vive la poche!" *Le Flambeau*, 4, June 19, 1915.

Hackspiel-Mikosh, Elizabeth. "Uniforms and the creation of ideal masculinity." In *The Men's Fashion Reader*, Peter McNeil and Vicki Karaminas, eds., 117–29. Oxford: Berg, 2009.

"Historique des titres de presses numérisés." Available at: https://p7.storage.canalblog.com/78/35/1046708/98477633.pdf (accessed July 26, 2020).

Kuchta, David. *The Three-Piece Suit and Modern Masculinity: Studies on the History of Societies and Cultures*, Victoria Bonnell and Lynn Hunt, eds. Berkeley and Los Angeles, CA, and London: University of California Press, 2002.

"Le Flambeau." *Le Flambeau*, 1, May 29, 1915.

Le Naour, Jean-Yves. "'Il faut sauver notre pantalon': La Première Guerre Mondiale et le sentiment masculin d'inversion du rapport de domination." *Cahiers d'histoire: Revue d'histoire critique* 84 (2001). Available at: http://chrhc.revues.org/1866.

"Leur Congrès." *Le Figaro*, April 12, 1896.

Navet-Bouron, Françoise. "La Censure et la Femme pendant la Première Guerre Mondiale." In *Guerres Mondiales et conflits contemporains* 198 (2000): 43–51. Available at: http://www.jstor.org/stable/2573z675 (accessed June 15, 2019).

Pinson, Guillaume. "La Femme masculinisée dans la presse française de la Belle Époque." In *Clio: Histoire, femmes et societies* 30 (2009): 211–30. Available at: http://clio.revues.org/9471 (accessed June 15, 2019).

Roberts Mary, Louise. "Making the modern girl French: From New Woman to *Éclaireuse*." In *The Modern Girl Around the World: Consumption, Modernity & Globalization*, Alice Eve Weinbaum, Lynn M. Thomas, Priti Ramamurthy, Uta G. Poiger, Madeleine Y. Dong, and Tani E. Barlow, eds., 77–95. Durham, NC: Duke University Press, 2009.

Steele, Valerie. *Paris Fashion: A Cultural History*, 2nd edn. Oxford: Berg, 1998.

Thébaud, Françoise. "Penser la guerre à partir des femmes et du genre: L'Exemple de la Grande Guerre." *Astérion* 2 (2004). Available at: http://asterion.revues.org/103 (accessed June 15, 2019).

Tilburg, Patricia. "Mimi Pinson goes to war: Taste, class and gender in France, 1900–18," In *Gender & History* 23, 1 (April 2011): 92–110.

Tournier, Jeanne. "Comment on fait soi-même une robe à la mode," *Le Flambeau*, 25, November 13, 1915.

Tournier, Jeanne. "Un Peu d'élégance." *Le Flambeau*, 25, November 13, 1915.

Tournier, Jeanne. "Un Peu d'élégance Pratique." *Le Flambeau*, 26, November 20, 1915.

Uzanne, Octave. *Parisiennes de ce temps en leurs divers milieux, états et conditions: Études pour servir à l'histoire des femmes, de la Société, de la Galanterie Française, des moeurs contemporaines et de l'égoïsme masculin*. Paris: Mercure de France, 1910.

Vogel, Lucien. "*La Gazette du Bon Ton* et la guerre," *La Gazette du Bon Ton: Art, Modes et Frivolités*, 8–9, Summer 1914.

19

Is beauty useless?

Fashion, gender, and British wartime society in Punch Magazine, 1915

Andrea Kollnitz

"The war, in fact, as all wars do had a deadening effect on fashion, and there is little of interest to record until the conflict was over."[1] Those are the words of James Laver in his *Costume and Fashion: A Concise History* from 1969. The quote presents the end of half a page on fashion at the outbreak of the First World War in Great Britain. Laver assumes fashion ended in 1914 and was "picked up again" in 1919.[2] Laver's survey, as well as several others on (British) fashion history, exemplifies a perspective on fashion as identified, interpreted, and evaluated through its historical changes and innovations, and thereby more or less leaves out the war years of 1914–18.[3] As Cheryl Buckley states, when looking at representations of British female fashion during wartime:

> Discussion of women's fashion in Britain during the First World War has been surprisingly generalized and lacking in detailed primary research. Typically, characterized by a number of "truisms"; it has been summed up thus: that uniforms were worn most of the time; that fashion was temporarily suspended; and that practical clothing predominated.[4]

As an alternative perspective, Buckley claims that "Fashion, as both social and cultural artifact and as representational process, was increasingly discursive during the period of the First World War and it provided a highly charged space in which femininity, modernity and class identity were negotiated."[5]

Agreeing with Buckley's focus on fashion as an important site for the construction of (new) identities, this article will problematize an established and generalizing classification of British fashion as "suspended" during the First World War and will instead look at this imagined gap as a crucial period of fashion distinction. Through an analysis of the visual fashion discourse in the satirical images of the British satirical magazine *Punch* during the year 1915, it will investigate the representation of fashion as a tool of conservatism, identity negotiation, and a provider of social security during a period of rising insecurity on all possible levels.

This essay will argue that during wartime, fashion gains special significance through its power to establish distinctive visual codes and to manifest constant stereotypical identities in order to resist an on-going and seemingly uncontrollable political and social change. The choice of the year 1915 as focus for this case study is not only based on the need for delimitation, but also highlights the peculiar state of British society during the first year of the war. In 1915, British society was already aware of and observing the war on the continent while still only partially participating on the battleground. The historian Adrian Gregory has identified different stages of war awareness in Britain. He defines the period 1914–16 as a transition "from spectatorship to participation" and "from volunteering to compulsion."[6]

I see this transitional state in British society as a period of insecurity and acclimation where fashion and dress came to play an exceptionally important role in the visual performance of social transformation. A look at the cartoons in *Punch* from 1915 shows how fashion serves as distinctive "costume" in the social dramas enacted in the cartoons and helped shape the identities or "role characters" performed within the jokes. While these costumes can be related to their actual use in contemporary society and politics, they also bear visual rhetorical significance in the images per se.

Punch, or The London Charivari, founded in 1841 as a counterpart to the French humoristic magazine *Le Charivari*, was a weekly illustrated journal containing news, satirical texts and cartoons, poems, reports on cultural and sports events etc. It was one of the first examples of what the publisher Charles Knight in 1862 called "picture journalism" with an important function of providing visual news for the contemporary reader.[7] *Punch* also played a pivotal role in developing the cartoon as a major visual and narrative element in international print media. Since its beginnings, it presented a rich number of fashion-related cartoons and caricatures that were meant to entertain, but also provide effective socio-political commentary for the contemporary British educated reader.[8]

While not all of these cartoons are explicitly about fashion, fashion plays a crucial performative role in all of them. Accordingly, this study examines cartoons that use fashion/s and dress as visual signifiers of the social roles and relationships they present. The fashion images and jokes in *Punch* are interpreted as performative in their staging of contemporary British society as they express, emphasize, and demarcate distinctive "characters" in their different "costumes". In accordance with Erving Goffman's metaphorical understanding of social relationships as a theatre, developed in *The

Presentation of Self in Everyday Life, these costumes are examined as a perceivable *front* or mask with a crucial function on the social stage; here, that stage frames the gender and class relationships of contemporary society.[9]

Starting from examples that focus on conspicuous female fashionability and its different significations, this article will identify diverse role characters, dramatic scenarios, and visual tropes which are repeated, manifested, or also transformed throughout the year of 1915. Those gender and class identities are, furthermore, closely related to questions of national identity, or rather national duty, which direct and color the roles staged in the public debate of *Punch*.[10] As demonstrated by Shuchuan Yan, the magazine had used fashion metaphorically to "stir nationalist sentiments" since its beginnings in 1841. In her investigation of *Punch* caricatures in the context of gender, nation, and Victorian fashion discourse she considers "*Punch* as not simply a humorous weekly magazine, but as an important vehicle for the dissemination of media narrative into nationalist discourse" relying "on the conceptual axes of gender and power to evoke the myths of nation through the rhetoric of fashion."[11] The following visual discourse analysis of *Punch* will take a similar approach.

The examined cartoons cannot really be called caricatures as their humor is predominantly created by the texts added to images that most of the time could be read as realistic classical drawings without expressing the illustrators' specific personal stylistic signatures.[12] The seemingly objective and "matter-of-fact" depiction of contemporary British society in those drawings makes them even more effective as tools of documentation of an actual social situation performed by actors in naturalistic contemporary apparel. As Lou Taylor argues, cartoons can be considered "'average' images of supposedly typical period characters who were instantly recognizable to the contemporary reader."[13] Disregarding the subtexts, some of them could almost be read as fashion illustrations.

Yet, following Roland Barthes' emphasis on the semiotic functioning of textual captions as "anchorage" and "relay" in order to direct and complete the visual messages in an image, this analysis will also focus on the interaction of image and text and the latter's impact on the meanings of fashion.[14] The stereotypical visual impression of the fashioned personalities in the cartoons is further directed and confirmed by the textual captions. The verbal conversations between the presented characters further define, dramatize, and distinguish social roles. Image and text work together in constructing types that indicate and affect on-going social developments.

Looking at the semiotic meanings and performative effects of the cartoons, it is finally crucial to highlight the textual formulations defining and demarcating the "role characters" of the theatrical "scenes" performed by *Punch* for the British readers' audience. The cartoons stage so called "scenes" enacted by roles such as "Bright youths," "Youthful Lieutenants," "Mothers," "Ladies," "Wives," etc., all of them characters and stereotypes with neutral facial traits and physical shapes but dressed in conspicuous costumes and fashions that stand out through their stereotypical, recognizable features and speak of their function, or malfunction, in contemporary national society.

Creative transformation

A first look will highlight female fashion and fashion practices typically emerging from the restrictive conditions of wartime fashion consumption. While much focus has been given to the masculinization of female dress and identity during the First World War in adaption of male military uniform, this article examines a type of more feminine attires presented in the cartoons of *Punch* during 1915. Some of these images are explicitly about fashion—which plainly refutes Laver's argument on the "deadening" effect of the war on fashion. They both celebrate and ridicule the creativity of the fashionable woman facing war restrictions and "the standard dress."

One such series of images drawn by Lewis Baumer (1870–1963), one of the main cartoonists of *Punch* active during a period of 50 years, covers a whole page and is titled "The standard dress comes home' with the caption: "It has been suggested, in connection with the Thrift campaign, that all ladies should adopt one form of evening dress, as men do, and one only."[15] This cartoon is early evidence of a project to create a National Standard Dress—a multifunctional garment supposed to be worn at any occasion and time of the day to be established, but never realized, in Great Britain in 1918.[16] The first image shows an elegant lady dressed in a plain dark dress, gazing sadly into the mirror, with her somber maid in the background. In the next image, both the lady and maid are happier and start to dance. The lady's body, style, and mood are visibly brightened and transformed. Following her mistress's orders, the maid has removed, cut, draped and rearranged the conservative, long, rigid and concealing dress from the first image into a short skirted one, with a dynamically swinging silhouette that reveals bare arms and a wide décolleté. The stiff, depressed, and conservatively dressed woman from the first image has transformed into an exuberant, happy, and fashionably dressed figure reminiscent of a chorus girl.

In another example of creative female transformation, also drawn by Baumer, a conspicuously so called "fashionable mother," "stricken by remorse by the cry of her children" who wonder why they cannot have any new clothes, chooses to transform her own garments into three costumes for her children.[17] Her mink muff and scarf are turned into a hat and bodice for her youngest, her high lace collar becomes a hat for her second, and the different layers of her flounced skirt are turned into skirts for her two elder daughters. The mother herself remains fashionable, though in a simpler and less extravagant style. While we do not know who actually executes the transformative design and construction of these new garments, the idea and initiative seems to come from the mother, familiar with both practical and stylistic matters of fashion. All four characters are turned from sad and subdued personalities into fashion mannequins proudly showing off their new apparel.

While these two image series are not focused on change in fashionable trends, they show fashion as a field of female creative activity and personal transformation which cannot be suppressed even in times of restriction. Yet, while applauding women's creative capabilities, the jokes also criticize women.

As Lucy Noakes states: "[t]he female concern with individual appearance and dress was out of place in a militarised society, where uniformity of dress was seen to echo uniformity of purpose."[18]

Still, even in wartimes *Punch* features cartoons that focus on novelties in fashion as such, which again contradicts the generalizing idea of a stagnation in British fashion during the war established by some fashion historians. Showing "Miss Kensington Gore as she was—and is" one cartoon, again by the obviously fashion-aware Lewis Baumer, juxtaposes two contrasting images of the same woman: on the left, she is drawn with a fashionable hat that covers her eyes and a wide décolleté that reveals her neck and part of her chest. On the right, her dress highlights opposite features: the upper part of the face is revealed, while her mouth and chin are hidden under an exaggerated version of a large plissé collar.[19]

Both versions communicate a lack of visibility when it comes to showing the face of Miss Kensington Gore. She is hiding behind fashions that consequently make her appear distant, suspicious, and unreachable for the (male) spectator. This cartoon stems from a long history of fashion discourse wherein predominantly male writers and caricaturists comment on the quickly-changing female fashion in openly misogynist ways. It also implies that the viewer and reader of early twentieth century *Punch* were predominantly male and that these men applied what Laura Mulvey coined as a male, objectifying gaze.[20]

Accordingly, cartoons focusing on conspicuous fashionable trends worn by vain young women socialites who showed off in the streets or parks of London—the name Miss Kensington Gore seems to allude to an important promenade street in central London close to Hyde Park—can be seen as a historical convention within fashion caricatures that ridicule and shed light on quickly passing trends and the ephemerality of (female) fashions.[21] They show that fashion development and its doubtful influence on the female gender was seen as an on-going process, even during the war.

Heartless vanity and fashionable ignorance

While the images analyzed so far may be read as praising wartime fashion creativity, they also hint at the supposed superficiality of (female) fashion consumers who kept to their fashionable needs despite the war. A more outspoken critique against such vain feminine concerns comes from a visual theme that more openly opposes female and male positions during the first year of war. A fashion-plate-like image by C. A. Shepperson shows three elegantly dressed lady-friends with fashionable V-necked dresses and hats with conspicuous feather and veil decorations chatting away on a London bridge; the cartoon depicts a so-called "fond" upper class mother complaining: "Isn't the war dreadful? And so awkward when poor Sylvia is just coming out."[22] The lack of men during war reduced the audience for fashionable debutantes and the cartoon makes the point that women, particularly the upper class, cared about nothing more than matchmaking and social distinction.

In an even more aggressive and openly accusative mode, a cartoon title used several times during 1915, mainly by the cartoonist and artist Arthur Wallis Mills (1878–1940), states the "People we should like to see interned."[23] In a British society with an intensifying class struggle and rising Republican and Democratic values, the people that "we"—that is, on the one hand, literally the editors and artists of *Punch,* and on the other, the readership they represent and address, or the educated British middle class—would want to see interned were exclusively upper-class women in fashionable attires.

Thus, one cartoon shows a lady—wearing a narrow black dress, large white fur muff, high hat with long and thin feathers in the newest Parisian style—accompanied by a small dog with a large bow, telling her more modest hosts: "You really must dine with us on Sunday. I shall have a couple of the dinkiest little wounded subs to show you."[24] This cartoon speaks to a macabre social phenomenon: the showing off of male war victims in high-society circles and their objectification or even fetishization by the beautiful and frivolous female representatives of the upper class. In her study on the First World War British army uniform, Jane Tynan points to the centrality of the public image of the ordinary soldier and a general curiosity on soldiering and the soldier's body as "[m]yths and memories of the war [that] are formed around the figure of the uniformed soldier."[25] Such mythification may be part of the superficial and heartless sensationalism exemplified above.

Another cartoon by Mills with the title "More people we should like to see interned" shows two ladies in dark elegant dresses, fur muffs, hats with feather decorations, with painted lips and shingled hair (Figure 19.1). One woman is quite fat, the other extremely thin. They have come to see a hospital

Figure 19.1 *Arthur Wallis Mills, "More people we should like to see interned,"* Punch, *March 24, 1915. Punch Cartoon Library/TopFoto.*

nurse who comes across as a model of normality in contrast to the two ridiculous visitors; the nurse is average in body shape and, the reader is led to assume, rational in mind. In the background the reader glimpses three wounded soldiers. "Well, we'll bring the car tomorrow, and take some of your patients for a drive. And, by-the-by, nurse, you might look out some with bandages that show—the last party might not have been wounded at all, as far as anybody in the streets could see."[26]

In those jokes the reader observes drastic contrasts and polarizations, both in social and in visual terms: the antithetical staging of elegance and conspicuous beauty or superficial fashion against the wounded, damaged, uniformed, or poorly dressed young soldiers who are to be shown off like freaks makes the soldiers signifiers of truth, honest patriotic commitment, and genuine misery while the ladies and their fashions become repellent examples of selfishness, falsity, and stupidity. Upper-class ladies come forward as representatives of a useless class. They belong to a passive and shallow feminine sphere that should be interned in order to gain true understanding of the war.

A final example of this trope of irresponsible female shallowness comes from a cartoon, again by Mills, depicting a young lady, showing off her charming profile under a veiled hat and exposing her tiny pointed fashionable boot. She leans forward to ask an invalid soldier lying in bed, whose face is almost totally covered by bandages: "Now, chatter away, and tell me all about it."[27] Her light, transparent veil could be seen as a metaphor for the lightness and insubstantiality of her speech. It contrasts with the much stronger, stable, and useful fabrics providing the bandages and slings for the surrounding war victims. Bodies, fashions/clothes and fabrics as well as words become metaphors and interact in creating an opposition between different worlds and values. Fashionable ephemerality and insubstantiality is put in contrast to functional authenticity, reliability, and substantial material value.

Discourse on female fashion is thus repeatedly interwoven with messages on female stupidity, naiveté, or careless ignorance, not only in objectifying upper-class women but also in family scenarios where mothers play a pivotal role. A number of images stage conspicuously elegant mothers who respond to their innocent children's revealing questions. Even though the mothers are not the main focus of these cartoons, they dominate the "stage" through their fashionable appearances. Their presence serves to represent and create a superficial feminine sphere in which ignorance on the serious matters of war is emphasized. In six different cartoons, mothers with their children are either shown strolling in English parks and the countryside, or resting and relaxing in their sofas; that is, they are always represented in inactive poses. These poses highlight their bodies and silhouettes in the most advantageous way, much like in fashion illustrations printed in the female fashion press.

For example, one such cartoon by the illustrator F. H. Townsend shows a promenading mother with her pretty little girl; the girl is wearing a lace dress and is clumsily trying to imitate the marching soldiers in the background.[28] Again, the joke is activated through the physical contrast between the true male militia in the background and the superficial imitation enacted by the female population. Another cartoon by Shepperson shows a mother who looks and poses like a fashion model, in a tight, black dress combined with abundant white fur accessories, and a flat broad hat of the newest model, standing on a lawn with a mansion in the background.[29] Such a pose could be taken from a fashion drawing were it not for the smartly dressed little boy with his rifle. Sandy, "member of a martial family, returning from tea with some friends of a like age," complains about his friends not having any weapons in their home. "Why, you wouldn't know there was a war on!" Here, the superficiality of the aristocracy is shown off not only through the fashionable looks of its female members, but also through its sons, who treat the tools of war as toys, while seeing themselves as contributors in defending the nation.

In another example by the same illustrator, the focus is again on fashion: a smartly dressed "Vicar's Daughter" on a promenade in the countryside, leans elegantly on her walking stick and reveals a pointed shoe. She asks a little girl where she has acquired her nice khaki mittens.[30] The girl answers: "Daddy sent them home from the front at Christmas." Again fashion is shown in its deceitful character, misinterpreted by a naive female mind who thinks only about looks, while the authentic meaning and true value of the garment in focus lies in its use at the war front.

In a final example, drawn by Baumer, the cruelty of war in contrast to the ignorant and irresponsible comfort of bourgeois life-style is emphasized when an innocent young girl, sitting on the floor, tells her beautifully coiffed and dressed mother, who is sitting on the sofa and reading the newspaper, "Oh, Mother! How I wish I was an angel!"[31] The mother asks, "Darling! What makes you say that?" "Oh," the child replies, "because then, Mother, I could drop bombs on the Germans." Reality and lack of reality, true war efforts and naive imagination, are juxtaposed in a macabre joke which is staged in an elegant feminine sphere.

(Feminine) looks versus (masculine) function

As the *Punch* jokes analyzed have shown so far, feminine fashionability and a lifestyle which ignored the war were commonly opposed to or juxtaposed with masculine war efforts. This was done through the written dialogues and the narrative content of the cartoons, but also through the visual (and metaphorical) contrasting of female fashion with military attire—mostly drawn as uniforms. As Cheryl Buckley has written:

> [War] offered men the escape from the routines of social, economic and sexual responsibilities; it released them from the private sphere of the home—the feminine world—and propelled them into "the domain of the masculine, the army or navy, to the world of discipline, obedience, action." The spaces of war were clearly articulated as masculine, whereas women's spaces, particularly those of middle-class women, were predominantly represented as domestic.[32]

Catriona Pennell extends Buckley's assertion, writing, "The entire home front was morally subordinated to the fighting soldier."³³

Though clearly part of a male sphere of war, the role of the male uniform on the stage of British First World War society created by *Punch* is manifold. Jane Tynan states that: "[a]s a motif for transformation, the uniform appeared to signify symbolic distinctions between military and civilian, the link between home and battlefront."³⁴ Such a distinction is confirmed through the uniform's links to the simplicity ideals of anti-fashion. It stands for practical functionality, heroism, and patriotic commitment, not only when worn at the front, but also when displayed at the wounded victims at home and contrasted against feminine fashion.

However, in some contexts, uniforms in *Punch* connoted masculine vanity, pretentious exposition of rank, and superficial fashionability. One "scene" (as the caption calls it), drawn by Shepperson, shows a "youthful 2nd Lieutenant trying on his new uniform, which has just arrived."³⁵ His mother comments: "I don't like all that decoration on the sleeve, dear. Couldn't you have it taken off?" Pointing out the fashionable, decorative aspects of the uniform, the young man's mother reveals her own (female) misunderstanding of the uniform—thinking about the uniform in terms of fashion. The cartoon also evokes male vanity, masquerade, and "dressing up" or "costuming" that takes place when young, bourgeois, civil men attempt to turn themselves into military men.

Several cartoons by Shepperson reveal the interactions between mothers or other elderly female relatives and their progeny, as seen through the trope of the mother commenting on the uniform. The young men in these cartoons have similar facial traits—long, thin faces with inexpressive eyes in the form of tiny dots as well as small mouths and noses. They are drawn as rather feminine characters; lacking virility, they appear too weak to even defend themselves against the women who control them with their sharp eyes and critical comments. Another "Dear Old Lady" cartoon by Shepperson depicts an old aunt speaking to her small-eyed, feeble "nephew" about war economy: "Well, you do look nice, Reggie, dear; but don't you think you might wear out your old uniform first and keep this one for Sundays?"³⁶ The joke attacks both the stupidity of the aunt who fails to grasp the true function of military dress (a garment that protects men in battle and serves to distinguish their rank), and also the listless, young, weak upper-class or bourgeois men, who seem transported into military roles which they cannot live up to, in spite of their new apparel.

Military or war-related garments, accessories, and tools such as uniforms, arms and protective gear are recurrently shown as superficial objects opposed to their real function in cartoons that are used to ridicule women as well as men. Thus, one such cartoon by Baumer illustrates a fashionably dressed mother with a pretty profile, her shining shoes slightly uplifted, her scared daughter at her side. A merchant shows her two versions of gas masks, explaining: "Well, Madam, we sell a good many of both. The solid rubber is perhaps the more serviceable article, but the other is generally considered the more becoming" (Figure 19.2).³⁷ Very clearly, utility and beauty are not compatible when it comes

"WELL, MADAM, WE SELL A GOOD MANY OF BOTH. THE SOLID RUBBER IS PERHAPS THE MORE SERVICEABLE ARTICLE, BUT THE OTHER IS GENERALLY CONSIDERED THE MORE BECOMING."

Figure 19.2 Lewis Baumer, "Well, Madam, we sell a good many of both . . .," Punch, August 18, 1915. Punch Cartoon Library/TopFoto.

down to the difficult choice of which gas mask to acquire in order to provide protection for those who until then were mostly concerned about superficial matters of outer appearance.

While joking, *Punch* addresses the phenomenon of marketing of gas masks to civilians, not least worrying mothers. As Susan R. Grayzel writes, such jokes "expressed some of the outrage on the use of chemical weapons . . . The choice was seemingly about the type of protection, but the prospect of women and children needing to safeguard themselves from a weapon of such horror was no joke."[38] Grayzel also highlights the role of mothers and women's "relational response to the war" as that of worrying less about themselves than about their loved ones—a pattern that seems to be confirmed by several mother–child or mother–son jokes in *Punch*.[39]

Another case of looks prioritized over function comes from a cartoon of a conspicuously slim, elegant, "Bright Youth," drawn by Shepperson, with a lorgnette, oiled hair, and a walking stick, who chats with a similarly fashionable young lady, dressed much like Shepperson's previously mentioned mother with her narrow black dress and the white furs.[40] Gazing at a uniformed officer who has just passed by, the "Bright Youth" reflects: "Yes, I'm thinkin' of gettin' a commission in something. What about joinin' that crowd with the jolly little red tabs on their collars? They look so doocid smart." The scene stages the trope of the unemployed dandy with his superficial motivations for joining the army; this trope is not unconnected to the weak, uniformed sons and nephews analyzed above.

Another recurring female stereotype used in the discussion of male uniforms is, of course, the role of the "wife." In a cartoon by Baumer, the "Wife of an Officer (just starting for the Dardanelles)," takes her tea dressed in a elegant flounced dress; revealing her smart shoes with crossed ribbons covering the calves, she boasts: "My husband's got an inflated waistcoat."[41] To which a "Sympathetic Old Lady" answers: "Dear, dear, dear! I do hope it won't involve an operation." Once again, these cartoons reveal that what women are concerned about shows ignorance about what really matters. The title of this cartoon confirms the joke on "Our volunteer reserve."[42]

Further examples make clear that the hitherto sketched discourse on what one might call both men's and women's "abuse" of the uniform as a fashion garment was connected to an urgent and much debated question in the British society of 1915. Namely, the different aspects of recruitment and volunteering, the so-called and largely women-based home defense, and the different ways in which the male and female population tried or pretended to try to take responsibility for their home country. According to Gregory, in 1914 and 1915, Britain raised the second largest volunteer army in history thanks in part to propagandistic recruitment meetings with spectators cheering for the brave recruits. However, a large number of soldiers were still acting on compulsion and bribery and the majority of the male population chose not to "volunteer."[43]

Showing off military identity for spectators was a status-enhancing action. Thus dressing up in uniforms, in public or at private occasions, could serve a man's vicarious performance and representation of military responsibility in spite of not participating on the actual battlefront. As Gregory writes, "Once in uniform, men became 'patriots' whatever the initial impulse for volunteering had been..."[44] Further, Pennell writes:

> The experience of volunteering involved all members of society regardless of gender, and also of class and age. Whilst some men enlisted out of a desire to protect their wives, mothers, sisters and daughters, women were actively involved in encouraging men to enlist—or publicly humiliating them if they did not.[45]

Such anxieties are certainly reflected in several of the jokes mentioned above, as well as in the following example: In another cartoon by Baumer, a sweet-looking, fashionable, young "Admiring Wife who has been to watch her husband's corps drill in uniform for the first time" speaks to her much older husband. (The reader understands this as a typical marriage of convenience). "I thought you all looked splendid my dear," the wife declares, "There's just one thing I should like to suggest; and that is that you all wear socks to match your puttees." The wife's superficiality colors the figure of the husband, who, drawn as old and engaged in the "feminine" and passive act of tea-drinking, appears impotent and weak. His masquerading in military costume seems to be mainly about visual effects rather than true strength and efficiency.

Good (visual) impressions are also what counted for upper-class ladies drawn wearing luxurious coats while they purchased military accessories for their husbands or sons. In a cartoon by Frederick Pegram, a "Lady" in a dark, lavish fur coat asks a vendor for studs for her son. When the "shopman" asks if they are for the front, she replies, "No—home defence."[46] Similarly, in a joke by Baumer entitled "Doing her bit," another Lady ("about to purchase military headgear") tells her sheepish-looking husband, sitting on a sofa in the background: "I know it's more expensive than the others, dear, but—well, you see, you're too old to enlist, and I really feel we ought to do *something*!"[47] This scene also exemplifies the so-called relief work that non-combatants volunteered for "in an effort to make their response to the war equal to the soldiers' sacrifice."[48] As Pennell wrote, "Those who could not fight, particularly women, could contribute by supporting the troops and comforting their families in a time of need. This kind of work also shielded non-combatants from accusations of 'not doing their bit.'"[49]

Yet, as the joke in *Punch* shows, some of these women and men were obviously suspected of just showing off. Besides the motif of unmanliness that is indicated by women taking charge of men's military "fashion," the *Punch* reader once again finds warfare reduced to superficial garments whose inauthentic use made them far from functional. These cartoons offer another version of *Punch*'s commentary on the hypocrisy and cowardice of the upper class hiding away in home defense, instead of making a real effort at the front.

Making a real man

Crucial aspects of masculinity and its staging or negotiation through uniforms are revealed in *Punch* jokes about the symbolic transformation uniforms may affect in a male character. Thus, in a cartoon by Frank Reynolds, a "Near-sighted Old Lady" who is called "a keen Recruiter," mistakes a life-size cartoon figure of Charlie Chaplin in his typical tramp attire as a fit young man: "Now look at that young fellow. A couple of months in the army would make a new man of him!"[50] The belief in the transformative effect of war as a state that brings out ideal masculinity and manhood is thus clearly related to dress and visual appearance. Reflecting on the impact of uniforms and physical discipline, Jane Tynan discusses how "the civilian body can easily be exchanged for a military body" and "preparations for war centered on bodily transformations." In wartime, Tynan writes, "popular culture had a role in recruitment in inviting civilians to alter their habits and "'become' soldiers through the inviting prospect of discipline and adornment."[51]

Returning to the question of volunteering, several *Punch* cartoons reveal how men don the uniform as a way to quickly engage in the war "effort" without much effort at all. Again drawn by Baumer, who seems to especially engage in the theme of the Volunteer reserve, a small, listless boy called "Bobbie" stands in the living room with his mother and sister, who all look unenthusiastically at the father "exhibit[ing] his new Volunteer uniform." "Well! Mother—I say! This brings war home to us, doesn't it?," Bobbie declares.[52] The use of the word "exhibiting" reveals the performative aspect of the uniform as a theatrical costume for an insincere and unfit male character who is drawn with puffy cheeks, glasses, and a slightly protruding belly. The father, the cartoon implies, can only pretend to be a real war hero. Only the children are deceived by this masquerade.

Besides elder men with physical traits that make them inadequate for military service at the front, another recurring theme in the *Punch* cartoons are the aforementioned "thin" young men demonstrating different versions of irresponsibility, often signaled by their clothing. A cartoon by Mills consists of three images showing a uniform transforming only the outside appearance, but not the inner morals of its wearer.[53] The series is called "Reversion to type." Its first picture shows a young man "before the war," in smart suit and hat, striking a fashionable pose, smoking and nonchalantly swinging his walking stick in the air. The second picture shows the same young man in the "First weeks of war," standing upright in a proper uniform, holding an officer's straight stick, with a listless face (much like the boys analyzed above); his body expresses the stiffness and inactivity of someone who is unsure of what to do. The third picture in the series shows the young fellow having come "back to the old form." He is now dressed in a combination of the military jacket with its belts and badges and the wide cap and trousers from "before the war." He is drawn smoking, swinging with his officer's stick, and strolling in a happy manner and in an irresponsibly careless mood.

While the first image signifies a dandy's nonchalance, the second shows the empty artificiality of a dressed up figure that does not really fit into his clothes. The third reveals the man's ingrained immorality, sloppiness, and lack of moral character, symbolized by his spineless mixing of different styles and types of masculinity.

Another example of the symbolic transformative power of the uniform, again by Baumer, expresses clear class critique.[54] A first image in the cartoon shows how "Sir Benjamin Goldmore and his junior clerk used to pass one another if they met in the city" (Figure 19.3). The second shows "how they pass one another now," that is, in 1915, when the junior clerk has not only enlisted, but then surpasses his boss in military rank. While the first picture contrasts the formal dark suit and shining top hat of an upright wealthy businessman against a young, subdued clerk who bows while taking off his hat for Sir Goldmore, with his thick cigar and haughty profile, the roles are exchanged in the second picture. Now the earlier rich and—as his name implies—greedy Sir Goldmore is dressed in simple soldier's garments and putties, and it is he who blushingly salutes his young clerk, who is haughtily passing by, shoulders back, neck out, and elegantly dressed in an officer's uniform with a pretty young lady at his side. The two men's new positions lead to new outfits, bodies, and body language. The war and its visual (dress) codes have removed traditional roles and social positions.

Figure 19.3 Lewis Baumer, "How Sir Benjamin Goldmore and his junior clerk...," Punch, April 28, 1915. Punch Cartoon Library/TopFoto.

The spectacle of war

The study so far has shown that in 1915, *Punch*'s cartoonists seem less concerned with the real-political happenings in Europe than with the gender and class questions raised in England that were being renegotiated in the light of the beginning war and its demands. The notion of "spectatorship" as an initial position of British society in connection with a common myth about British war enthusiasm in 1914 and 1915 is clearly exemplified in two series of jokes that mainly appeared during the summer months, both relating to entertainment during weekend trips and vacation.[55] These also react to what Pennell has identified as "changing landscapes," or visual changes, affected by the war, especially in the area of London and the surrounding countryside.[56]

The first set of cartoons partly imitates advertisements announcing the sensational zeppelins, which could be observed at certain locations. It exposes fashionable couples as naïve spectators viewing the zeppelins as entertainment ignoring their function as weapons of warfare. One such false advertisement (author unnamed), called "A hint to the railway companies," shows a romantic scene of an elegant couple gazing dreamily at a night sky where two zeppelins fly, one of them dropping a bomb into the glittering surface of the sea.[57] The caption says "Be in the movement and go to Northend—on Sea. Frequent zeppelin displays."

Just as fashionable and mundane, and just as naïvely detached from war's actual concerns, are an upper-class couple in another cartoon by Shepperson, evidently dressed for an evening at the theatre or the opera. The husband, wearing a lorgnette, and the lady, displaying her elegant high-heeled shoes on the night streets of London, ask a police officer, "Oh, have you seen the zeppelin? Which way did it go?" The policeman answers, "Up the street opposite, madam, and first turning on the left."[58]

A third example, drawn by Townsend, shows "A Zeppelin Picnic" consisting of a group of young people in relaxed summer outfits, resting on the grass and engaging in typical picnic socializing. All of them, though, even their dog, wear gas masks under their fashionable sun hats.[59] In all three cases, upper-class fashionability is made to symbolize an unawareness of the proximity of the war, a trivialization of the war's gravity, and mundane sensationalism of warfare. These jokes and fake ads hark back to the earlier analyzed examples criticizing the curiosity with and fetishization of the soldiers wounded in war.

While the cartoons examined above mainly deal with the upper class, the leisurely pleasures of the middle class were also criticized in jokes that demonstrated the naive spectacularization of war in Great Britain. Fashion and costume had a distinctive role to play in scenarios where military uniforms were opposed to the relaxed holiday garb and bathing outfits worn by an "audience" ignorant of the war's severity.

The entire issue of *Punch* published on July 7, 1915, was devoted to the pleasures of summer holiday.[60] Here the reader finds fake touristic advertisements captioned: "Spend your holidays on the famous Cleekton Links. New Bunkers. New Hazards."[61] The illustration depicts smartly dressed golfers of both sexes watching and trying to enter a military zone. On the same page, an elegant lady strolls between two uniformed men, with the accompanying caption: "Come to Breezy Brightsmouth. More Soldiers to the Square Yard than in Any Other Spot in England." Here, the soldiers and warzones become an objectified spectacle, expressed through the absurdity of civilians clad in casual summer and sporting fashions that have invaded the spaces of the unformed male militia.

Another version of the war as a tourist attraction is revealed in the images of bathers playing "war" in a cartoon titled "War-time holidays."[62] It shows different scenes of holiday activities such as, "A hint to beach photographers," depicting a photographer offering two passing men in summer suits the opportunity to pose behind a wooden backdrop with cutout faces of soldiers engaging in gunfire. Listless, ignorant, and irresponsible young men enjoying their holiday are invited to act and dress up as soldiers, as are the fashionable female consumers who, in the next image, are given the fashion tip, "Bathing costumes should have the military touch." The illustration shows a model wearing a swimming suit inspired by the Scottish militia's uniform.

As Lucy Noakes discussed in her article on British women and the First World War military uniform, the pejorative notion of females "playing at being soldiers" was widespread as "[w]omen in uniform walked a fine line between expressing patriotism and threatening both the continuity of gender roles and the status of combatant men."[63] Such gender anxiety was confirmed in these *Punch* cartoons as well as in several other cartoons on volunteering women in uniform printed in other issues.[64] Military identity is thus presented as a superficial game and a source of entertainment for people who ignored the ongoing war and its atrocities. In these cartoons, life continued as usual for an unknowing and selfish segment of the population who preferred to watch the war from a safe distance.

Conclusion

The First World War restructured gender identities. Yet, in the British wartime society depicted and criticized by *Punch*, questions of gender were tightly interwoven with questions of class, professional roles and national identity. As Pennell writes when explaining how the First World War was constructed as a "National Cause" in public British opinion:

> Explaining why Britain was at war involved constructing heroes, victims, scapegoats, and villains, however simplistic or idealistic. It was not enough to vilify the enemy: what Britain stood for in wartime had to be defined. Often these ideas were latent in peacetime but came to the fore once the nation was in crisis. Values, beliefs, and codes of behaviour that were inherent and implicit in Edwardian society, became explicit.[65]

In conclusion then, we may ask ourselves which costumed characters *Punch* demarcates as the actual national heroes in British First World War society? Who are the ideal Brits that are indirectly performed in the jokes about male and female stereotypes that do *not* properly engage in national service? The figures that are depicted to readers as "good," "useful," and "normal" in *Punch* are mainly nurses and wounded soldiers. That is, ordinary lower or middle-class men and women, clad in plain, functional dress, with inconspicuous bodies, and who act with rational human behavior; good citizens beyond gender-specific expressiveness, class-distinction, and interest in self-fashioning of any kind.

These brave men and women who serve their nation are staged in contrast to the ones "we would like to see interned"—the ones whose beauty, fashion and self-display come forward as deceptive and morally weakening. In spite of its aesthetic qualities, fashionable appearance was most of the time suspected of leading to false pretensions, empty role-play, passive nonchalance, and alienation from reality in a time when true commitment and strong actions were demanded.

As a final citation from *Punch,* the following poem from 1916 seems to summarize the magazine's, and probably the dominating British public opinion:

> You who when the world is mourning
> Only think of self-adorning
> Sadden Punch, your friend.[66]

The cartoonists of *Punch* staged fashionable and superficial versions of female and male citizens in order to satirically demarcate their opposite—that is, ideal and functional women and men who worked and fought for their nation. Maybe the moralizing discourse against fashion exemplified by *Punch* has contributed to dress history mainly focusing on sartorial styles that emphasize efficiency, practicality, normality, and usefulness and their practical function during the First World War. Buying into the largely pejorative tone on fashion and fashion practices that the jokes have communicated, historians may have unconsciously erased, hidden, or silenced other stories on fashion and fashionability as less politically correct in the (dress) history of the Great War in Britain. Rather than merely looking at and laughing at Punch's cartoons, a close analysis of the discourse, rhetoric, and representation of fashion within the magazine reveals the function of fashion as a performative instrument of power. "Undressing" the role-play enacted in these cartoons, means "undressing" different gender-related or sociopolitical agendas.

Notes

1 James Laver, *Costume and Fashion: A Concise History*, reprint (London: Thames & Hudson, 2002 [1969]), 229f.

2 Ibid., 230.

3 Other examples are Christopher Breward, *Fashioning London: Clothing and the Modern Metropolis* (Oxford: Berg, 2004); Lou Taylor and Elizabeth Wilson, *Through the Looking Glass: A History of Dress from 1860 to the Present Day* (London: BBC Books, 1989) or Elizabeth Wilson, *Adorned in Dreams: Fashion and Modernity* (London: I.B. Tauris, 2007).

4 Cheryl Buckley, "'De-Humanised females and Amazonians': British wartime fashion and its representation in *Home Chat*, 1914–1918," *Gender & History* 14, 3 (November 2002): 516.

5 Ibid., 524.

6 Adrian Gregory, "From spectatorship to participation: From volunteering to compulsion 1914–1916," in *The Last Great War: British Society and the First World War* (Cambridge: Cambridge University Press, 2008), 70–111.

7 Janice Carlisle, *Picturing Reform in Victorian Britain* (Cambridge: Cambridge University Press, 2012), 13.

8 As the introduction to its first edition in 1841 states, *Punch* "has the honour of making his appearance every SATURDAY, and continues, from week to week, to offer to the world all the fun to be found in his own and the following heads: politics, fashions, police, reviews, fine arts, music and the drama, sporting, and the facetiae (1841: iii–iv)." Further, *Punch* is well-known for redefining the concept of *cartoon* in its July 1 issue of 1843, where it announced "the publication of several exquisite designs, to be called PUNCH-CARTOONS!"—transforming the meaning of cartoon from a design for an art object to its now familiar meaning of "a humorous image in black and white," ibid., 89.

9 Erving Goffman, *The Presentation of Self in Everyday Life* (Edinburgh: University of Edinburgh, 1956), 14f.

10 See also my earlier study on the relationships between nation and gender in the visual fashion discourse of cultural and satirical magazines in Germany and Sweden during the 1910s and 1920s. Andrea Kollnitz, "The devil of fashion: Women, fashion and the nation in early-twentieth-century German and Swedish cultural magazines," in *Fashion in Popular Culture: Literature, Media and Contemporary Studies*, Joseph H. Hancock II, Toni Johnson-Woods, and Vicki Karaminas, eds. (Bristol and Chicago, IL: Intellect 2013), 225–41.

11 Shu-chuan Yan, "'Politics and petticoats': Fashioning the nation in *Punch* Magazine 1840s–1880s," *Fashion Theory* 15, 3 (2011): 346f.

12 See Carlisle on the almost realistic style developed in *Punch's* engraved illustrations. Carlisle, *Picturing Reform*, 14.

13 Lou Taylor, *The Study of Dress History* (Manchester and New York: Manchester University Press, 2002), 140.

14 Roland Barthes, "Rhetoric of the image," in *Image, Music, Text*, Stephen Heath, ed. and trans. (New York: Hill and Wang 1977), 32–51.

15 *Punch*, August 18, 1915.

16 As the *Encyclopedia of Fashion* writes: "In 1918 the British government introduced a new garment called a 'National Standard Dress,' a simple loose, mid-calf dress made with no hooks and eyes. Because cotton and wool were needed for the war effort, the National Standard Dress was made from silk and was intended to be an all-purpose dress that could be worn for any occasion, any time of day or evening," "Civilian Dress in Wartime," *Encyclopedia of Fashion*, at: http://www.fashionencyclopedia.com/ (accessed July 29, 2020); see also Laver, *Costume and Fashion*, 230.

17 *Punch*, December 1, 1915.

18 Lucy Noakes, "'Playing at being Soldiers?': British women and military uniform in the First World War," in *British Popular Culture and the First World War*, Jessica Meyer, ed. (Leiden and Boston, MA: Brill, 2008), 129.

19 *Punch*, November 17, 1915.

20 On fashion discourse and dress and morality, see Aileen Ribeiro, *Dress and Morality* (London: Berg, 2003). On the male gaze, see Laura Mulvey, "Visual pleasure and narrative cinema," in *Film Theory and Criticism: Introductory Readings*, Leo Braudy and Marshall Cohen, eds. (New York: Oxford Univerisyt Press, 1999), 833–44.

21 For further case studies on early-twentieth-century European fashion discourse on fashion, gender, and the nation, see also Kollnitz, "The devil of fashion."

22 *Punch*, July 28, 1915.

23 The jokes come also with titles in other variations, such as "people we 'ought to,'" "more people we . . ." See also the following examples.

24 *Punch*, January 20, 1915.

25 Jane Tynan, "'Tayloring in the trenches': The making of First World War British Army uniform," in *British Popular Culture*, Meyer, ed., 71.

26 *Punch*, March 24, 1915.

27 Ibid., April 28, 1915.

28 Ibid., June 3, 1915.

29 Ibid., March 17, 1915.

30 Ibid., May 5, 1915.

31 Ibid., February 3, 1915.

32 Buckley, "'De-Humanised females and Amazonians,'" 518. Buckley is referring to Susan Kingsley Kent, *Making Peace: The Reconstruction of Gender in Interwar Britain* (Princeton, NJ: Princeton University Press, 1993), 12f.

33 Catriona Pennell, *A Kingdom United: Popular Responses to the Outbreak of the First World War in Britain and Ireland* (Oxford: Oxford University Press, 2012), 77.

34 Tynan, "'Tayloring in the trenches,'" 71.

35 *Punch*, August 11, 1915.

36 Ibid., October 20, 1915.

37 Ibid., August 18, 1915.

38 Susan R. Grayzel, "The Baby in the Gas Mask: Motherhood, Wartime Technology, and the Gendered Division Between the Fronts During and After the First World War" in *Gender and the First World War*, eds. Christa Hämmerle, Oswald Überegger, and Birgitta Bader Zaar (London: Palgrave Macmillan, 2014), 132.

39 Ibid., 127f.

40 *Punch*, February 17, 1915.

41 Ibid., October 20, 1915.

42 Ibid., March 17, 1915.

43 Gregory, *The Last Great War*, 73ff.

44 Ibid., 81.

45 Pennell, *A Kingdom United*, 158.

46 *Punch*, January 27, 1915.

47 Ibid.

48 Pennell, *A Kingdom United*, 76.

49 Ibid.

50 *Punch*, July 28, 1915.

51 Tynan, "'Tayloring the trenches,'" 90.

52 *Punch*, February 17, 1915.

53 Ibid., July 28, 1915.

54 Ibid., April 28, 1915.

55 On the myth of British war enthusiasm, see Pennell, *A Kingdom United*, 3–6.

56 Ibid., 205–9.

57 *Punch*, September 15, 1915.

58 Ibid., November 10, 1915.

59 Ibid., July 7, 1915.

60 "Mr. Punch's Holiday Pages," ibid.

61 Ibid., 18.

62 Ibid., 27.

63 Noakes, "'Playing at being soldiers?,'" 143.

64 See, for example, *Punch*, December 15, 1915, where a "Gallant Highland officer" is "taking a Lady Volunteer's salute," by spreading out his kilt like a skirt and smiling while the "Lady" in uniform takes a "masculine" pose with severe facial expression.

65 Pennell, *A Kingdom United*, 57.

66 *Punch*, March 22, 1916, quoted in Noakes, "'Playing at being Ssoldiers,'" 129.

References

Barthes, Roland. "Rhetoric of the image." In *Image, Music, Text*, Stephen Heath, ed. and treans., 32–51. New York: Hill and Wang 1977.
Breward, Christopher. *Fashioning London: Clothing and the Modern Metropolis*. Oxford and New York: Berg, 2004.
Buckley, Cheryl. "'De-Humanised females and Amazonians': British wartime fashion and its representation in *Home Chat*, 1914–1918. *Gender & History* 14, 3 (November 2002): 516–36.
Carlisle, Janice. *Picturing Reform in Victorian Britain*. Cambridge: Cambridge University Press, 2012.
Goffman, Erving. *The Presentation of Self in Everyday Life*. Edinburgh: University of Edinburgh, 1956.
Grayzel, Susan R. "The baby in the gas mask: Motherhood, wartime technology, and the gendered division between the fronts during and after the First World War." In *Gender and the First World War*, Christa Hämmerle, Oswald Überegger, and Birgitta Bader Zaar, eds., 127–43. London: Palgrave Macmillan, 2014.
Gregory, Adrian. *The Last Great War: British Society and the First World War*. Cambridge: Cambridge University Press, 2008. See especially chapter 3, "From spectatorship to participation: From volunteering to compulsion 1914–1916," 70–111.
Kingsley Kent, Susan. *Making Peace: The Reconstruction of Gender in Interwar Britain*. Princeton, NJ: Princeton University Press, 1993.
Kollnitz, Andrea, "The devil of fashion: Women, fashion and the nation in early-twentieth-century German and Swedish cultural magazines," in *Fashion in Popular Culture: Literature, Media and Contemporary Studies*, Joseph H. Hancock II, Toni Johnson-Woods, and Vicki Karaminas, eds., 225–41. Bristol and Chicago, IL: Intellect 2013.
Laver, James. *Costume and Fashion: A Concise History*, reprint. London: Thames & Hudson, 2002 [1969].
Mulvey, Laura, "Visual pleasure and narrative cinema." In *Film Theory and Criticism: Introductory Readings*, Leo Braudy and Marshall Cohen, eds., 833–44. New York: Oxford University Press, 1999.
Noakes, Lucy. "'Playing at being soldiers?': British women and military uniform in the First World War." In *British Popular Culture and the First World War*, Jessica Meyer, ed., 123–45. Leiden and Boston, MA: Brill, 2008.
Pennell, Catriona. *A Kingdom United: Popular Responses to the Outbreak of the First World War in Britain and Ireland*. Oxford: Oxford University Press, 2012.
Punch Magazine, 1915.

Referenced issues:
  Punch, January 20, 1915.
  Punch, January 27, 1915.
  Punch, February 3, 1915.

Punch, February 17, 1915.
Punch, March 17, 1915.
Punch, March 24, 1915.
Punch, April 28, 1915.
Punch, May 5, 1915.
Punch, June 3, 1915.
Punch, July 7, 1915.
Punch, July 28, 1915.
Punch, August 11, 1915.
Punch, August 18, 1915.
Punch, September 15, 1915.
Punch, October 20, 1915.
Punch, November 10, 1915.
Punch, November 17, 1915.
Punch, December 1, 1915.
Punch, December 15, 1915.

Ribeiro, Aileen. *Dress and Morality*. London: Berg, 2003.
Taylor, Lou. *The Study of Dress History*. Manchester and New York: Manchester University Press, 2002.
Taylor, Lou and Elizabeth Wilson. *Through the Looking Glass: A History of Dress from 1860 to the Present Day*. London: BBC Books, 1989.
Tynan, Jane. "'Tayloring in the trenches': The making of First World War British Army uniform." In *British Popular Culture and the First World War*, Jessica Meyer, ed. Leiden and Boston, MA: Brill 2008.
Wilson, Elizabeth. *Adorned in Dreams: Fashion and Modernity*. London: I.B. Tauris, 2007.
Yan, Shu-chuan, "'Politics and petticoats': Fashioning the nation in *Punch* Magazine 1840s–1880s," *Fashion Theory* 15, 3 (2011): 345–71.

Notes on Contributors

Maude Bass-Krueger is Professor in the Art History, Music, and Theatre Studies Department at Ghent University, Belgium. She received her MA in History from Sciences-Po in Paris, with her thesis on French fashion during the First World War, and her PhD in Material Culture, Decorative Arts, and Design History from the Bard Graduate Center in New York. Her doctoral dissertation was on the discipline of dress history in France in the nineteenth century. She co-curated the exhibition *Mode & Guerre, 14/18*, which opened at the Bibliothèque Forney in Paris in 2017 in Paris in 2017. The American version of the exhibition, titled *French Fashion, Women, and the First World War*, opened at the Bard Graduate Center in New York in 2019 and was accompagnied by a book of the same name. Her research interests cover French fashion historiography, architectural drawings in nineteenth-century France, and the relationship between fashion and architecture.

Nele Bernheim is a joint PhD candidate in History at the University of Antwerp and Art History at Ghent University, Belgium. She holds an MA in Fashion and Textile Studies from the Fashion Institute of Technology, New York and a MA in Art Sciences from the Vrije Universiteit Brussel. Her research interests focus on the history of Belgian fashion in the twentieth century, which is at the heart of the study of her doctoral dissertation, "Norine Couture, Brussels: The embodiment of the Belgian avant-garde, 1915–1952." She lectures on Fashion History at the Royal Academy of Fine Arts in Ghent and the École nationale supérieure des arts visuels de La Cambre in Brussels. In 2015, she co-curated the exhibition *The Belgians: An Unexpected Fashion Story* at the Centre for Fine Arts (BOZAR) in Brussels and is the co-editor of the book of the same name.

Emily Brayshaw, PhD, is Honorary Research Fellow at the University of Technology Sydney, Australia. She also works as a costume designer. Her areas of research include Broadway Revue and Parisian Music Hall costuming from 1890 to 1930; the intersection of fashion, dress, and costume within the performance costumes of classical musicians; the aesthetics of the Bauhaus; knitting in performance costume; and fashion, dress, costume, and trauma during the First World War.

Jérémie Brucker is Associate Professor at the Université d'Angers and holds a PhD in Contemporary History. He presented his thesis, "Avoir l'étoffe. Une histoire du vêtement professionnel en France des années 1880 à nos jours" (Dressing the part: Professional clothing in France from 1880 to the Present Day), at the Université d'Angers in 2019. This thesis is in the process of being published.

Manuel Charpy is Research Fellow at the Centre national de la recherche scientifique (CNRS) in Paris, France, and Director of the InVisu laboratory (CNRS/Institut national d'histoire de l'art INHA). His areas of interest include material and visual cultural history in Europe, the United States, and Western and Central Africa. He is now leading a study on the history of confection in France and on the use of European clothing in Congo, from the nineteenth century to today. He co-founded the journal *Modes pratiques, revue d'histoire du vêtement et de la mode* with Patrice Verdière.

Marguerite Coppens, PhD, is Honorary Chief-Curator of the Musées royaux d'Art et d'Histoire, Brussels. She is the author of numerous publications and has curated exhibitions dedicated to the history of lace and costume. Marguerite is the Honorary President of the International Council of Museums' (ICOM) Belgian National Committee, and her research interest also covers museology. She is the Honorary President and administrator of the Association française d'histoire du textile (AFET) in Paris.

Amy de la Haye is Professor of Dress History and Curatorship and joint director of the Research Centre for Fashion Curation at London College of Fashion, University of the Arts London. Her research interests focus on subcultures; the history of London's elite fashion industry; fashion designer archives; worn and perished dress; and fashion and biography. In 1991–9, she was Curator of 20th Century Dress at the Victoria and Albert Museum. Amy has a long-term interest in the Women's Land Armies during both world wars. She curated the exhibition *The Land Girls: Cinderellas of the Soil* and wrote the accompanying catalogue of the same title (2009). She was an editor of *The Handbook of Fashion Studies* (2013), co-author, with Valerie D. Mendes, of *Lucile* and *Worth: Portrait of an Archive* (2009) and, with Judith Clark, of *Exhibiting Fashion: Before & After 1971* (2014). She is co-curator, with Colleen Hill, of *Ravishing: The Rose in Fashion* (Museum at the Fashion Institute of Technology, New York) and author of the accompanying publication (2020).

Burcu Dogramaci, is Professor of Art History at the Ludwig-Maximilians-Universität of Munich. Her research focuses on exile, migration and flight; fashion history and theory; architecture and urbanity. Her main books include, as co-editor *Arrival Cities. Migrating Artists and New Metropolitan Topographies in the 20th Century* (2020) and *Handbook of Art and Global Migration. Theories, Practices, and Challenges* (2019). She is editor of *Textile Moderne / Textile Modernism* (2019) and author of

Heimat. Eine künstlerische Spurensuche (2016) and Wechselbeziehungen. *Mode, Malerei und Fotografie im 19. Jahrhundert* (2011). She has been awarded an ERC Consolidator Grant for the project METROMOD (2017–2022), which focuses on six exile metropolises for modern artists.

Waleria Dorogova is an art, design and fashion historian. She completed her PhD in 2022 at the University of Bonn with a dissertation on the first history of the Franco-American fashion house Boué Sœurs. She is currently working on two exhibitions of Sonia Delaunay, one for Kunstmuseen Krefeld and the other for the Bard Graduate Center in New York..

Hayley Edwards-Dujardin is an art and fashion historian and an independent curator. She received her MA in Art History from L'École du Louvre, Paris, and her MA in Fashion Curation, from the London College of Fashion. She teaches Fashion History, Visual Culture and Fashion Theory in Paris. Her research interests and publications cover the relationship between art and fashion; modern and contemporary fashion theory; fashion and the self; decorative arts; history of contemporary fashion; modern architecture; and fashion photography. Her main books include *Rechercher la mode* (2020), the art history book collection, *Ça c'est de l'art* and *Petite Anthologie de la Mode* (2022).

Birgit Haase is Professor of Art History, Fashion History, and Fashion Theory at Hamburg University of Applied Sciences in the Department of Design. She holds a PhD in Art History from the University of Hamburg, with a thesis on the relation between fashion and art in the French Second Empire. She also received a degree in Clothing Technology. Her research interests cover the history of European clothing; the correlation of art and fashion, especially of the nineteenth and twentieth centuries; fashion theory; and object-based clothing research. She is currently working on a monograph about the fashion designer Christoph Drecoll.

Sara Hume is Associate Professor and Curator of the Kent State University Museum, Ohio. She holds an MA in Museum Studies: Costume and Textiles from the Fashion Institute of Technology and a PhD in History from the University of Chicago. Her research in the history of dress has focused on the relationship between evolving fashionable aesthetics and the underlying forces of economic and political change. She is currently completing a book which examines the development and preservation of regional dress practices in Alsace in the face of pressure both from political conflict and mainstream fashion.

Marta Kargól received her MA in History and History of Art at Jagielloński University in Krakow. In 2013, she received her PhD in Cultural Anthropology for the dissertation "Tradition in fashion: Dutch regional dress within contemporary culture," which was published in 2015. Her research interests include the history of dress and fashion in the nineteenth and twentieth centuries; heritage of regional dress; economic and gender aspects of homemade clothing; and contemporary textile art. She is the co-author of two exhibition catalogues, as well as numerous academic and popular articles. She has worked as Assistant Curator for the exhibition *Women of Rotterdam* (Museum of Rotterdam, 2017). Since 2016, she has been writing about textile art for the Dutch magazine, *Textiel Plus*.

Andrea Kollnitz is Associate Professor of Art History at the Department of Culture and Aesthetics at Stockholm University. After completing her PhD on "The national identity of art: On German and Austrian modernism in Swedish art criticism, 1908–1934" (2008), she worked as a senior lecturer at the Centre for Fashion Studies at Stockholm University until 2018. Her research is focused on art and nationalism; art and fashion discourses during the early twentieth century; the Nordic avant-garde from transnational perspectives; the avant-garde artist's role and self-fashioning; fashion and art during modernism; and fashion photography and fashion image. She is co-editor of the books *Fashion and Modernism* (2018) and *A Cultural History of the Avant-Garde in the Nordic Countries, Vol. 2: 1925–1950* (2019). She is currently working on a monograph about the surrealist artist Leonor Fini and her self-performances as well as co-editing the anthology *Fashion, Performance & Performativity* (2020).

Sophie Kurkdjian is Associate Researcher at the Institut d'Histoire du Temps Présent (IHTP-CNRS) in Paris, France. After completing her PhD on the history of fashion press at the beginning of the twentieth century, she worked as a Researcher at the Bibliothèque Nationale de France. Thereafter, she joined the Fédération de la Haute Couture et de la Mode, where she was in charge of the archives of the Chambre syndicale de la mode parisienne. In 2018, she co-created Culture(s) de Mode, a network of scholars who research fashion. She teaches Fashion History and Fashion Media History at the Université Paris 1 and Sciences Po. Sophie curated the exhibition *Mode et Femmes, 14/18* at the Bibliothèque Forney in Paris, in 2017 and *French Fashion, Women, and the First World War* at the Bard Graduate Center in New York, in 2019. Her work centers on Parisian fashion and its global influences, and appropriations, circulations, and transfers in the nineteenth and twentieth centuries.

Nigel Lezama, PhD, is a specialist in critical fashion and luxury studies, and nineteenth-century French literature. He teaches at Brock University in Canada. In May 2017, he co-organized the conference, "Nouveau Reach: Past, Present & Future of Luxury," in Toronto. Some recent works include: "Re-thinking Luxury in the Museum Fashion Exhibition," which appeared in *Luxury: History, Culture, Consumption* (2020); "Status, Votive Luxury, and Labour: The Female Rapper's Delight" (2019) in *Fashion Studies*; and, "Mo' Money, Mo' Problems: Hip Hop and Luxury's Uneasy Partnership" (2018) in *The Oxford Handbook of Hip Hop Music Studies*. His co-edited volume *Canadian Critical Luxury Studies Recentring Luxury* is forthcoming in 2021.

Zsolt Mészáros, PhD, is a curator at the Petőfi Literary Museum, Budapest. His research interests focus on fashion media; fashion and gender; and Parisian haute couture's network in Central Europe in the nineteenth and early twentieth centuries. He was Visiting Researcher at INHA, Paris, in 2018, where he worked on "La Tournée européenne de Paul Poiret (1911)." He is the author of "Reflections on the gender aspects of World War One: Commemoration projects and historiography in Hungary," in *L'Homme: European Review of Feminist History* (2018) and of "L'élégance genrée: Étude comparative entre le premier volume de *Monsieur* et de *Vogue* français (1920)," in *Visual Design: The Periodical Page as a Designed Surface* (2019).

Enrica Morini is Professor of Contemporary Fashion at IULM University in Milan. She holds a BA in History of Art Criticism. Enrica Morini has published *Fashion History from the Eighteenth to the Twenty-First Century* (2011) as well as numerous essays on ready-to-wear, Italian and French fashion, youth style, and the relationships between art and fashion. She has worked as a curator on exhibitions, focusing on post-war Italian fashion and fashions of the sixties and the seventies. In 2003, she co-curated with Margherita Rosina, a display about the impact of the First World War on the lives and style of women, *Le Donne, la moda, la guerra. Emancipazione femminile e moda durante la Prima guerra mondiale* (Women, Fashion, War: Women's Emancipation and Fashion during the First World War).

Georgina Ripley is Senior Curator of Modern and Contemporary Fashion and Textiles at National Museums Scotland (NMS), where she oversees the collections dating from 1850 to the present day. She holds an MA in the History of Dress from the Courtauld Institute of Art, London, and previously worked for National Galleries of Scotland, Museums Galleries Scotland, the Royal Academy of Arts, London, and the Warner Textile Archive, Braintree, Essex. She is the editor of a forthcoming publication on the little black dress which will accompany a temporary exhibition (postponed to 2023); she has curated the touring exhibition *Body Beautiful: Diversity on the Catwalk* (2019) and was Lead Curator for the museum's permanent Fashion & Style gallery, which opened in 2016. Her special interests include constructs of masculinity in contemporary menswear and image-making, with a focus on intersectionality; she is also conducting ongoing research into Jean Muir (fl. 1962–95) and her archive, which forms part of the National Museums' collection.

Margherita Rosina is Professor of Fashion History and Research at Università degli Studi, Milan, and Visiting Lecturer of Textile and Fashion History, IULM University, Milan. From 2007 to 2016, she was the Director of the Museo Studio del Tessuto at the Fondazione Antonio Ratti, Como. Her research interests focus on ancient and contemporary textiles. She is the author of numerous publications related to the history of textiles, with particular focus on twentieth-century Italian fabrics. She has also curated exhibitions on the same subject.

Mary Lynn Stewart is Professor Emerita at Simon Fraser University in Burnaby, British Columbia. She is the author of *Dressing Modern Frenchwomen: Marketing Haute Couture, 1919–1939* (2008), "Haute couture and the Art Deco Exhibition of 1925: A turning point," in *The Routledge Companion to Art Deco*, Michael Windover and Brigid Elliott, eds. (2019), "Copying and copyrighting haute couture," *French Historical Studies* (2005), and "Marketing fabrics and femininity in interwar France," *Textile History* (2004).

Guillaume de Syon, PhD, teaches History at Albright College in Reading, Pennsylvania, and is Visiting Scholar in History at Franklin & Marshall College in Lancaster, Pennsylvania. He is the author of *Zeppelin! Germany and the Airship, 1900–1939* (2002), and of numerous articles and chapters on the cultural history of technology. At present, he is working on a history of airline advertising as reflected in food, technology, and uniforms.

Index

Page numbers in *italics* refer to figures.

A Társaság (The Society) 237, 238
Adam, Helen Pearl 52, 93
advertisements 235, *235*
Africa 213, 220, 221–2
agricultural workers *see* Women's Land Army
Aine-Montaillé, Jean 20, 21–2
Alfred-Marie 63, 81
Algemeen Handelsblad 136, 139, 140
Algeria 213, 220
Alsace, dress practices in 108–18, *109*
    background to Alsace 108–10
    clothing workshops 112–13
    department stores 111–12
    French and German fashion 111
    introduction to 9, 14 n. 18
    motion pictures 115, *116*
    post-war parade 117–18
    propaganda, French 114–17, *116*
    traditional dress 110, 113–14
Alsace (film, 1916) 115, *116*
Alsen, Ola 65
Amies de la dentelle (Friends of Lace) 123, 125–6, 127
Anne-Marie 82
Antwerp Six 83
aprons 37–8, *38*
army surplus *see* secondhand uniforms in France
Arnoux, Guy 192
Auernheimer, Raoul 236
austerity measures 50
Australia 97
Austria 20, 62, 78, 236
avant-garde, influence of 81–2, 83
aviators' uniforms in France 197–204, *199*, *201–2*, *204*
    conclusion 203–4
    flight suits and other items 200–2, *201–2*, *204*
    introduction 197–8
    at rest 202–3
    before the war 198
    wartime inspiration 199–200
Az Érdekes Újság (The Interesting Journal) 239

balaclavas 141, 201, 202
Balard, Germain 280
Barbier, Georges 93, 96
Bárczy, István 234
Barrès, Commander 200, 202
Barthes, Roland 290
Bastia, Jean, *Masculine Fashion* (1916) 233
Bauhaus 252, 256 n. 20
Baumer, Lewis 291, 292, 295, 296, 297, 298, 299–300
Belgian Relief 125
Belgium 8–9, 72–84
    beginning of Belgian fashion 83–4
    clothing 74–5, *75*
    education 122–3, 131
    fashion, as defiance 77–8
    fashion magazines 78–80, *79*
    historical context 72–3
    lace industry 123–4, 125–9, 127–9, 131
    Norine Couture 75–6, *76*, 77, 80–2, *81*, 83
    patriotic colors 156, *156*
    wartime economy 124–5
    wartime life 73–4, 77
Belle Époque 72, 91, 94, 95
Benda, Georges Kugelmann 93, 94, 96
Bendel, Henri 53
Berthelot, Marcellin 221
Bismarck, Otto von 246
Blumer, Herbert 197
Boisson & Fesquet 155, 156–7, 158

Bordeaux, Henry 215
Bosselt, Rudolf, *Krieg und deutsche Mode* (War and German Fashion) (1915) 250, 253
Boué Sœurs 8, 29–41
    America, marketing in 38–40
    America, visits to 31–3, *32*
    Americanization of 40–1
    background 29
    at the beginning of the war 29–31
    New York branch 33–4
    patriotic nationalism of 35–9, *36*, *38*
    smuggling plot 34–5
    transatlantic travel, dangers of 35
    workshop 34
bows, religious affiliations of 110
Brachfeld, Sándor 239
Braillon 184, 185, 189
Braun, Auguste 117
Brazil 211, 220
breeches 169, 171–2, 173, *174*
Brooks, Margaret 171, 173
Buckley, Cheryl 288, 295
Budapesti Hírlap 234
Bulletin de L'Office du Travail (Bulletin of the Work Office) 130
Bulletin des Usines de Guerre (Bulletin on War Factories) 187, *188*
Bureau de l'Habillement 215–16
buyers
    American 17, 18, 19, 23 n. 1
    copying by 22
Buzenet, Marianne 22

Callot Sœurs 52, 158
Calvé, Emma 35
Cappiello, Leonetto 93, *94*
    Pupazzi var Cappiello (Cappiello's Italian Puppets) (1918) 100, *101*
Carelsen, Geertruida 143
cartes de nuances (hue cards) 156
cartoons
    anti-German 93–4
    of German fashion 59, *60*
    of Land Girls 170, *171*
    in *Punch*
        conclusion 303–4
        feminine vs. masculine 295–9, *297*
        of Gaby Deslys 99
        introduction 289–90
        making a real man 299–300, *300*
        spectacle of war 301–3
        transformations 291–2
        vanity and ignorance 292–5
    of women in workwear 191, *192*
Castel 200
Castelanu, Francis de 220
Chambe, René 117, 198
Chambre Syndicale de la Couture Parisienne (Trade Association of Parisian Couture) 20, 21–2, 40
Chavent Père & Fils 155
Chéruit 158
Cleveland Manufacturing Company 175
coats
    civilian 160 n. 9
    military 201–2, *202*
    style of 31–2, 239
cockades 35–6, 113, 158–9
Cocteau, Jean 92, 95
    Parade (1917) 93
colonial use of uniforms 211, 213, 220–2
colors
    beige 51, 57 n. 21
    blue 53
    Boué collection, 1914–15 32
    Feldgrau (field gray) 65–6
    green 53, 55
    horizon blue 186, 199
    hue cards 156–7
    khaki 173, 239
    Lucile 47–8, *48*, 56 n. 6
    of menswear in Hungary 239
    patriotic 50, 65, 92, 154, 155, *156*, 157
    of pilots' uniform 203, 204, *204*
    practical 51
    restricted 96
    of selvedges 154
    of silk fabrics 153, 154, *156*
Comité du Travail Féminin (Committee for Female Labor) 186–7, *188*–9, 190
Commard, Madame 188–9
Commission for Relief in Belgium 125
Como, silk production 151–9
Concours des Cocardes de Mimi Pinson (Contest of the Mimi Pinson Cocardes) 36
conferences 4–5, 5–6

copying
    by German fashion designers 249–51
    of haute couture 17–18, 20, 21–2, 35
    of patterns 138
    by Paul Poiret 250–1
costume parties 61
costumes *see* feathered showgirls
couture industry, introduction to 6, 8–9
coveralls 185, 187–8, 188–9, 191, *192*
    see also overalls
Craik, Jennifer 172
Croswell, Olive 173–4
culottes 189
Cummings, H. P. 179
customs tariffs 20, 34

Dagullion, Jean 203–4
Dartey (Anette Osterlind) 62
De Baets, Elvira 75, *75*
De Fransche Modejournalen (The French Fashion Magazine) 138
De Gracieuse (The Gracious) 135, 137, 138–9, *139–40*
De Mode 140
De Schaepdrijver, Sophie 72
De Vlaamsche Post (The Flemish Post) 77, 78
De Witte, Baron 222
deconstructivist garments 83
department stores
    in Alsace 111–12
    in America 35, 40, 96
    uniform sold in 175
    workwear in 184, 185, 193
Der Kunstwart 249–50
Deschryver, Norine 75, *76*
Deslys, Gaby 92, 95, 98–101
Deutsch, Ernst 65
Deutscher Werkbund (German Association of Craftsmen) 246–7, 248, 251
Die Herrenwelt (The Menswear) 234
diseases and secondhand clothes 212
Distinguished Service Ribbon 176
Divat és Mûvészet (Fashion and Art) 237
dolls 116–17
domestic production 141–4, *142–3*
Dr. Jutassy 235, *235*
drivers 201–2
Dry Goods Reporter, The 154
Duff Gordon, Lucy, Lady *see* Lucile

Duguet, Camille 273, 277–80, 278–9, 283
Dulac, Léon 189
D'Ulmes, Tony (Berthe Rey) 263
Durand, Marguerite 182, 191
duster coveralls 185, 189
Duval, Paul 94
dyes 153, 186

education 122–3, 131
Edwards, Nina 158
Élégances: Grand magazine de la femme (Elegance: Grand Magazine for Women) 79–80
Elegante Welt 61, 62, 63, 64, 65, 66
Elisabeth, Queen of Belgium 74, 123–4
embroidery 37, 66, 144
engineers 198
Étévé, Albert 198
Etreillis, Jeanne d' 29, 30, 31, 34, 35
evening wear
    lampshade tunic 61
    by Lucile 47–8, *48*, 49, 50, 53, 54, 55
    menswear 239
exhibitions 5

Fabiano, Fabien 191
fabrics
    alternatives 238, 252
    Boué Sœurs collection 32
    French 22, 31
    "Lucile look" 47–8, *48*
    restrictions on 96, 160 n. 9
    silk 151–9
factories
    clothing production 137–8
    clothing worn in 185, 186–8, 189, 190, 191, *192*, 193
    silk production in Italy 151–9
    uniform production and refurbishment 216–17
    wages in France 183–4
fashion and textile industries, introduction to 9–10
fashion writing in Germany 12, 246–54
    conclusion 253–4
    fashion and politics 253
    fashion industry, creation of 251–2
    French fashion, against 249–51
    introduction 246–9, *247–9*
Faure-Favier, Louise 273, 274–6, *274*, 282–3
Faustin I, emperor of Haiti 211, 221

feathered showgirls 9, 91–102
    Gaby Deslys 92, 95, 98–101
    Laisse les Tomber! revue (1917) 92
    music halls in Paris 94–5
    ostrich feathers, return of 95–7
    Paris 1917 93–4
    plumes and Paris 91–2
    sources of feathers 97–8
Fédération des Métaux (Federation of Metalworkers) 191
female workwear in France 11, 182–93
    conclusion 193
    everyday clothes at work 183–4
    feminism, attitudes of 191
    images of workwear 191–3, *192*
    institutional attitudes 190–1
    introduction 182–3
    masculinization of women 188–9
    menswear for women 185–8
    for replacement workers 184–5, *185*
Fémina 61
feminine vs. masculine in *Punch* 295–9, *297*
feminism and clothing 191, 276–7
Férfi Divat (Men's Fashion) 232
Fermo Fossati 1871 154–5
Figaro 211, 217
FISAC (Fabbriche Italiane di Seterie A. Clerici Sa) 152–3
Fisher, Miss L. M. 176
Flaubert, Gustave, *L'Éducation sentimentale* (Sentimental Education) (1869) 280
flight suits 200
flour sacks, reused 125
Folies Bergère 94
Fonck, René 204
Fondazione Antonio Ratti (FAR) 151, 155, 156, 157, 158
food aid 125
footwear *see* shoes
Forbes, Angela, Lady 52
Foulsham and Banfield, Ltd. 100
France
    Alsace, dress practices in 9, 14 n. 18, 108–18, *109*
    aviators' uniforms 197–204, 199, 201–2, *204*
    education 122, 131
    fashion industry, introduction to 3–4, 6, 8
    feathered showgirls 9, 91–102
    female workwear 11, 182–93
    influence on Alsace 111
    lace industry 123–4, 129–30, 131
    magazines in 12, 272–83

    menswear in 233
    Parisian haute couture in the USA 6, 8, 17–23
    ribbons 157–9, *159*
    secondhand uniforms 11, 208–23
    silk in Italian collections 155–7
    women, attitudes towards 275, 276–83
François, Henri 189
Franklin Simon & Co 40
Friedlaender, Max J., *Echt und unecht* (Genuine and Counterfeit) (1929) 251
Fuller, Loie 157

gas masks 296–7, *297*
gay iconography of uniforms 220
gender and fashion
    feminism and clothing 4, 191, 276–7
    masculinity 232, 236
    masculinization of women 172, 188–9, 191, 192, 277–8
    in *Punch* 288–304
Genio, Buon 261, 262, 263
Genoni, Rosa 261
gentleman, as masculine ideal 236
Gentlewoman, The 51
Germany
    Alsace, annexation of 109–10, 111–12, 118
    clothing workshops 112–13
    fashion writing in 12, 246–54
    haute couture, copying of 18, 20, 22
    kriegskrinoline (war crinoline) 8, 59–67, *60*
    rationing of clothing 113
    words for items of clothing 235–6
Gesmar, Charles 92, 102
Gignoux, Régis 239
Gilded Age 17
Glenn, Susan 50
Globe, The 173
Glyn, Elinor 52
goat skins 200, *202*
Gochet, Alexis Marie 222
Goffman, Erving 289–90
Good Service Ribbon 175, *176*
Goreczky, István 237
Graeffe, Constance Ellis 74
Grande Encyclopédie 211
Grandmaison, Léonce de 217
Grayzel, Susan R. 297
Greer, Howard 49
Gregory, Adrian 289, 298

Guazzaroni, Teresita 265
Guynemer, Georges 203, *204*

Haas-Heye, Otto 63
Haiti 211, 221
Hansi 113–14, *114*
Harlingue, Albert 100
Harper's Bazaar 52, 53
Harrods 175
Harsányi, Zsolt 239
hats
    for aviators 198, 199, *199*
    for Land Girls 178
    for men 239, *240*
    with ostrich feathers 91, 95, 96
    ribbons for 158–9
Hederer, General Fernand 200
Heine, Thomas Theodor, *Die enttäuschte Pariserin* (The disappointed Parisian) (1916) 59, *60*
Heitland, Margaret A. 173
hemlines 21, 31–2, 63, 191
Henner, Jean-Jacques, *L'Alsace. Elle Attend* (1871) 113
Herborth, August 111
Het Volk (The People) 137, 138
Hickson Inc. 35
Hirsch 140
Hirschfeld, Magnus 63
holidays 302
home working
    lace, in Belgium 123–4, 125, 126
    silk, in Italy 151–2
homemade clothing 141–4, *142–3*
Hoppé, Emil Otto 100
hospitals, sale of secondhand clothes from 209, 212
Hungary, menswear in 231–41

Imperial War Museum (IWM) 169, 174
import taxes 20, 34
industrial clothing production 137–8
inside out clothing 83
Italy
    fashion magazine *Margherita* 12, 260–7
    silk produced in 151–9

jackets 238–9

Kálnoki, Izidor 239
Kaufhaus Louvre 111–12

Kaufhaus Modern 112
Kellogg, Charlotte 126
Kitchener, Herbert 157
Knight, Charles 289
knitting 141–3, *142–3*, 144, 214
kriegskrinoline see war crinoline

La Baïonnette 94, 191, *192*
La Bataille syndicaliste (The Syndicalist Battle) 191–2
La Belle Jardinière 184, 185, 193
"la Françoise" coverall 188–9, *190*
La Fronde 191
La Gazette du Bon Ton (The Gazette of Good Taste) 18, 19, 21, 52, 93
La Grande Encyclopédie 221
La Mode 1915 (Fashion 1915) 78–9
La Vie heureuse (The Happy Life) 278–9
La Vie parisienne 96
La Voix des femmes (The Women's Voice) 191–2
lace industry in France and Belgium 10, 122–31
    Belgian wartime lace industry 74, 125–9, *127–9*
    Belgium at war 124–5
    conclusion 131
    French lace during the war 129–30
    handmade lace, promotion of 123–4
Laisse les Tomber! revue 92, 95, 99, 100
lampshade tunic 61
Land Girls *see* Women's Land Army
Landswoman, The 167, 169, 171, 174–5, 176, 177–8
Laver, James 288
Le Boucher, Léon 189
Le Carnet de la Semaine (The Weekly Notebook) 233
Le Figaro 239
Le Flambeau: Grand Magazine de Luxe Hebdomadaire (The Torch: Weekly Luxury Magazine) 12, 272–83
    Camille Duguet, columns by 277–80, *278–9*
    conclusion 282–3
    feminism in 276–7
    introduction 272–4, *273*
    Jeanne Tournier, columns by 181, 280–2
    Louise Faure-Favier, columns by 274–7
Le Foyer 215
Le Gaulois (The Gaul) 233, 235
Le Naour, Jean-Yves 278
Le Pêle-Mêle 236, 238, 239
Le Style parisien (The Parisian Style) 19, 21, 62
Le Temps 238

L'Écho de Paris 214
legal issues 34–5
Les Élégances parisiennes 95, 96, 97
Les Jolies modes (The Pretty Fashions) 74–5, 79, 80
Les Modes de Paris 96, 158
L'Expansion Belge 222
lice 212
L'Illustration 214
lingerie dress 36, 37
Lloyd George, David 165, 166
London
    feathers in 97
    male fashions 236, 237
    silk sold to 154
    during the war 19, 30, 52
    see also Lucile
Louisiana Purchase Exposition (1904) 20
Louvre (department store) 111–12
Lucile 8, 46–56
    in America 49, 50, 51
    attitude to clothes 49, 55
    clients of 52
    daywear 51
    fashion and morale 53, 54, 55
    introduction 46–7
    "Lucile look" 47–8, 48, 56 n. 6
    surviving garments 49–50

Macy's 96
magazines
    in Belgium 78–80, *79*
    in France 12, 272–83
    in Hungary, for men 232, 236, 237, 238
    in Italy 12, 260–7
    in the Netherlands 135, 138, 141, 143–4
Magritte, René 81, *81*
Magyar Figaró (Hungarian Figaro) 232, 233–4, *233*
Magyar Iparmûvészet (Hungarian Decorative Arts) 234
Maison Lewis 96, 98, 99
Maison Martin Margiela 83
male gaze 292
Mangold, Béla Kolos 234, 237
Marc, Lt. 203
Marchal, Sergeant 197
Margherita 12, 260–7
    call for Italian fashion 263–6
    on colors 154
    conclusion 266–7
    introduction 260–1
    on silk industry 151, 152, 153
    on war and women 261–3
Margiela, Martin 83
Mark, Bernard 203
markets in Paris 209, 210
Marsh, Eva 174
masculine ideals 236
masculinization of women 172, 188–9, 191, 192, 277–8
Massy, Jules Robert de 209
May, Mrs. Jack 50, 51
Mazier, Captain Louis 198
McLoughlin, Marie 3
men, stereotypes of in cartoons 296, 297–8
menswear for women 185–8
menswear in Hungary 12, 231–41
    conclusion 240–1
    English fashion, influence of 236–7
    industry, crisis of 237–8
    introduction 231–2
    soldier vs. civilian discourse 232–4, *233*
    styles, changes in 238–40
    vocabulary, German 235–6
Mercantile and Financial Times 33
Merrheim, Alphonse 191
military influence 36–7
military ribbons 158
Mills, Arthur Wallis 293–4, 293, 300
Missionaries of Mary 215
Mistinguett 101–2
modernism and fashion 59, 64–6
Modes Élégantes (Elegant Fashions) 79, *79*
Montegut, Sylvie 29, 30, 34, 35
Mornand, Felix 211
moustaches 240
Mulvey, Laura 292
music halls 94–5
Musidora, Mlle 96
Muthesius, Hermann
    Der Deutsche nach dem Kriege (The German after the War) 247, *248*
    "Deutsche Mode" (German Fashion) 249–50, 251, 253
    Die Zukunft der deutschen Form (The Future of German Form) (1915) 246, *247*

National Standard Dress 55–6, 58 n. 43, 291
Navet-Bouron, Françoise 275

Netherlands, clothing production in 10, 134–45
   conclusion 144–5
   daily life 135–6
   domestic couture 141–4, *142–3*
   fashion during the war 138–41, *139–40*
   garment industry, pre-war 136
   industrial clothing production 137–8
   magazines 135, 138, 141, 143–4
   nurse uniforms 137
   suffrage 136
Neue Freie Presse (New Free Press) 236
neutrality
   in Italy 261–2
   in the Netherlands 136
New York Herald 35, 96
New York Times 96, 219
New Zealand Herald 97
Newcastle Daily Journal 177
Nicholls, Horace W. 170, 178
Noakes, Lucy 292, 303
Norine Couture 75–6, *76*, 80–2, *81*, *83*
nostalgic imagery 53, 63, 94–5, 279–80
nurses 137, 184

objectifying gaze 292
Œuvre de la Cocarde (Cocarde Charity Workshop) 35–6
Offterdinger, Annie, *Modebild II* (Two dancing women) (1916) 63, *64*
Onze Kleeding (Our Clothing) 135, 137, 144
Osterline, Anette (Dartey) 62
ostrich feathers 91–2, 95–6, 97–8, 99, 100
overalls 171, 175, *176*
   see also coveralls
Owen, Nellie 166, 168

painted clothes 81, 83
Panama–Pacific International Exposition (1915) 20–1
Panofsky, Erwin, *Kopie oder Fälschung* (Copy or Forgery) (1928) 251
Paquin 52, 159
parades, in Alsace 110, 117–18
Paris
   in 1917 93–4
   feathers, use of 91–2
   haute couture in the USA 6, 8, 17–23
   impact of war on fashion industry 51, 52
   influence on the Netherlands 138–40
   music halls 94–5

   secondhand markets in 209, 210
   shows in America 52
Parravicini & Co. 153–4
patriotic clothes 50, 99
patriotic colors 50, 65, 92, 154, 155, 156, *156*, 157
patriotic consumption in Hungary 234
patriotic nationalism of Boué Sœurs 35–9, *36*, *38*
patterns, from magazines 135, 141–4, *142–3*
Peek & Cloppenburg 140
Pégoud, Adolphe 200, *201*
Pegram, Frederick 299
Pelletier, Madeleine 188
Pennell, Catriona 296, 298, 299, 301, 303
Picasso, Pablo 93
picture dresses 47–8, *48*, 53
picture journalism 289
pilots 198, 199, *199*, 200, 201–2, *202*, 203, 204, *204*
Pinchetti, Pietro 154
Pinson, Mimi 36, 158, 280, 282
pockets 51, 276
Poiret, Paul
   copying, prevention of 18
   Germany and Austria, influence of 250–1
   lampshade tunic 61
   marketing to USA 21
   military coat *7*
   shop in New York 22
   style of 67 n. 6
political rallies, in Alsace 110, 117–18
pompons 97–8
postal workers 188, 193
postcards 115–16, 170, 171, 192
prices
   of clothing 138, 175, 184, 185, 189
   of lace 127
   of secondhand uniforms 210
   of shoes 138
print sources, introduction to 11–13
production of clothing
   domestic production 141–4, *142–3*
   factories 137–8
   uniform production and refurbishment 216–17
propaganda
   Belgian lacemakers 127, *127*
   British 50, 167
   French, in Alsace 114–17, *116*
   Hungarian vocabulary 234, 235–7, *235*
Prothero, Rowland 167

Punch
    fashion, gender and society 13, 288–304
        conclusion 303–4
        feminine vs. masculine 295–9, *297*
        introduction 288–90
        making a real man 299–300, *300*
        spectacle of war 301–3
        transformations 291–2
        vanity and ignorance 292–5
    on National Service 99
    on ostrich feathers 97

Queen, The 50, 55–6, 173, 179

railways, women working in 182
Ramazzotti, Amelia Brizzi 263
rationing of clothing 113
Ratti, Antonio 151, 155
refugees 130, 135–6, 137, 141
refurbishment of uniforms 217
Réjane (Gabrielle Charlotte Réju) 115, *116*
religious affiliations of bows 110
Renoir, Jean, *The Grand Illusion* (1937) 200
Resal, Louis 201, 202
restrictions on materials 96, 160 n. 9
Revue d'Hygiène et de Police Sanitaire (Review of Hygiene and Police Sanitation) 212
revues 92, 94–5, 96, 99, 100
Rey, Berthe 263
Reynolds, Frank 299
ribbons 154, 156, 157–9, *159*
Ribeiro, Aileen 47
Rittenhouse, Anne 30
robe peinte (painted dress) 81
Roberts, Mary Lou 4
Rosselli, Amelia 265
Roubaud, Louis 35
Roussel, Christine 35
Ruck, Berta, *A Land Girl's Love Story* (1919) 171

sabers 198
Sackville-West, Vita 172
Satie, Erik 93
scarves 178, 202
Schwabe, Randolph 178
secondhand clothes 11, 74, 175
secondhand uniforms in France 11, 208–23
    American, sale of 219
    charity initiatives 214–15, *214–16*
    colonies, restrictions on trade 213
    conclusion 222–3
    of demobilized men 218–19
    disease, association with 212
    distribution and export of 211
    impersonations, fear of 213, 219–20
    indigenous people, wearing of 220–2, *221*
    introduction 208
    markets in Paris 209, *210*
    military supply 209–10
    subversive use of 220
    symbolic significance of 220
    as trophies 219
    war time reuse 215–18
selvedges 154
Senegal 213
service industries 185
sewing workshops 112–13
Shepperson, C. A. 292, 294–5, 296, *297*, 302
shoes
    ankle boots 62, *63*
    boots for Land Girls 166, 175
    prices 138
shop of Boué Sœurs in New York 33–4
shops *see* department stores
shortages
    of clothing 113
    of dyes 153
    of fabric 31
    in France 96
    of mannequins 51
    in the Netherlands 137–8
    of thread 129
showgirls *see* feathered showgirls
silk produced in Italy 151–9
    Fermo Fossati 1871 154–5
    FISAC silk-mill 152–3
    French silk in Italian collections 155–7
    Parravicini & Co. 153–4
    ribbons 157–9, *159*
skirt-culottes 189
skirts
    hoop skirts 61
    length of 21, 31–2, 63, 191
    in the Netherlands 139–40, *139–40*
    width of 32, 62–3, 140

Slade, Henry Aye de 203
smocks 171, 184, 187, 193
South Africa 97
South America 23, 220
Spindler, Charles 112
sportswear 277, *278*
St. Louis World's Fair (1904) 20
Stahl, Fritz 254
Stanley, Henry Morton 221
Steele, Valerie 95
Stern, Norbert 111, 248, 249, 252
    Die Weltpolitik der Weltmode (1915) 253
strikes 93
suffrage 4, 136
suit jackets 238–9
Syndicat de Défense de la Grande Couture Française (Syndicate for the Defense of French Haute Couture) 18, 21, 22
Syndicat de la Couture Parisienne 96
Szabó Hírlap (Tailor's Journal) 234
Szabó Otthon (Home of the Tailor) 231, 236
Szende-Dárday, Olga 236

Tableau Général du Commerce 211
Talbot, Dame Meriel L. 166, 167–8
Taylor, Lou 3, 93, 95–6, 290
Tedeschi, Virginia Treves (Buon Genio) 261, 262, 263
Thébaud, Françoise 190, 276
Thomas, Albert 186–7, 189
ties 154, 155
Tilburg, Patricia 282
Toulouse-Lautrec, Henri de, *La Troupe de Mademoiselle Eglantine* (Mademoiselle Eglantine's troupe) (1896) 95
Tournier, Jeanne 273–4, 280–2, 283
Town Topics 33
Townsend, F. H. 294–5, 302
trade fairs 20
traditional costume
    of Alsace 109, 110, 113–18, 114, *116*
    in the Netherlands 144
transatlantic travel, dangers of 35
trousers 172
    see also breeches
Trübner, Alice 63
Tynan, Jane 293, 296, 299
Tyrer, Nicola 178

underclothes, for men 141, *143*
uniforms
    aviators' uniforms in France 197–204, 199, 201–2, *204*
    in cartoons of *Punch* 296, 298, 300, *301*
    influence of 65, 275
    introduction to 10–11
    masculinity, associated with 232
    menswear, influence on 239
    military ribbons 158
    myths of 293
    nurse 137, 184
    secondhand uniforms 11, 208–23
    Women's Land Army 10, 165–79
unions and workwear 190–1
United Kingdom 52, 219, 236, 237
    see also London; Lucile; Women's Land Army
United States of America
    Boué Sœurs marketing in 38–40
    Boué Sœurs visits to 31–4, *32*
    buyers 17, 18, 19, 23 n. 1
    department stores 35, 40, 96
    designers 19
    fashion shows 52
    Lucile in 49, 50, 51
    Parisian haute couture in 6, 8, 17–23
    sale of surplus uniforms 219
Uzanne, Octave 277

Van Hecke, Paul-Gustave 72, 75–8, 76, 80, 82
Van de Woestijne, Karel 74, 78, 82, 83
Vanna, Donna 265
Variety 94, 99
Verhaegan, Pierre 124
Verhaegen, Pierre 221
Vienna 62, 78
Vigée Le Brun, Elisabeth, *Madame Molé-Raymond* (1786) 38
Villalba, Marquise of 262
Villemot, Jean, *Les Usines de guerre* (1917) 191, *192*
Viviani, René 183
Vlossak, Elizabeth 115
Vogue 19, 20, 22, 33, 37, 55
Volterra, Léon 99
volunteering 298, 299–300
Vrouw en haar Huis (The Woman and Her Home) 135, 143

wages
    in Belgium 125, 126
    in France 130, 182, 183–4
    of Land Girls in Britain 175
waistline 21, 31–2, 61, 63–4
waiters 185, *186*
Waltz, Jean-Jacques "Hansi" 113–14, *114*
Wanamaker, John 21
war crinoline 8, 59–67, *60*
    conclusion 66–7
    German perspective 61–4, 252
    introduction 59–60, *60*
    modernism of 64–6
    prewar genealogy 61
    van Hecke on 77–8
war lace 127, *128*
Warnod, André 208, 210, 220
weapons 198
Weber, Helene Marie 277
Weingarten, Morris 22
West Australian 97
White, Bonnie 174, 178
Wiener Werkstätte 62
Wieselthier, Vally, *Im Tierpark* (At the Zoological Garden) (1916) 62
Wilson, Elizabeth 64–5
Wimmer-Wisgrill, Eduard 62
Wolseley, Frances, 2nd Viscountess 170
women
    attitudes in France 275, 276–83
    home working in Belgium 125
    lacemakers 123–4, 126, 127, *127*, 130, 131
    in the Netherlands 136–7
    roles of 4
    stereotypes of in cartoons 291, 293–9, *293, 297*
    and traditional dress in Alsace 110, 113–18

war work in Italy 262–3
    in workshops 112–13
    workwear in France 182–93
Women's Land Army 10, 165–79
    awards of merit 175–6, *176*
    conclusion 178–9
    creation of 167–8
    introduction to 165–6
    uniform
        allocation of 168–9
        biography of 170
        conduct when wearing 172–3
        democracy of 174–5
        design of 170–2
        examples of 169–70
        individualism of 175, 177–8
        responses to 173–4
        sources for research 170
    unsuitable clothing 167
Women's National Land Service Corps (WNLSC) 166, 167
Women's Wear Daily 19, 20, 21–2
wool
    in Italy 151, 152
    prices in Hungary 241 n. 1
    restrictions on 96, 160 n. 9
workshops
    in Alsace 112–13
    Boué Sœurs 34
    secondhand clothes 74
workwear *see* female workwear in France; Women's Land Army
Worth 19, 139, 158

Yan, Shu-chuan 290

zeppelins 301–2